Honoré de Balzac

Modeste Mignon and Other Stories

Honoré de Balzac

Modeste Mignon and Other Stories

ISBN/EAN: 9783744751513

Printed in Europe, USA, Canada, Australia, Japan

Cover: Foto ©Thomas Meinert / pixelio.de

More available books at **www.hansebooks.com**

H. DE BALZAC

MODESTE MIGNON

AND OTHER STORIES

TRANSLATED BY

CLARA BELL

WITH A PREFACE BY

GEORGE SAINTSBURY

PHILADELPHIA

THE GEBBIE PUBLISHING CO., Ltd.

1898

CONTENTS

LIST OF ILLUSTRATIONS

Drawn by D. Murray-Smith.

PREFACE.

"MODESTE MIGNON" occupies a very peculiar place in Balzac's works—a place indeed, which, though for the form's sake more than anything else the author has connected it with the rest of the "Comédie" by some repetition of personages, is almost entirely isolated. I think it has puzzled some devoted Balzacians—so much so that I have seen it omitted even from lists of his works suitable to "the young person," in which it surely should have had an eminent place. As it is distinctly late—it was written in 1844, and nothing of combined magnitude and first-class importance succeeded it except "Les Parents Pauvres"—it may not impossibly serve as a basis for the expectation that if Balzac, after his re-establishment in Paris as a wealthy personage, had received a new lease of life and vigor instead of a sentence of death, we might have had from him a series of works as different from anything that he had composed before as "Modeste Mignon" is from her sisters.

In saying this, I do not mean to put the book itself in the very first class of its author's work. It is too much of an experiment for that—of an experiment as far as the heroine is concerned, the boldness and novelty of which is likely to be underestimated by almost any reader, unless he be a literary student who pays strict attention to times and seasons. Even in England (though Charlotte Brontë was planning her at this very time) the willful, unconventional heroine was something of a novelty; and when it is remembered how infinitely stricter was the standard of the French *ingénue*, until quite recently, than it ever, even in the depths of the eighteenth century, was in England, the audacity of the conception of Modeste may be at least generally appreciated. And it is specially important to observe that though the author puts in Charles

Mignon's mouth a vindication of the French process of tying
a girl hand and foot and handing her over to the best bidder
as a husband, instead of allowing her to choose for herself,
Modeste's audacity in pursuing the opposite method is crowned
with complete success, if not with success of exactly the kind
that she anticipated. Except the case of Savinien de Portenduère and Ursule Mirouët, hers is, so far as I can remember,
the only example in the whole "Comédie" of a love-marriage
which, as we are told, was wholly successful, without even
vacillations on the wife's part or relapses on the husband's.
It is true that, with a slight touch of cowardice or concession,
Balzac has made Modeste half a German ; but this is a very
venial bowing in the porch, not the chancel, of the House of
Rimmon.

Whether the young lady is as entirely successful and as entirely charming as she is undeniably audacious in conception,
is not a point for equally positive pronouncement. Just as it
was probably necessary for Balzac, in order not to outrage the
feelings of his readers too much, to put that Teutonic strain in
Modeste, so he had, in all probability, to exhibit her as
capricious and almost unamiable, in order to attain the fitness
of things in connection with so terrible a young person. It
is certain that even those who by no means rejoice in pattern
heroines, even those who "like them rather wicked," may
sometimes think Modeste nasty in her behavior to her family,
to Butscha, and, perhaps, to her future husband. She is, for
instance, quite wrong about the whip, which she might have
refused altogether, but could not with decency accept from
one person and refuse from another. But what has just been
said will cover this and other petulances and outbursts. So
" shoking " a young person (it is very cheerful and interesting
to think how much more exactly that favorite *vox nihili* of
French speech expresses French than English sentiment) could
not but behave " shokingly."

Most of the minor characters are good : Butscha, a difficult and, in any case, slightly improbable personage, is, in his own way, very good, indeed. It was probably necessary for Balzac, in turning the usual scheme of the French novel upside down, to provide a rather timid hero for such a masterful heroine; and it must be admitted that Ernest de la Brière is a rather preternaturally good young man. Still, he is not mawkish; and except that he should not have given Modeste quite such a valuable present, he behaves more like a gentleman in the full English sense than any other of Balzac's heroes.

The very full, very elaborate, and very unfavorable portrait of Canalis offers again much scope for difference of mere taste and opinion, without the possibility of laying down a conclusion very positively. Even if tradition were not unanimous on the subject, it would be quite certain that Canalis is a direct presentment of Lamartine, from whom he is so ostentatiously dissociated. And there can, of course, be no two opinions as to the presentment being very distinctly unfavorable—much more so than the earlier introductions of this same Canalis, which are either complimentary or colorless for the most part, though his vanity is sometimes hinted at. I do not know whether Balzac had any private quarrel with the poet, or whether Lamartine's increasing leanings toward republicanism exasperated the always monarchical novelist. But it is certain that Canalis cuts rather a bad figure here—that Lamartine was actually supposed to have married for money—and that the whole thing has more of the nature of a personal attack than anything else in Balzac, except the outbreak against Sainte-Beuve in "Un Prince de la Bohème."

Perhaps it should be added that the practice of correspondence between incognitas and men of letters, not unknown in any country, has been rather frequent and famous in France. The chief example is, of course, that interchange of communications between Mérimée and Mlle. Jenny Dacquin, which had such important results for literature, and such not unimportant ones for the parties concerned. Balzac himself rejoiced in a Modeste called Louise, whom, however, he seems never to have seen ; and there is little doubt that Lamartine the actual was attacked, as the fictitious Canalis boasts that he was, by scores of such persons. The chief instance I can think of in which such a correspondence led to matrimony was that of Southey and his second wife, Caroline Bowles.

The history of "Modeste Mignon" is short and simple. It was first given to the public in the spring and summer of 1844 by the "Journal des Débats," and before the end of the year it appeared in four volumes, published by Roux and Cassanet. It had here seventy-five chapter divisions, with headings. In 1845, scarcely twelve months after its first appearance, it took its place in the "Comédie."

The story of "Honorine" contains some of Balzac's profoundest observations, better stated than is usual, or, at least, invariable, with him. The best of all are certain axioms, disputed rather than disputable, as to the difference of men's and women's love. The book suffers to some extent from that artistic fault of the recitation, rather than the story proper, to which he was so prone, and perhaps a little from the other proneness—so constantly to be noted in any complete critique of him—to exaggerate and idealize good as well as ill. But it is, as his abomination Sainte-Beuve said of another matter, an *essai noble* (a great sketch) ; and it is not, as Sainte-Beuve also said of that matter which had nothing to do with Balzac, an *essai pâle* (light sketch).

"Facino Cane" first saw the light in the "Chronique de Paris" of March 17, 1836. Next year it became an "Étude Philosophique" (Philosophical Study). It had another grouped appearance with "Albert Savaron," etc., in 1843, and entered the "Comédie" the year after.

G. S.

MODESTE MIGNON.

To a Polish Lady.

Daughter of an enslaved land, an angel in your love, a demon in your imagination, a child in faith, an old man in experience, a man in brain, a woman in heart, a giant in hope, a mother in suffering, a poet in your dreams, and Beauty itself withal—this work, in which your love and your fancy, your faith, your experience, your suffering, your hopes, and your dreams, are like chains by which hangs a web less lovely than the poetry cherished in your soul—the poetry whose expression when it lights up your countenance is, to those who admire you, what the characters of a lost language are to the learned—this work is yours.

DE BALZAC.

IN the beginning of October, 1829, Monsieur Simon-Babylas Latournelle, a notary, was walking up the hill from le Havre to Ingouville arm in arm with his son, and accompanied by his wife. By her, like a page, came the notary's head clerk, a little hunchback named Jean Butscha. When these four persons—of whom two at least mounted by the same way every evening—reached the turn in the zigzag road (like what the Italians call a Cornice), the notary looked about him to see whether any one might overhear him from some garden terrace above or below, and as an additional precaution he spoke low.

"Exupère," said he to his son, "try to carry out in an intelligent manner, without guessing at the meaning, a little manœuvre I will explain to you; and even if you have a suspicion, I desire you will fling it into the Styx which every

(1)

notary or law-student ought to keep handy for other people's
secrets. After paying your respects, homage, and devoir to
Madame and Mademoiselle Mignon, to Monsieur and Madame Dumay, and to Monsieur Gobenheim, if he is at the
chalet, when silence is restored, Monsieur Dumay will take
you aside; look attentively—I allow you—at Mademoiselle
Modeste all the time he is talking to you. My worthy friend
will ask you to go out for a walk and return in about an hour,
at about nine o'clock, with a hurried air; try to seem quite out
of breath, then whisper in his ear, but loud enough for Mademoiselle Modeste to hear: ' The young man is coming ! ' "

Exupère was to start for Paris on the following day to
begin his law studies. It was this prospect of departure which
had led Latournelle to propose to his friend Dumay that his
son should play the assistant in the important conspiracy
which may be suspected from his instructions.

"Is Mademoiselle Modeste suspected of carrying on an
intrigue?" asked Butscha timidly of his mistress.

"Hsh—Butscha!" replied Madame Latournelle, taking
her husband's arm.

Madame Latournelle, the daughter of the registrar of the
lower court, considers herself justified by her birth in describing her family as parliamentary. These pretensions account
for the efforts made by the lady, whose face is rather too red
and rough, to assume the majesty of the tribunal whose ver-
dicts are recorded by her father. She takes snuff, holds herself as stiff as a post, gives herself airs of importance, and
looks exactly like a mummy that has been galvanized into
life for a moment. She tries to give her sharp voice an aristocratic tone, but she no more succeeds in that than in concealing her defective education. Her social value is indisputable when you look at the caps she wears, bristling with
flowers, the false fronts plastered on her temples, and the
gowns she chooses. How could the stores get rid of such
goods if it were not for such as Madame Latournelle?

This worthy woman's absurdities might have passed almost unremarked, for she was essentially charitable and pious, but that nature, which sometimes has its little jest by turning out these grotesque creations, gave her the figure of a drum-major so as to display the devices of her provincial mind. She has never been out of le Havre, she believes in the infallibility of le Havre, she buys everything at le Havre, and gets her dresses there; she speaks of herself as Norman to the finger-tips; she reverences her father and adores her husband. Little Latournelle was bold enough to marry this woman when she had attained the post-matrimonial age of thirty-three, and they contrived to have a son. As he might anywhere have won the sixty thousand francs which the registrar had to settle, his unusual courage was set down to a wish to avoid the irruption of the Minotaur, against which his personal attractions would hardly have guaranteed him if he had been so rash as to set his house on fire by bringing home a pretty, young wife. The notary had, in fact, simply discerned the good qualities of Mademoiselle Agnès—her name was Agnès—and remarked how soon a wife's beauty is a thing of the past to her husband. As to the insignificant youth to whom the registrar gave his Norman name at the font, Madame Latournelle was so much astonished to find herself a mother at the age of thirty-five years and seven months, that she would even now find milk to suckle him withal if he needed it—the only hyperbole which can give a notion of her maternal mania.

"How handsome my boy is!" she would say to her little friend Modeste Mignon, without any ulterior motive, as she looked at him on their way to church, her beautiful Exupère leading the way.

"He is like you," Modeste Mignon would reply, as she might have said, "What bad weather!"

This sketch of the woman, a mere accessory figure, seems necessary when it is said that Madame Latournelle had for three years past been the chaperon of the young girl for whom the notary and his friend Dumay were laying one of those snares which, in the "Physiologie du Mariage," I have called mouse-traps.

As for Latournelle, imagine a good little man, as wily as the purest honesty will allow, but whom every stranger would take for a rogue at first sight of the singular face, to which every one at le Havre is accustomed. Weak eyes, always red, compel the worthy lawyer to wear green spectacles to protect them. Each eyebrow, thinly marked with down, projects about a line beyond the brown tortoise-shell rim of the glasses, thus making a sort of double arch. If you never happen to have noticed in some passer-by the effect of these two semicircles, one above the other and divided by a hollow, you cannot conceive how puzzling such a face may be; especially when this face is pale and haggard, and ends in a point like that of Mephistopheles, which painters have taken from the cat, and this is what Babylas Latournelle is like. Above those vile green spectacles rises a bald skull, with a wig all the more obviously artificial because it seems endowed with motion and is so indiscreet as to show a few white hairs straggling below it all around, while it never sits straight on the forehead. As we look at this estimable Norman, dressed in black like a beetle, on two legs like pins, and know him to be the most honest soul living, we wonder, but cannot discover, what is the reason of such contradictory physiognomies.

Jean Butscha, a poor, abandoned foundling, of whom the Registrar Labrosse and his daughter had taken charge, had risen to be head clerk by sheer hard work, and was lodged and fed by his master, who gave him nine hundred francs a year. With no appearance of youth and almost a dwarf, he had made Modeste his idol; he would have given his life for her. This poor creature, his eyes, like two slow matches under thickened eyelids, marked by the smallpox, crushed by a mass of woolly hair, encumbered by his huge hands, had lived under the gaze of pity from the age of seven. Is not this enough to account

for him in every way?   Silent, reserved, exemplary in his
conduct, and religious, he wandered through the vast expanse
marked on the map of the realm of Love, as Love without
Hope, the barren and sublime wilderness of Longing.   Modeste had nicknamed this grotesque clerk "The Mysterious
Dwarf." This led Butscha to read Walter Scott's romance, and
he said to Modeste—

"Would you like to have a rose from your Mysterious
Dwarf in case of danger?"

Modeste hurled the soul of her adorer down into its mud
hovel again by one of the terrible looks which young women
fling at men whom they do not like.   Butscha had called
himself *le clerc obscure* (the obscure clerk), not knowing that
the pun dated back to the origin of coats-of-arms; but he,
like his master's wife, had never been away from le Havre.

It is perhaps necessary, for the benefit of those who do not
know that town, to give a word of explanation as to whither
the Latournelle family was bound, the head clerk evidently
being included.   Ingouville is to le Havre what Montmartre
is to Paris, a high hill with the town spread at its foot; with
this difference, however—that the sea and the Seine surround
the town and the hill; that le Havre is permanently limited
by enclosing fortifications; and, finally, that the mouth of
the river, the port and the docks, form a scene quite unlike
that offered by the fifty thousand houses of Paris.

At the foot of Montmartre an ocean of slates displays its
rigid blue waves; at Ingouville you look down on what might
be moving roofs stirred by the wind.   This high ground, ·
which, from Rouen to the sea, follows the course of the river,
leaving a wider or narrower margin between itself and the
water, contains treasures of picturesque beauty with its towns,
its ravines, its valleys, and its meadows, and rose to immense
value at Ingouville after 1818, from which year dates the
prosperity of le Havre.   This hamlet became the Auteuil, the
Ville-d'Avray, the Montmorency of the merchants, who built

themseleves terraced villas on this amphitheatre, to breathe the
sea-air sweetened by the flowers of their magnificent gardens.
These bold speculators rest there from the fatigues of the counting-house and the atmosphere of the closely packed houses,
with no space between them—often not even a courtyard, the
inevitable result of the growth of the population, the un-
yielding belt of the ramparts and the expansion of the docks.

And, indeed, how dreary is the heart of the town, how
glad is Ingouville! The law of social development has made the
suburb of Graville sprout into life like a mushroom ; it is larger
now than le Havre itself, clinging to the foot of the slope like
a serpent.   Ingouville, on the ridge, has but one street ; and,
as in all such places, the houses looking over the Seine have an
immense advantage over those on the opposite side of the
road, from which the view is shut out, though they stand like
spectators, on tiptoe, to peep over the roofs.   Here, however,
as everywhere else, compromises have been exacted.   Some
of the houses perched on the top occupy a superior position,
or enjoy a right of view which compels their neighbor to keep
his buildings below a certain height.   Then the broken rocky
soil has cuttings here and there for roads leading up to the
amphitheatre, and through these dips some of the plots
get a glimpse of the town, the river, or the sea.   Though it
is not precipitous, the high ground ends rather suddenly in a
cliff; from the top of the street, which zigzags up the steep
slope, coombes are visible where villages are planted : Saint-
Adresse, two or three Saints-who-knows-who, and coves where
the sea roars.   This side of Ingouville, almost deserted, is in
striking contrast to the handsome villas that overlook the Seine
valley.   Are the gales a foe to vegetation ?   Do the merchants
shrink from the expense of gardening on so steep a slope?
Be this as it may, the traveler by steamboat is startled at finding the coast so bare and rugged to the west of Ingouville—a
beggar in rags next to a rich man sumptuously clothed and
perfumed.

In 1829, one of the last houses toward the sea—now, no doubt, in the middle of Ingouville—was called, perhaps is still called, the chalet. It had been originally a gatekeeper's lodge, with a plot of garden in front. The owner of the villa to which it belonged—a house with a paddock, gardens, an aviary, hot-houses, and meadows—had a fancy to bring this lodge into harmony with the splendor of his residence, and had it rebuilt in the style of an English cottage. He divided it by a low wall from his lawn, graced with flowers, borders and the terrace of the villa, and planted a hedge close to the wall to screen it. Behind this cottage, called the chalet in spite of all he could do, lie the kitchen-garden and orchards. This chalet—a chalet without cows or dairy—has no fence from the road but a paling, of which the wood has become invisible under a luxuriant hedge.

Now, on the other side of the road, the opposite house has a similar paling and hedge. Being built under special conditions it allows the town to be seen from the chalet.

This little house was the despair of Monsieur Vilquin, the owner of the villa. And this is why: The creator of this residence, where every detail loudly proclaimed, "Here millions are displayed!" had extended his grounds into the country solely, as he said, not to have his gardeners in his pocket. As soon as it was finished, the chalet could only be inhabited by a friend.

Monsieur Mignon, the first owner, was greatly attached to his cashier, and this story will prove that Dumay fully returned the feeling; he therefore offered him this little home. Dumay, a stickler for formalities, made his master sign a lease for twelve years at three hundred francs a year; and Monsieur Mignon signed it willingly, saying, "Consider, my dear Dumay, you are binding yourself to live with me for twelve years."

In consequence of events to be here related, the estates of Monsieur Mignon, formerly the richest merchant in le Havre, were sold to Vilquin, one of his opponents on 'Change. In his delight at taking possession of the famous Villa Mignon, the purchaser forgot to ask for this lease to be canceled. Dumay, not to hinder the sale, would at that time have signed anything Vilquin might have required; but when once the sale was completed, he stuck to his lease as to a revenge. He stayed in Vilquin's pocket, in the heart of the Vilquin family, watching Vilquin, annoying Vilquin; in short, Vilquin's gad-fly. Every morning, at his window, Vilquin felt a surge of violent vexation as he saw this gem of domestic architecture, this chalet which had cost sixty thousand francs, and which blazed like a ruby in the sunshine.

An almost exact comparison! The architect had built the cottage of the finest red-bricks, pointed with white. The window-frames are painted bright green and the timbers a yellow-brown. The roof projects several feet. A pretty fretwork balcony adorns the first floor, and a verandah stands out like a glass cage from the middle of the front. The first floor consists of a pretty drawing-room and a dining-room divided by the bottom landing of the stairs, which are of wood designed and decorated with elegant simplicity. The kitchen is at the back of the dining-room, and behind the drawing-room is a small room which, at this time, was used by Monsieur and Madame Dumay as their bedroom. On the second floor the architect has planned two large bedrooms, each with a dressing-room, the verandah serving as a sitting-room; and above these, in the roof, which looks like two cards leaning against each other, are two servants' rooms, attics, each with a dormer window, but fairly spacious.

Vilquin had the meanness to build a wall on the side next the kitchen-garden and orchard. Since this act of vengeance, the few square yards secured to the chalet by the lease are like a Paris garden. The outbuildings, constructed and painted to match the chalet, back against the neighboring grounds.

The interior of this pleasant residence harmonizes with the

exterior. The drawing-room, floored with polished iron-wood, is decorated with a marvelous imitation of Chinese lacquer. Myriad-colored birds and impossible green foliage, in fantastic Chinese drawing, stand out against a black background, in panels with gilt frames. The dining-room is completely fitted with pine-wood carved and fretted, as in the high-class peasants' houses in Russia. The little anteroom, formed by the landing, and the staircase are painted like old oak, to represent Gothic decoration. The bedrooms, hung with chintz, are attractive by their costly simplicity. That in which the cashier and his wife slept is wainscoted, like the cabin of a steamship. These shipowners' vagaries account for Vilquin's fury. This ill-starred purchaser wanted to lodge his son-in-law and his daughter in the cottage. This plan, being known to Dumay, may subsequently explain his Breton obstinacy.

The entrance to the chalet is through a trellised iron gate, with lance-heads, standing some inches above the paling and the hedge. The little garden, of the same width as the pompous lawn beyond, was just now full of flowers—roses, dahlias, and the choicest and rarest products of the hot-house flora; for another subject of grievance to Vilquin was that the pretty little hot-house, madame's hot-house as it was called, belongs to the chalet, and divides the chalet from the villa—or connects them, if you like to say so. Dumay indemnified himself for the cares of his place by caring for the conservatory, and its exotic blossoms were one of Modeste's chief pleasures. The billiard-room of Vilquin's villa, a sort of passage-room, was formerly connected with this conservatory by a large turret-shaped aviary, but after the wall was built, which blocked out the view of the orchard, Dumay bricked up the door.

"Wall for wall!" said he.

"You and Dumay have both gone to the wall!" Vilquin's acquaintances on 'Change threw in his teeth; and every day the envied speculator was hailed with some new jest.

In 1827 Vilquin offered Dumay six thousand francs a year and ten thousand francs in compensation if he would cancel the lease; the cashier refused, though he had but a thousand crowns laid by with Gobenheim, a former clerk of his master's. Dumay is indeed a Breton whom fate has planted out in Normandy. Imagine the hatred for his tenants worked up in Vilquin, a Norman with a fortune of three million francs. What high treason to wealth to dare prove to the rich the impotence of gold! Vilquin, whose desperation made him the talk of le Havre, had first offered Dumay the absolute freehold of another pretty house, but Dumay again refused. The town was beginning to wonder at this obstinacy, though many found a reason for it in the statement, "Dumay is a Breton."

In fact, the cashier thought that Madame and Mademoiselle Mignon would be too uncomfortable anywhere else. His two idols dwelt here in a temple worthy of them, and at least had the benefit of this sumptuous cottage, where a dethroned king might have kept up the majesty of his surroundings, a kind of decorum which is often lacking to those who have fallen. The reader will not be sorry perhaps to have made acquaintance with Modeste's home and habitual companions; for, at her age, persons and things influence the future as much as character does, if, indeed, the character does not derive from them certain ineffaceable impressions.

By the Latournelles' manner as they went into the chalet, a stranger might have guessed that they came there every evening.

"Already here, sir?" said the notary, on finding in the drawing-room a young banker of the town, Gobenheim, a relation of Gobenheim-Keller, the head of the great Paris house. This young fellow, who was lividly pale—one of those fair men with black eyes, in whose fixed gaze there is something fascinating—who was as sober in speech as in habits, dressed in black, strongly built, though as thin as a

consumptive patient, was a constant visitor to his former master's family and the cashier's house, far less from affection
than from interest ; whist was played there at two sous a point,
and evening dress was not insisted on ; he took nothing but a
few glasses of *eau sucrée*, and need offer no civilities in return.   By his apparent devotion to the Mignons he got credit
for a good heart ; and it excused him from going into society
in le Havre, from useless expenditure, and disturbing the
arrangements of his domestic life.   This youthful devotee of
the golden calf went to bed every evening at half-past ten, and
rose at five in the morning.   Also, being certain of secrecy
in Latournelle and Butscha, Gobenheim could analyze in their
presence various knotty questions, benefit by the notary's
gratuitous advice and reduce the gossip on 'Change to its true
value.   This sucking gold-eater (*Gobe-or*, a witticism of Butscha's) was of the nature of the substances known to chemistry
as absorbents.   Ever since disaster had overwhelmed the house
of Mignon, to which he had been apprenticed by the Kellers
to learn the higher branches of maritime trade, no one at the
chalet had ever asked him to do a single thing, not even a
simple commission ; his answer was known beforehand.   This
youth looked at Modeste as he might have examined a penny
lithograph.

"He is one of the pistons of the huge machine called
trade," said poor Butscha, whose wit betrayed itself by little
ironies, timidly uttered.

The four Latournelles greeted, with the utmost deference,
an old lady dressed in black, who did not rise from the armchair in which she sat, for both her eyes were covered with
the yellow film produced by cataract.   Madame Mignon may
be painted in a sentence.   She attracted attention at once by
the august expression of those mothers whose blameless life is
a challenge to the strokes of fate, though fate has taken them
as a mark for its shafts, who form the larger class of Niobes.
Her white wig, well curled and well put on, became her cold

white face, like those of the burgomasters' wives painted by
Mirevelt. The extreme neatness of her dress—velvet shoes,
a lace collar, a shawl put on straight—bore witness to Modeste's tender care for her mother.

When a minute's silence—as predicted by the notary—
reigned in the pretty room, Modeste, seated by her mother,
for whom she was embroidering a kerchief, was for a moment
the centre of all eyes. This inquisitiveness, concealed under
the commonplace questions always asked by callers, even
those who meet every day, might have betrayed the little
domestic plot against the girl, even to an indifferent person ;
but Gobenheim, more than indifferent, noticed nothing ; he
lighted the candles on the card-table. Dumay's attitude made
the situation a terrible one for Butscha, for the Latournelles,
and, above all, for Madame Dumay, who knew that her husband was capable of shooting Modeste's lover as if he were a
mad dog. After dinner, the cashier had gone out for a walk,
taking with him two magnificent Pyrenean dogs, whom he
suspected of treason, and, had therefore, left with a farmer,
formerly a tenant of Monsieur Mignon's ; then, a few minutes
before the Latournelles had come in, he had brought his pistols from their place by his bed, and had laid them on the
chimney-shelf, without letting Modeste see it. The young
girl paid no attention to all these arrangements—strange, to
say the least of it.

Though short, thick-set, and battered, with a low voice,
and an air of listening to his own words, this Breton, formerly a lieutenant in the Guard, has determination and presence of mind so plainly stamped on his features that, in
twenty years, no man in the army had ever tried to make
game of him. His eyes, small and calmly blue, are like two
specks of steel. His manners, the expression of his face, his
mode of speech, his gait, all suit his short name of Dumay.
His strength, which is well known, secures him against any
offense. He can kill a man with a blow of his fist ; and, in

fact, achieved this doughty deed at Botzen, where he found himself in the rear of his company, without any weapon, and face to face with a Saxon.

At this moment, the man's set but gentle countenance was sublimely tragical ; his lips, as pale as his face, betrayed convulsive fury subdued by Breton determination ; his brow was damp with slight perspiration, visible to all, and understood to be a cold moisture. The notary knew that the upshot of all this might be a scene in an assize court. In fact, the cashier was playing a game for Modeste's sake, where honor, fidelity, and feelings of far more importance than any social ties, were at stake ; and it was the outcome of one of those compacts of which, in the event of fatal issues, none but God can be the judge. Most dramas lie in the ideas we form of things. The events which seem to us dramatic are only such as our soul turns to tragedy or comedy, as our own nature tends.

Madame Latournelle and Madame Dumay, charmed with keeping watch over Modeste, both had an indescribable artificial manner, a quaver in their voice, which the object of their suspicions did not notice, she seemed so much absorbed by her work. Modeste laid each strand of cotton with an accuracy that might be the envy of any embroiderer. Her face showed the pleasure she derived from the satin-stitch petal that put the finish to a flower. The hunchback, sitting between Madame Latournelle and Gobenheim, was swallowing tears and wondering how he could get round to Modeste, and whisper two words of warning in her ear. Madame Latournelle, by placing herself in front of Madame Mignon, had cut off Modeste with the diabolical ingenuity of a pious prude. Madame Mignon, silent, blind, and whiter than her usual pallor, plainly betrayed her knowledge of the ordeal to which the girl was to be subjected. Now, at the last moment, perhaps she disapproved of the stratagem, though deeming it necessary. Hence her silence. She was weeping in her heart. Exupère, the trigger of the trap, knew nothing whatever of the piece in which chance had cast him for a part. Gobenheim was as indifferent as Modeste herself seemed to be —a consequence of his nature.

To a spectator in the secret, the contrast between the utter ignorance of one-half of the party and the tremulous tension of the others would have been thrilling. In these days, more than ever, novel-writers deal largely in such effects; and they are in their rights, for nature has at all times outdone their skill. In this case, as you will see, social nature—which is nature within nature—was allowing itself the pleasure of making fact more interesting than romance, just as torrents produce effects forbidden to painters and achieve marvels by arranging or polishing stones so that architects and sculptors are amazed.

It was eight o'clock. At this season of the year it is the hour of the last gleam of twilight. That evening the sky was cloudless, the mild air caressed the earth, flowers breathed their fragrance, the grinding gravel could be heard under the feet of persons returning from their walk. The sea shone like a mirror.

There was so little wind that the candles on the table burned with a steady flame though the windows were half-open. The room, the evening, the house—what a setting for the portrait of this young creature, who at the moment was being studied by her friends with the deep attention of an artist gazing at "Margherita Doni," one of the glories of the Pitti palace. Was Modeste, a flower enshrined like that of Catullus, worthy of all these precautions? You have seen the cage; this is the bird:

At the age of twenty, slender and delicately made, like one of the sirens invented by English painters to grace a book of beauty, Modeste, like her mother before her, bears the engaging expression of a grace little appreciated in France, where it is called sentimentality, though among the Germans it is the poetry of the heart suffusing the surface, and displayed in affectation by simpletons, in exquisite manners by sensible girls.   Her most conspicuous feature was her pale gold hair, which classed her with the women called, no doubt in memory of Eve, *blondes celestes* (heavenly fair), whose sheeny skin looks like silk paper laid over the flesh, shivering in the winter or reveling in the sunshine of a look, and making the hand envious of the eye.   Under this hair, as light as marabout feathers, and worn in ringlets, the brow, so purely formed that it might have been drawn by compasses, is reserved and calm to placidity, though bright with thought ; but when or where could a smoother one be found, or more transparently frank ?   It seems to have a lustre like pearl.   Her eyes, of grayish blue, as clear as those of a child, have all a child's mischief and innocence, in harmony with the arch of eyebrows scarcely outlined, as lightly touched in as those painted in Chinese faces.   This playful innocence is accentuated by nacreous tones, with blue veins round the eyes and on the temples, a peculiarity of those delicate complexions.   Her face, of the oval so often seen in Raphael's Madonnas, is distinguished by the cool, maidenly flush of her cheeks, as tender as a China rose, on which the long lashes of her transparent eyelids cast a play of light and shade.   Her throat, bent over her work, and slender to fragility, suggests the sweeping lines dear to Leonardo.   A few freckles, like the patches of the past century, show that Modeste is a daughter of earth and not one of the creations seen in dreams by the Italian school of Angelico.   Lips, full but finely curved, and somewhat satirical in expression, betray a love of pleasure.   Her shape, pliant without being frail, would not scare away motherhood, like that of girls who seek to triumph through the unhealthy pressure of stays.   Buckram, steel, and stay-lace never improved or formed such serpentine lines of elegance, resembling those of a young poplar swayed by the wind.   A pearl-gray dress, long in the waist, and trimmed with cherry-colored gimp, accentuated the pure bust and covered the shoulders, still somewhat thin, over a deep muslin tucker, which betrayed only the outline of the curves where the bosom joins the shoulders. At the sight of this countenance, at once vague and intelligent, with a singular touch of determination given to it by a straight nose with rosy nostrils and firmly-cut outlines—a countenance where the poetry of an almost mystical brow was belied by the voluptuous curve of the mouth—where, in the changing depths of the eyes, candor seemed to fight for the mastery with the most accomplished irony—an observer might have thought that this young girl, whose quick ear caught every sound, whose nose was open to the fragrance of the blue flower of the ideal, must be the arena of a struggle between the poetry that plays around the daily rising of the sun and the labors of the day, between fancy and reality. Modeste was both curious and modest, knowing her fate, and purely chaste, the virgin of Spain rather than of Raphael.

She raised her head on hearing Dumay say to Exupère, "Come here, young man," and, seeing them talk together in a corner of the room, she fancied it was about some commission for Paris. She looked at the friends who surrounded her as if astonished at their silence, and exclaimed with a perfectly natural air—

"Well, are you not going to play?" pointing to the green table that Madame Latournelle called the altar.

"Let us begin," said Dumay, after dismissing Exupère.

"Sit there, Butscha!" said Madame Latournelle, placing the table between the clerk and the group formed by Madame Mignon and her daughter.

"And you—come here," said Dumay to his wife, desiring her to stay near him.

Madame Dumay, a little American of six-and-thirty, secretly wiped away her tears; she was devoted to Modeste and dreaded a catastrophe.

"You are not lively this evening," said Modeste.

" We are playing," said Gobenheim, sorting his hand.

However interesting the situation may seem, it will be far more so when Dumay's position with regard to Modeste is explained. If the brevity of the style makes the narrative dry, this will be forgiven for the sake of hastening to the end of this scene, and of the need, which rules all dramas, for setting forth the argument.

Dumay—Anne-François-Bernard—born at Vannes, went as a soldier in 1799, joining the army of Italy. His father, a president of the revolutionary tribunal, had distinguished himself by so much vigor that the country was too hot to hold the son when his father, a second-rate lawyer, perished on the scaffold after the 9th of Thermidor. His mother died of grief; and Anne, having sold everything he possessed, went off to Italy at the age of twenty-two, just as our armies were defeated. In the department of the Var he met a young man who, for similar reasons, was also in search of glory, thinking the battlefield less dangerous than Provence.

Charles Mignon, the last survivor of the family to whom Paris owes the street and the hotel built by Cardinal Mignon, had for his father a crafty man, who wished to save his estate of la Bastie, a nice little fief under the Counts of Provence, from the clutches of the revolution. Like all nervous people in those days, the Comte de la Bastie, now Citizen Mignon, thought it healthier to cut off other heads than to lose his own. This supposed terrorist vanished on the 9th of Thermidor, and was thenceforth placed on the list of *émigrés*. The fief of la Bastie was sold. The pepper-caster towers of the dishonored château were razed to the ground. Finally, Citizen Mignon himself, discovered at Orange, was killed with his wife and children, with the exception of Charles Mignon, whom he had sent in search of a refuge in the department of the Hautes-Alpes. Charles, stopped by these shocking tidings, awaited quieter times in a valley of Mont

2

Genèvre. There he lived till 1799 on a few louis his father had put into his hand at parting. At last, when he was three-and-twenty, with no fortune but his handsome person— the southern beauty which, in its perfection, is a glorious thing, the type of Antinous, Hadrian's famous favorite—he resolved to stake his Provençal daring on the red field of war, regarding his courage as a vocation, as did many another. On his way to headquarters at Nice he met the Breton.

The two infantrymen, thrown together by the similarity of their destiny and the contrast of their nature, drank of the torrent from the same cup, divided their allowance of biscuit, and were sergeants by the time peace was signed after the battle of Marengo.

When war broke out again, Charles Mignon got leave to be transferred to the cavalry, and then lost sight of his comrade. The last of the Mignons of la Bastie was, in 1812, an officer of the Legion of Honor and major of a cavalry regiment, hoping to be reinstated as Comte de la Bastie and made colonel by the Emperor. Then, taken prisoner by the Russians, he was sent with many more to Siberia. His traveling companion was a poor lieutenant, in whom he recognized Anne Dumay, with no decoration, brave indeed, but hapless, like the millions of rank-and-file with worsted epaulettes, the web of men on which Napoleon painted the picture of his Empire. In Siberia, to pass the time, the lieutenant-colonel taught his comrade arithmetic and writing, for education had seemed unimportant to his Scævola parent. Charles found in his first traveling companion one of those rare hearts to whom he could pour out all his griefs while confiding all his joys.

The Provençal had, ere this, met the fate which awaits every handsome young fellow. In 1804, at Frankfort-on-the-Main, he was adored by Bettina Wallenrod, the only daughter of a banker, and married her with all the more enthusiasm because she was rich, one of the beauties of the town, and he was still only a lieutenant with no fortune but the most un-

certain prospects of a soldier of that time. Old Wallenrod, a
decayed German Baron—bankers are always barons—was enchanted to think that the handsome lieutenant was the sole
representative of the Mignons of la Bastie, and approved the
affections of the fair Bettina, whom a painter—for there was
a painter then at Frankfort—had taken for his model of an
ideal figure of Germany. Wallenrod, who already thought
of his grandsons as Comtes de la Bastie-Wallenrod, invested
in the French funds a sufficient sum to secure to his daughter
thirty thousand francs a year. This dower made a very small
hole in his coffers, seeing how small a capital was required.
The Empire, following a practice not uncommon among
debtors, rarely paid the half-yearly dividends. Charles, indeed, was somewhat alarmed at this investment, for he had
not so much faith in the Imperial Eagle as the German Baron
had. The phenomenon of belief, or of admiration, which is
only a transient form of belief, can hardly exist in illicit com-
panionship with the idol. An engineer dreads the machine
which the traveler admires, and Napoleon's officers were the
stokers of his locomotive when they were not the fuel. Baron
von Wallenrod-Tustall-Bartenstild then promised to help the
young people. Charles loved Bettina Wallenrod as much as
she loved him, and that is saying a great deal; but when a
Provençal is fired, anything seems natural to him in the matter
of feeling. How could he help worshiping a golden-haired
woman who had stepped out of a picture by Albert Dürer, an
angel of good temper, with a fortune famous in Frankfort?

So Charles had four children, of whom only two daughters
were alive at the time when he poured out his sorrows on the
Breton's heart. Without knowing them, Dumay was fond of
these two little girls, the effect of the sympathy so well understood by Charles, who shows us the soldier as fatherly to
every child. The elder, named Bettina Caroline, was born in
1805; the second, Marie Modeste, in 1808. The unhappy
lieutenant-colonel, having had no news of those he loved,

came back on foot in 1814, with the lieutenant for his companion, all across Russia and Prussia. The two friends, for whom any difference of rank had ceased to exist, arrived at Frankfort just as Napoleon landed at Cannes. Charles found his wife at Frankfort, but in mourning; she had had the grief of losing the father who adored her, and who longed always to see her smiling, even by his death-bed. Old Wallenrod did not survive the overthrow of the Empire. At the age of seventy-two he had speculated largely in cotton, believing still in Napoleon's genius, and not knowing that genius is as often the slave of events as their master.

The last of the Wallenrods, the true Wallenrod-Tustall-Bartenstild, had bought almost as many bales of cotton as the Emperor had sacrificed men during his tremendous campaign in France.

"I am tying in cotton" (I am dying in clover), said this father to his daughter, for he was of the Goriot species, trying to beguile her of her grief, which terrified him, "and I tie owing noting to noboty"—and the Franco-German died struggling with the French language his daughter loved.

Charles Mignon, happy to have saved his wife and daughters from this double shipwreck, now returned to Paris, where the Emperor made him lieutenant-colonel of the Cuirassiers of the Guard and commander of the Legion of Honor. The colonel at last was general and Count, after Napoleon's first success; but his dream was drowned in torrents of blood at Waterloo. He was slightly wounded, and retired to the Loire, leaving Tours before the troops were disbanded.

In the spring of 1816 Charles realized the capital of his thirty thousand francs a year, which gave him about four hundred thousand francs, and decided on going to make his fortune in America, leaving a country where persecution already pressed hardly on Napoleon's soldiers. He went from Paris to le Havre, accompanied by Dumay, whose life he had saved in one of the frequent chances of war, by taking

him behind him on his horse in the confusion that ended the
day of Waterloo.   Dumay shared the colonel's opinions and
despondency.   Charles, to whom the Breton clung like a dog,
for the poor infantryman worshiped the two little girls, thought
that Dumay's habits of obedience and discipline, his honesty
and his attachment, would make him a servant not less faithful than useful.   He therefore proposed to him to take service
under him in private life.   Dumay was very happy to find
himself adopted into a family with whom he hoped to live
like mistletoe on an oak.

While awaiting an opportunity of sailing, choosing among
the ships, and meditating on the chances offered in the various ports of their destination, the colonel heard rumors of the
splendid fortunes that the peace held in store for le Havre.
While listening to a discussion between two of the natives,
he saw a means of making his fortune, and set up forthwith as
a shipowner, a banker, and a country gentleman.   He invested
two hundred thousand francs in land and houses, and freighted
a ship for New York with a cargo of French silks bought at
Lyons at a low figure.   Dumay sailed on the vessel as his
agent.   While the colonel was settling himself with his family
in the handsomest house in the Rue Royale, and studying the
science of banking with all the energy and prodigious acumen
of a Provençal, Dumay made two fortunes, for he returned
with a cargo of cotton bought for a mere song.   This transac-
tion produced an enormous capital for Mignon's business.
He then purchased the villa at Ingouville, and rewarded
Dumay by giving him a small house in the Rue Royale.

The worthy Breton had brought back with him from New
York with his bales a pretty little wife, who had been chiefly
attracted by his nationality as a Frenchman.   Miss Grummer
owned about four thousand dollars (twenty thousand francs),
which Dumay invested in his colonel's business.   Dumay,
now the *alter ego* of the shipowner, very soon learned book-
keeping, the science which, to use his phrase, distinguished the

sergeant-majors of trade. This guileless soldier, whom fortune
had neglected for twenty years, thought himself the happiest
man in the world when he saw himself master of a house—
which his employer's munificence furnished very prettily—of
twelve hundred francs a year of interest on his capital, and
of three thousand six hundred francs in salary. Never in his
dreams had Lieutenant Dumay hoped for such prosperity; but
he was even happier in feeling himself the hub of the richest
merchant's house in le Havre.

Madame Dumay had the sorrow of losing all her children
at their birth, and the disasters of her last confinement left her
no hope of having any; she therefore attached herself to the
two Mignon girls as affectionately as Dumay, who would not
have loved his own children so well. Madame Dumay, the
child of agriculturists, accustomed to a thrifty life, found two
thousand four hundred francs enough for herself and her
housekeeping. Thus, year by year, Dumay put two thousand
and some hundred francs into the Mignon concern. When
the master made up the annual balance, he added to the
cashier's credit a bonus in proportion to the business done.
In 1824 the sum to the cashier's account amounted to fifty-
eight thousand francs. Then it was that Charles Mignon,
Comte de la Bastie, a title that was never mentioned, crowned
his cashier's joy by giving him a lease of the chalet, where
we now find Modeste and her mother.

Madame Mignon's deplorable condition had its cause in
the catastrophe to which Charles' absence was due, for her
husband had left her a still handsome woman. It had taken
three years of sorrow to destroy the gentle German lady, but
it was one of those sorrows which are like a worm lying at
the heart of a fine fruit. The sum-total of her woes is easily
stated: Two children who died young had stamped a double
ci-git on a soul which could never forget. Charles' captivity
in Siberia had been to this dear and loving heart a daily
death. The disasters of the great Wallenrod house and the

unhappy banker's death on his empty money-bags, coming in the midst of Bettina's suspense about her husband, was a final blow. The joy of seeing him again almost killed this German floweret. Then came the second overthrow of the Empire, and their plans for emigration had been like relapses of the same fit of fever.

At last ten years of constant prosperity, the amusements of her home-life, the handsomest house in le Havre, the dinners, balls, and entertainments given by the successful merchant, the magnificence of the Villa Mignon, the immense respect and high esteem enjoyed by her husband, with the undivided affection of this man, who responded to perfect love by love equally perfect—all these had reconciled the poor woman to life.

Then, at the moment when all her doubts were at rest, and she looked forward to a calm evening after her stormy day, a mysterious disaster, buried in the heart of the double household, and presently to be related, came like a summons from misfortune. In 1826, in the midst of a party, when all the town was ready to return Charles Mignon as its deputy, three letters (from New York, London, and Paris) came like three hammer-strokes on the glass house of prosperity. In ten minutes ruin swooped down with vulture's wings on this unheard-of good fortune, like the frost on the Grande Armée in 1812. In one night which he spent with Dumay over the books, Charles Mignon was prepared for the worst. It would absorb everything he possessed, not excepting the furniture, to pay everybody.

"Le Havre," said the colonel to the lieutenant, "shall never see me in the mud. Dumay, I will take your sixty thousand francs at six per cent.——"

"At three, colonel."

"At nothing, then," said Charles peremptorily. "I make you my partner in my new enterprise. The 'Modeste,' which is no longer mine, sails to-morrow ; the captain takes me with him. You—I place you in charge of my wife and daughter. I shall never write. No news is good news."

Dumay, still but a lieutenant, had not asked his colonel by a word what his purpose was.

"I suspect," said he to Latournelle, with a knowing air, "that the colonel has laid his plans."

On the following morning, at break of day, he saw his master safe on board the good ship "Modeste," bound for Constantinople. Standing on the vessel's poop, the Breton said to the Provençal—

"What are your last orders, colonel?"

"That no man ever goes near the chalet!" cried the father, with difficulty restraining a tear. "Dumay, guard my last child as a bull-dog might. Death to any one who may try to tempt my second daughter! Fear nothing, not even the scaffold. I would meet you there!"

"Colonel, do your business in peace. I understand. You will find Mademoiselle Modeste as you leave her, or I shall be dead! You know me, and you know our two Pyrenean dogs. No one shall get at your daughter. Forgive me for using so many words."

The two soldiers embraced as men who had learned to appreciate each other in the heart of Siberia.

The same day the "Courrier du Havre" published this terrible, simple, vigorous, and honest leading paragraph:

"The house of Charles Mignon has suspended payment, but the undersigned liquidators pledge themselves to pay all the outstanding debts. Bearers of bills at date can at once discount them. The value of the landed estate will completely cover current accounts.

"This notice is issued for the honor of the house and to prevent any shock to general credit on the Havre Exchange.

"Monsieur Charles Mignon sailed this morning in the 'Modeste' for Asia Minor, having left a power-of-attorney

"DUMAY, GUARD MY LAST CHILD AS A BULL-DOG MIGHT."

D. MURRAY SMITH.

to enable us to realize every form of property, even landed estate.

> "DUMAY, Liquidator for the Banking Account.
> "LATOURNELLE, Notary, Liquidator for the Houses and Land in Town and Country.
> "GOBENHEIM, Liquidator for Commercial Bills."

Latournelle owed his prosperity to Monsieur Mignon's kindness; he had, in 1817, lent the notary a hundred thousand francs to buy the best business in le Havre. The poor lawyer, without any pecuniary resources, was by that time forty years old; he had been a head clerk for ten years, and looked forward to being a clerk for the rest of his days. He was the only man in le Havre whose devotion could compare with Dumay's, for Gobenheim took advantage of this bankruptcy to carry on Mignon's connection and business, which enabled him to start his little banking concern. While universal regret was expressed on 'Change, on the quays, and in every home; while praises of a blameless, honorable, and beneficent man were on every lip, Latournelle and Dumay, as silent and as busy as emmets, were selling, realizing, paying, and settling up. Vilquin gave himself airs of generosity, and bought the villa, the town-house, and a farm, and Latournelle took advantage of this first impulse to extract a good price from Vilquin.

Every one wanted to call on Madame and Mademoiselle Mignon, but they had obeyed Charles and taken refuge at the chalet the very morning of his departure, of which at the first moment they knew nothing. Not to be shaken in his purpose by their grief, the courageous banker had kissed his wife and daughter in their sleep. Three hundred cards were left at the door. A fortnight later the most complete oblivion, as Charles had prophesied, showed the two women the wisdom and dignity of the step enjoined on them.

Dumay appointed representatives of his master at New York,

London, and Paris. He followed up the liquidation of the three banking houses to which Mignon's ruin was due, and between 1826 and 1828 recovered five hundred thousand francs, the eighth part of Charles' fortune. In obedience to the orders drawn up the night before his departure, Dumay forwarded this sum at the beginning of 1828, through the house of Mongenod at New York, to be placed to Monsieur Mignon's credit. All this was done with military punctuality, excepting with regard to the retention of thirty thousand francs for the personal needs of Madame and Mademoiselle Mignon. This, which Charles had ordered, Dumay did not carry out. The Breton sold his house in the town for twenty thousand francs, and gave this to Madame Mignon, reflecting that the more money his colonel could command, the sooner he would return.

"For lack of thirty thousand francs a man sometimes is lost," said he to Latournelle, who bought the house at his friend's price ; and there the inhabitants of the chalet could always find room. Many were the pleasant hours that Madame Mignon, her daughter, Modeste, and also Lieutenant Dumay and his ever-watchful wife, passed in that hospitable retreat. Butscha's wit constantly entertained them.

This, to the famous house of Mignon, le Havre, was the outcome of the crisis which, in 1825–26, upset the principal centres of commerce, and caused—if you remember that hurricane—the ruin of several Paris bankers, one of them the president of the chamber of commerce. It is intelligible that this tremendous overthrow, closing a civic reign of ten years, might have been a death-blow to Bettina Wallenrod, who once more found herself parted from her husband, knowing nothing of his fate, apparently as full of peril and adventure as Siberian exile ; but the trouble that was really bringing her to the grave was to these visible griefs what an ill-starred child is to the commonplace troubles of a family—a child that gnaws and devours its home. The fatal stone that had struck this mother's heart was a tombstone in the little cemetery of Ingouville, on which may be read :

BETTINA CAROLINE MIGNON

AGED TWO-AND-TWENTY

PRAY FOR HER !

1827.

This inscription is for the girl who lies there what many an epitaph is for the dead—a table of contents to an unknown book. Here is the book in its terrible epitome, and it may explain the pledge demanded and given in the parting words of the colonel and subaltern.

A young man, extremely handsome, named Georges d'Estourny, came to le Havre on the common pretext of seeing the sea, and he saw Caroline Mignon. A man of some pretense to fashion, and from Paris, never lacks some introductions ; he was therefore invited by the intervention of a friend of the Mignons to an entertainment at Ingouville. He fell very much in love with Caroline and her fortune and schemed for a happy issue. At the end of three months he had played every trick of the seducer, and run away with Caroline. The father of a family who has two daughters ought no more to admit a young man to his house without knowing him than he should allow books or newspapers to lie about without having read them. The innocence of a girl is like milk which is turned by a thunder-clap, by an evil smell, by a hot day, or even by a breath.

When he read his eldest daughter's farewell letter, Charles Mignon made Madame Dumay set out instantly for Paris. The family alleged the need for a change of air suddenly prescribed by the family doctor, who lent himself to this necessary pretext ; but this could not keep the town from gossiping about her absence.

"What, such a strong girl, with the complexion of a Spaniard, and hair like jet! She, consumptive!"

"Yes—so they say. She did something imprudent——"

"Ah, ha!" cried some Vilquin.

"She came in from a ride bathed in perspiration and drank iced water, at least so Dr. Troussenard says."

By the time Madame Dumay returned, the troubles of the Mignons were an exhausted subject; no one thought anything more of Caroline's absence or the return of the cashier's wife.

At the beginning of 1827 the newspapers were full of the trial of Georges d'Estourny, who was proved guilty of constant cheating at play. This young pirate vanished abroad without thinking anything more about Mademoiselle Mignon, whose money value was destroyed by the bankruptcy at le Havre. Before long Caroline knew that she was deserted and her father a ruined man. She came home in a fearful state of mortal illness, and died a few days afterward at the chalet. Her death, at any rate, saved her reputation. The malady spoken of by Monsieur Mignon at the time of his daughter's elopement was very generally believed in, and the medical orders which had sent her off, it was said, to Nice.

To the very last the mother hoped to save her child. Bettina was her darling, as Modeste was her father's. There was something touching in this preference: Bettina was the image of Charles, as Modeste was of her mother. They perpetuated their love in their children. Caroline, a Provençal, inherited from her father the beautiful blue-black hair, like a raven's wing, which we admire in the daughters of the south, the hazel, almond-shaped eye as bright as a star, the olive complexion with the golden glow of a velvety fruit, the arched foot, the Spanish bust that swells beneath the bodice. And the father and mother were alike proud of the charming contrast of the two sisters.

"A demon and an angel!" people used to say, without ill meaning, though it was prophetic.

After spending a month in tears in her room, where she insisted on staying and seeing no one, the poor German lady came forth with her eyes seriously injured. Before she lost her sight she went, in spite of all her friends, to look at Caroline's tomb. This last image remained bright in her darkness, as the red spectre of the last object we have seen remains when we shut our eyes in bright daylight. After this terrible and twofold disaster, Dumay, though he could not be more devoted, was more anxious than ever about Modeste, now an only child, though her father knew it not. Madame Dumay, who was crazy about Modeste, like all women who have no children, overpowered her with her deputy motherhood, but without disobeying her husband's orders. Dumay was distrustful of female friendships. His injunctions were absolute.

"If ever any man, of whatever age or rank, speaks to Modeste," said Dumay, "if he looks at her, casts sheep's eyes at her, he is a dead man. I will blow his brains out and surrender myself to the public prosecutor. My death may save her. If you do not wish to see me cut my throat, fill my place unfailingly when I am in town."

For three years Dumay had examined his pistols every night. He seemed to have included in his oath the two Pyrenean dogs, remarkably intelligent beasts; one slept in the house, the other was sentinel in a kennel that he never came out of, and he never barked; but the minute when those dogs should set their teeth in an intruder would be a terrible one for him.

The life may now be imagined which the mother and daughter led at the chalet. Monsieur and Madame Latournelle, frequently accompanied by Gobenheim, came almost every evening to visit their friends and play a rubber. Conversation would turn on business at le Havre, on the trivial events of country-town life. They left between nine and ten. Modeste went to put her mother to bed; they said their prayers together, they talked over their hopes, they spoke of

the dearly loved traveler.   After kissing her mother, Modeste
went to her own room at about ten o'clock.   Next morning
Modeste dressed her mother with the same care, the same
prayers, the same little chat.   To Modeste's honor, from the
day when her mother's terrible infirmity deprived her of one
of her senses, she made herself her waiting-maid, and always
with the same solicitude at every hour, without wearying of
it, or finding it monotonous.   Her affection was supreme,
and always ready, with a sweetness rare in young girls, and
that was highly appreciated by those who saw her tenderness.
And so Modeste was, in the eyes of the Latournelles and of
Monsieur and Madame Dumay, the jewel I have described.
Between breakfast and dinner, on sunny days, Madame Mignon and Madame Dumay took a little walk as far as the shore,
Modeste assisting, for the blind woman needed the support of
two arms.

A month before the scene in which this digression falls as
a parenthesis, Madame Mignon had held council with her
only friends, Madame Latournelle, the notary, and Dumay,
while Madame Dumay was giving Modeste the little diversion
of a long walk.

"Listen, my friends," said the blind woman, "my daughter
is in love.   I feel it.   A strange change has come over her,
and I cannot think how you have failed to observe it——"

"Bless my stars!" the lieutenant exclaimed.

"Do not interrupt me, Dumay.   For the last two months
Modeste has dressed herself with care as if she were going to
meet some one.   She has become excessively particular about
her shoes; she wants her foot to look nice, and scolds Madame Gobain the shoemaker.   Some days the poor child sits
gloomy and watchful, as if she expected somebody; her voice
is short and sharp, as though by questioning her I broke in
on her expectancy, her secret hopes; and then, if that somebody has been——"

"Bless my stars!"

"Sit down, Dumay," said the lady. "Well, then Modeste is gay. Oh! you do not see that she is gay; you cannot discern these shades, too subtle for eyes to see that have all nature to look at. Her cheerfulness betrays itself in the tones of her voice, accents which I can detect and account for. Modeste, instead of sitting still and dreaming, expends her light activity in flighty movement. In short, she is happy! There is a tone of thanksgiving even in the ideas she utters. Oh, my friends, I have learned to know happiness as well as grief. By the kiss my poor Modeste gives me I can guess what is going on in her mind: whether she has had what she was expecting, or is uneasy. There are many shades in kisses, even in those of a young girl—for Modeste is innocence itself, but it is not ignorant innocence. Though I am blind, my affection is clairvoyante, and I implore you—watch my daughter."

On this, Dumay, quite ferocious; the notary as a man who is bent on solving a riddle; Madame Latournelle as a duenna who has been cheated; and Madame Dumay, who shared her husband's fears—all constituted themselves spies over Modeste. Modeste was never alone for a moment. Dumay spent whole nights under the windows, wrapped in a cloak like a jealous Spaniard; still, armed as he was with military sagacity, he could find no accusing clue. Unless she were in love with the nightingales in Vilquin's park, or some goblin prince, Modeste could have seen no one, could neither have received nor given a signal. Madame Dumay, who never went to bed till she had seen Modeste asleep, hovered about the roads on the high ground near the chalet with a vigilance equal to her husband's. Under the eyes of these four Arguses, the blameless child, whose smallest actions were reported and analyzed, was so absolutely acquitted of any criminal proceedings, that the friends suspected Madame Mignon of a craze, a monomania. It devolved on Madame Latournelle, who

herself took Modeste to church and home again, to tell the
mother that she was under a mistake.

"Modeste," said she, "is a very enthusiastic young person;
she has passions for this one's poetry and that one's prose.
You could not see what an impression was made on her by
that executioner's piece (a phrase of Butscha's, who lent wit
without any return to his benefactress), called 'Le Dernier
Jour d'un condamné' (The Condemned's Last Day); but
she seemed to me beside herself with her admiration of that
Monsieur Hugo. I cannot think where that sort of people
(Victor Hugo, Lamartine, and Byron were what Madame
Latournelle meant by *that sort*) go to find their ideas. The
little thing talked to me about 'Childe Harold;' I did not
choose to have the worst of it; I was fool enough to set to
work to read it that I might be able to argue with her. I
don't know whether it is to be set down to the translation,
but my heart heaved, my eyes were dizzy. I could not get
on with it. It is full of howling comparisons, of rocks that
faint away, of the lava of war!

"Of course, as it is an Englishman on his travels, one
must expect something queer, but this is really too much!
You fancy you are in Spain, and he carries you up into the
clouds above the Alps; he makes the torrents and the stars
speak; and then there are too many virgins! You get sick
of them. In short, after Napoleon's campaigns we have had
enough of flaming shot and sounding brass which roll on
from page to page. Modeste tells me that all this pathos
comes from the translator, and I ought to read the English.
But I am not going to learn English for Lord Byron when I
would not learn it for Exupère! I much prefer the romances
of Ducray-Duménil to these English romances! I am too
thoroughly Norman to fall in love with everything that comes
from abroad, and especially from England——"

Madame Mignon, notwithstanding her perpetual mourning,
could not help smiling at the idea of Madame Latournelle

reading "Childe Harold." The stern lady accepted this smile as approbation of her doctrines.

"And so, my dear Madame Mignon, you mistake Modeste's imaginings, the result of her reading, for love affairs. She is twenty. At that age a girl loves herself. She dresses to see herself dressed. Why, I used to make my little sister, who is dead now, put on a man's hat, and we played at gentleman and lady—— You, at Frankfort, had a happy girlhood, but let us be just: Modeste here has no amusements. In spite of our readiness to meet her lightest wishes, she knows that she is guarded, and the life she leads has little pleasure to offer a girl who could not, as she can, find something to divert her in books. Take my word for it, she loves no one but you. Think yourself lucky that she falls in love with nobody but Lord Byron's corsairs, Walter Scott's romantic heroes, or your Germans, Count Egmont, Werther, Schiller, and all the other *ers.*"

"Well, madame?" said Dumay respectfully, alarmed by Madame Mignon's silence.

"Modeste is not merely ready for love; she loves somebody," said the mother obstinately.

"Madame, my life is at stake, and you will no doubt allow me—not for my own sake, but for my poor wife's and for the colonel's, and all our sakes—to try to find out which is mistaken—the watch-dog or the mother."

"It is you, Dumay! Oh, if I could but look my daughter in the face!" sobbed the poor blind woman.

"But who is there that she can love?" replied Madame Latournelle. "As for us—I can answer for my Exupère."

"It cannot be Gobenheim, whom we hardly see for nine hours out of the week since the colonel went away. Besides, he is not thinking of Modeste—that crown-piece made man! His uncle, Gobenheim-Keller, told him, 'Get rich enough to marry a Keller!' With that for a programme, there is no fear that he will even know of what sex Modeste is. Those

3

are all the men we see here. I do not count Butscha, poor
little hunchback. I love him; he is your Dumay, madame,"
he said to the notary's wife. "Butscha knows very well that
if he glanced at Modeste it would cost him a combing *à la
mode de Vannes.* Not a soul ever comes near us. Madame
Latournelle, who since—since your misfortune, comes to take
Modeste to church and bring her home again, has watched
her carefully these last days during the mass, and has seen
nothing suspicious about her. And then, if I must tell you
everything, I myself have raked the paths round the house for
the last month, and I have always found them in the morning
with no footmarks."

"Rakes are not costly nor difficult to use," said the German lady.

"And the dogs?" asked Dumay.

"Lovers can find sops for them," replied Madame Mignon.

"I could blow out my own brains if you are right, for I
should be done for," cried Dumay.

"And why, Dumay?"

"Madame, I could not meet the colonel's eye if he were
not to find his daughter, especially now that she is his only
child; and as pure, as virtuous as she was when he said to me
on board the ship, 'Do not let the fear of the scaffold stop
you, Dumay, when Modeste's honor is at stake.'"

"I know you both—how like you!" murmured Madame
Mignon, much moved.

"I will wager my eternal salvation that Modeste is as innocent as she was in her cradle," quoth Madame Dumay.

"Oh, I will know all about it," replied Dumay, "if
Madame la Comtesse will allow me to try a plan, for old soldiers are knowing in stratagems."

"I allow you to do anything that may clear up the matter
without injuring our last surviving child."

"And what will you do, Anne," asked his wife, "to find
out a young girl's secret when it is so closely kept?"

"All of you obey me exactly," returned the lieutenant, "for you must all help."

This brief account, which, if elaborately worked up, would have furnished forth a complete picture of domestic life—how many families will recognize in it the events of their own home!—is enough to give a clue to the importance of the little details previously given of the persons and circumstances of this evening, when the lieutenant had undertaken to cope with a young girl, and to drag from the recesses of her heart a passion detected by her blind mother.

An hour went by in ominous calm, broken only by the hieroglyphical phrases of the whist-players: "Spade! Trump! Cut! Have we the honors? Two trebles! Eight all! Who deals?"—phrases representing in these days the great emotions of the aristocracy of Europe. Modeste stitched, without any surprise at her mother's taciturnity. Madame Mignon's pocket-handkerchief slipped off her lap on to the floor; Butscha flew to pick it up. He was close to Modeste, and as he rose whispered in her ear, "Be on your guard!"

Modeste raised astonished eyes, and their light, pointed darts as it seemed, filled the hunchback with ineffable joy.

"She loves no one," said the poor fellow to himself, and he rubbed his hands hard enough to flay them.

At this moment Exupère flew through the garden and into the house, rushing into the drawing-room like a whirlwind, and said in Dumay's ear, "Here is the young man!"

Dumay rose, seized his pistols, and went out.

"Good God! Supposing he kills him!" cried Madame Dumay, who burst into tears.

"But what is going on?" asked Modeste, looking at her friends with an air of perfect candor, and without any alarm.

"Something about a young man who prowls round the chalet!" cried Madame Latournelle.

"What then?" said Modeste. "Why should Dumay kill him?"

"*Sancta simplicitas!*" said Butscha, looking at his master as proudly as Alexander gazes at Babylon in Lebrun's picture.

"Where are you going, Modeste?" asked her mother, as her daughter was leaving the room.

"To get everything ready for you to go to bed, mamma," replied Modeste, in a voice as clear as the notes of a harmonica.

"You have had all your trouble for nothing," said Butscha to Dumay when he came in.

"Modeste is as saintly as the Virgin on our altar!" cried Madame Latournelle.

"Ah, good heavens! Such agitation is too much for me," said the cashier. "And yet I am a strong man."

"I would give twenty-five sous to understand one word of what you are at this evening," said Gobenheim; "you all seem to me to have gone mad."

"And yet a treasure is at stake," said Butscha, standing on tiptoe to speak into Gobenheim's ear.

"Unfortunately, I am almost positive of the truth of what I say," repeated the mother.

"Then it now lies with you, madame," said Dumay quietly, "to prove that we are wrong."

When he found that nothing was involved but Modeste's reputation, Gobenheim took his hat, bowed, and went away, carrying off ten sous, regarding a fresh rubber as hopeless.

"Exupère, and you Butscha, leave us," said Madame Latournelle. "Go down to the town. You will be in time to see one piece; I will treat you to the play."

As soon as Madame Mignon was left with her four friends, Madame Latournelle glanced at Dumay, who, being a Breton, understood the mother's persistency, and then at her husband fidgeting with the cards, and thought herself justified in speaking.

"Come, Madame Mignon, tell us what decisive evidence has struck your ear?"

"Oh, my dear friend, if you were a musician, you, like me, would have heard Modeste's tone when she sings of love."

The piano belonging to the two sisters was one of the few feminine luxuries among the furniture brought from the town-house to the chalet. Modeste had mitigated some tedium by studying without a master. She was a born musician, and often played to cheer her mother. She sang with natural grace the German airs her mother taught her. From this instruction and this endeavor had resulted the phenomenon, not uncommon in natures prompted by a vocation, that Modeste unconsciously composed purely melodic strains, as such composition is possible without a knowledge of harmony. Melody is to music what imagery and feeling are to poetry, a flower that may blossom spontaneously. All nations have had popular melodies before the introduction of harmony. Botany came after flowers. Thus Modeste, without having learned anything of the technique of painting beyond what she had gathered from seeing her sister work in water-colors, could stand enchanted before a picture by Raphael, Titian, Rubens, Murillo, Rembrandt, Albert Dürer, or Holbein; that is to say, the highest ideal of each nation. Now, for about a month, Modeste had more especially burst into nightingale songs, into new strains so poetical as to arouse her mother's attention, surprised as she was to find Modeste bent on composition and trying airs to unfamiliar words.

"If your suspicions have no other foundation," said Latournelle to Madame Mignon, "I pity your sensitiveness."

"When a young girl sings in Brittany," said Dumay, now grave again, "the lover is very near."

"I will let you overhear Modeste improvising," said the mother, "and you will see!——"

"Poor child!" said Madame Dumay. "If she could but know of our anxiety, she would be in despair; and she would tell us the truth, especially if she knew all it meant to Dumay.''

"To-morrow, my friends, I will question Modeste," said Madame Mignon; "and perhaps I shall achieve more by affection than you have gained by ruse.''

Was the comedy of the " Ill-guarded Daughter " being enacted here, as it is everywhere and at all times, while these worthy Bartolos, these spies, these vigilant watch-dogs failed to scent, to guess, to detect the lover, the conspiracy, the smoke of the fire ?

This was not the consequence of any defiance between a prisoner and her gaolers, between the tyranny of the dungeon and the liberty of the captive, but merely the eternal repetition of the first drama played as the curtain rose on the new creation : Eve in Paradise. Which, in this case, was right— the mother or the watch-dog ?

None of the persons about Modeste understood the girl's heart—for, be assured, the soul and the face were in unison. Modeste had transplanted her life into a world of which the existence is as completely denied in our days as the New World of Christopher Columbus was denied in the sixteenth century. Fortunately, she could be silent, or she would have been thought mad.

We must first explain the influence that past events had had on the girl. Two especially had formed her character, as they had awakened her intelligence. Monsieur and Madame Mignon, startled by the disaster that had come upon Bettina, had, before their bankruptcy, resolved on seeing Modeste married, and their choice fell on the son of a wealthy banker, a native of Hamburg, who had settled at le Havre in 1815, and who was under some obligations to them. This young man—Francisque Althor—the dandy of le Havre, handsome in the style which captivates the Philistine, what the English call a heavy-weight—florid, healthy coloring, firm flesh, and square shoulders—threw over his bride-elect, at the news of

their disaster, so completely that he had never since set eyes
on Modeste, or on Madame Mignon, or on the Dumays.
Latournelle having made so bold as to speak to the father,
Jacob Althor, on the subject, the old German had shrugged
his shoulders, and replied, "I do not know what you mean."

This reply, repeated to Modeste to give her experience,
was a lesson she understood all the better because Latournelle
and Dumay made voluminous comments on this base desertion. Charles Mignon's two daughters, spoiled children as
they were, rode, had their own horses and servants, and enjoyed fatal liberty. Modeste, finding herself in command of
a recognized lover, had allowed Francisque to kiss her hand,
and put his arm round her to help her to mount; she had
accepted flowers and the trifling gifts of affection which are
the burden of paying court to a young lady; she worked him
a purse, believing in bonds of that kind, so strong to noble
souls, but mere cobwebs to the Gobenheims, Vilquins, and
Althors.

In the course of the spring, after Madame Mignon and her
daughter had moved into the chalet, Francisque Althor went
to dine with the Vilquins. On catching sight of Modeste
beyond the wall of the lawn, he looked away. Six weeks
after, he married Mademoiselle Vilquin—the eldest. Thus
Modeste learned that she, handsome, young, and well born,
had for three months been simply Mademoiselle Million. So
Modeste's poverty, which was of course known, was a sentinel
which guarded the ways to the chalet quite as well as the Dumays' prudence and the Latournelles' vigilance. Mademoiselle
Mignon was never mentioned but with insulting pity: "Poor
girl! what will become of her? She will die an old maid."
"What a hard lot! After seeing all the world at her feet,
and having a chance of marrying Althor, to find that no one
will have anything to say to her?" "Such a life of luxury,
my dear! and to have sunk to penury!"

Nor were these insults spoken in private and only guessed

by Modeste; more than once she heard them uttered by the
young men and girls of the town when walking at Ingouville,
who, knowing that Madame and Mademoiselle Mignon lived
at the chalet, discussed them audibly as they went past the
pretty little house. Some of the Vilquins' friends wondered
that these ladies could bear to live so near the home of their
former splendor. Modeste, sitting behind closed shutters,
often heard such impertinence as this: "I cannot think how
they can live there!" one would say to another, walking
round the garden, perhaps to help the Vilquins to be rid of
their tenants. "What do they live on? What can they do
there? The old woman is gone blind! Is Mademoiselle
Mignon still pretty? Ah, she has no horses now. How
dashing she used to be!"

As she heard this savage nonsense spoken by envy, foul-
mouthed and surly, and tilting at the past, many girls would
have felt the blood rise to their very brow; others would
have wept; some would have felt a surge of rage; but Modeste
smiled as we smile at a theatre, hearing actors speak. Her
pride could not descend to the level which such words, rising
from below, could reach.

The other event was even more serious than this mercenary
desertion. Bettina Caroline had died in her sister's arms;
Modeste had nursed her with the devotion of a woman, with
the inquisitiveness of a maiden imagination. The two girls,
in the watches of the night, had exchanged many a confidence. What dramatic interest hung around Bettina in the
eyes of her innocent sister! Bettina knew passion only as
misfortune; she was dying because she had loved. Between
two girls every man, wretch though he be, is a lover. Passion
is the one thing really absolute in human life; it will always
have its own. Georges d'Estourny, a gambler, dissipated
and guilty, always dwelt in the memory of these two young
things as the Parisian dandy of the Havre parties, the cyno-
sure of every woman—Bettina believed that she had snatched

him from Madame Vilquin's flirtations—and, to crown all,
Bettina's successful lover. In a young girl her worship is
stronger than social reprobation. In Bettina's mind, justice
had erred ; how should she have condemned a young man by
whom she had been loved for six months, loved with passion
in the mysterious retreat where Georges hid her in Paris, that
he might preserve his liberty. Thus Bettina, in her death,
had inoculated her sister with love.

The sisters had often discussed the great drama of passion,
to which imagination lends added importance ; and the dead
girl had taken Modeste's purity with her to her grave, leaving
her not perhaps all-knowing, but, at any rate, all-curious. At
the same time, remorse had often set sharp pangs in Bettina's
heart, and she lavished warnings on her sister. In the midst
of her revelations, she never failed to preach obedience in
Modeste, absolute obedience to her family. On the eve of
her death, she implored her sister to remember the pillow she
had soaked with her tears, and never to imitate the conduct
her sufferings could scarcely expiate. Bettina accused herself
of having brought the lightning down on those dear to her ;
she died in despair at not receiving her father's forgiveness.
In spite of the consolations of religion, which was softened
by such deep repentance, Bettina's last words, in a heart-
rending cry, were, "Father ! Father ! "

"Never give your heart but with your hand," said she to
Modeste, an hour before her death ; "and, above all, accept
no attentions without my mother's consent or papa's."

These words, touching in their simple truth and spoken in
the hour of death, found an echo in Modeste's mind, all the
more because Bettina made her take a solemn vow. The
poor girl, with prophetic insight, drew from under her pillow
a ring on which she had had engraved *Pense à Bettina*, 1827
—"Remember Bettina"—instead of a motto, sending it by
the hand of her faithful servant Françoise Cochet, to be done
in the town. A few minutes before she breathed her last

sigh, she placed this ring on her sister's finger, begging her to wear it till she should be married. Thus, between these two girls there had been a strange succession of acute remorse and artless descriptions of that brief summer which had been so soon followed by the autumn winds of desertion, while tears, regrets, and memories were constantly overruled by a dread of evil.

And yet this drama of the young creature seduced, and returning to die of a dreadful disorder under the roof of elegant poverty, the meanness of the Vilquins' son-in-law, and her mother's blindness, resulting from her griefs, only account for the surface of Modeste's character, with which the Dumays and the Latournelles had to be content, for no devotion can fill the mother's place. This monotonous life in the pretty chalet, among the beautiful flowers grown by Dumay; these habits, as regular as the working of a clock; this provincial propriety; these rubbers at cards by which she sat knitting; this silence, only broken by the moaning of the sea at the equinoxes; this monastic peace covered the stormiest kind of life—the life of ideas, the life of the spiritual world.

We sometimes wonder at the lapses of young girls, but that is when they have no blind mother to sound with her stick the depths of the maiden heart undermined by the caverns of fancy.

The Dumays were asleep when Modeste opened her window, imagining that a man might pass by—the man of her dreams, the knight who would take her on a pillion, defying Dumay's pistols. In her dejection after her sister's death, Modeste had plunged into such constant reading as was enough to make her idiotic. Having been brought up to speak two languages, she was mistress of German as well as of French; then she and Caroline had learned English of Madame Dumay. Modeste, who, in such matters, found little supervision from her uncultivated companions, fed her soul on the masterpieces of modern English, German, and French literature—Lord Byron,

Goethe, Schiller, Walter Scott, Hugo, Lamartine, Crabbe, Moore, the great works of the seventeenth and eighteenth centuries, history and the theatre, romance from Rabelais to Manon Lescaut, from Montaigne's "Essays" to Diderot, from the "Fabliaux" to "La Nouvelle Héloïse," the thoughts of three countries furnished her brain with a medley of images. And her mind was beautiful in its cold guilelessness, its repressed virginal instincts, from which sprang forth, flashing, armed, sincere, and powerful, an intense admiration for genius. To Modeste, a new book was a great event; she was so happy over a great work as to alarm Madame Latournelle, as we have seen, and saddened when it failed to take her heart by storm.

But no gleam of this lurid flame ever appeared on the surface; it escaped the eye of Lieutenant Dumay and his wife as well as of the Latournelles; but the ear of the blind mother could not fail to hear its crackling. The deep contempt which Modeste thenceforth conceived for all ordinary men soon gave her countenance an indescribably proud and shy expression which qualified its German simplicity, but which agrees with one detail of her face; her hair, growing in a point in the middle of her forehead, seems to continue the slight furrow made by thought between her brows, and makes this shy look perhaps a little too wild.

This sweet girl's voice—before his departure Charles Mignon used to call her his little "Solomon's slipper," she was so clever—had acquired delightful flexibility of accent from her study of three languages. This advantage is yet further enhanced by a suave fresh quality which goes to the heart as well as to the ear. Though her mother could not see the hope of high destiny stamped on her daughter's brow, she could study the changes of her soul's development in the tones of that amorous voice.

After this period of ravenous reading, there came to Modeste a phase of the singular faculty possessed by a lively imagination ; of living as an actor in an existence pictured as in a dream; of representing things wished for with a vividness so keen that it verges on reality ; of enjoying them in fancy, of devouring time even, seeing herself married, grown old, attending her own funeral, like Charles V.—in short, of playing out the drama of life, and at need that of death too.

As for Modeste, she played the drama of love. She imagined herself adored to the height of her wishes, and passing through every social phase. As the heroine of some dark romance, she loved either the executioner or some villain who died on the scaffold, or else, like her sister, some penniless fop, whose misdemeanors were the affair of the police court. She pictured herself as a courtesan, and laughed men to scorn in the midst of perpetual festivities, like Ninon. By turns, she led the life of an adventuress or of a popular actress, going through the vicissitudes of a Gil Blas or the triumphs of Pasta, Malibran, Florine. Satiated with horrors, she would come back to real life. She married a notary, she ate the dry bread of respectability, she saw herself in Madame Latournelle. She accepted a laborious life, facing the worries of accumulating a fortune ; then she began to romance again : she was loved for her beauty ; the son of a peer of France, artistic and eccentric, read her heart, and discerned the star which the genius of a Staël had set on her brow. At last her father returned a millionaire. Justified by experience, she subjected her lovers to tests, preserving her own freedom ; she owned a splendid château, servants' carriages, everything that luxury has most curious to bestow ; and she mystified her lovers till she was forty, when she accepted an offer.

This edition of the "Arabian Nights," of which there was but one copy, lasted nearly a year, and brought Modeste to satiety of invention. She too often held life in the hollow of her hand ; she could say to herself very philosophically, and too seriously, too bitterly, too often, "Well; and then?" not to sink now to her waist in those depths of disgust, into

which men of genius fall who are too eager to escape by the
vast labor of the task to which they have devoted themselves.
But for her rich nature and her youth, Modeste would have
retired to a cloister. This satiety flung the girl, still soaked
in Catholic feeling, into a love of goodness and of the infinitude of heaven. She conceived of charity as the occupation
of her life ; still she groped in forlorn gloom as she found
there no aliment for the fancy that gnawed at her heart like a
malignant insect in the cup of a flower. She calmly sewed
on baby clothes for poor women ; and she listened absently
to Monsieur Latournelle grumbling at Monsieur Dumay for
trumping a thirteenth, or forcing him to play his last trump.
Faith led Modeste into a strange path. She fancied that by
becoming irreproachable in the Catholic sense, she might
achieve such a pitch of sanctity that God would hear her and
grant her desires.

"'Faith,' as Jesus Christ says, 'can remove mountains ;'
the Saviour made His apostle walk on the Lake of Tiberias,
while I only ask of God to send me a husband," thought she.
"That is much easier than going for a walk on the sea."

She fasted all through Lent, and did not commit the smallest
sin ; then she promised herself that on coming out of church
on a certain day she would meet a handsome young man,
worthy of her, whom her mother would approve, and who
would follow her, madly in love. On the day she had fixed
for God to send her this angel without fail, she was persistently followed by a horrible beggar ; it poured with rain ;
and there was not one young man out of doors. She went
down to the quay to see the English come on shore, but every
Englishman had an English damsel almost as handsome as
herself, and Modeste could not see anything like a "Childe
Harold" who had lost his way. At that stage tears rose to her
eyes as she sat, like Marius, on the ruins of her imaginings.
One day when she made an appointment with God for the
third time, she believed that the elect of her dreams had come

into the church, and she dragged Madame Latournelle to
look behind every pillar, imagining that he was hiding out
of delicacy. Thenceforth she concluded that God had no
power. She often made conversations with this imaginary
lover, inventing question and answer, and giving him a very
pretty wit.

Thus it was her heart's excessive ambition, buried in romance, which gave Modeste the discretion so much admired
by the good people who watched over her; they might have
brought her many a Francisque Althor or Vilquin *fils*, she
would not have stooped to such boors. She required simply
and purely a man of genius; talent she thought little of, as a
barrister is nothing to a girl who is set on an ambassador.
She wished for riches only to cast them at her idol's feet.
The golden background against which the figures of her
dreams stood out was less precious than her heart overflowing
with a woman's delicacy; for her ruling idea was to give
wealth and happiness to a Tasso, a Milton, a Jean-Jacques
Rousseau, a Murat, a Christopher Columbus. Vulgar sorrows
appealed but little to this soul, which longed to extinguish
the stake of such martyrs unrecognized during their lifetime.
Modeste thirsted for unconfessed suffering, the great anguish
of the mind.

Sometimes she imagined the balm, she elaborated the tenderness, the music, the thousand devices by which she would
have soothed the fierce misanthropy of Jean-Jacques. Again
she fancied herself the wife of Lord Byron, and almost entered
into his scorn of realities, while making herself as fantastic as
the poetry of Manfred, and into his doubts while making him
a Catholic. Modeste accused all the women of the seventeenth century as guilty of Molière's melancholy.

" How is it," she wondered, "that some living, wealthy,
and beautiful woman does not rush forth to meet every man
of genius, to make herself his slave like Lara, the mysterious
page?"

As you see, she had quite understood the English poet's wail, as sung by Gulnare. She greatly admired the conduct of the young English girl who came to propose to the younger Crébillon, who married her. The story of Sterne and Eliza Draper was a joy to her for some months; as the imaginary heroine of a similar romance she studied the sublime part of Eliza again and again. The exquisite feeling so gracefully expressed in those letters filled her eyes with the tears which, it is said, never rose to those of the wittiest of English writers.

Modeste thus lived for some time by her sympathy, not merely with the works, but with the personal character of her favorite authors. Goldsmith, the author of "Obermann," Charles Nodier, Maturin—the poorest, the most unhappy were her gods; she understood their sufferings, she entered into their squalor, blending with heaven-sent visions; she poured on them the treasures of her heart; she pictured herself clearly as supplying the comforts of life to these artists, martyrs to their gifts. This noble compassion, this intuitive knowledge of the difficulties of work, this worship for talent, is one of the rarest vagaries that ever beat its wings in a woman's soul. At first it is like a secret between her and God, for there is nothing dazzling in it, nothing to flatter her vanity—that potent auxiliary of all actions in France.

From this third phase of her ideas there was born in Modeste a violent desire to study one of these anomalous lives to the very heart of it, to know the springs of thought, the secret sorrows of genius, and what it craves, and what it is. And so, in her, the rashness of phantasy, the wanderings of her soul in a void, her excursions into the darkness of the future, the impatience of her undeveloped love to centre in an object, the nobleness of her notions of life, her determination to suffer in some lofty sphere rather than to paddle in the slough of provincial life as her mother had done, the vow she had made to herself never to go wrong, to respect her parents' home, and never bring to it anything but joy—

all this world of feeling at last took shape: Modeste purposed to be the wife of a poet, an artist; a man, in short, superior to the crowd; but she meant to choose him, and to subject him to a thorough study, before giving him her heart, her life, her immense tenderness freed from all the different trammels of passion.

She began by reveling in this pretty romance. Perfect tranquillity possessed her soul. Her countenance was gradually colored by it. She became the lovely and sublime image of Germany that you have seen, the glory of the chalet, the pride of Madame Latournelle and the Dumays. Thus Modeste lived a double life. She humbly and lovingly fulfilled all the trivial tasks of daily life at the chalet, using them as a check to hold in the poem of her ideal existence, like the Carthusians, who order their material life by rule, and occupy their time to allow the soul to develop itself in prayer.

All great intellects subject themselves to some mechanical employment to obtain control of thought. Spinoza ground lenses, Bayle counted the tiles in a roof, Montesquieu worked in his garden. The body being thus under control, the spirit spreads its wings in perfect security. So Madame Mignon, who read her daughter's soul, was right. Modeste was in love; she loved with that Platonic sentiment which is so rare, so little understood—the first illusion of girlhood, the subtlest of feelings, the heart's daintiest morsel. She drank deep draughts from the cup of the unknown, the impossible, the visionary. She delighted in the blue bird of the Maiden's Paradise, which sings far away, on which none may lay hands, which lets itself be seen, while the shot of no gun can ever touch it; its magical colors, like the sparkling of gems, dazzle the eye, but it is never more seen when once reality appears—the hideous Harpy bringing witnesses and the *maire* in her train. To have all the poetry of love without the presence of the lover! How exquisite an orgy! What a fair chimera of all colors and every plumage!

This was the trifling foolish accident which sealed the girl's fate.

Modeste saw on a bookseller's counter a lithographed portrait of de Canalis, one of her favorites. You know what libels these sketches are, the outcome of an odious kind of speculation which falls upon the persons of celebrated men, as if their faces were public property. So Canalis, caught in a Byronic attitude, offered to public admiration his disordered hair, his bare throat, and the excessively high forehead proper to every bard. Victor Hugo's brow will lead to as many heads being shaved as there were suckling field-marshals who rushed to die on the strength of Napoleon's glory.

Modeste was struck by this head, made sublime by commercial requirements; and on the day when she bought the portrait, one of the finest books by Arthès had just come out. Though it may sound to her discredit, it must be confessed that she long hesitated between the illustrious poet and the illustrious prose writer. But were these two great men unmarried? Modeste began by securing the co-operation of Françoise Cochet, the girl whom poor Bettina Caroline had taken with her from le Havre and brought back again. She lived in the town, and Madame Mignon and Madame Dumay would employ her for a day's work in preference to any other. Modeste had this somewhat homely creature up into her room; she swore that she would never cause her parents the smallest grief, nor exceed the limits imposed on a young lady; she promised Françoise that in the future, on her father's return, the poor girl should have an easy life, on condition of her keeping absolute secrecy as to the service required of her. What was it? A mere trifle, a perfectly innocent thing. All that Modeste asked of her accomplice was that she should post certain letters and fetch the replies, addressed to Françoise Cochet.

The bargain concluded, Modeste wrote a polite note to Dauriat, the publisher of Canalis' poems, in which she asked

4

him, in the interests of the great poet, whether Canalis was
married, begging him to address the answer to Mademoiselle
Françoise, poste restante, au Havre.   Dauriat, who, of course,
could not take such a letter seriously, sent a reply concocted
in his private room by five or six journalists, each in turn
adding his jest :

"MADEMOISELLE :—Canalis (Baron de), Constant-Cyr-
Melchior, member of the French Academy, born in 1800 at
Canalis, Corrèze ; stands five feet four, is in good condition,
vaccinated, thoroughbred, has served his term under the con-
scription, enjoys perfect health, has a small landed estate in
Corrèze, and wishes to marry, but looks for great wealth.

"His arms are, party per pale gules a broad axe or, and
sable a shell argent ; surmounted by a baron's coronet ; supporters, two larches proper.   The motto *Or et fer* (gold and
iron) has never proved auriferous.

" The first Canalis, who went to the Holy Land in the first
crusade, is mentioned in the Chronicles of Auvergne as carrying no weapon but an axe, by reason of the complete indigence in which he lived, and which has ever since weighed
on his posterity.   Hence, no doubt, the blazon.   The axe
brought him nothing but an empty shell.   This noble baron
became famous, having discomfited many infidels, and he
died at Jerusalem, without either gold or iron, as bare as a
worm, on the road to Ascalon, the ambulance service having
not yet been called into existence.

" The castle of Canalis—the land yields a few chestnuts—
consists of two dismantled towers joined by a wall, remarkable for its superior growth of ivy, and it pays twenty-two
francs to the revenue.

" The publisher, undersigned, begs to remark that he pays
Monsieur de Canalis ten thousand francs per volume for his
poetry.   He does not give his empty shells for nothing.

" The Bard of the Corrèze lives at Rue de Paradis-Poisson-

nière, No. 29, which is a suitable situation for a poet of the
Seraphic School.　Worms (*les vers*) are a bait for gudgeon.
Letters must be prepaid.

"Certain noble dames of the Faubourg Saint-Germain,
often, it is said, make their way to paradise and patronize the
divinity.　King Charles X. thinks so highly of this great poet
as to believe him capable of becoming a statesman.　He has
recently made him an officer of the Legion of Honor, and,
what is more to the purpose, master of appeals, attached to
the ministry for foreign affairs.　These functions in no way
keep the great man from drawing a pension of three thousand
francs from the fund devoted to the encouragement of art
and letters.　This pecuniary success causes, in the publishing
world, an eighth plague which Egypt was spared—a plague
of worms (*les vers*)!

"The last edition of the works of Canalis, printed on hand-
made paper, large 8vo, with vignettes by Bixiou, Joseph Bridau, Schinner, Sommervieux, and others, printed by Didot,
is in five volumes, price nine francs, postpaid."

This letter fell like a paving-stone on a tulip.　A poet as
master of appeals, in the immediate circle of a minister,
drawing a pension, aiming at the red rosette, adored of the
ladies of the Faubourg Saint-Germain!　Was this at all like
the threadbare poet wandering on the quays, melancholy and
dreamy, overwrought by work, and climbing up to his garret
again loaded with poetic inspiration?　At the same time,
Modeste saw through the jest of the envious publisher, which
conveyed, "I made Canalis!　I made Nathan!"　Then she
re-read Canalis' verses, very catching verses, full of hypocrisy,
and which require a few words of analysis if only to explain
her infatuation.

Canalis is distinguished from Lamartine, the chief of the
Seraphic School, by a sort of sick-nurse blarney, a perfidious
sweetness, and exquisite correctness.　If the chief, with his

sublime outcry, may be called an eagle, Canalis, all rose and
white, is a flamingo.   In him women discern the friend they
yearn for, a discreet confidant, their interpreter, the being
who understands them, and who explains them to themselves.

The broad margins with which Dauriat had graced his last
edition were covered with confessions scribbled in pencil by
Modeste, who sympathized with this dreamy and tender soul.
Canalis has not life in his gift ; he does not breathe it into his
creations ; but he knows how to soothe vague sufferings such
as Modeste was a victim of.   He speaks to girls in their own
language, lulling the pain of the most recent wounds, and
silencing groans and even sobs.   His talent does not consist
in preaching loftily to the sufferer, in giving her the medi-
cine of strong emotions ; he is content to say in a musical
voice which commands belief : "I am unhappy, as you are ;
I understand you fully ; come with me, we will weep together
on the bank of this stream, under the willows !"   And they
go ! and listen to his verse, as vacuous and as sonorous as the
song of a nurse putting a baby to sleep !   Canalis—like
Nodier in this—bewitches you by an artlessness, which in the
prose writer is natural but in the poet elaborately studied, by
his archness, his smile, his fallen flowers, his childlike philosophy.   He mimics the language of early days well enough to
carry you back to the fair field of illusion.

To an eagle we are pitiless ; we insist on the quality of the
diamond, flawless perfection ; but from Canalis we are satisfied with the orphan's mite ; everything may be forgiven him.
He seems such a good fellow, human above everything.
These seraphic airs succeed with him, as those of a woman
will always succeed if she acts simplicity well—the startled,
youthful, martyred, suffering angel.

Modeste, summing up her impressions, felt that she trusted
that soul, that countenance, as attractive as Bernardin de
Saint-Pierre's.   She paid no heed to the publisher.   And so,
at the beginning of the month of August, she wrote the fol-

lowing letter to this Dorat of the sacristy, who even now is regarded as one of the stars of the modern Pleiades:

I.

To Monsieur de Canalis.

"Many times ere now, monsieur, I have intended to write you—and why? You can guess: to tell you how much I delight in your talent. Yes, I feel a longing to express to you the admiration of a poor country-bred girl, very solitary in her nook, whose sole joy is in reading your poetry. From René I came to you. Melancholy tends to reverie. How many other women must have paid you the homage of their secret thoughts! What chance have I of being of the elect in such a crowd! What interest can this paper have, though full of my soul, above all the perfumed letters which beset you? I introduce myself with more to perplex you than any other woman. I intend to remain unknown, and yet ask your entire confidence, as if you had known me a long time.

"Answer me, be kind to me. I do not pledge myself to tell my name some day, still I do not positively say no. What more can I add to this letter? Regard it, monsieur, as a great effort, and allow me to offer you my hand—oh, a very friendly hand—that of your servant,

"O. D'ESTE-M.

"If you do me the favor of replying, address your letter, I beg, to Mademoiselle F. Cochet, Poste Restante, le Havre."

Now every damsel, whether romantic or not, can imagine Modeste's impatience during the next few days! The air was full of tongues of flame; the trees looked like plumage; she did not feel her body; she floated above nature! The

earth vanished under her tread. Wondering at the powers of
the postoffice, she followed her little sheet of paper through
space; she was glad, as we are glad at twenty at the first
exercise of our will.   She was bewitched, possessed, as people were in the middle ages.   She pictured to herself the
poet's lodgings, his room; she saw him opening the letter,
and she made a million guesses.

Having sketched his poetry, it is necessary here to give
an outline of the man.   Canalis is small and thin, with an
aristocratic figure; dark; gifted with a foolish face and a
rather insignificant head, that of a man who has more vanity
than pride.   He loves luxury, display, and splendor.   Fortune is a necessity to him more than to most other men.   No
less proud of his birth than of his talent, he has swamped
his ancestors by too-great personal pretensions.   After all,
the Canalises are neither Navarreins, nor Cadignans, nor
Grandlieus, nor Nègrepelisses; however, nature has done
much to support his pretensions. He has the eyes of Oriental
lustre that we look for in a poet, a very pretty refinement of
manner, a thrilling voice; but a mannerism that is natural to
him almost nullifies these advantages.   He is an actor in
perfect good faith.   He displays a very elegant foot—it is an
acquired habit.   He has a declamatory style of talk, but it
is his own.   His affectation is theatrical, but it has become a
second nature.   These faults, as we must call them, are in
harmony with an unfailing generosity, which may be termed
carpet-knightliness in contrast to chivalry.   Canalis has not
faith enough to be a Don Quixote, but he is too high-minded
not to take invariably the nobler side in any question.   His
poetry, which comes out in a miliary eruption on every possible occasion, is a great disadvantage to the poet, who is not
indeed lacking in wit, but whose talent hinders his wit from
developing.   He is the slave of his reputation; he aims at
seeming superior to it.

Hence, as frequently happens, the man is completely out

of tune with the products of his mind. The author of these insinuating, artless poems, full of tender sentiment, of these calm verses as clear as lake-ice, of this caressing womanish poetry, is an ambitious little man, buttoned tightly into his coat, with the air of a diplomat, dreaming of political influence, stinking of the aristocrat, scented and conceited, thirsting for a fortune that he may have an income equal to his ambitions, and already spoiled by success under two aspects —the crown of bays and the crown of myrtle. A salary of eight thousand francs, a pension of three thousand, two thousand from the Académie, a thousand crowns of inherited income—a good deal reduced by the agricultural requirements of the Canalis estate, and the ten thousand francs he gets from his poems one year with another—twenty-five thousand francs a year in all.

To Modeste's hero this income was all the more precarious because he spent, on an average, five or six thousand francs a year more than he received, but hitherto the King's privy purse and the secret funds of the ministry had made up the deficit. He had composed a hymn for the coronation, for which he had been rewarded with a service of plate ; he refused a sum of money, saying that the Canalises owed their homage to the King of France. The cavalier King smiled, and ordered from Odiot a costly version of the well-known lines from " Zaïre : "

> " What! Rhymester, did you ever hope to vie
> With Charles the Tenth in generosity?"

Canalis had drained himself dry, to use a picturesque vulgarism ; he knew that he was incapable of inventing a fresh form of poetry ; his lyre has not seven strings, it has but one ; and so long had he played on it that the public left him now no choice but to use it to hang himself, or be silent. De Marsay, who could not endure Canalis, had uttered a sarcasm

of which the poisoned dart had pierced the poet's conceit to
the quick.

"Canalis," he had said, "strikes me as being just like the
man of whom Frederick the Great spoke after a battle, as the
trumpeter who had never ceased blowing the same note
through his penny pipe!"

Canalis was anxious to become a political personage, and as
a beginning made capital of a journey he had taken to Madrid when the Duc de Chaulieu was ambassador, accompany-
ing him as *attaché*—but to the Duchess, as the jest went in
fashionable drawing-rooms. How often has a jest sealed a
man's fate! Colla, the erewhile President of the Cisalpine
Republic, and the greatest advocate in Piémont, is told by a
friend, at the age of forty, that he knows nothing of botany;
he is nettled, he becomes a Jussieu, cultivates flowers, invents
new ones, and publishes, in Latin, the "Flora of Piémont,"
the work of ten years!

"Well, after all, Canning and Chateaubriand were statesmen," said the extinguished poet, "and in me de Marsay
shall find his master!"

Canalis would have liked to write an important political
work; but he was afraid of getting into trouble with French
prose, a cruelly exacting medium to those who have acquired
the habit of taking four Alexandrine lines to express one idea.
Of all the poets of the day, only three—Victor Hugo,
Théophile Gautier, and de Vigny—have been able to conquer
the double glory of a poet and a prose-writer, which was also
achieved by Voltaire, Molière, and Rabelais. It is one of
the rarest triumphs in French literature, and distinguishes a
poet far above his fellows. Our poet of the Faubourg Saint-
Germain was therefore very wise to try to find shelter for his
chariot under the guardian roof of a government office.

When he was made master of appeals, he felt the need of
a secretary, a friend who might fill his place on many occasions, cook his affairs with publishers, see to his fame in the

newspapers, and, at a pinch, support him in politics—in short, who would be his satellite. Several men, famous in art, science, or letters, have one or two such followers in Paris, a captain in the Guards, or a court chamberlain, who live in the beams of their sunshine, a sort of aides-de-camp intrusted with delicate tasks, allowing themselves to be compromised at need, working round the idol's pedestal, not quite his equals, not quite his superiors; men bold in puffery, the first in every breach, covering his retreats, looking after his business, and devoted to him so long as their illusions last or till their claims are satisfied. Some at last perceive that their Great Man is ungrateful; others feel that they are being made use of; many weary of the work; and few indeed are satisfied by the mild interchange of sentiment, the only reward to be looked for from an intimacy with a superior man, and which satisfied Ali, raised by Mahomet to his own level. Many, deluded by their self-conceit, think themselves as clever as their Great Man. Devotion is rare, especially without reward and without hope, as Modeste conceived of it.

Nevertheless, a Menneval is occasionally to be met with; and, in Paris more than anywhere, men love to live in the shade and to work in silence, Benedictines who have lost their way in a world which has no monastery for them. These valiant lambs bear in their deeds and in their private lives the poetry which writers put into words. They are poets at heart, in their secluded meditations, in their tenderness, as others are poets on paper, in the fields of intellect, and at so much a verse, like Lord Byron—like all those who live, alas! by ink, which in these days is the water of Hippocrene, for which the government is to blame.

It was a young consulting referendary of the court of exchequer who constituted himself the poet's secretary; he was attracted by the poet's fame, and the future prospects of this vaunted political genius, and led by the advice of Madame d'Espard, who thus played the Duchesse de Chaulieu's cards

for her ; and Canalis made much of him, as a speculator does
of his first shareholder. The beginnings of this alliance had
quite an air of friendship. The younger man had already
gone through a course of the same kind with one of the ministers who fell in 1827 ; but the minister had taken care to
find him a place in the exchequer.

Ernest de la Brière, at that time seven-and-twenty, decorated with the Legion of Honor, with nothing in the world
but the emoluments of his office, had the habit of business,
and, after hanging about the private room of the prime minister for four years, he knew a good deal. He was gentle,
amiable, with an almost maidenly soul, full of good feeling,
and he hated to be seen in the foreground. He loved his
country, he yearned to be of use, but brilliancy dazzled him.
If he had had his choice, the place of secretary to a Napoleon
would have been more to his mind than that of prime
minister.

Ernest, having become the friend of Canalis, did great
things for him, but in eighteen months he became aware of the
shallowness of a nature which was poetical merely in its literary expression. The truth of the homely proverb, "The
cowl does not make the monk," is especially applicable in
literature. It is most rare to find a talent and character in
harmony. A man's faculties are not the sum-total of a man.
This discord, of which the manifestations are startling, is the
outcome of an unexplored—a perhaps unexplorable—mystery.
The brain and its products of every kind—since in the arts
the hand of man carries out his brain—form a world apart
that flourishes under the skull, perfectly independent of the
feelings, of what are called the virtues of a citizen, of the
head of a family, of a private householder. And yet this is
not final ; nothing in man is final. It is certain that a
debauchée will exhaust his talent in orgies, and a drunkard
drown it in his libations, while a good man can never acquire
talent by wholesome decency ; but it is also almost proved that

Virgil, the poet of love, never loved a Dido; and that Rousseau, the pattern citizen, had pride enough to furnish forth a whole aristocracy. Nevertheless, Michael Angelo and Raphael showed the happy concord of talent and character. Hence talent is in men, as far as the individual is concerned, what beauty is in women—a promise. Let us give twofold admiration to the man whose heart and character are equally perfect with his talent.

Ernest, when he detected under the poet an ambitious egoist—the worst species of egoist, for some are amiable—felt a singular diffidence about leaving him. Honest souls do not easily break their bonds, especially those they have voluntarily accepted. The secretary, then, was on very good terms with the poet when Modeste's letter was flying through the mail, but on the good terms of constant self-effacement. La Brière felt he owed Canalis something for the frankness with which he had revealed himself. And indeed, in this man, who will be accounted great so long as he lives, and made much of, like Marmontel, his defects are the seamy side of brilliant qualities. But for his vanity, his pretentious conceit, he might not have been gifted with that sonorous verbiage which is a necessary instrument in the political life of the day. His shallowness is part of his rectitude and loyalty; his ostentation is paired with liberality. Society profits by the results; the motives may be left to God.

Still, when Modeste's letter arrived, Ernest had no illusions left as to Canalis. The two friends had just breakfasted and were chatting in the poet's study; he was at that time living in first-floor rooms looking out on a garden, beyond a courtyard.

"Ah!" cried Canalis, "I was saying the other day to Madame de Chaulieu that I must cast forth some new poem; admiration is running low, for it is some time since I have had any anonymous letters——"

"An unknown lady?"

"Unknown! A d'Este, and from le Havre! It is evidently an assumed name!"

And Canalis handed the letter to la Brière. This poem, this veiled enthusiasm—in short, Modeste's very heart—was recklessly exposed by the gesture of a coxcomb.

"It is a grand thing," said the young accountant, "thus to attract the chastest feelings, to compel a helpless woman to shake off the habits forced upon her by education, by nature, by society, to break through conventionalities—— What privileges genius commands! A letter like this in my hand, written by a girl, a genuine girl, without reservation, with enthusiasm——"

"Well?" said Canalis.

"Well, if you had suffered as much as Tasso, you ought to find it reward enough!" exclaimed la Brière.

"So we tell ourselves at the first or at the second letter," said Canalis. "But at the thirtieth!—— but when we have discovered that the young enthusiast is an old hand! but when at the end of the radiant path traveled over by the poet's imagination we have seen some English old maid sitting on a milestone and holding out her hand! but when the angel, by post, turns into a poor creature, moderately good-looking, in search of a husband!—— Well, then, the effervescence subsides."

"I am beginning to think," said la Brière, smiling, "that glory has something poisonous in it, like certain gorgeous flowers."

"Beside, my dear fellow," Canalis went on, "all these women, even when they are sincere, have an ideal to which we rarely correspond. They never tell themselves that a poet is a man, and a tolerably vain one, as I am accused of being; it never occurs to them that he is rough-ridden by a sort of feverish excitement which makes him disagreeable and uncertain. They want him to be always great, always splendid; they never dream that talent is a disease; that Nathan lives on Florine; that d'Arthez is too fat; that Joseph Bridau is too thin; that Béranger can go on, foot; that the divinity may foam at the mouth. A Lucien de Rubempré, a verse-writer and a pretty fellow, is a phœnix. So why go out of your way to receive bad compliments and sit under the cold shower-bath of a disillusioned woman's helpless stare?"

"Then the true poet," said la Brière, "ought to remain hidden, like God, in the centre of his universe, and be visible only in his creations!"

"Then glory would be too dearly paid for," replied Canalis. "There is some good in life, I tell you," said he, taking a cup of tea. "When a woman of birth and beauty loves a poet, she does not hide herself in the gallery or the stage-box of a theatre, like a duchess smitten by an actor; she feels strong enough and sufficiently protected by her beauty, by her fortune, by her name, to say, as in every epic poem, 'I am the nymph Calypso, and I love Telemachus.' Mystification is the resource of small minds. For some time now I have never answered such masqueraders——"

"Oh! how I could love a woman who had come to me!" cried la Brière, restraining a tear. "It may be said in reply, my dear Canalis, that it is never a poor creature that rises to the level of a celebrated man; she is too suspicious, too vain, too much afraid. It is always a star, a——"

"A princess," said Canalis, with a shout of laughter, "who condescends to him, I suppose? My dear fellow, such things happen once in a century. Such a passion is like the plant that flowers once in a hundred years. Princesses who are young, rich, and handsome have too much else to do; they are enclosed, like all rare plants, within a hedge of silly men, well-born and well-bred, and as empty as an alder-stem. My dream, alas! the crystal of my dream hung with garlands of flowers all the way hither from la Corrèze, and with what fervor! But no more of that!—it is in fragments, at my feet, long since. No, no, every anonymous

letter is a beggar! And what demands they make. Write
to this young person, assuming her to be young and pretty,
and you will see! You will have your hands full. One cannot, in reason, love every woman. Apollo, or, at any rate,
the Apollo Belvedere, is a consumptive dandy who must save
his strength.''

"But when a woman comes to you like this," argued
Ernest, "her excuse must lie in her certainty that she can
eclipse the most adored mistress in tenderness, in beauty—
and then a little curiosity——''

"Ah!" said Canalis, "my too youthful Ernest, you must
allow me to be faithful to the fair Duchess, who is all my joy!''

"You are right—too right," replied Ernest.

Nevertheless, the young secretary read and re-read Modeste's letter, trying to guess the mind behind it.

"But there is nothing extravagant in it, no appeal to your
genius, only to your heart," he said to Canalis. "This perfume of modesty and the exchange proposed would tempt
me——''

"Sign it yourself; answer her, and follow up the adventure
to the end; it is a poor bargain that I offer you," exclaimed
Canalis, with a smile. "Go on; you will have something to
tell me in three months' time, if it lasts three months.''

Four days after Modeste received the following letter,
written on handsome paper, under a double cover, and sealed
with the arms of Canalis:

II.

To Mademoiselle O. d' Este-M.

"MADEMOISELLE:—Admiration for great works—admitting
that mine may be great—implies a certain holy simplicity
which is a defense against irony and a justification, in the
eyes of every tribunal, of the step you have taken in writing

me. Above all, I must thank you for the pleasure which such a testimonial never fails to give, even when undeserved, for the writer of verse and the poet alike secretly believe themselves worthy of them, self-love is a form of matter so far from repellent of praise. The best proof of friendship that I can give to an unknown lady in return for this balm, which heals the stings of criticism, is surely to share with her the harvest of my experience, at the risk of scaring away her living illusions.

" Mademoiselle, the noblest palm a young girl can bear is that of a saintly, pure, and blameless life. Are you alone in the world? That is a sufficient answer. But if you have a family, a father, or a mother, consider all the sorrows that a letter like yours may entail—written to a poet whom you do not know. Not every writer is an angel; they have their faults. Some are fickle, reckless, conceited, ambitious, dissipated; and imposing as innocence must be, chivalrous as a French poet may be, you might find more than one degenerate bard willing to encourage your affection only to betray it. Then your letter would not be interpreted as I read it. He would find a meaning in it which you have not put there, and which in your innocence you do not even suspect. Many authors, many natures !

" I am extremely flattered by your having thought me worthy to understand you ; but if you had addressed yourself to an insincere talent, to a cynic whose writings were melancholy while his life was a continual carnival, you might have found at the end of your sublime imprudence some bad man, a dangler behind the scenes, or a wine-shop hero ! You, under the arbor of clematis where you dream over poetry, cannot smell the stale cigar smoke which depoetizes the manuscript ; just as when you go to a ball, dressed in the dazzling products of the jeweler's skill, you never think of the sinewy arms, the toilers in their shirt-sleeves, the wretched workshops whence spring these radiant flowers of handicraft.

"Go further. What is there in the solitary life of reverie that you lead—by the seashore, no doubt—to interest a poet whose task it is to divine everything, since he must describe everything? Our young girls here are so highly accomplished that no daughter of Eve can vie with them! What reality was ever so good as a dream? And you now, you, a young girl brought up to be the duteous mother of a family, what would you gain by an initiation into the terrible excitement of a poet's life in this appalling capital, to be defined only as a hell we love.

"If you took up your pen, prompted by the wish to enliven your monotonous existence as an inquisitive girl, has not this a semblance of depravity? What meaning am I to attribute to your letter? Are you one of a caste of reprobates, seeking a friend at a distance? Are you cursed with ugliness, and do you feel you have a noble soul with none to trust? Alas!—a sad conclusion—you have either gone too far or not far enough. Either let it end here, or, if you persist, tell me more than in the letter you have already written.

"But, mademoiselle, if you are young, if you have a family, if you feel that you bear in your heart a heavenly spikenard, to be shed, as the Magdalen shed hers on Christ's feet, suffer yourself to be appreciated by some man who is worthy of you, and become what every good girl should attain—an admirable wife, the virtuous mother of children. A poet is the poorest conquest any young woman can aspire to; he has too much vanity, too many salient angles which must run counter to the legitimate vanity of a wife, and bruise the tenderness which has no experience of life. The poet's wife should love him for long before marrying him; she must resign herself to be as charitable and as indulgent as the angels, to all the virtues of motherhood. These qualities, mademoiselle, exist only as a germ in a young girl.

"Listen to the whole truth; do I not owe it you in return for your intoxicating flattery? Though it may be glorious to marry a great celebrity, a woman soon discovers that a man, however superior, is but a man like all others. He then the less fulfills her hopes, because miracles are expected of him. A famous poet is then in the predicament of a woman whose overpraised beauty makes us say, ‘I had pictured her as handsomer;’ she does not answer to the requirements of the portrait sketched by the same fairy to whom I owe your letter—Imagination!

“Again, great qualities of mind develop and flourish only in an invisible sphere; the poet’s wife sees only the unpleasant side of it; she sees the jewels made instead of wearing them. If the brilliancy of an exceptional position is what fascinates you, I warn you, its pleasures are soon exhausted. You would be provoked to find so much that is rough in a situation which from afar looks so smooth, so much ice on a glittering height! And then, as women never have set foot in the world of difficulty, they presently cease to value what they once admired, when they fancy that they have understood the workmanship at a glance.

“I will conclude with a last reflection, which you will do wrong to mis-read as an entreaty in disguise; it is the advice of a friend. A communion of souls cannot be complete excepting between two persons who are prepared to conceal nothing. Could you show yourself as you really are to a stranger? I pause before the consequences of such a notion.

“Accept, mademoiselle, all the respect we owe to every woman, even to those who are unknown, and who wear a mask.”

To think that she had carried this letter between her skin and her stays, under the scorching busk, for a whole day!—— that she had postponed reading it till an hour when everybody was asleep, till midnight, after waiting for the solemn hour in the pangs of a fiery imagination!—— that she had blessed the poet, had read in fancy a thousand letters, had

5

conceived of everything excepting this drop of cold water
shed on the most diaphanous visions of fancy, and destroying
them as prussic acid destroys life.   It was enough to make
her hide her face—as Modeste did—under her sheets, though
she was alone, and put out the candle, and weep.

All this happened in the early days of July.   Modeste presently got up, paced her room, and then opened the window.
She wanted air.   The scent of flowers came up to her with
the peculiar freshness of night-perfumes.   The sea, lighted up
by the moon, twinkled like a mirror.   A nightingale was
singing in the Vilquins' park.

"Ah! there is the poet!" said Modeste to herself, her
anger dying out.

The bitterest reflections crowded on her mind.   She was
stung to the quick; she wanted to read the letter again.   She
re-lighted the candle, and studied this careful production, till
at last she heard the early voices of real life.

"He is in the right, and I am in the wrong," thought she.
"But how could I expect to find one of Molière's old men
under the star-spangled robe of a poet?"

When a woman or a girl is caught red-handed, she feels
intense hatred of the witness, the first cause, or the object of
her folly.   And so Modeste, genuine, natural, and coy, felt
her heart swell with a dreadful longing to trample on this
essence of rectitude and throw him into some abyss of contradiction, anything she could devise to pay him back this
stunning blow.

The pure-hearted child, whose head alone had been cor-
rupted by her reading, by her sister's long agony, and by the
perilous meditations of her solitude, was roused by a sunbeam
falling on her face.   She had lain for three hours tacking
about on the immense ocean of doubt.   Such nights are never
forgotten.

Modeste went at once to her little lacquer table, her father's
gift, and wrote a letter dictated by the infernal spirit of re-

venge which disports itself at the bottom of a young girl's heart :

III.

To Monsieur de Canalis.

" MONSIEUR :—You are certainly a great poet, but you are something better—an honest man. After showing so much frank loyalty to a young girl on the verge of an abyss, have you enough to reply without the least hypocrisy or evasion to this question—

" Would you have written the letter I have received in answer to mine—would your ideas, your language, have been the same if some one had whispered in your ear, what may be true : ' Mademoiselle O. d'Este-M. has six millions of francs, and does not want to have a simpleton for her master ? '

" For one moment admit this hypothesis for a fact. Be as honest with me as with yourself; fear nothing, I am superior to my twenty years ; nothing that is genuine can injure you in my estimation. When I shall have read that confession, if, indeed, you vouchsafe to make it to me, you shall have an answer to your first letter.

"After admiring your talent, which is often sublime, allow me to do homage to your delicacy and rectitude, which compel me to sign myself

" Your humble servant,

" O. d'ESTE-M."

When this note was placed in la Brière's hands, he went out to walk on the boulevards, tossed in his soul like a light bark in the tempest when the wind blows every minute from a different point of the compass. One of the young men of whom we meet so many—a true Parisian—would have summed up the case in these words, "An old hand ! " But to a young

fellow whose soul is lofty and refined, this sort of implied
oath, this appeal to veracity, had the power to arouse the three
judges that lurk at the bottom of every conscience. And
Honor, Truth, and Justice, rising erect, as it were, thus cried
aloud.

"Ah ! my dear Ernest," said Truth, " you certainly would
not have written a lecture to a rich heiress. No, no, my boy,
you would have set off, nose on, for le Havre, to find out
whether the young lady was handsome, and you would have
been much aggrieved by the preference given to genius. And
if you only could have tripped your friend up, and have made
yourself acceptable in his place, Mademoiselle d'Este would
have been divine ! " " What," said Justice, " you pity yourselves, you men of brains or wit, and without cash, when you
see rich girls married to men whom you would not employ as
porters ; you run amuck against the sordidness of the age,
which is eager to wed money with money, and never to unite
some fine young fellow full of talent to a rich and high-born
beauty ; now here is one who rebels against the spirit of the
time, and the poet retorts with a blow on the heart ! " " Rich
or poor, young or old, handsome or plain, this girl is in the
right, she has brains, she casts the poet into the mire of self-
interest," cried Honor. " She deserves a sincere, noble, and
honest reply ; and, above all, the true expression of your
thought ! Examine yourself. Sound your heart, and purge
it of its meanness ! What would Molière's Alceste say ? "
And la Brière, starting from the Boulevard Poissonnière, lost
in meditation, walked so slowly that at the end of an hour he
had but just reached the Boulevard des Capucines. He returned by the quays to the exchequer, at that time situated near
the Sainte-Chapelle. Instead of verifying accounts, he sat
under the spell of his perplexities.

" She has not six millions, that is clear," said he to himself;
" but that is not the question——"

Six days later Modeste received the following letter :

IV.

To Mademoiselle O. d'Este-M.

"MADEMOISELLE :—You are not a d'Este. That is an assumed name to conceal your own. Are such revelations as you request due to a person who is false as to her identity? Attend ; I will answer your question by asking another, Are you of illustrious parentage? of noble birth? of a family of townsfolk?

"Morality indeed cannot change ; it is one ; but its obligations vary in different spheres. As the sun sheds a different light on different aspects, producing the variety we admire, morality makes social duty conform to rank and position. What is a peccadillo in the soldier is a crime in the general, and *vice versâ*. The proprieties are not the same for a peasant-girl who reaps the field, for a workwoman at fifteen sous a day, for the daughter of a small shopkeeper, for a young girl of the middle class, for the child of a rich commercial house, for the heiress of a noble family, for a daughter of the race of Este. A king must not stoop to pick up a gold coin, and a workman must turn back to look for a piece of ten sous he has dropped, though both alike ought to observe the laws of economy. A d'Este owning six millions of francs may wear a broad-brimmed hat and feathers, flourish a riding whip, mount an Arab horse, and come as an Amazon in gold lace, followed by a groom, to say to a poet, 'I love poetry, and I desire to expiate the wrongs done by Leonora to Tasso,' while the daughter of a merchant would be simply ridiculous in imitating her.

"To what social class do you belong? Answer truly, and I will as truly reply to the question you ask me.

"Not being so happy as to know you, though already bound to you by a sort of poetical communion, I do not like

to offer you any vulgar homage. It is already a triumph of
mischief for you perhaps to have perplexed a man whose
books are published."

The young accountant was not lacking in the skill of fence
which a man of honor may allow himself. By return of post
he received this reply:

V.

To Monsieur de Canalis.

"You are more and more cautious, my dear poet. My
father is a count. The most distinguished member of our
family was a cardinal, in the days when cardinals were the
equals of kings. At the present day our race, almost extinct,
ends in me; but I have the necessary quarterings to admit
me to any court or any chapter. In short, we are a match
for the Canalises. Excuse my not forwarding our coat-of-
arms.

"Try to write as sincerely as I do. I await your reply to
know whether I may still subscribe myself, as now,

"Your servant,

"O. D'ESTE-M."

"What advantage the young person takes of her position!"
exclaimed la Brière. "But is she truthful?"

It is not for nothing that a man has been for four years a
minister's private secretary; that he has lived in Paris and
watched its intrigues; and the purest soul is always more or
less intoxicated by the heady atmosphere of the Empress City.
La Brière, rejoicing that he was not Canalis, secured a place
in the mail-coach for le Havre, after writing a letter in which
he promised a reply by a certain day, excusing the delay by
the importance of the confession required of him and the
business of his office. He took the precaution of obtaining

from the director-general of the mails a line enjoining silence
and compliance on the head of the office at le Havre. He
could thus wait to see Françoise Cochet arrive at the office,
and quietly follow her home. Guided by her, he mounted
the hill of Ingouville, and saw Modeste Mignon at the window
of the chalet.

"Well, Françoise?" asked the girl.

"Yes, mademoiselle, I have one."

Ernest, struck by this celestially fair type of beauty, turned
on his heel, and inquired of a passer-by the name of the owner
of that splendid residence.

"That?" asked the native, pointing to the great house.

"Yes, my good fellow."

"Oh, that belongs to Monsieur Vilquin, the richest shipowner of the place, a man who does not know how much he
has."

"I know of no Cardinal Vilquin in history," said the accountant to himself, as he went down the town again, to
return to Paris.

Of course, he questioned the postmaster as to the Vilquin
family. He learned that the Vilquins owned an immense
fortune; that Monsieur Vilquin had a son and two daughters,
one of them married to young Monsieur Althor. Prudence
saved la Brière from showing any adverse interest in the
Vilquins; the postmaster was already looking at him with
suspicion.

"Is there no one at the house just now beside the family?"
he asked.

"Just at present the Hérouville family is there. There
is some talk of a marriage between the young Duke and the
second Mademoiselle Vilquin."

"There was a famous Cardinal d'Hérouville," thought la
Brière, "in the time of the Valois; and, under Henry IV.,
the terrible marshal, who was created duke."

Ernest returned, having seen enough of Modeste to dream

of her; to believe that, rich or poor, if she had a noble soul, he would gladly and unhesitatingly make her Madame la Brière, and he, therefore, determined to still carry on the correspondence.

Do your utmost, hapless Frenchwomen, to remain unknown, to weave the very least little romance in the midst of civilization which takes note on public squares of the hour when every hackney cab comes and goes, which counts every letter and stamps them twice at the exact hours when they are posted and when they are delivered, which numbers the houses, which registers each floor on the schedule of taxes, after making a list of the windows and doors, which ere long will have every acre of land, down to the smallest holdings and its most trifling details, laid down on the broad sheets of a survey—a giant's task, by command of a giant! Try, rash maidens, to evade—not, indeed, the eye of the police, but the ceaseless gossip which, in the poorest hamlet, scrutinizes your most trivial acts, counts the dishes at the préfet's dessert, and sees the melon-rind outside the door of the small annuitant, which tries to hear the chink of gold when Economy adds it to her treasury, and every evening, over the fire, sums up the incomes of the village, of the town, of the department!

Modeste, by a commonplace mistake, had escaped the most innocent espionage, for which Ernest already blamed himself. But what Parisian could endure to be the dupe of a little country girl? Never be duped! This odious maxim is a solvent for all man's noble sentiments. From the letter he wrote, where every lash of the scourge of conscience has left its mark, the reader may easily imagine the conflict of feelings to which the honest youth was a prey.

A few days later, Modeste, sitting at her window on a fine summer day, read the following pages:

VI.

To Mademoiselle O. d' Este-M.

" MADEMOISELLE :—Without hypocrisy, yes, if I had been sure that you had an immense fortune, I should have acted quite differently. Why? I have sought the reason, and it is this : There is in us an inborn feeling, developed, too, to an extreme by society, which urges us to seek and to seize happiness. Most men confound happiness with the means to happiness, and in their eyes fortune is its chief element. I should therefore have endeavored to please you, spurred by the social instinct that has in all ages made wealth a religion. At least, I think so. The wisdom which substitutes good sense for impulse is not to be looked for in a man who is still young ; and when the prey is in sight, the animal instinct lurking in the heart of man urges him on. Thus, instead of a lecture, I should have sent you compliments and flattery.

"Should I have respected myself? I doubt it. Mademoiselle, in such a case, success brings absolution ; but as to happiness, that is another matter. Should I not distrust my wife if I won her thus? Most certainly. Your action would, sooner or later, have resumed its true character ; your husband, however great you might deem him, would at last have reproached you for having humiliated him ; and you, sooner or later, might have learned to despise him. An ordinary man cuts the gordian knot of a marriage for money with the sword of tyranny. A strong man forgives. The poet bewails himself. This, mademoiselle, is the answer given by my honesty.

" Now, attend to me well. Yours is the triumph of having made me reflect deeply, both on you, whom I know not enough, and on myself, whom I know but little. You have had the skill to stir up the evil thoughts that grovel at the

bottom of every heart; but in me the outcome has been a
generous something, and I hail you with my most grateful
blessings, as, at sea, we hail a lighthouse warning us of rocks
where we might have been wrecked.

"And now for my confession, for I would not lose your
esteem nor my own for the price of all the treasures on earth.
I was bent on knowing who you were.   I have just come back
from le Havre, where I saw Françoise Cochet, followed her to
Ingouville, and saw you in your magnificent villa.   You are
as lovely as a poet's dream of woman ; but I know not whether
you are Mademoiselle Vilquin hidden under Mademoiselle
d'Hérouville, or Mademoiselle d'Hérouville hidden under
Mademoiselle Vilquin.   Though all is fair in war, I blush at
playing the spy, and I paused in my investigations.   You
piqued my curiosity ; owe me no grudge for having been so
womanly, is it not a poet's privilege?   Now I have opened
my heart to you ; I have let you read it ; you may believe in
the sincerity of what I am about to add.   Brief as was the
glimpse I had of you, it was enough to modify my opinion.
You are a poet and a poem even before being a woman.   Yes,
there is in you something more precious than beauty ; you
are the ideal of art, of fancy.

"The step you took, blamable in a young girl fated to a
commonplace existence, is different in one gifted with such a
character as I suppose you to have.   Among the vast number
of beings flung by chance into social life to make up a
generation, there are exceptions.   If your letter is the outcome
of long political musing on the lot which the law reserves for
women ; if, carried away by the vocation of a superior and
cultivated mind, you have wished to know something of the
intimate life of a man to whom you concede the chance en-
dowment of genius, in order to create a friendship with a
soul akin to your own, exempt from vulgar conditions, and
evading all the limitations of your sex—you are, indeed, an
exception !   The law which is good to measure the actions

of the crowd is then very narrow to qualify your determination. But then the words of my first letter recur in all their meaning, 'You have done too much or not enough.'

"Once more accept my thanks for the service you have done me in compelling me to probe my heart; for you have cured me of the error, common enough in France, of regarding marriage as a means to fortune. In the midst of the disturbance of my conscience a sacred voice has spoken. I have solemnly sworn to myself to make my own fortune, that my choice of a wife may never be determined by mercenary motives. Finally, I have blamed and repressed the unbecoming curiosity you aroused in me. You have not six millions. It would be impossible at le Havre that a young lady possessed of such a fortune should remain unknown, and you would have been betrayed by the pack of those aristocratic families which I see in pursuit of heiresses here in Paris, and which has sent the King's chief equerry on a visit to your Vilquins. So the sentiments I express are put forward as a positive rule, apart from all romance or statement of fact.

"Now, prove to me that you have one of those souls which we allow to disobey the common law, and you will grant in your mind that this second letter is in the right as well as the first. You are destined to a middle-class life; obey the iron law that holds society together. You are a superior woman, and I admire you; but if you are bent on yielding to the instinct you ought to repress, I pity you; these are the conditions of the social state. The admirable moral of the domestic epic 'Clarissa Harlowe' is that the victim's love, though legitimate and sincere, leads to her ruin, because it has its rise and progress in defiance of her family. The family, silly and cruel as it is, is in its rights as against Lovelace. The family is society.

"Believe me, for a girl, as for a wife, her glory will always consist in restraining her ardent whims within the strictest

limits of propriety. If I had a daughter who might become
a Madame de Staël, I would wish that she might die at fifteen.
Can you think, without the acutest regret, of your own child
exhibited on the stage of celebrity and parading to win the
applause of the mob? However high a woman may have
raised herself in the secret poetry of her dreams, she must
sacrifice her superiority on the altar of family life. Her soaring moods, her genius, her aspirations toward the lofty and
the sublime, all the poem of a girl's soul belongs to the man
she accepts, the children she may bear. I discern in you a
secret ambition to enlarge the narrow circle of life to which
every woman is condemned, and to bring passion and love
into your marriage. Ah! it is a beautiful dream; it is not
impossible; it is difficult; but it has been realized to bring
incompatible souls—forgive me a word which has become
ridiculous—to desperation.

"If you look for a sort of Platonic regard, it can only lead
you to despair in the future. If your letter was a sport, play
no more. And so this little romance ends, does it not? It
will not have been altogether barren of fruit; my honesty has
taken up arms; and you, on your part, have learned something certain about social life. Turn your gaze on real life,
and throw the transient enthusiasm to which literature has
given birth into the virtues of your sex. Farewell, mademoiselle; do me the honor of granting me your esteem. Since
seeing you—or her whom I believe to be you—your letter has
seemed to me quite natural; so fair a flower would instinctively turn toward the sun of poetry. So love poetry still, as
you doubtless love flowers and music, the sumptuous grandeur
of the sea, the beauties of Nature—all as ornaments of the
soul; but remember all I have had the honor of telling you
about poets. Be sure you do not marry an ass; seek with
care for the mate God has created for you. There are, take
my word for it, many clever men capable of appreciating you
and of making you happy. If I were rich, and you were

poor, I would some day lay my fortune and my heart at your
feet, for I surely believe that you have a soul full of riches and
of loyalty ; and I would intrust you with my life and honor
in the fullest confidence.   Once more farewell, fair daughter
of fair Eve.''

On reading this letter—at one gulp, like a drink of cold
water in a desert—the mountain weighing on Modeste's heart
was lifted ; then, perceiving the mistakes she had made in
carrying out her scheme, she corrected them at once by
making some wrappers for Françoise, on which she wrote her
own address at Ingouville, desiring her to come no more to
the chalet.   Thenceforth Françoise was to go home, place
each letter as it came from Paris in one of these wrappers,
and privily repost it in the town.   Modeste promised herself
always to meet the postman, standing at the front door at the
hour when he should pass.

As to the feelings excited in Modeste by this reply, in which
poor la Brière's noble heart throbbed under the brilliant mask
of Canalis, they were as infinite as the waves which rolled up
to die one after another on the shore, while, with her eyes
fixed on the ocean, she gave herself up to the joy of having
harpooned an angel's soul, so to speak, in the sea of Paris, of
having discerned that in a really superior man the heart may
sometimes be on a par with genius, and of having been well
advised by the voice of presentiment.   A mastering interest
would henceforth inspire her life.   The enclosure of her
pretty home, the wires of her cage were broken.   Thought
could soar on widespread wings.

   '' Oh, dear father,'' she cried, looking across to the horizon,
'' make us very rich ! ''

   Her answer, which Ernest de la Brière read five days later,
will tell more than any comments can the feelings of her mind
at this time :

VII.

To Monsieur de Canalis.

"MY FRIEND :—Let me call you so—you have enchanted me, and I would not have you other than you are in this letter—the first ; oh, let it not be the last ! Who but a poet could ever have so perfectly excused and understood a girl ?

"I wish to speak to you with the same sincerity as that which dictated the opening lines of your letter.

"In the first place, happily, you do not know me. I can tell you, gladly, that I am neither that frightful Mademoiselle Vilquin nor that most noble and most faded Mademoiselle d'Hérouville, who hovers between thirty and fifty, and cannot make up her mind to a creditable age. Cardinal d'Hérouville flourished in church history before the cardinal who is our only pride, for I do not count lieutenant-generals, or abbés who write small volumes of too big verse, as celebrities.

"Also, I do not live in the Vilquins' gorgeous villa ; thank God, not the millionth part of a drop of their blood, chilled in many a counting-house, flows in my veins. I am by birth partly German, partly a child of Southern France ; in my brain lurks Teutonic sentiment, and in my blood the energy of the Provençal. I am of noble birth both on my father's and my mother's side ; through my mother I have connections on every page of the 'Almanach de Gotha.' But I have taken every precaution ; it is not in the power of any man, not even of the police, to lift my disguise. I shall remain shrouded, unknown. As to myself and my belongings, *mes propres*, as they say in Normandy, be quite easy ; I am at least as good-looking as the little person—happy, though she knows it not—on whom your eyes fell ; and I do not think myself a pauper, though I am not attended in my walks by ten sons of peers ! I have even seen the contemptible farce played in my behoof of the heiress adored for her millions.

"Finally, make no attempt to find me, not even to win a bet. Alas! though free, I am guarded; in the first place, by myself, and then by brave folk, who would not hesitate to stick a knife in your heart if you tried to penetrate this retreat. I say this, not to incite your courage or your curiosity; I believe no such sentiments are needed to arouse your interest in me or to secure your attachment.

"I now proceed to reply to the second and greatly enlarged edition of your sermon:

"Shall I make a confession? When I found you so suspicious, taking me for a Corinne—how her improvisations have bored me!—I said to myself that many a tenth Muse had, ere now, led you by the tow-line of curiosity into her inmost vales, and proposed to you to taste the fruits of her school-girl Parnassus. Be quite easy, my friend; though I love poetry, I have no copies of verses in my blotting-book; my stockings are, and will remain, perfectly white. You will not be bored by any 'trifles' in one or two volumes. In short, if I should ever say to you, 'Come,' you know now that you will not find an old maid, ugly and penniless——

"Oh! my friend, if you could only know how much I regret that you should have come to le Havre! You have altered the aspect of what you call my romance. God alone can weigh in His Almighty hands the treasure I had in store for a man great enough, confiding and clear-sighted enough, to set out on the strength of my letters, after having made his way step by step through all the recesses of my heart, and to come to our first meeting with the guilelessness of a child! I dreamed of such innocence in a genius; you have marred that treasure. I forgive you; you live in Paris; and, as you say, a poet is a man.

"Will you, therefore, take me to be a silly school-girl, cherishing the enchanted garden of illusions? Nay, do not amuse yourself with throwing stones at the broken windows of a long-ruined castle. You, a man of wit, how is it that you never guessed that Mademoiselle d'Este had already read herself the lecture contained in your first letter? No, my dear poet, my first note was a pebble flung by a boy loitering along the highway, who thinks it fun to startle a landowner reading his tax-paper under shelter of his fruit trees; or, rather, was the line carefully fixed by a fisherman from the top of a rock by the seashore, in hope of a miraculous draught.

"All you say so beautifully about family ties has my approbation. The man I shall love, and of whom I shall think myself worthy, shall have my heart and my life with my parents' consent. I would neither distress nor startle them; I am certain of overruling them, and they have no prejudices. Again, I am strong enough to defy the illusions of my fancy. I have built a stronghold with my own hands, and have allowed it to be fortified by the unbounded devotion of those who watch over me as a treasure—not that I am not strong enough to defend myself in open fight; for, I may tell you, fate has clothed me in well-tempered armor on which is stamped the word DISDAIN. I have the deepest horror of everything which suggests self-interest, of all that is not entirely noble, pure, and disinterested. Without being romantic, I worship the beautiful and the ideal; though I have been romantic, all to myself, in my dreams. And so I could recognize the truth—true even to platitude—of what you wrote me as to social life.

"For the present, we are only, and can only be, friends. Why seek a friend among the unknown? you will ask. Your person is unknown to me; but your mind and heart are known to me; I like them, and I am conscious of infinite feelings in my soul, which demand a man of genius as their only confidant. I do not want the poem of my heart to be wasted; it shall be as beautiful for you as it would have been for God alone. What a precious thing is a trusty comrade to whom we may say what we will! Can you reject the unspoiled blossoms of a genuine girl? They will fly to you as gnats fly to the sunbeams. I am sure that your intellect has never before won you such a success—the confidences of a young girl. Listen to her prattle, accept the songs she has hitherto sung only for herself.

"By-and-by, if our souls are really akin, if on trial our characters agree, some day an old white-haired retainer will await you, standing by the roadside, and conduct you to a châlet, a villa, a castle, a palace—I do not yet know of what type that temple of Hymen may be—brown and gold, the colors of Austria, which marriage has made so powerful—nor whether such a conclusion may be possible; but confess that it is poetical, and that Mademoiselle d'Este has good ideas. Does she not leave you free? Does she come on jealous tiptoe to glance round Paris drawing-rooms? Does she lay on you the task of some high emprise, the chains which paladins of old voluntarily hung on their arm? What she asks of you is a really spiritual and mystical alliance.

"Come, come to my heart whenever you are unhappy, wounded, weary. Tell me everything, conceal nothing; I shall have balm for all your sorrows. I, my friend, am but twenty; but my mind is fifty, and I have unhappily known through another, my second self, the horrors and ecstasies of passion. I know all that the human heart can possibly contain of meanness and infamy, and yet I am the most honest girl living. No; I have no illusions left; but I have something better—faith and religion. There, I have played first in our game of confidences.

"Whoever my husband may be, if he is my own choice, he may sleep in peace; he might sail for the Indies, and on his return he would find me finishing the tapestry begun at his departure; no eyes would have looked into mine, no man's voice would have tainted the air in my ear; in every stitch he might find a line of the poem of which he was the

6

hero. Even if I should have been taken in by a fair and
false exterior, that man would have every flower of my
thought, every refinement of my tenderness, all the wordless
sacrifices of proud and never suppliant resignation. Yes, I
have vowed to myself never even to go out with my husband
when he does not want me; I will be the divinity of his
hearth. This is my human religion. But why should I not
test and choose the man to whom I shall be what life is to the
body? Does a man ever find life an inconvenience? What
is a wife who annoys her husband? Not life, but a sickness.
By life, I mean the perfect health which makes every hour an
enjoyment.

"To return to your letter, which will always be dear to
me. Yes, jesting apart, it really contains what I had hoped
for—the expression of prosaic sentiments, which are as necessary to family life as air is to the lungs, and without which
happiness is out of the question. What I hoped for in my
friend was that he should act as an honest man, think as a
poet, love as women love; and this is now, beyond a doubt,
no longer a chimera.

"Farewell, my friend. At present I am poor. That is
one of the reasons which makes me cling to my mask, my
incognito, my impenetrable fortress.

"I read your last poem in the 'Revue,' and with what
delight, after having mastered the austere and secret loftiness
of your soul!

"Will it aggrieve you greatly to be told that a girl be-
seeches God fervently in your behalf, that she makes you her
one thought, and that you have no rival in her heart but her
father and mother? Can there be any reason why you should
reject these pages that are full of you, that are written for
you, that none but you will read? Repay me in kind. I am
as yet so little a woman that your effusions, so long as they
are genuine and full, will suffice for the happiness of your

"O. D'ESTE-M."

"Great heavens! am I in love with her already?" exclaimed the young referendary, when he discovered that he had been sitting for an hour with this letter in his hand, after having read it. "What must I do next? She believes she is writing to our great poet. Ought I to carry on the deception? Is she a woman of forty or a girl of twenty?"

Ernest was fascinated by the abyss of the unknown. The unknown is dark infinitude, and nothing is more enthralling. From that murky vastness flash fires which rend it from time to time, and light up visions like those of Martin. In a life as full as that of Canalis, an adventure of this kind is swept away like a cornflower among the boulders of a torrent; in that of a young referendary awaiting the reinstatement in power of the party of which his patron was the representative, and who, as a precaution, was dry-nursing Canalis for parliament, this pretty girl—his imagination persistently believed her to be the fair-haired damsel he had seen—was bound to find a place in his heart, and commit all the ravages caused by a romance when it breaks into a humdrum existence, like a wolf into a farmyard. So Ernest thought a great deal about his unknown correspondent, and he replied by the following letter—an elaborate and pretentious letter, but already betraying some passion by its tone of annoyance:

VIII.

To Mademoiselle O. d'Este-M.

"MADEMOISELLE:—Is it quite fair in you to come and establish yourself in a poor poet's heart with the admitted purpose of leaving him to his fate if he should not be to your mind, and bequeathing to him perennial regrets after showing him, for a few minutes, an image of perfection were it but assumed, or, at least, a first promise of happiness?

"I was wanting in foresight when I requested the letter in

which you have begun the display of your elegant assortment of ideas. A man may well fall in love with a stranger who can unite so much daring with so much originality, such fancy with such feeling. Who but would long to know you after reading these first confidences? It is only by a really great effort that I preserve my balance when I think of you, for in you are combined all things that can disturb a man's heart and brain. So I take advantage of the remains of coolness I am able to preserve to put the case humbly before you.

"Do you believe, mademoiselle, that letters which are more or less truthful in relation to life as it really is, and more or less insincere, since the letters we may write to each other must be the expression of the moment when we send them forth, and not the general outcome of our characters —do you believe, I ask, that, however fine they may be, these letters can ever take the place of the expression of ourselves we should give through the practical evidence of daily life? Each man is twofold. There is the invisible life of the spirit, which letters may satisfy, and the mechanical life, to which we attach, alas! more importance than you, at your age, can imagine. These two existences ought both to agree with the ideal you cherish, and this, it may be said, very rarely happens.

"The pure, spontaneous, disinterested homage of a solitary soul, at once well-informed and chaste, is one of those heavenly flowers whose color and fragrance are a consolation for every grief, every wound, every mortification entailed by a literary life in Paris; and I thank you with a fervor equal to your own; but after this poetical exchange of my woes in return for the pearls of your charity, what can you expect? I have neither the genius nor the splendid position of Lord Byron; above all, I have not the halo of his artificial damnation and his imaginary social grievances; but what would you have hoped for from him in similar circumstances? His friendship, no doubt. Well, he, who ought only to have

been proud, was eaten up by an offensive and sickly vanity
which discouraged friendship. I, who am a thousand times
less great than he—may not I, too, have such discords of nature
as to make life unpleasing, and turn friendship into the most
difficult burden? What will you get in return for your dreams?
The vexations of a life which will not be wholly yours.

"The bargain is a mad one, for this reason: The poetry of
your dreams is but a plagiarism. A young German girl, not
half-German, like you, but wholly German, in the intoxication
of her twenty years, adored Goethe; she made him her friend,
her religion, her god, knowing that he was married. Frau
Goethe, a good German soul, a poet's wife, lent herself to
this worship with very shrewd complacency—which failed to
cure Bettina! But what was the end? The ecstatic married
some substantial worthy German. Between ourselves let us
confess that a girl who should have made herself the hand-
maid of a genius, who should have raised herself to his level
by understanding him, and have adored him piously till her
death—as one of those divine figures might have done that
painters have represented on the doors of their mystical
shrines—and who, when Germany should lose Goethe, would
have retired to some wilderness never more to see mankind—
as Lord Bolingbroke's lady did—let us confess that this girl
would have lived forever in the poet's glory as Mary Magdalen
does in the blood-stained triumph of the Saviour.

"If this is sublime, what do you say to the converse of it?

"Being neither Lord Byron nor Goethe, but merely the
writer of a few approved poems, I cannot claim the honors of
worship. I have little in me of the martyr. I have a heart, but
I am also ambitious, for I have to make my fortune, and I am
yet young. See me as I am. The King's favor and the patronage of his ministers afford me a decent maintenance; I
have all the habits of a very commonplace man. I go to
evening parties exactly like the first fool you meet; but my
carriage-wheels do not run, as the present times require,

on ground made solid under me by securities in the state funds.

"Though I am not rich, I have not, on the other hand, the distinction conferred by a garret, by neglected work, by glory in penury, on certain men of greater merit than mine; for instance, on d'Arthez.

"What prosaic fifth act will you not find for the enchanted fancy of your young enthusiasm? Let it rest here. If I have been so happy as to seem to you an earthly wonder, you will have been to me something radiant and supernal, like a star that blazes and vanishes. Let nothing tarnish this episode in our lives. By remaining as we are, I may love you, going through one of those mad passions which break down every obstacle and light fires in the heart, which are alarming by their violence out of all proportion to their duration; and, supposing that I should succeed in pleasing you, we must end in the vulgarest way—marriage, housekeeping, and children. Oh, Bélise and Henriette Chrysale in one, can that be? So, farewell."

IX.

To Monsieur de Canalis.

"MY FRIEND:—Your letter gave me as much pain as pleasure. Perhaps we may soon find it all pleasure to read each other's letters. Understand me. We speak to God; we ask of Him many things; He remains speechless. Now, I want to have from you the answers God never gives us. Cannot such a friendship as that of Mademoiselle de Gournay and Montaigne be repeated? Have you not known the household of Sismonde de Sismondi, at Geneva, the most touching home-life ever seen, and of which I have been told—something like that of the Marchese and Marchesa di Pescara, happy even in their old age? Good heavens! is it impossible that there should be two harps, which, though at a distance, respond to each other as in a symphony, and vibrate so as to produce delicious harmony? Man alone, in all creation, is at once the harp, the musician, and the hearer.

"Do you see me fretting after the manner of ordinary women? Do I not know that you go into society and see the handsomest and cleverest women in Paris? Can I not imagine that one of those sirens might embrace you in her cold scales, and that it is she who has sent the answer that grieves me by its prosaic reflections? There is, my friend, something more beautiful than these flowers of Parisian blandishment; there is a flower that grows at the height of those Alpine peaks called men of genius; the pride of humanity, which they fructify by shedding on it the clouds they collect with their heads in the skies; that flower I intend to cultivate and to make it open, for its wild, sweet perfume will never fail us; it is perennial.

"Do me the honor to believe that in me there is nothing common. If I had been Bettina—for I know to whom you allude—I would never have been Frau von Arnim; and if I had been one of Lord Byron's loves, I should at this moment be in a convent. You have touched me in a sensitive spot.

"You do not know me; you will know me. I feel in myself a sublime something which may be spoken of without vanity. God has implanted in my soul the root of that hybrid plant I have mentioned as native to Alpine heights, and I will not stick it in a flower-pot at my window to see it perish. No, that gorgeous and unique blossom, full of intoxicating fragrance, shall not be dragged through the vulgarities of life; it is yours—yours without a glance having blighted it, yours for ever. Yes, dear one, yours are all my thoughts, even the most secret, the most mad; yours is the heart of a girl without reserve; yours an infinite affection. If I do not like you personally, I shall not marry.

"I can live the life of the heart, the life of your mind, of your feelings; they please me, and I shall always be, as I am now, your friend. There is beauty of nature in you, and that is enough for me. There lies my life. Do not disdain a pretty young handmaiden who, for her part, does not shrink from the idea of being some day the poet's old housekeeper, in some sort his housewife, in some sort his commonsense, in some sort his wealth. This devoted maid, so precious in your lives, is pure, disinterested Friendship, to whom everything is revealed; who listens sometimes with a shake of the head, and who sits late, spinning by the light of the lamp, to be at hand when the poet comes home, soaked by the rain or out of sorts. This is my destiny if I am never to be a happy and faithfully attached wife: I can smile on one as on the other.

"And do not suppose that France will be deeply aggrieved if Mademoiselle d'Este does not give her two or three children, or refuses even to be a Madame Vilquin, or the like. I, for my part, shall never be an old maid. I shall make myself a motherhood by beneficence, and by secretly sharing the existence of a great man, to whom I shall dedicate all my thoughts and all my earthly efforts. I have the utmost horror of the commonplace. If I should be free and rich—and I know I am young and handsome—I will never become the property of some simpleton under the excuse of his being the son of a peer of France; nor of some good-looking man, who would be the woman of the two; nor of any man who would make me blush twenty times a day at the thought that I was his. Be quite easy on that score.

"My father adores my wishes too much ever to contravene them. If my poet likes me, if I like him, the glorious palace of our love will be built so high that it will be absolutely inaccessible to misfortune. I am an eaglet; you will see it in my eye. I will not repeat what I have already told you, but I put it into fewer words when I assure you that I shall be of all women the most glad to be as completely the captive of love, as I am at this moment of my father's will.

"Come, my friend, let us reduce to the truth of romance what has come upon us by my free-will.

"A girl of lively imagination shut up in a turret is dying to run about in a park which only her eyes can explore; she invents a way of opening her bars, she springs out of window, climbs the park wall, and goes off to sport at her neighbor's. It is the eternal comedy!—— Well, that girl is my soul, the neighboring park is your genius. Is it not most natural? Was a neighbor ever heard of who complained of his trellis being damaged by pretty feet?

"So much for the poet; but must the ultra-reasonable hero of Molière's comedies have reasons? Here are plenty. My dear Géronte, marriages are commonly made in direct opposition to commonsense. A family makes inquiries as to a young man. If this Léandre, provided by a friendly gossip, or picked up in a ball-room, has robbed no one, if he has no visible stain, if he has as much money as is expected, if he has come from college or has had a legal training, thus satisfying the usual ideas of education, he is allowed to call on a young lady, dressed to receive him from the moment when she gets up, instructed by her mother to be careful of what she says, and enjoined to keep anything of her soul or heart from being read in her countenance by assuming a set smile, like a dancer finishing a pirouette; she is armed with the most positive instructions as to the perils of showing her true character, and advised not to appear too distressingly knowing. The parents, when all the points of interest are satisfactorily settled between them, are simple-minded enough to recommend the young people to know all they can of each other during the few moments when they are alone, when they talk together, when they walk out—without any kind of freedom, for they know that they are tied already. Under such conditions a man dresses his mind as carefully as his person, and the girl on her side does the same. This miserable farce, carried on with gifts of flowers and jewels and places at the play, is what is called courting a girl.

"This is what I rebel against, and I mean to make legal marriage the outcome of a long marriage of souls. In all a girl's life this is the only moment when she needs reflection, insight, and experience. Her liberty and happiness are at stake, and you place neither the dice nor the box in her hands; she bets on the game; she is but a looker-on. I have the right, the will, and the power to work out my own woe, and I will use them—as my mother did when, guided by instinct, she married the most generous, devoted, and loving of men, who bewitched her one evening by his beauty. I know you to be single, a poet, and handsome. You may be sure that I never should have chosen for my confidant one of your brethren in Apollo who was married. If my mother was attracted by a handsome face, which is perhaps the genius of form, why should not I be attracted by mind and form combined? Shall I know you better after studying you by correspondence than after beginning by the vulgar method of so many months of courting? ' That is the question,' saith Hamlet.

"My plan, my dear Chrysale, has at least the advantage of not compromising our persons. I know that love has its illusions, and every illusion has its morrow. Therein lies the reason why so many lovers part who believed themselves bound for life. The true test lies in suffering and in happiness. When, after standing this double test of life, two beings have shown all their faults and good qualities, and have learned each other's characters, they may go to the tomb hand in hand; but, my dear Argante, who tells you that our little drama has no future before it?—— And, at any rate, shall we not have had the pleasure of our correspondence?

"I await your commands, monseigneur, and remain, with all my heart, yours obediently,   O. D'ESTE-M."

X.

To Mademoiselle O. d' Este-M.

"You are a demon ! I love you. Is that what you want, extraordinary girl ? Perhaps you only wish to divert your leisure in the country by looking on at the follies of which a poet is capable ? That would be a very wicked thing. Your two letters betray just enough of mischief to suggest the doubt to a Parisian. But I am no longer master of myself; my life and future hang on the answer you may send me. Tell me whether the certain possession of an unbounded affection given to you, in defiance of social conventionalities, can touch you ; if you will allow me to visit you? There will still be ample room for doubt and agony of mind in the question whether I shall personally be agreeable to you. If your answer is favorable, I alter my life, and bid adieu to many vexations which we are so foolish as to call happiness.

" Happiness, my dear, beautiful, unknown one, is what you have dreamed it ; a perfect fusion of feelings, an absolute harmony of souls, a keen sense of ideal beauty—so far as God vouchsafes it to us here below—stamped on the common actions of a life whose round we are bound to follow ; above all constancy of heart, far more precious than what we call fidelity. Can anything be called a sacrifice when the end is the supremest good, the dream of poets and of maidens, the poem to which on entering life—as soon as the spirit tries its wings—every lofty mind looks up with longing, brooding eyes, only to see it dashed to pieces against a stumbling-stone as hard as it is vulgar ; for almost every man sees the foot of reality set down at once on that mysterious egg which hardly ever hatches out ?

" I will not as yet tell you of myself, of my past, of my character, nor of an affection—almost motherly on one side,

and on mine almost filial—in which you have already wrought
a change with results in my life that may explain the word
sacrifice. You have made me forgetful, not to say ungrateful.
Is that enough to satisfy you? Oh! speak! Say one word,
and I shall love you till my eyes are closed in death, as Pescara loved his wife, as Romeo loved his Juliet, and as faithfully. Our life—mine, at any rate—will be that untroubled
happiness of which Dante speaks as being the atmosphere of
his ' Paradiso '—a poem infinitely superior to his ' Inferno.'

"Strange to say, it is not myself, but you, whom I doubt
in the long meditations in which I have allowed myself—like
you, perhaps—to follow the chimerical course of a dream-
life. Yes, dear one, I feel in me the strength to love thus, to
go on my way to the tomb gently, slowly, always smiling,
arm in arm with the woman I love, without a cloud on the
fair weather of my soul. Yes, I have courage enough to look
forward to our old age together, to see us both with white
hair, like the venerable historian of Italy, still inspired by the
same affection, but changed by the spirit of each season.

" You see, I can no longer be no more than your friend.
Though Chrysale, Oronte, and Argante, you say, have come
to life again in me, I am not yet so senile as to drink of a cup
held by the fair hands of a veiled woman without feeling a
fierce desire to tear away the domino, the mask, and to see
her face. Either write no more or give me hope. I must
have a glimpse of you, or throw up the game. Must I say
farewell? Will you allow me to sign myself,

"YOUR FRIEND?"

XI.

To Monsieur de Canalis.

" What flattery! How quickly has grave Anselme turned
into a dashing Léandre! To what am I to ascribe such a

change? Is it to the black I have scribbled on white, to the ideas which are to the flowers of my soul what a rose drawn in black-lead pencil is to the roses of the garden? Or to the remembrance of the girl you took for me, who is to my real self what a waiting-maid is to her mistress? Have we exchanged parts? Am I reason, and are you folly?

"A truce to this nonsense. Your letter made me acquainted with intoxicating joys of soul, the first I have not owed to family feelings. What, a poet has asked, are the ties of blood which weigh so heavily on ordinary souls in comparison with those which heaven forges for us of mysterious sympathies? Let me thank you—no, there are no thanks for such things. Blessings on you for the happiness you have given me; may you be happy with the gladness you poured into my soul.

"You have explained to me some apparent injustice in social life. There is something brilliant in glory, something masculine which becomes men alone, and God has prohibited women from wearing this halo while giving us love and tenderness with which to refresh the brows on which its awful light rests. I feel my mission, or, rather, you have confirmed me in it.

"Sometimes, my friend, I have risen in the morning in a frame of inconceivable sweetness. A sort of peace, tender and divine, gave me a sense as of heaven. My first thought was like a blessing. I used to call these mornings my German *levers*, to distinguish them from my southern sunsets, full of heroic deeds of battles, of Roman festivals, and of ardent verse. Well, after having read the letter into which you breathed a fever of impatience, I felt in my heart the lightness of one of those heavenly awakenings, when I loved air and nature, and felt myself destined to die for some one I loved. One of your poems, 'Le Chant d'une jeune fille,' describes these delicious hours when gladness is sweet, when prayer is a necessity, and it is my favorite piece. Shall I put all my flattery into one line: I think you worthy to be me!

"Your letter, though short, allowed me to read your heart. Yes, I could guess your tumultuous impulses, your excited curiosity, your plans, all the faggots carried (by whom) for the pyre of your heart. But I do not yet know enough of you to comply with your request. Understand, dear one, it is mystery which allows me the freedom that betrays the depths of my soul. When once we have met, farewell to our knowledge of each other.

"Shall we make a bargain? Was the first we made a bad one for you? You gained my esteem by it. And admiration supported by esteem is a great thing, my friend. First write me a sketch of your life in a few words; then tell me about your life in Paris, day by day, without any disguise, as if you were chatting to an old friend; well, then, after that I will carry our friendship a step further. I will see you, my friend, that I promise you; and it is a great deal.

"All this, dear, I warn you, is neither an intrigue nor an adventure; it cannot result in any kind of an 'affair' of gallantry, as you men say among yourselves. My life is involved in it, and, moreover—a thing which sometimes causes me terrible remorse as to the thoughts I send flying to you in flocks—not less involved is the life of a father and mother I adore, whom I must satisfy in my choice, and who in my friend must find a son.

"How far can you lordly souls, to whom God has given the wings of angels, but not always their perfections, yield to the family and its petty needs? A text I have pondered over already! Although before going forth to you I said in my heart, 'Be bold!' it has not quaked the less on the road, and I have never deceived myself either as to the roughness of the way or the difficulties of the mountain I had to climb. I have followed it all out in long meditations. Do I not know that men as eminent as you are have known the love they have inspired quite as well as that they have felt; that they have had more than one romance; and that you, above all, while cherishing those thoroughbred chimeras which a woman will buy at any cost, have gone through more final than first chapters? And yet I could say to myself, 'Be bold!' because I have studied the geography of the high peaks of humanity that you accuse of coldness—studied them more than you think. Did you not say of Byron and Goethe that they were two colossal masses of egoism and poetry? Ah, my friend, you there fall into the error of superficial minds; but it was, perhaps, generosity on your part, false modesty, or the hope of evading me.

"The vulgar may be allowed, but you may not, to regard the results of hard work as a development of the individual. Neither Lord Byron, nor Goethe, nor Walter Scott, nor Cuvier, nor any inventor belongs to himself; they are all the slaves of an idea; and this mysterious power is more jealous than a woman, it absorbs them, it makes them or kills them for its own advantage. The visible outcome of this concealed life resembles egoism in its effects; but how dare we say that a man who has sold himself for the delight, the instruction, or the greatness of his age is an egoist? Is a mother accused of selfishness when she sacrifices everything for her child? Well, the detractors of genius do not discern its teeming maternity, that is all.

"The poet's life is so perpetual a sacrifice that he needs a gigantic organization to enable him to enjoy the pleasures of an ordinary life. Hence, if, like Molière, he insists on living the life of feelings while giving them expression in their most acute crises, what disasters come upon him! for to me the comic side of Molière, as overlaying his private life, is really horrible. The magnanimity of genius seems to me almost divine, and I have classed you with that noble family of egoists so called. Oh! if I had found shallowness, self-interest, and ambition where, as it is, I admire all the flowers of the soul that I love best, you cannot know what slow suffering would have consumed me. I found disappointment sitting at the portal of my sixteenth year; what should I have done if at twenty I had found fame a liar, and the man who, in his writings, had expressed so many of the sentiments buried in my heart, incapable of understanding that heart when disclosed to him alone?

"Do you know, my friend, what would have become of me? I am going to admit you to the very depths of my soul. Well, I should have said to my father, 'Bring me any son-in-law to your mind; I give up all free-will; get me married to please yourself!'—and the man might have been a notary, a banker, avaricious, stupid, provincial, as tiresome as a rainy day, as vulgar as a parish voter; he might have been a manufacturer or some brave but brainless soldier—he would have found in me his most resigned and attentive slave. But then—dreadful suicide at every instant!—my soul would never have unfolded in the life-giving beams of the sun it worships. Not a murmur should ever have revealed to my father, my mother, or my children the suicide of the being who is at this moment shaking its prison-bars, flashing lightnings from its eyes, flying to you on outspread pinions, perching like a Polyhymnia in the corner of your study, breathing its atmosphere, and gazing at everything with a mildly inquisitive eye. Sometimes in the fields, where my husband might have taken me, I should have escaped a little way from my babes, and, seeing a lovely morning, would secretly have shed a few very bitter tears. Finally, in my heart, and in the corner of a drawer, I should have stored a little comfort for every girl betrayed by love, poor poetical souls dragged into torments by a smiling face!

"But I believe in you, my friend. This faith purifies the most fantastic notions of my secret ambition, and sometimes —see how frank I can be—I long to be in the middle of the story we have just begun, so assured am I of my feelings, such strength for love do I feel in my heart, such constancy founded on reason, such heroism to fulfill the duty I am creating for myself in case love should ever turn to duty.

"If it were given to you to follow me to the splendid seclusion where I picture our happiness, if you could know my schemes, you might utter some terrible sentence about madness, and I should perhaps be cruelly punished for sending so much poetry to a poet. Yes, I want to be a living spring, to be as inexhaustible as a beautiful country during the twenty years which nature allows us to shine in. I will keep satiety at a distance by refinements and variety. I will be brave for my love as other women are for the world. I will vary happiness, lend wit to tenderness, and piquancy to faithfulness. I am ambitious; I will kill my past rivals, dispel superficial troubles by the sweetness, the proud self-devotion of a wife, and, for a whole lifetime, give such care to the nest as a bird gives for only a few days. This immense dower ought, and could, only be offered to a great man before being dropped into the mire of vulgar conventionality.

"Now, do you still think my first letter a mistake? A gust of some mysterious will flung me toward you, as a tempest may carry a rose-bush to the heart of a stately willow. And in the letter I keep here—next my heart—you have exclaimed like your ancestor when he set out for the crusades, ' It is God's will ! '

"You will be saying, ' How she chatters ! ' All those about me say, ' Mademoiselle is very silent ! '

"O. D'ESTE-M."

These letters seemed very original to those persons to whose kindness the author of the " Comédie Humaine " is beholden for them; but their admiration for this duel between two minds crossing their pens, while their faces were hidden by the strictest incognito, may not be generally shared. Of a hundred spectators, eighty perhaps will be tired of this assault of arms. So the respect due to the majority—even to a possible majority—in every country enjoying a constitutional government, advises the suppression of eleven more letters

7

exchanged by Ernest and Modeste during the month of September; if a flattering majority should clamor for them, let us hope that it may one day afford me the means of restoring them here.

Tempted on by a wit as audacious as the heart beneath seemed to be adorable, the poor private secretary's really heroic feelings gave themselves the rein in those letters, which each reader's imagination may conceive of as finer than they really are, when picturing this harmony of two unfettered souls. Ernest, indeed, lived only on those dear scraps of paper, as a miser lives on those sent forth by the bank; while in Modeste a deep attachment had grown up in the place of the pleasure of bringing excitement into a life of celebrity, and being, in spite of distance, its chief element. Ernest's affection completed Canalis' glory. Alas! it often takes two men to make one perfect lover, just as in literature a type can only be produced by a compound of the peculiarities of several different characters. How often has a woman said in a drawing-room after some intimate talk: " That man would be my ideal as to his soul, but I feel that I love that other who is no more than a fancy of my senses! "

The last letter written by Modeste, which here follows, gives us a glimpse of the " Isle of Pheasants," whither the divagations of this correspondence was conducting our lovers:

XII.

To Monsieur de Canalis.

" Be at le Havre on Sunday; go into the church after the one o'clock service, walk round it two or three times, go out without speaking to any one, without asking anybody a question; wear a white rose in your button-hole. Then return to Paris, you will there find an answer. This answer will not be such as you expect, for, I must tell you, the future is not yet in my hands. But should I not be really mad to say *yes* without having seen you? When I have seen you, I can say *no* without offense. I am sure to remain unrecognized."

This was the letter Modeste had sent off the very day before that on which the futile struggle between herself and Dumay had taken place. So she was happy in looking forward with yearning impatience to Sunday, when her eyes would prove her intuitions, her heart, to be right or wrong—one of the most solemn moments in a woman's life, made, too, as romantic as the most enthusiastic girl could desire by three months of communion soul to soul.

Everybody, excepting her mother, had taken this torpor of expectancy for the placidity of innocence. However stringent the laws of family life and religious bonds, there are still Julies d'Étanges and Clarissas—souls which, like a brimming cup, overflow under the divine touch. Was not Modeste splendid in the fierce energy she brought to bear on repressing her exuberant youth, and remaining concealed? Let us confess that the memory of her sister was more potent than any social limitations; she had sheathed her will in iron that she might not fail her father or her family. But what a turbulent upheaval! and how could a mother possibly fail to perceive it!

On the following day Modeste and Madame Dumay led Madame Mignon out into the noonday sun to her bench among the flowers. The blind woman turned her pale, withered face toward the ocean, inhaled the scent of the sea, and took Modeste's hand in her own, for the girl was sitting by her mother. Even as she was about to question her child, the mother hesitated between forgiveness and remonstrance, for she knew that this was love, and to her, as to the false Canalis, Modeste seemed exceptional.

"If only your father may be here in time! If he delays much longer, he will find you alone of those he loved!

Promise me once more, Modeste, never to leave him," she said, with motherly persuasiveness.

Modeste raised her mother's hands to her lips and kissed them softly, as she replied—

" Need I tell you so again ? "

" Ah, my child, you see, I myself left my father to go to my husband! And my father was alone too; I was his only child—— Is that what God is punishing me for, I wonder? All I ask you is to marry in agreement with your father's choice, to keep a place for him in your heart, not to sacrifice him to your happiness; to keep him in the bosom of your family. Before I lost my sight I made a note of my wishes; he will carry them out; I have enjoined on him to keep the whole of his fortune, not that I have a thought of distrusting you, but can one ever be sure about a son-in-law? I, my child, was I prudent? A flash of an eye settled my whole life. Beauty, the most deceitful of shows, spoke the truth to me ; but if it should ever be the same with you, poor child, swear to me that if appearances should carry you away, as they did your mother, you would leave it to your father to make inquiries as to the character, the heart, and the previous life of the man of your choice, if you make a choice."

" I will never marry without my father's consent," replied Modeste.

On hearing this answer, her mother sat in complete silence, and her half-dead countenance showed that she was pondering on it, as blind people ponder, meditating on her daughter's tone in speaking it.

" You see, my child," said Madame Mignon, after a long silence, " the thing is this : If Caroline's wrong-doing is killing me by inches, your father would never survive yours ; I know him ; he would blow his brains out ; there would neither be life nor happiness on earth for him——"

Modeste walked away a few steps, and returned in a minute.

" Why did you leave me ? " asked Madame Mignon.

"You made me cry, mamma," said Modeste.

"Well, my angel, kiss me then. You love no one here? You have no one paying attentions to you?"

"No, mamma," said the little Jesuit.

"Can you swear to that?"

"Really, truly!" cried Modeste.

Madame Mignon said no more; she still doubted.

"In short, if you should choose a husband, your father would know all about it?"

"I promised that to my sister and to you, mother. What sin do you suppose I could commit when every minute I read on my finger, 'Remember Bettina!' Poor little sister!"

At the moment when the words, "Poor little sister!" were followed by an interval of silence between Modeste and her mother, from whose darkened eyes fell tears which Modeste could not check even by falling at Madame Mignon's knees and crying, "Forgive me; forgive me, mamma!" at that very moment the worthy Dumay was mounting the hill of Ingouville at a rapid pace, an abnormal incident in the cashier's life.

Three letters had once brought them ruin; one had brought fortune back to them. That morning Dumay had received, by the hand of a captain just returned from the China seas, the first news he had had of his patron and only friend.

To Monsieur Dumay, formerly Cashier to the firm of Mignon.

"MY DEAR DUMAY:—Barring misadventure by sea, I shall follow closely on the vessel by which I am forwarding this letter; I would not leave the ship to which I am accustomed. I told you no news was to be good news; but the first words of this letter will rejoice you, for those words are, I have at least seven millions of francs! I am bringing a large part of it in indigo, a third in good bills on London and Paris, and

another third in bright gold.   The money you sent me enabled
me to make the sum I had determined on—two millions for
each of the girls, and comfort for myself.

" I have been dealing wholesale in opium for the Canton
houses, all ten times as rich as I am.   You have no notion in
Europe of what the rich China merchants are.   I traveled
from Asia Minor, where I could buy opium cheap, to Canton,
where I sold it in bulk to the firms that deal in it.

" My last voyage was to the Malay archipelago, where I could
buy indigo of the first quality with the proceeds of the opium
trade.   Perhaps I may find that I have five or six hundred
thousand francs more, as I am valuing my indigo only at cost
price.

" I have been quite well all the time ; never an ailment.
That is the reward of traveling for one's children !   At the
beginning of the second year I was able to purchase the
' Mignon,' a nice brig of seven hundred tons burthen, built
of teak, and lined with the same, and copper-bottomed ; fitted
throughout to suit my convenience.   This, too, is worth something.   The seafaring life, the constant change needed in my
trading, and hard work, as being in a way my own captain
on the high seas, have all kept me in excellent health.

" To speak of all this is to speak of my two girls and my
dear wife !   I hope that on hearing of my ruin the wretch who
robbed me of my Bettina may have deserted her, and the
wandering lamb have returned to the cottage.   She, no doubt,
will need a larger dower.

" My three women and my good Dumay—you have all four
been constantly in my thoughts during these three years.
Dumay, you are a rich man.   Your share, beside my own
fortune, amounts to five hundred and sixty thousand francs,
which I am forwarding to you by a draft, payable to yourself
only, by the firm of Mongenod, who are advised from New
York.   A few months more and I shall see you all again—
well, I hope.

"Now, my dear Dumay, I write to you only, because I wish you to keep the secret of my fortune, and I leave it to you to prepare my dear ones for the joy of my return. I have had enough of trade, and I mean to leave le Havre.

"The choice of my sons-in-law is a very serious matter. It is my intention to repurchase the estate and château of la Bastie, to endow it with an entailed settlement of a hundred thousand francs a year at least, and to petition the King to confer my name and titles on one of my sons-in-law. You, my dear Dumay, know the misfortune that befell us in consequence of the fatal splendor given by wealth. By that I wrecked the honor of one of my daughters. I carried back to Java the most wretched of fathers—an unhappy Dutch merchant, with nine millions of francs, whose two daughters had been both carried off by villains! We wept together like two children. So I will not have the amount of my fortune known.

"I shall not land at le Havre, but at Marseilles. My mate is a Provençal, an old retainer of my family, whom I have enabled to make a little fortune. Castagnould will have my instructions to repurchase la Bastie, and I shall dispose of my indigo through the firm of Mongenod. I shall place my money in the Bank of France, and come home to you, professing to have made no more than about a million of francs in merchandise. My daughters will be reputed to have two hundred thousand francs apiece. Then my great business will be to decide which of my sons-in-law may be worthy to succeed to my name, my arms, and my titles, and to live with us; but they must both be, as you and I are, absolutely steady, firm, loyal, and honest men.

"I have never doubted you, old boy, for a single instant. I have felt sure that my dear and admirable wife, with yours and yourself, will have drawn an impassable fence round my daughter, and that I may press a kiss full of hope on the pure brow of the angel that remains to me. Bettina Caroline, if you have been able to screen her fault, will have a fortune. After trying war and trade, we will now go in for agriculture, and you must be our steward.   Will that suit you?

"And so, old friend, you are master of your line of conduct to the family, to tell them, or to say nothing of my success.   I trust to your judgment; you are to say just what you think right. In four years there may have been many changes of character. I make you the judge; I so greatly fear my wife's tender weakness with her daughters.

"Farewell, my dear old Dumay.   Tell my wife and daughters that I have never failed to embrace them in my heart every day, morning and evening.   The second draft, for forty thousand francs, payable, like the other, to you alone, is for my wife and daughters to go on with.

"Your master and friend,

"CHARLES MIGNON."

"Your father is coming home," said Madame Mignon to her daughter.

"What makes you think that, mamma?" asked Modeste.

"Nothing could make Dumay run but having that news to bring us."

Modeste, lost in her own thoughts, had not seen nor heard Dumay.

"Victory!" shouted the lieutenant from the gate.   "Madame, the colonel has never been ill, and he is coming home—— He is coming on the 'Mignon,' a good ship of his own, which, with the cargo he describes to me, must be worth eight or nine hundred thousand francs.   But he urgently begs you will say nothing about it; the disaster to our poor, lost child has eaten deeply into his heart."

"He has made room in it for a grave then," said Madame Mignon.

"And he ascribes this disaster—as seems to me most probable—to the greed which a large fortune excites in young

men. My poor colonel hopes to find the lost lamb among us
here. Let us rejoice among ourselves, and say nothing to
anybody, not even to Latournelle if possible. Mademoiselle,"
he added to Modeste apart, " write a letter to your father to
tell him of the loss in the family and its terrible consequences, so as to prepare him for the dreadful sight that awaits
him ; I will undertake that he shall get the letter before arriving at le Havre, for he will be obliged to come through Paris ;
write fully, you have plenty of time ; I will take the letter
on Monday ; on Monday, no doubt, I shall have to go to
Paris——"

Modeste was now afraid lest Dumay and Canalis should
meet ; she was eager to go up to her room and write to put
off the assignation.

" Tell me, mademoiselle," Dumay went on in the humblest
tone, but standing in her path, " that your father will find
his daughter without a feeling in her heart but that which was
in it when he left—of love for her mother."

" I have sworn to my sister and my mother—I have sworn
to myself to be my father's comfort, his joy, and his pride,
and—I—will be," replied Modeste, with a haughty and scornful glance at Dumay. " Do not mar my joy at knowing that
my father will soon be among us again by any offensive suspicions. A young girl's heart cannot be hindered from beating ; you do not wish me to be a mummy ? I belong to my
family ; but my heart is my own. If I love any one, my
father and mother shall be told of it. Are you satisfied, monsieur ? "

" Thank you, mademoiselle," replied Dumay. " You have
restored me to life. But you might at least have called me
Dumay, even when giving me a slap in the face ! "

" Swear to me," said her mother earnestly and beseechingly,
" that you have never exchanged a word or a glance with any
young man."

" I can swear it," said Modeste, smiling, and looking at

Dumay, who was studying her with a mischievous smile like a girl's, when playing off some joke.

"Can she really be so false?" exclaimed Dumay, when Modeste had gone into the house.

"My daughter Modeste may have her faults," said the mother, "but she is incapable of a lie."

"Well, then, let us make ourselves easy," replied the lieutenant, "and be satisfied that misfortune has now closed its account with us."

"God grant it!" said Madame Mignon. "You will see him, Dumay; I can only hear him—— There is much sadness in my joy."

Modeste, meanwhile, though happy in the thought of her father's return, was, like Pierrette, distressed to see all her eggs broken. She had hoped for a larger fortune than Dumay had spoken of. She was ambitious for her poet, and wished for at least half of the six millions of which she had written in her second letter. Thus absorbed by her double happiness, and annoyed by the grievance of her comparative poverty, she sat down to her piano, the confidant of so many girls, who tell it their anger and their wishes, expressing them in their way of playing.

Dumay was talking to his wife, walking to and fro below her window, confiding to her the secret of their good fortune, and questioning her as to her hopes, wishes, and intentions. Madame Dumay, like her husband, had no family but the Mignon family. The husband and wife decided on living in Provence, if the Count should go to Provence, and to leave their money to any child of Modeste's that might need it.

"Listen to Modeste," said Madame Mignon to them; "only a girl in love could compose such a melody without any knowledge of music."

Homes may burn, fortunes may collapse, fathers may come back from their travels, empires may fall, cholera may ravage the town—a girl's love pursues its flight as nature keeps her course, or that horrible acid discovered by chemistry which might pierce through the earth if it were not absorbed in the centre.

This is the melody Modeste had improvised to some verses which must be quoted here, though they are to be found in the second volume of poems published by Dauriat; for, to adapt them to the air, the young composer had broken the rhythm by some changes which might puzzle the admirers of a poet who is sometimes too precise.

And here, too, since modern typography allows of it, is Modeste's music, to which her exquisite expression lent the charm we admire in the greatest singers—a charm that no printing, were it phonetic or hieroglyphic, could ever represent:

A MAIDEN'S SONG.

Come a -
wake, my heart, for the soaring lark Wings her
upward flight as she chants her lay. Sleep no
more, my heart, for the vi - o - let Breathes her

incense to God   at break of day.   Ev'ry

blos - som re - fresh'd,   and soft - ly un - clos - ing,

Op - ens an   eye   to be - hold   it - self   fair. In each

chalice a   gem,   a   dew - drop re - pos - ing,

Mir - rors its hues Ere it dies in the air. We

feel in the breeze that the an-gel of flowers Has

kiss'd ev' - ry rose as he pass'd in the night, Has

guarded their beauty through all the dark hours, Their

first smile is his in the sweet morning light.

Then a - wake, my heart, for the soaring lark

Wings her ear-ly flight, and chants her lay.

Night and sleep be-gone! my heart, the vi - o - let

To God her in-cense breathes at break of day.

Night and sleep begone! my heart, the vi - o - let To

God her in - cense breathes at break of day.

"It is pretty," said Madame Dumay. "Modeste is very musical; that is all."

"She has the very devil in her!" exclaimed the cashier, for the mother's dread had entered into his soul and made his blood run cold.

"She is in love," returned Madame Mignon.

By her success in communicating her conviction as to Modeste's secret passion on the irrefragable evidence of that melody, Madame Mignon chilled the cashier's joy over his patron's return and success. The worthy Breton went off to the town to do his day's business at Gobenheim's; then, before going home to dinner, he called on the Latournelles to mention his fears, and once more to request their help and coöperation.

"Yes, my good friend," said Dumay on the threshold, as he took leave of the notary, "I am of madame's opinion. She is in love, sure enough; beyond that the devil only knows!—— I am disgraced!"

"Do not worry yourself, Dumay," said the little notary. "We certainly, among us all, must be a match for that little lady. Sooner or later every girl who is in love does something rash which betrays her secret; we will talk it over this evening."

So all these persons, devoted to the Mignon family, were still a prey to the same anxiety as had tormented them before the experiment that the old soldier had expected to be deci-

8

sive.   The futility of all these struggles so spurred Dumay's
conscience that he would not go to Paris to fetch his fortune
before he had discovered the clue to this enigma.   All these
hearts, caring far more for sentiment than for self-interest,
understood that unless he found this daughter innocently pure,
the colonel might die of grief on finding Bettina dead and
his wife blind.   The unhappy Dumay's despair made so deep
an impression on the Latournelles that they forgot their loss of
Exupère, whom they had sent off to Paris that morning.
During the dinner hour, when the three were alone, Monsieur
and Madame Latournelle and Butscha turned the matter over
under every aspect and considered every conceivable hypothesis.

"If Modeste were in love with any one at le Havre, she
would have quaked last night," said Madame Latournelle,
"so her lover must be elsewhere."

"She swore this morning to her mother, in Dumay's presence, that she had not exchanged a glance or a word with a
living soul," said the notary.

"Then she loves as I do!" said Butscha.

"And how do you love, my poor boy?" asked Madame
Latournelle.

"Madame," replied the little hunchback, "I love all to
myself, from afar, almost as far as from hence to the stars."

"And how do you get there, you great goose?" said
Madame Latournelle, smiling at him.

"Ah, madame, what you take to be a hump is the sheath
for my wings."

"Then this explains your seal!" laughingly exclaimed the
lawyer.

The clerk's seal was a star; the motto, *Fulgens, sequar*—
Shine, and I will follow you—the device of the house of
Chastillonest.

"A beautiful creature may be as diffident as the most hideous," said Butscha, as if talking to himself.   "Modeste is

quite clever enough to have feared lest she should be loved only for her beauty.''

Hunchbacks are wonderful creatures, and due entirely to civilization ; for, in the scheme of nature, weak or deformed beings ought to perish. A curvature or twist of the spinal column gives to these men, who seem to be nature's outcasts, a flashing look, in which is concentrated a greater quantity of nervous fluids than other men can command, in the very centre where they are elaborated and act, and whence they are sent forth like a light to vivify their inmost being. Certain forces are the result, detected occasionally by magnetism, but most frequently lost in the waste-places of the spiritual world. Try to find a hunchback who is not gifted in some remarkable way, either with a cheerful wit, superlative malignity, or sublime kindliness. These beings, privileged beings though they know it not, live within themselves as Butscha did, when they have not exhausted their splendidly concentrated powers in the battle they have fought to conquer obstacles and remain alive.

In this way we may explain the superstitious and popular traditions, which we owe to the belief in gnomes, in frightful dwarfs, in misshapen fairies—the whole race of *la bouteille*, as Rabelais has it, that contain rare balsams and elixirs.

Thus Butscha almost read Modeste ; and with the eagerness of a hopeless lover, of a slave ever ready to die like the soldiers who, deserted and alone amid Russian snows, still shouted *" Vive l'Empereur ! "* he dreamed of discovering her secret for himself alone.

As his chief and Madame Latournelle walked up to the chalet, he followed them with a very anxious mien, for it was imperative that he should conceal from every watchful eye, from every listening ear, the snare in which he meant to entrap the girl. There should be a flashing glance, a start detected, as when a surgeon lays his finger on a hidden injury.

That evening Gobenheim did not join them ; Butscha was

Monsieur Dumay's partner against Monsieur and Madame
Latournelle.   At about nine o'clock, while Modeste was
absent preparing her mother's room, Madame Mignon and
her friends could talk openly ; but the poor clerk, stricken by
the conviction which had come on him too, seemed as far
away from the discussion as Gobenheim had been the night
before.

"Why, Butscha, what ails you?" exclaimed Madame Latournelle, astonished at him.   "One might think you had
lost all your relations!"

A tear started to the poor fellow's eye—a foundling, deserted by a Swedish sailor, and his mother dead of grief in
the workhouse!

"I have no one in the world but you," he replied in husky
tones ; "and your compassion is too pious ever to be with-
drawn from me, for I will never cease to deserve your kindness."

The answer struck an equally sensitive chord in those
present, that of delicacy.

"We all love you, Monsieur Butscha," said Madame Mignon with emotion.

"I have six hundred thousand francs of my own!" cried
the worthy Dumay.   "You shall be a notary at le Havre,
and Latournelle's successor."

The American, for her part, had taken the poor hunchback's hand and pressed it.

"You have six hundred thousand francs!" cried Latournelle, pricking up his ears at this speech, "and you let these
ladies stay here!   And Modeste has no horse!   And she no
longer has lessons in music, in painting, in——"

"Oh, he has only had the money a few hours," exclaimed
the American.

"Hush!" exclaimed Madame Mignon.   While this was
going on, the dignified Madame Latournelle had recovered
herself.   She turned to Butscha.

"My dear boy," said she, "you have so much affection around you that I never considered the particular bearing of a common phrase as applied to you; but you may thank me for my blunder, since it has shown you what friends you have earned by your beautiful nature."

"Then you have some news of Monsieur Mignon?" asked the notary.

"He is coming home," said Madame Mignon; "but we must keep it secret. When my husband hears how Butscha has clung to us, and that he has shown us the warmest and most disinterested friendship when the world turned its back on us, he will not leave you to provide for him entirely, Dumay. And so, my friend," she added, trying to turn towards Butscha, "you may proceed at once to deal with Latournelle——"

"He is of full age, five-and-twenty," said Latournelle. "And, on my part, it is paying off a debt, my dear fellow, if I give you the refusal of my practice."

Butscha kissed Madame Mignon's hand, wetting it with his tears, and showed a tearful face when Modeste opened the drawing-room door.

"Who has been distressing my mysterious dwarf?" she asked.

"Oh, mademoiselle, do we children nursed in sorrow ever shed tears of grief? I have just received such marks of attachment that I was moved with tenderness for all those in whom I liked to believe I had found relations. I am to be a notary; I may grow rich. Ah, ha! Poor Butscha may some day be rich Butscha. You do not know what audacity exists in this abortion!" he exclaimed.

The hunchback struck himself hard on his cavernous breast, and placed himself in front of the fireplace after giving Modeste a look that stole like a gleam from under his heavy, drooping eyelids; for in this unforeseen conjuncture he had found his chance of sounding his sovereign lady's heart.

For an instant Dumay fancied that the clerk had dared
aspire to Modeste ; he exchanged looks with his friends which
were understood by all, and which made them gaze at the
little hunchback with a sort of dread mingled with curiosity.

"I—I too—have my dreams," Butscha went on, not taking
his eyes off Modeste.

The girl looked down instinctively, in a way which was a
revelation to the clerk. "You love romances ; allow me, in
the midst of my joy, to confide my secret to you, and you
will tell me if the end of the romance I have dreamed of for
my life is possible—— If not, of what use is fortune. To
me, more than to any one else, money is happiness, since to
me happiness means the enriching of the one I love ! You
who know so many things, mademoiselle, tell me whether a
man can be loved independently of his person—handsome or
ugly, and for his soul alone?"

Modeste looked up at Butscha. It was a terrible, questioning look, for at this moment Modeste shared Dumay's suspicions. "When I am rich, I shall look out for some poor but
beautiful girl, a foundling like myself, who has suffered much,
and is very unhappy ; I will write to her, comfort her, be her
good genius ; she shall read my heart, my soul ; she shall
have all my wealth, in both kinds—my gold, offered with
great delicacy, and my mind, beautified by all the graces
which the misfortune of birth has denied to my grotesque
form ! And I will remain hidden, like a cause which science
seeks. God perhaps is not beautiful. The girl will naturally
be curious and want to see me ; but I shall tell her that I am
a monster of ugliness, I will describe myself as hideous——"

At this, Modeste looked hard in his face. If she had said,
"What do you know of my love affairs?" it could not have
been more explicit.

"If I am so happy as to be loved for the poetry of my
soul !—if, some day, I might seem to that woman to be only
slightly deformed, confess that I shall be happier than the

handsomest of men, that even a man of genius beloved by
such a heavenly creature as you are——''

The blush that mounted to Modeste's face betrayed almost
the whole of the girl's secret to the hunchback.

"Well, now, if a man can enrich the girl he loves, and
charm her heart irrespective of his person, is that the way to
be loved? This has been the poor hunchback's dream—
yesterday's dream; for to-day your adorable mother has given
me the clue to my future treasure by promising to facilitate
my acquiring an office and connection. Still, before becoming a Gobenheim, I must know whether such a horrible transformation will achieve its end. What do you think, mademoiselle, on your part?"

Modeste was so taken by surprise that she did not observe
Butscha's appeal to her judgment. The lover's snare was
better contrived than the soldier's; for the poor girl, quite
bewildered, stood speechless.

"Poor Butscha!" said Madame Latournelle to her hus-
banand, "is he going mad?"

"You want to play the fairy tale of Beauty and the Beast,"
said Modeste at last, "and you forget that the Beast is turned
into Prince Charming."

"Do you think so?" said the dwarf. "Now I have always
imagined that transformation to symbolize the phenomenon
of the soul becoming visible and eclipsing the body by its
radiant glory. If I should never be loved, I shall remain
invisible, that is all! You and yours, madame," said he to
his mistress, "instead of having a dwarf at your command,
will have a life and fortune."

Butscha returned to his seat, and said to the three players,
affecting perfect calmness—

"Who deals?"

But to himself he was saying with grief, "She wants to be
loved for her own sake; she is corresponding with some sham
great man, but how far has she gone?"

"My dear mamma, it has struck a quarter to ten," said Modeste to her mother.

Madame Mignon bid her friends good-night, and went to bed.

Those who insist on loving in secret may be watched over by Pyrenean dogs, mothers, Dumays, Latournelles—they are in no danger from these; but a lover! It is diamond cut diamond, fire against fire, wit against wit, a perfect equation, of which the terms are equal and interchangeable.

On Sunday morning Butscha was beforehand with Madame Latournelle, who always went to escort Modeste to mass, and stayed cruising about outside the chalet, waiting for the postman.

"Have you a letter for Mademoiselle Modeste this morning?" he asked of that humble functionary as he approached.

"No, monsieur, no——"

"We have been good customers of the government for some time past!" exclaimed the clerk.

"I believe you!" replied the postman.

Modeste from her room saw and heard this little interview; she posted herself at her window at this hour, behind the Venetian shutter, to watch for the postman.

She went down and out into the little garden, where, in a husky voice, she called out, "Monsieur Butscha!"

"Here am I, mademoiselle," said the hunchback, coming to the little gate, which Modeste herself opened.

"Will you tell me whether you include among your titles to the affection of a woman the disgraceful espionage you choose to exercise?" asked the girl, trying to overwhelm her slave by her gaze and queenly attitude.

"Yes, mademoiselle," he proudly replied. "I had never imagined," he added in a low voice, "that a worm could do good service to a star! But so it is. Would you rather have your heart read by your mother, Monsieur Dumay, and Madame Latournelle than by a poor creature, almost an outcast

from life, who is yours as much as one of the flowers you cut
to gratify you for a moment ?   They all know that you love ;
I alone know how.   Take me as you would take a watch-dog ;
I will obey you, I will protect you, I will never bark, and I
will have no opinions about you.   All I ask is that you will
let me be of some use to you.   Your father placed a Dumay
in your menagerie ; try a Butscha, and you will find it quite
another story !   A poor Butscha, who asks for nothing, not
even for a bone."

"Well, I will take you on trial," said Modeste, who only
wished to be rid of so sharp a guardian.   " Go at once to all
the hotels at Graville and le Havre, and ask if a M. Arthur
has arrived from England——"

" Listen, mademoiselle," said Butscha respectfully, but interrupting Modeste, " I will just go for a walk on the beach,
and that will be all that is necessary, for you do not wish me
to go to church, that is all."

Modeste looked at the hunchback in blank astonishment.

" Yes, mademoiselle, though you have wrapped your face in
wadding and a handkerchief, you have no cold ; though you
have a double veil to your hat, it is only to see without being
seen."

" What endows you with so much penetration ? " cried
Modeste, reddening.

" Why, mademoiselle, you have no stays on !   A cold would
not require you to disguise your figure by putting on several
petticoats, to hide your hands in old gloves, and your pretty
feet in hideous boots, to dress yourself anyhow, to——"

" That will do," said she.   " But, now, how am I sure
that you will obey me ? "

" My master wanted to go to Sainte-Adresse, and was rather
put out ; but as he is really very kind, he would not deprive
me of my Sunday.   Well, I will propose to him that we
should go——"

" Go then, and I shall trust to you——"

"Are you sure you will not want me at le Havre?"

"Quite. Listen, mysterious dwarf, and look up," she said, pointing to a cloudless sky. "Can you see the track left by the bird that flew across just now? Well, my actions, as pure as that pure air, leave no more trace than that. Reassure Dumay and the Latournelles, reassure my mother; and be sure that this hand" (and she held out to him a slender little hand with upturned finger-tips, transparent to the light) "will never be given away, never even warmed by the kiss of what is called a lover, before my father's return."

"And why do you want me to keep away from church to-day?"

"Do you cross-question me, after all I have done you the honor to tell you and require of you?"

Butscha bowed without replying, and hastened home, enraptured at thus entering the service of his anonymous mistress.

An hour later Monsieur and Madame Latournelle came to fetch Modeste, who complained of a dreadful toothache.

"I really had not strength to dress," said she.

"Well, then, stay at home," said the notary's wife.

"No, no. I will go and pray for my father's safe return," replied Modeste; "and I thought that if I wrapped up well, it would do me more good than harm to go out."

So Mademoiselle Mignon set out alone with Latournelle. She would not take his arm for fear of being questioned as to the internal tremor that agitated her at the idea of so soon seeing her great poet. One look, the first, was about to decide her future existence.

Is there in the life of man a more exquisite moment than that of the first promised meeting? Can the feelings that lie buried in his heart, and that then burst into life, ever be known again? Can he ever again feel the pleasure that he finds, as did Ernest de la Brière, in choosing his best razors, his finest shirts, spotless collars, and impeccable clothes? We deify everything that is associated with that supreme hour. We imagine poems in our hearts, secret poems as beautiful as the woman's, and on the day when each reads the other's soul all is over! Is it not the same with these things as with the blossom of those wild fruits, at once sharp and sweet, lost in forest depths, the delight of the sun, no doubt; or, as Canalis says in "The Maiden's Song," the gladness of the plant itself which the Angel of Flowers has allowed to see its own beauty.

This leads to the reflection that la Brière, a modest soul, like many another penurious being for whom life begins with toil and money difficulties, had never yet been loved. He had arrived at le Havre the night before, and had at once gone to bed like a coquette, to efface every trace of his journey; and he had now, after taking a bath, just completed a carefully advantageous toilet. This, perhaps, is the place for giving a full-length portrait of him, if only to justify the last letter Modeste was ever to write to him.

Born of a good family at Toulouse, distantly connected with that minister who took him under his patronage, Ernest has the well-bred air which comes of an education begun from the cradle; the habit of business has given it solidity without effort, for pedantry is the rock on which precocious gravity is commonly wrecked. Of medium height, his face is attractively refined and gentle; his complexion warm, though colorless, was at that time set off by a slender mustache and a small imperial, a *virgule à la Mazarin.* But for these manly witnesses, he would, perhaps, have looked too much like a girl dressed up, so delicate is the cut of his face and lips, so natural is it to attribute to a woman teeth of transparent enamel and almost artificial evenness. Add to these feminine characteristics a voice as sweet as his looks, as gentle as his turquoise-blue eyes, with Oriental lids, and you will perfectly understand how it was that the minister had nicknamed his young private secretary Mademoiselle de la Brière. His broad, smooth forehead, framed under thick black hair, has a dreamy look that does not contradict the expression of his countenance, which is wholly melancholy. The prominence of the eyebrows, though delicately arched, overshadows the eyes, and adds to this look of melancholy by the sadness—a physical sadness, so to speak —that the eyelids give when they half-close the eyes. This secret bashfulness, to which we give the name of modesty, characterizes his features and person. The whole result will, perhaps, be better understood if we add that the theory of perfect drawing demands greater length in the shape of the head, more space between the chin, which ends abruptly, and the forehead, on which the hair grows too low. Thus the face looks flattened. Work had already graven a furrow between the eyebrows, which were thick, and too nearly met, like those of all jealous natures. Though la Brière was as yet slight, his figure was one of those which, developing late, are most unexpectedly stout at the age of thirty or thirty-five years.

The young man might very well have typified, to those who are familiar with French history, the royal and mysterious personality of Louis XIII., with his melancholy diffidence for no known reason, pallid under his crown, loving the fatigue of hunting, and hating work; so timid with his mistress as to respect her virtue, so indifferent to his friend as to leave him to be beheaded; explicable only by his remorse at having avenged his father on his mother—either a Catholic Hamlet or the victim of some incurable malady. But the canker-worm which paled the King's cheek and unnerved his strength was as yet, in Ernest, no more than simple distrust of himself, the shyness of a man to whom no woman had ever said, "How I love you!" and, above all, wasted self-sacrifice. After hearing the knell of a monarchy in the fall of a minister, the poor boy had found in Canalis a rock hidden under tempting mosses; he was seeking a despotism to worship; and this uneasiness, that of a dog in search of a master, gave him the expression of the King who found his. These clouds and feelings, this "pale cast" over his whole person, made his face far more attractive than the young secretary himself imagined, annoyed as he was sometimes to find himself classed by women as a *beau ténébreux*— gloomily handsome; a style gone quite out of fashion at a time when every man would gladly keep the clarions of advertisement for his own exclusive use.

So Ernest the diffident had sought the adornment of the most fashionable clothes. For this interview, when everything would depend on first sight, he donned black trousers and carefully polished shoes, a sulphur-colored waistcoat, revealing an excessively fine shirt fastened with opal studs, a black necktie, and a short blue coat, which looked as if it had been glued to his back and waist by some new process; his rosette graced the button-hole. He wore smart kid gloves of the color of Florentine bronze, and held in his left hand a light cane and his hat, with a certain Louis-quatorze air; thus showing, as the sacred place demanded, his carefully combed hair, on which the light shed satin-like reflections. Standing sentry under the porch from the very beginning of the service, he studied the church while watching all the Christians, more especially those in petticoats, who came to dip their fingers in the holy water.

As Modeste came in, an inner voice cried out, "'Tis he!" That coat and figure, so essentially Parisian, the rosette, the gloves, the walking-cane, the scented hair—none of these things were native to le Havre. And when la Brière turned to look at the notary's tall and showy wife, the little notary himself and the bundle—a word dedicated to this sense by women—under which Modeste had concealed herself, though she was fully prepared, the poor child was stricken to the heart by the aspect of this romantic countenance, in the bright daylight from the open door. She could not be mistaken; a small white rose almost hid the rosette. Would Ernest recognize his unknown fair hidden under an old hat and a double veil? Modeste was so fearful of the clairvoyance of love that she walked with an elderly shuffle.

"Wife," said Latournelle, as he went to his place, "that man does not belong to le Havre."

"So many strangers come through," replied that lady to her husband.

"But do strangers ever think of coming to see our church, which is not more than two centuries old?"

Ernest remained in the porch all through the service without seeing any woman who realized his hopes. Modeste, on her part, could not control her trembling till near the end. She was agitated by joys which she alone could have described. At last she heard on the pavement the step of a gentleman, for, mass being over, Ernest was walking round the church, where no one remained but the *dilettanti* of prayer, who became to him the object of anxious and piercing scrutiny. He remarked the excessive trembling of the prayer-book held by the veiled lady as he passed her; and as she was the only one who hid her face, he conceived some suspicions, confirmed by Modeste's dress, which he studied with the care of an inquisitive lover.

When Madame Latournelle left the church, he followed her at a decent distance, and saw her, with Modeste, go into the house in the Rue Royale, where Mademoiselle Mignon usually waited till the hour of vespers. Ernest studied the house, decorated with escutcheons, and asked of a passer-by the name of the owner, who was mentioned almost with pride as Monsieur Latournelle, the first notary of le Havre.

As he lounged down the Rue Royale, trying to catch a glimpse of the interior of the house, Modeste could see her lover; she then declared herself to be too ill to attend vespers, and Madame Latournelle kept her company. So poor Ernest had his cruise for his pains. He dared not go to loiter about Ingouville; he made it a point of honor to obey, and returned to Paris after writing a letter while waiting for the coach, and posting it for Françoise Cochet to receive next morning with the postmark of le Havre.

Monsieur and Madame Latournelle dined at the chalet every Sunday, taking Modeste home after vespers. As soon as the young lady felt better, they all went up to Ingouville, followed by Butscha. Modeste, quite happy, now dressed herself beautifully. As she went down to dinner she forget all about her disguise of the morning, and her cold, and sang—

> " Night and sleep begone ! My heart, the violet
> To God her incense breathes at break of day ! "

Butscha felt a thrill as he beheld Modeste, she seemed to him so completely changed ; for the wings of love fluttered, as it were, on her shoulders ; she looked like a sylph, and her cheeks glowed with the divine hue of happiness.

" Whose words are those which you have set to such a pretty air?" Madame Mignon asked her daughter.

" They are by Canalis, mamma," she replied, turning in an instant to the finest crimson, from her neck to the roots of her hair.

"Canalis !" exclaimed the dwarf, who learned from Modeste's tone and blush all of her secret that he as yet knew not. " He, the great poet, does he write ballads ? "

"They are some simple lines," replied she, " to which I have ventured to adapt some reminiscences of German airs."

" No, no, my child," said Madame Mignon ; " that music is your own, my dear."

Modeste, feeling herself grow hotter and hotter, went out into the garden, taking Butscha with her.

"You can do me a great service," said she, in an undertone. " Dumay is affecting discretion to my mother and me as to the amount of the fortune my father is bringing home, and I want to know the truth. Has not Dumay, at different times, sent papa five hundred and something thousand francs?

My father is not the man to stay abroad four years simply to double his capital. Now a ship is coming in that is all his own, and the share he offers Dumay amounts to nearly six hundred thousand francs."

"We need not question Dumay," said Butscha. "Your father had lost, as you know, four millions of francs before his departure, these he has no doubt recovered; he would certainly have given Dumay ten per cent. of his profits; so, from the fortune the worthy Breton confesses to, my chief and I calculate that the colonel's must amount to six or seven millions——"

"Oh, father!" cried Modeste, crossing her arms and raising her eyes to heaven, "you have given me a second life!"

"Oh, mademoiselle, you love a poet! A man of that stamp is more or less of a Narcissus. Will he love you as he ought? A craftsman in words, always absorbed in fitting sentences together, is very fatiguing. A poet, mademoiselle, is not poetry—any more than the seed is the flower."

"Butscha, I never saw such a handsome man!"

"Beauty, mademoiselle, is a veil which often serves to hide many imperfections."

"He has the most angelic heart that heaven——"

"God grant you may be right," said the dwarf, clasping his hands. "May you be happy! That man, like yourself, will have a slave in Jean Butscha. I shall then no longer be a notary; I shall give myself up to study—to science——"

"And why?"

"Well, mademoiselle, to bring up your children, if you will condescend to allow me to be their tutor—— Oh! if you would accept a piece of advice! Look here, let me go to work my own way. I could ferret out this man's life and habits, could discover if he is kind, if he is violent or gentle, if he will show you the respect you deserve, if he is capable of loving you perfectly, preferring you to all else, even to his own talent——"

" What can it matter if I love him ? " said she simply.

" To be sure, that is true," cried the hunchback.

At this moment Madame Mignon was saying to her friends: " My daughter has this day seen the man she loves."

" Can it be that sulphur-colored waistcoat that puzzled you so much, Latournelle ? " at once ejaculated the notary's wife. " That young man had a pretty white rosebud in his button-hole and——"

" Ah ! " said the mother, "a token to be known by ! "

" He wore the rosette of the Legion of Honor," Madame Latournelle went on. " He is a charming youth ! But we are all wrong ; Modeste never raised her veil, she was huddled up like a pauper, and——"

" And she said she was ill," added the notary. " But she has thrown off her mufflers, and is perfectly well now ! "

" It is incomprehensible ! " said Dumay.

" Alas ! it is as clear as day," said the notary.

" My child," said Madame Mignon to Modeste, who came in, followed by Butscha, " did you happen to see in church this morning a well-dressed little man with a white rose in his buttonhole, and the rosette——"

" I saw him," Butscha hastily put in, seeing by the attention of the whole party what a trap Modeste might fall into. " It was Grindot, the famous architect, with whom the town is treating for the restoration of the church. He came from Paris, and I found him this morning examining the outside as I set out for Sainte-Adresse."

"Oh ! he is an architect ! He puzzled me greatly," said Modeste, to whom Butscha had secured time to recover herself.

Dumay looked askance at Butscha. Modeste, put on her guard, assumed an impenetrable demeanor. Dumay's suspicions were excited to the highest pitch, and he resolved to go next day to the mayor and ascertain whether the expected architect had in fact been at le Havre. Butscha, on his part,

9

very uneasy as to Modeste's ultimate fate, decided on starting
for Paris to set a watch over Canalis.

Gobenheim arrived in time to play a rubber, and his presence repressed the ferment of feeling. Modeste awaited her
mother's bedtime almost with impatience; she wanted to write,
and this is the letter her love dictated to her when she thought
that every one was asleep:

XIII.

To Monsieur de Canalis.

"Oh, my best-beloved friend, what vile libels are your portraits displayed in the print-sellers' windows! And I who was
happy with that detestable lithograph! I am quite shy of
loving such a handsome man. No, I cannot conceive that
Paris women can be so stupid as not to see, one and all, that
you are the fulfillment of their dreams. You neglected! You
loveless! I do not believe a word you have said about your
obscure and laborious life, your devotion to an idol till now
vainly sought for. You have been too well loved, monsieur;
your brow, as pale and smooth as a magnolia petal, plainly
shows it, and I shall be wretched.

"What am I now? Ah! why have you called me forth to
life? In one instant I felt that I had shed my ponderous
chrysalis! My soul burst the crystal which held it captive; it rushed through my veins. In short, the cold
silence of things suddenly ceased to me; everything in
nature spoke to me. The old church to me was luminous;
its vault, glittering with gold and azure, like that of an
Italian church, sparkled above my head. The melodious
strains, sung by angels to martyrs to make them forget their
anguish, sounded through the organ! The hideous pavement
of le Havre seemed like a flowery path. I recognized the sea

as an old friend, whose language, full of sympathy, I had
never known well enough. I saw how the roses in my garden
and greenhouse had long worshiped me, and whispered to me
to love! They all smiled on me on my return from church;
and, to crown all, I heard your name of Melchior murmured by
the flower-bells; I saw it written on the clouds! Yes, I am,
indeed, alive, thanks to you—poet more beautiful than that
cold and prim Lord Byron, whose face is as dull as the English
climate. Wedded to you by one only of your Oriental
glances which pierced my black veil, you transfused your
blood into my veins, and it fired me from head to foot. Ah,
we do not feel life like that when our mothers bring us into
the world! A blow dealt to you would fall on me at the same
instant, and my existence henceforth can only be accounted
for by your mind. I know now the purpose of the divine
harmony of music; it was invented by the angels to express
love.

"To be a genius and handsome, too, my Melchior, is too
much. A man should have a choice at his birth. But when
I think of the treasures of tenderness and affection you have
lavished on me, especially during this last month, I wonder
whether I am dreaming! Nay, you must be hiding some
mystery. What woman could give you up without dying
of it? Yes, jealousy has entered my heart with such love
as I could not believe in! Could I imagine such a conflagration?

"A new and inconceivable vagary! I now wish you were
ugly! What follies I committed when I got home! Every
yellow dahlia reminded me of your pretty waistcoat, every
white rose was a friend, and I greeted them with a look which
was yours, as I am wholly! The color of the gentleman's
well-fitting gloves—everything, to the sound of his step on
the flagstones—everything is so exactly represented by my
memory that, sixty years hence, I shall still see the smallest
details of this high day, the particular hue of the atmosphere,

and the gleam of the sunbeam reflected from a pillar; I shall hear the prayer which your advent broke into; I shall breathe the incense from the altar; and I shall fancy that I feel above our heads the hands of the priest who was giving us the final benediction just as you went past. That good Abbé Marcellin has married us already. The superhuman joy of experiencing this world of new and unexpected emotions can only be equaled by the joy I feel in telling you of them, in rendering up all my happiness to him who pours it into my soul with the unstinting bounty of the sun. So no more veils, my beloved! Come, oh, come back soon! I will unmask with joy.

"You have, no doubt, heard of the firm of Mignon of le Havre? Well, in consequence of an irreparable loss, I am the sole heiress of the family. Do not scorn us, you who are descended from one of the heroes of Auvergne. The arms of Mignon de la Bastie will not dishonor those of Canalis. They are *gules, a bend sable charged with three besants, in each quarter a patriarchal cross or,* surmonted by a cardinal's hat, and the cord and tassels as mantling. My dear, I will be faithful to our motto, *Una fides, unus Dominus!* One faith and one Lord.

"Perhaps, my friend, you will think there is some irony in my name after all I have here confessed. It is Modeste. Thus, I did not altogether cheat you in signing 'O. d'Este-M.' Nor did I deceive you in speaking of my fortune; it will, I believe, amount to the sum which has made you so virtuous. And I know so surely that to you money is so unimportant a consideration, that I can write of it unaffectedly. At the same time, you must let me tell you how glad I am to be able to endow our happiness with the freedom of action and movement that wealth gives, the power of saying, 'Let us go——' when the fancy takes us to see a foreign land, of flying off in a comfortable carriage, seated side by side, without a care about money; and happy, too, to give you the right of saying to the King, ' I have such a fortune as you require in your peers ! '

"In this, Modeste Mignon can be of some service to you, and her money will find noble uses. As to your humble servant, you have seen her once, at her window in a wrapper. Yes, the fair-haired daughter of Eve was your unknown correspondent; but how little does the Modeste of to-day resemble her whom you then saw! She was wrapped in a shroud, and this other—have I not told you so?—has derived from you the life of life. Pure and permitted love, a love that my father, now at last returning from his travels and with riches, will sanction, has uplifted me with its childlike but powerful hand from the depths of the tomb where I was sleeping. You awoke me as the sun awakes the flowers. The glance of her you love is not now that of the bold-faced little Modeste ! Oh, no ; it is bashful, it has glimpses of happiness, and veils itself under chaste eyelids. My fear now is that I cannot deserve my lot. The King has appeared in his glory ; my liege has now a mere vassal, who implores his forgiveness for taking such liberties, as the thimble-rigger with loaded dice did after cheating the Chevalier de Grammont.

"Yes, beloved poet, I will be your ' Mignon,' but a happier Mignon than Goethe's, for you will leave me to dwell in my native land, won't you?—in your heart.

"As I write this bridal wish, a nightingale in the Vilquins' park has just answered for you. Oh ! let me quickly hear that the nightingale, with his long-drawn note, so pure, so clear, so full, inundating my heart with love and gladness, like an annunciation, has not lied.

"My father will pass through Paris on his way from Marseilles. The house of Mongenod, his correspondents, will know his address ; go and see him, my dearest Melchior, tell him that you love me, and do not try to tell him how much I love you ; let that be a secret always between us and God ! I, dear adored one, will tell my mother everything. She, a

daughter of Wallenrod Tustall-Bartenstild, will justify me by
her caresses; she will be made happy by our secret and romantic poem, at once human and divine! You have the
daughter's pledge; now obtain the consent of the Comte de
la Bastie, the father of your own

" MODESTE.

"*P. S.*—Above all, do not come to le Havre without having
obtained my father's permission; and, if you love me, you
will be able to discover him on his way through Paris."

"What are you doing at this time of night, Mademoiselle
Modeste?" asked Dumay.

"I am writing to my father," she replied to the old soldier. "Did you not tell me that you were starting to-morrow?"

Dumay had no answer to this and went to bed, while
Modeste wrote a long letter to her father.

Next day Françoise Cochet, alarmed at seeing the Havre
postmark, came up to the chalet to deliver to her young mistress the following letter, and carry away that which Modeste
had written:

To Mademoiselle O. d' Este-M.

"My heart warns me that you were the woman, so carefully veiled and disguised, placed between Monsieur and Madame Latournelle, who have but one child, a son. Ah, dearly
loved one! if you are of humble rank, devoid of position,
distinction, or even fortune, you cannot imagine what my joy
would be. You must know me by this time; why not tell
me the whole truth? I am no poet excepting through love,
in my heart, and for you. Oh, what immense affection I
must have to stay here, in this Hôtel de Normandie, and not
walk up to Ingouville, that I can see from my windows!

Will you love me as I love you? To have to leave le Havre for Paris in such uncertainty! Is not that being punished for loving as if I had committed a crime? I have obeyed you blindly.

"Ah! let me soon have a letter; for, if you are mysterious, I have returned mystery for mystery, and I must at last throw off the mask of my incognito, and tell you how little I am a poet, abdicating the glory you have lent me."

This letter greatly disturbed Modeste; she could not withdraw her own, which Françoise had already posted by the time she read the last lines once more, puzzled as to their meaning; but she went up to her room, and wrote an answer, asking for explanations.

During these little incidents, others, equally small, were happening in the town, and were destined to make Modeste forget her uneasiness. Dumay, having gone early to le Havre, at once knew that no architect had arrived there the night before last. Furious at the lie told him by Butscha, which revealed a complicity which he was determined he would know the meaning of, he hurried from the mayor to the Latournelles.

"Where is your Master Butscha?" asked he of his friend the notary, on not finding the clerk in the office.

"Butscha, my dear fellow? He is on the road to Paris, whisked away by the steamboat. Early this morning, on the quay, he met a sailor, who told him that his father, the Swedish sailor, has come into some money. Butscha's father went to India, it would seem, and served some prince, a Mahratta, and he is now in Paris——"

"A pack of lies! Shameful! Monstrous! Oh, I will find that damned hunchback; I am going to Paris, and on purpose for that!" cried Dumay. "Butscha is deceiving us! He knows something about Modeste, and has never told us. If he dares meddle in the matter—— He shall never be a notary; I will cast him back on his mother, in the mire, in the——"

"Come, my friend, never hang a man without trying him," replied Latournelle, quite terrified at Dumay's exasperation.

After explaining on what his suspicions were founded, Dumay begged Madame Latournelle to stay at the chalet with Modeste during his absence.

"You will find the colonel in Paris," said the notary. "In the shipping news this morning, in the 'Commerce' newspaper, under the heading of Marseilles. Here, look!" he said, handing him the sheet, "The 'Bettina Mignon,' Captain Mignon, arrived October 16th, and to-day is the 17th. At this moment all le Havre knows of the master's return."

Dumay requested Gobenheim to dispense henceforth with his services; he then returned at once to the chalet, going in at the moment when Modeste had just closed her letters to her father and to Canalis. The two letters were exactly alike in shape and thickness, differing only in the address. Modeste thought she had laid that to her father over that to her Melchior, and had done just the reverse. This mistake, so common in the trifles of life, led to the discovery of her secret by her mother and Dumay.

The lieutenant was talking eagerly to Madame Mignon in the drawing-room, confiding to her the fresh fears to which Modeste's duplicity and Butscha's connivance had given rise.

"I tell you, madame," he exclaimed, "he is a viper we have warmed on our hearth; there is not room for a soul in these fag-ends of humanity."

Modeste had slipped the letter to her father into her pocket, fancying that it was the letter to her lover, and went down with that addressed to Canalis in her hand, hearing Dumay speak of starting immediately for Paris.

"What is wrong with my poor mysterious dwarf, and why

are you talking so loud?" said she at the door of the drawing-room.

" Butscha, mademoiselle, set out for Paris this morning, and you, no doubt, can say why! It must be to carry on some intrigue with the so-called little architect in a sulphur-colored waistcoat, who, unluckily for the hunchback's false-hood, has not yet been to le Havre."

Modeste was startled; she guessed that the dwarf had gone off to make his own inquiries as to the poet's manners and customs; she turned pale, and sat down.

"I will be after him; I will find him!" said Dumay. "That, no doubt, is the letter for your father?" he added, holding out his hand. "I will send it to Mongenod's—if only my colonel and I do not cross on the way."

Modeste gave him the lettter. Little Dumay, who could read without spectacles, mechanically read off the following address—

"Monsieur le Baron de Canalis, Rue de Paradis-Poisson-nière, No. 29!" he exclaimed. "What is the meaning of this?"

"Ah! my child, then he is the man you love!" cried Madame Mignon. "The verses that you set to music are by him——"

"And it is his portrait that you have upstairs in a frame!" added Dumay.

"Give me back that letter, Monsieur Dumay," said Modeste, drawing herself up, like a lioness defending her cubs.

"Here it is, mademoiselle," he replied. Modeste slipped the letter into her bosom, and held out to Dumay that addressed to her father.

"I know you to be capable of anything, Dumay," said she; "but if you move a single step toward Monsieur de Canalis, I will take one out of this house and never come back!"

"You will kill your mother!" replied Dumay, who went to call his wife.

The poor mother had fainted away, stricken to the heart by Modeste's threatening speech.

"Good-by, wife," said the Breton, embracing the little American. "Save the mother; I am going to save the daughter."

He left Modeste and Madame Dumay with Madame Mignon, made his preparations in a few minutes, and went down to le Havre. An hour later he set off by post with the swiftness which passion or interest alone can give to the wheels.

Madame Mignon soon revived under her daughter's care, and went up to her room, leaning on Modeste's arm; the only reproach she uttered when they were alone was to say, "Unhappy child! what have you done? Why hide anything from me? Am I so stern?"

"Why, of course, I was going to tell you everything," replied the girl in tears.

She told her mother the whole story; she read her all the letters and replies; she plucked the rose of her poem to pieces, petal by petal, to lay in the heart of the kind German lady; this took up half the day. When her confession was ended, and she saw something like a smile on the lips of the too indulgent blind woman, she threw herself into her arms with tears.

"Oh, mother!" she cried, in the midst of her sobs, "you whose heart is of gold, and all poetry, and like some choice vessel moulded by God to contain the one pure and heavenly love that can fill a whole life!—you whom I long to imitate by loving nothing on earth but my husband—you must know how bitter are these tears which I shed at this moment, which fall wet on your hands. The butterfly with iridescent wings, that beautiful second soul which your daughter has cherished with maternal care—my love, my sacred love, that inspired and living mystery—has fallen into vulgar hands that will tear its wings and its veil under the cruel pretext of enlightening me, of inquiring whether genius is as correct as a banker, if

my Melchior is capable of amassing dividends, if he has some
love affair to be unearthed, if he is not guilty in vulgar eyes
of some youthful episode, which to our love is what a cloud
is to the sun. What are they going to do? Here, feel my
hand; I am in a fever! They will kill me!"

Modeste, seized by a deadly shivering fit, was obliged to go
to bed, alarming her mother, Madame Latournelle, and
Madame Dumay, who nursed her while the lieutenant was
traveling to Paris, whither the logic of events transfers our
tale for the moment.

Men who are truly modest, like Ernest de la Brière, and
especially those who, though knowing their own value, are
neither loved nor appreciated, will understand the infinite
rapture in which the young secretary reveled as he read Modeste's letter. After discovering the wit and greatness of his
mind, his young and guileless but wily mistress thought him
handsome. This is the supremest flattery. Why? Because
beauty is no doubt the Master's signature on the work into
which He has infused His soul; it is the divinity made mani-
fest; and to see it where it does not exist, to create it by the
power of an enchanted eye, is—is it not?—the crowning
magic of love.

And the poor young fellow could exclaim to himself with
the ecstasy of an applauded author—

"At last I am loved!"

When once a woman, a courtesan, or an innocent girl has
let the words escape her, "How handsome you are!" even
if it be untrue, if the man allows the subtle poison of the
words to enter his brain, he is thenceforth tied by eternal
bonds to the bewitching liar, to the truthful or deluded
woman; she is his world; he thirsts for this testimony; he
would never weary of it, not even if he were a prince.

Ernest proudly paced his room; he stood in front of the
mirror—three-quarter face, in profile; he tried to criticise his

own features, but a diabolical, insinuating voice said to him, "Modeste is right!" and he came back to the letter and read it again. He saw the heavenly fair one, he talked to her! Then, in the midst of his rapture, came the overwhelming thought, "She believes me to be Canalis, and she is a millionaire!"

All his happiness fell with a crash, as a man falls when, walking in his sleep, he has reached the ridge of a roof, and, hearing a voice, steps forward and is dashed to pieces on the stones.

"But for the halo of glory, I should be ugly!" cried he. "What a horrible predicament I have gotten myself into!"

La Brière was too thoroughly the man of his letters, too entirely the pure and noble soul he had shown in them, to hesitate at the voice of honor. He at once resolved to go and confess everything to Modeste's father if he were in Paris, and to inform Canalis fully of the outcome of their very Parisian practical joke. To this sensitive young fellow the vastness of Modeste's fortune was a casting reason. Above all, he would not be suspected of having used the stimulation of this correspondence, though on his side so perfectly sincere, for filching a fortune. Tears stood in his eyes as he walked from his rooms in the Rue Chantereine to Mongenod the banker's, whose prosperity, connections, and prospects were partly the work of the minister to whom he himself was indebted.

At the time when la Brière was closeted with the head of the house of Mongenod, and acquiring all the information he needed in his strange position, such a scene was taking place in Canalis' house as Dumay's hasty departure might have led us to expect.

Dumay, like a true soldier of the imperial school, whose blood had been boiling all through his journey, conceived of a poet as an irresponsible fellow, a man who fooled in rhyme, living in a garret, dressed in black cloth white at all the

seams, whose boots sometimes had soles, whose linen was
anonymous, who always looked as if he had just dropped
from the clouds, when he was not scribbling as intently as
Butscha. But the ferment that muttered in his brain and
heart received a sort of cold shower-bath when he reached
the poet's handsome residence, saw a man cleaning a carriage
in the courtyard, found himself in a splendid dining-room
with another servant dressed like a banker, to whom the
groom had referred him, who looked him over from head to
foot as he said that Monsieur le Baron could not see any one.

"Monsieur le Baron has a meeting to-day," he added, "at
the council of state."

"Am I right?" asked Dumay. "Is this the house of Monsieur de Canalis, who writes poetry?"

"Monsieur le Baron de Canalis," said the footman, "is no
doubt the great poet you mean; but is also master of appeals
to the state council, and attached to the foreign office."

Dumay, who had come to box a rhymester's ears, to use his
own contemptuous expression, had found a state functionary.
The drawing-room where he was kept waiting, remarkable for
its magnificence, presented to his contemplation the row of
crosses that glittered on Canalis' evening coat, left by the
servant over the back of a chair. Presently he was attracted
by the sheen and workmanship of a silver-gilt cup, and the
words, "The gift of MADAME," struck his eye. Opposite
this, on a bracket, was a Sèvres vase, over which was engraved,
"Given by Madame la Dauphine." These silent warnings
restored Dumay to his commonsense, while the manservant
was asking his master whether he could receive a stranger, who
had come from le Havre on purpose to see him—his name
Dumay.

"What is he like?" asked Canalis.

"Has a good hat and the red ribbon."

At a nod of assent, the man went out, and returned an-
nouncing—

"Monsieur Dumay."

When he heard his own name, when he stood before Canalis in a study as costly as it was elegant, his feet on a carpet quite as good as the best in the Mignons' old house, when he met the glance prepared by the poet, who was playing with the tassels of a sumptuous dressing-gown, Dumay was so absolutely dumfounded that he left the great man to speak first.

"To what, monsieur, do I owe the honor of this visit?"

"Monsieur," Dumay began, still standing.

"If you have much to say, pray be seated," said Canalis, interrupting him; and the poet sank back into his large easy-chair, and crossed his legs, raising the upper one to rock his foot on a level with his eye, while staring hard at Dumay, who, to use his own soldier's phrase, "felt like a dummy."

"I am listening, monsieur," said the poet. "My time is precious; I am due at the office——"

"Monsieur," returned Dumay, "I will be brief. You have bewitched—how I know not—a young lady at le Havre—handsome, rich, the last and only hope of two noble families, and I have come to ask you your intentions."

Canalis, who for the last three months had been absorbed by serious matters, who aimed at promotion to the grade of commander of the Legion of Honor and to be minister to a German court, had totally forgotten the letter from le Havre.

"I?" cried he.

"You," replied Dumay.

"Monsieur," said Canalis, smiling, "I know no more what you mean than if you were talking Hebrew. I bewitch a young girl? I, who——?" A lordly smile curled the poet's lip. "Come, monsieur. I am not a boy that I should amuse myself by stealing poor wild fruit when I have ample orchards open to me, where the finest peaches in the world ripen. All Paris knows where my affections are placed. That there should be at le Havre a young lady suffering from some admiration, of which I am wholly unworthy, for the

verses I have written, my dear sir, would not astonish me!
Nothing is commoner. Look there! You see that handsome
ebony-box inlaid with mother-of-pearl, and fitted with iron
wrought as fine as lace. That coffer belonged to Pope Leo X.;
it was given to me by the Duchesse de Chaulieu, who had it
from the King of Spain. I have devoted it to the preservation of all the letters I receive from every part of Europe,
written by unknown women and girls. Oh! I have the
greatest respect for those posies of flowers culled from the
very soul, and sent to me in a moment of enthusiasm that is
indeed worthy of all respect. Yes, to me the impulse of a
heart is a noble and beautiful thing! Others, mocking spirits,
screw up such notes to light their cigars, or give them to
their wives for curl-papers; I—who am a bachelor, monsieur
—have too much delicate feeling not to treasure these artless
and disinterested offerings in a kind of tabernacle; indeed, I
hoard them with no little reverence, and when I am dying I
will see them burnt under my eyes. So much the worse for
those who think me ridiculous! What is to be said? I am
grateful by nature, and these testimonials help me to endure
the criticisms and annoyances of a literary life. When I
receive in my spine the broadside of an enemy in ambush
behind a newspaper, I look at that chest and say to myself,
'There are, here and there, a few souls whose wounds have
been healed, or beguiled or stanched by me——' "

This rodomontade, pronounced with the cleverness of a
great actor, petrified the little cashier, whose eyes dilated
while his astonishment amused the great poet.

"To you," the peacock went on, still spreading his tail,
"out of respect for a position I can sympathize with, I can
but propose that you should open that treasury and look there
for your young lady; but I never forget names. I know what
I am saying, and you are mistaken."

" And this is what happens to a poor girl in this gulf called
Paris!" cried Dumay. "The idol of her parents, the delight

of her friends, the hope, the darling of them all; the pride of her family, for whom six persons have made a rampart of their hearts and their fortunes against disaster!"

Dumay paused, and then went on—

"Well, monsieur, you are a great poet, and I am but a poor soldier. For fifteen years, while I served my country in the ranks, I felt the wind of many a bullet in my face, I crossed Siberia, where I was kept a prisoner, the Russians flung me on a truck like a bale of goods, I have endured everything; I have seen no end of my comrades die—— And you, monsieur, have sent such a chill through my bones as I never felt before!"

Dumay believed that he had touched the poet; he had flattered him—an almost impossible achievement, for the ambitious man had by this time forgotten the first phial of precious balm that praise, it seemed now long past, had broken on his head.

"You see, my brave friend," said the poet solemnly, as he laid his hand on Dumay's shoulder, feeling it a strange thing that he should be able to make a soldier of the Empire shiver, "this girl is everything to you—— But to society, what is she? Nothing. If at this moment the most important mandarin in China is closing his eyes and putting the Empire into mourning, does that grieve you deeply? In India the English are killing thousands of men as good as we are; and at this moment, as I speak, the most charming woman is there being burnt—but you have had coffee for breakfast all the same? Indeed, at this minute, here in Paris, you may find several mothers of families lying on straw and bringing a child into the world without a rag to wrap it in! And here is some delicious tea in a cup that cost five louis, and I am writing verses to make the ladies of Paris exclaim, '*Charming, charming! divine, exquisite! it goes to the heart!*'

"Social nature, like mother nature herself, is great at forgetting. Ten years hence you will be amazed at the step you have taken. You are in a city where we die, and marry, and worship each other at an assignation ; where a girl suffocates herself, while a man of genius and his cargo of ideas full of humanitarian benefits go to the bottom, side by side, often under the same roof, and knowing nothing of each other. And you come and expect us to swoon with anguish at this commonplace question, ' Is a certain young person at le Havre this or that, or is she not ? ' Oh, you really are———''

" And you call yourself a poet ! " cried Dumay. " But do you really feel nothing of what you depict ? "

" If we felt all the misery or joy that we describe, we should be worn out in a few months, like old shoes," said the poet, smiling. " Listen, you shall not have come from le Havre to Paris, and to me, Canalis, without having something to take back with you. Soldier ! "—and Canalis had the figure and gesture of an Homeric hero—" learn this from the poet, ' Every noble feeling in each of us is a poem so essentially individual that our best friend, our self, takes no interest in it. It is a treasure belonging to each alone——' ' ''

" Forgive me for interrupting you," said Dumay, who gazed at Canalis with horror, " but have you been to le Havre ? "

" I spent a night and day there in the spring of 1824 on my way to London."

" You are a man of honor," Dumay went on. " Can you give me your word of honor that you do not know Mademoiselle Modeste Mignon ? "

" This is the first time I ever heard her name," replied Canalis.

" Oh, monsieur," cried Dumay, " into what dark intrigue am I about to plunge ? May I count on you to help me in my inquiries ? For some one, I am certain, has been making use of your name. You ought to have received a letter yesterday from le Havre."

" I have received nothing ! You may be sure, monsieur,

10

that I will do all that lies in my power to be of service to you."

Dumay took leave, his heart full of anxiety, believing that hideous little Butscha had hidden himself in the semblance of the great poet to captivate Modeste ; while Butscha, on the contrary, as keen and clever as a prince who avenges himself, sharper than a spy, was making inquisition into the poet's life and actions, escaping detection by his insignificance like an insect working its way into the young wood of a tree.

The Breton had but just left when la Brière came into his friend's room.   Canalis naturally mentioned the visit of this man from le Havre.

" Hah ! " said Ernest, " Modeste Mignon !   I have come on purpose to speak about that affair."

" Bless me ! " cried Canalis, " do you mean to say I have made a conquest by proxy ? "

" Why, yes, that is the turning-point of the drama.   My friend, I am loved by the sweetest girl in the world, beautiful enough to shine among the beauties of Paris, with a heart and education worthy of Clarissa Harlowe ; she has seen me, she likes my looks—and she believes me to be the great poet Canalis.

" Nor is this all : Modeste Mignon is of good birth, and Mongenod has just told me that her father, the Comte de la Bastie, must have a fortune of something like six millions of francs.   This father has come home within three days, and I have just begged him to arrange an interview with me, at two o'clock—through Mongenod, who in his note mentioned that it concerned his daughter's happiness.   You will understand that before meeting the father I was bound to tell you everything."

"Among all the blossoms that open to the sunshine of fame," said Canalis with emphasis, " there is one glorious plant which, like the orange, bears its golden fruit amid the thousand united perfumes of wit and beauty! one elegant shrub, one true passion, one perfect happiness—and it has evaded me!'' Canalis kept his eyes on the carpet that Ernest might not read them. '' How,'' he went on after a pause, to recover his presence of mind, '' how is it possible, among the intoxicating scents of these fancy-paper notes, and these phrases that mount to the brain, to detect the genuine heart—the girl, the woman, in whom true love is hidden under the livery of flattery, who loves us for ourselves, and who offers us happiness? No one could do it but an angel or a demon, and I am only an ambitious master of appeals!

''Ah, my dear fellow, fame transforms us into a butt, a target for a thousand arrows. One of us owed his marriage to a copy of hydraulic verses; and I, even more ingratiating, more the ladies' man than he, shall have missed my chance —for you love this poor girl?'' said he, looking intently at la Brière.

'' Oh !'' cried la Brière.

''Well, then, be happy, Ernest,'' said the poet, taking his friend's arm and leaning on it. ''As it turns out, I shall not have been ungrateful to you! You are handsomely rewarded for your devotion, for I will be generously helpful to your happiness.''

Canalis was furious, but he could not behave otherwise, so he took the benefit of his ill-luck by using it as a pedestal. A tear rose to the young secretary's eye; he threw his arms about Canalis and embraced him.

'' Oh, Canalis, I did not half know you!''

'' What did you expect? It takes time to travel around the world,'' replied the poet with emphatic irony.

''Consider,'' said la Brière, ''that immense fortune?——''

'' Well, my friend, will it not be in good hands?'' cried Canalis, pointing his effusiveness by a charming gesture.

'' Melchior,'' said la Briere, ''I am yours in life and death.''

He wrung the poet's hands and went away hastily; he was
eager to see Monsieur Mignon.

At this hour the Comte de la Bastie was suffering all the
sorrows that had been lurking for him as their prey. He had
learned from his daughter's letter the facts of Bettina Caroline's death and her mother's blindness; and Dumay had
just told him the story of the terrible imbroglio of Modeste's
love affair.

"Leave me to myself," he said to his faithful friend.

When the lieutenant had closed the door, the unhappy
father threw himself on a couch and lay there, his head in his
hands, shedding the few thin tears that lie without falling under the eyelids of a man of fifty-six, wetting them, but drying
quickly and rising again, the last dews of the autumn of human
life.

"To have children you love and a wife you adore is to
have many hearts and offer them all to the dagger!" cried
he, starting to his feet with a furious bound and pacing the
room. "To be a father is to give one's self over to misfortune,
bound hand and foot. If I meet that fellow d'Estourny I will
kill him. Daughters! Who would have daughters? One
gets hold of a scoundrel; and the other, my Modeste, of what?
A coward, who deludes her under the gilt-paper armor of a
poet. If only it were Canalis! There would be no great
harm done. But this Scapin of a lover! I will throttle him
with my own hands!" said he to himself, with an involuntary
gesture of energetic atrocity. "And what then," he thought,,
"if my child should die of grief?"

Mechanically he looked out of the window of the Hôtel des
Princes, and came back to sit down on the divan, where he
remained motionless. The fatigue of six voyages to the
Indies, the anxieties of investments, the dangers he had met
and escaped, care and sorrow had silvered Charles Mignon's
hair. His fine military face, clean in outline, was bronzed

by the sun of Malaysia, China, and Asia Minor, and had assumed an imposing expression, which grief at this moment made sublime.

"And Mongenod tells me I can perfectly trust the young man who is to come to speak to me about my daughter!——"

Ernest de la Brière was just then announced by one of the servants whom the Comte de la Bastie had attached to him in the course of these four years, and had picked out from the crowd of men under him.

"You come, monsieur, with an introduction from my friend Mongenod?" said he.

"Yes," replied Ernest, gazing timidly at a face as gloomy as Othello's. "My name is Ernest de la Brière, connected, monsieur, with the family of the late prime minister; I was his private secretary when he was in office. At his fall, his excellency was good enough to place me in the court of exchequer, where I am now a first-class referendary, and where I may rise to be a master——"

"And what has all this to do with Mademoiselle de la Bastie?" asked Charles Mignon.

"Monsieur, I love her, and it is my unhoped-for happiness to be loved by her. Listen, monsieur," said Ernest, interrupting a terrible movement on the part of the angry father, "I have the strangest confession to make to you, the most ignominious for a man of honor. And the worst punishment of my conduct, which perhaps was natural, is not this revelation to you—I dread the daughter even more than the father."

Ernest then told the prologue of this domestic drama, quite simply, and with the dignity of sincerity; he did not omit the twenty and odd letters they had exchanged—he had brought them with him—nor the interview he had just had with Canalis. When the father had read all these letters, the poor lover, pale and suppliant, quaked before the fiery looks of the Provençal.

"Well, monsieur," said Mignon, "in all this, there is only one mistake, but it is all-important. My daughter has not six millions of francs; her fortune at most is two hundred thousand francs in settlement, and very doubtful expectations."

"Oh, monsieur!" cried Ernest, throwing his arms around Charles Mignon and hugging him, "you relieve me of a load that oppressed me. Now, perhaps, nothing will come in the way of my happiness! I have interest; I shall soon be master of the exchequer. If she had but ten thousand francs, if I had to accept nominal settlements, Mademoiselle Mignon would still be the wife of my choice; and to make her happy, as happy as you have made yours, to be a true son to you— yes, monsieur, for my father is dead—this is the deepest wish of my heart."

Charles Mignon drew back three steps, and fixed on la Brière a look that sank into the young man's eyes, as a poniard goes into its sheath; then he stood silent, reading in those fascinated eyes and on that eager countenance the most perfect candor and the purest truthfulness.

"Is fate at last wearied out?" said he to himself in an undertone. "Can I have found a paragon son-in-law in this youth?" He walked up and down the room in great excitement.

"Well, monsieur," he said at length, "you owe implicit obedience to the sentence you have come to ask, for otherwise you would at this moment be acting a mere farce."

"Indeed, monsieur——"

"Listen to me," said the father, nailing la Brière to the spot by a look. "I will be neither severe, nor hard, nor unjust. You must take the disadvantages with the advantages of the false position in which you have placed yourself. My daughter imagines that she is in love with one of the great poets of our day, whose fame chiefly has fascinated her. Well, then, ought not I, as her father, to enable her to choose between the celebrity which has seemed a lighthouse to her, and the humble reality thrown to her by chance in the irony it so often allows itself? Must she not be free to choose between you and Canalis. I trust to your honor to be silent as to what I have just told you concerning the state of my affairs. You and your friend, the Baron de Canalis, must come to spend the last fortnight of this month of October at le Havre. My house will be open to you both ; my daughter will have the opportunity of knowing you. Remember, you yourself are to bring your rival, and to allow him to believe all the fables that may be current as to the Comte de la Bastie's millions. I shall be at le Havre by to-morrow, and shall expect you three days later. Good-morning, monsieur."

Poor la Brière very slowly made his way back to Canalis. At that moment the poet, face to face with himself, could give himself up to the torrent of reflections that flow from that "second thought" which Talleyrand so highly praised. The first thought is the impulse of nature, the second that of society.

" A girl with six millions of francs ! And my eyes failed to discern the glitter of that gold through the darkness! With such a fortune as that, I can be a peer of France, count, ambassador! I have answered the most ordinary women, simpletons, intriguing girls who only wanted an autograph! And I rebelled against these *bal masqué* wiles on the very day when heaven sent me a chosen soul, an angel with wings of gold! Pooh! I will write a sublime poem, and the chance will come again ! What luck for that little la Brière, who spread his tail in my sunbeams ! And what plagiary. I am the model, and he is to be the statue ! This is playing the fable of 'Bertrand and Raton.' Six millions, and an angel, a Mignon de la Bastie ! An aristocratic angel, who loves poetry and the poet ! And I meanwhile display my muscles as a strong man, perform athletics, like Alcides, to astonish

this champion of physical strength by moral force—this brave
soldier full of fine feeling, this young girl's friend, who will
tell her I have a soul of iron.   I am playing Napoleon, when
I ought to show myself as a seraph!   I shall have won a
friend perhaps, and have paid dear for him; but friendship is
a fine thing.   Six millions—that is the price of a friend; a
man cannot have many at that figure!"

At this last point of exclamation la Brière came into his
friend's room; he was depressed.

"Well, what is the matter?" said Canalis.

"The father insists that his daughter shall be enabled to
choose between the two Canalis——"

"Poor boy!" said the poet, laughing.   "A clever man is
that father!"

"I have pledged my honor to take you to le Havre," said
la Brière dolefully.

"My dear boy," said Canalis, "if your honor is at stake,
you may depend upon me.   I will ask for a month's leave of
absence."

"Oh, Modeste is lovely!" cried la Brière in despair,
"and you will easily extinguish me!   Still, I was amazed to
find good fortune coming my way; I said to myself, it is all
a mistake!"

"Pooh!   We shall see," said Canalis with ruthless cheerfulness.

That evening, after dinner, Charles Mignon and his cashier
were flying, at the cost of three francs a stage to the postillion, from Paris to le Havre.   The father had completely
allayed his watch-dog's alarms as to Modeste's love affairs, had
released him from his responsibilities, and reassured him as to
Butscha's proceedings.

"Everything is for the best, my good old friend," said
Charles, who had made inquiries of Mongenod as to Canalis
and la Brière.   "We have two players for one part," he
added, laughing.

At the same time, he enjoined absolute silence on his old comrade as to the comedy about to be played at the chalet, and his gentle revenge, or, if you will, the lesson to be given by a father to his child. From Paris to le Havre was one long dialogue between the friends, by which the colonel learned the smallest events that had happened in his family during the past four years; and Charles told Dumay that Desplein, the great surgeon, was to come before the end of the month to examine the Countess' eyes and decide whether it would be possible to remove the cataract and restore her sight.

A few minutes before the breakfast hour at the chalet, the cracking of a whip, by a postillion counting on a large gratuity, announced the return of the two soldiers. Only the joy of a father coming home to his family after a long absence would give rise to such a detonation, and all the women were standing at the little gate.

There are so many fathers, and so many children—more fathers perhaps than children—who can enter the excitement of such a meeting, that literature is never required to depict it; happily! for the finest words, and poetry itself, are inadequate to such emotions. Perhaps, indeed, the sweeter emotions have no literary side.

Not a word was spoken that day that could disturb the happiness of the Mignon family. There was a truce between the father, the mother, and the daughter as to the mysterious love affair which had paled Modeste's cheek. She was up today for the first time. The colonel, with the delicate tenderness that characterizes a true soldier, sat all the time by his wife's side, her hand constantly held in his, and he watched Modeste, never tired of admiring her refined, elegant, and poetic beauty. Is it not by such small things that we know a man of true feeling?

Modeste, fearful of troubling the melancholy happiness of her father and mother, came from time to time to kiss the traveler's brow, and by kissing him so often seemed to wish to kiss him for two.

" Ah, darling child !   I understand you," said her father, pressing Modeste's hand at a moment when she was smothering him with affection.

" Hush ! " whispered Modeste in his ear, pointing to her mother.

Dumay's rather perfidious silence left Modeste very uneasy as to the results of his journey to Paris ; she now and then stole a look at the lieutenant, but could not penetrate that tough skin.   The colonel, as a prudent father, wished to study his only daughter's nature, and, above all, to consult his wife, before proceeding to a discussion on which the happiness of the whole family would depend.

" To-morrow, my dearest child, rise early," said he at night, " and, if it is fine, we will go for a walk together on the seashore.   We have to talk over your poems, Mademoiselle de la Bastie."

These words, spoken with a smile that was reflected on Dumay's lips, were all Modeste could know ; still, this was enough to allay her anxiety and to make her too curious to get to sleep till late, so busy was her fancy.

Next morning Modeste was dressed and ready before the colonel.

" You know everything, my dear father," said she, as soon as they had started on their way to the sea.

" I know everything—and a good many things that you do not know," replied he.

Thereupon the father and daughter walked some few steps in silence.

" Now, tell me, my child, how a daughter so worshiped by her mother could take so decisive a step as to write to a man unknown to her without asking that mother's advice? "

" Well, papa, because mamma would not have allowed it."

"And do you think, my child, that it was right? Though you have inevitably been left to bring yourself up, how is it that your reason or your insight — if modesty failed you—did not tell you that to act in such a way was to throw yourself at a man's head? Can it be that my daughter, my only child, lacks pride and delicacy? Oh! Modeste, you gave your father two hours of hell's torments in Paris; for, in point of fact your conduct, morally, has been the same as Bettina's, without having the excuse of seduction; you have been a coquette in cold blood, and that is love without heart, the worst vice of the Frenchwoman."

"I—without pride?" said Modeste in tears. "But he has never seen me!"

"*He* knows your name."

"I never let him know it till the moment when our eyes had set the seal to three months of correspondence, during which our souls had spoken to each other!"

"Yes, my dear mistaken angel, you have brought a kind of reason to bear on this madness which has compromised your happiness and your family."

"Well, after all, papa, happiness is the justification of such boldness," said she, with a touch of temper.

"Ah! Then it is merely boldness?" cried her father.

"Such boldness as my mother allowed herself," she answered hastily.

"Refractory child! Your mother, after meeting me at a ball, told her father, who adored her, the same evening that she believed she could be happy with me. Now, be candid, Modeste; is there any resemblance between love, at first sight it is true, but under a father's eye, and the mad act of writing to an unknown man?"

"An unknown man? Nay, papa, one of our greatest poets, whose character and life are under the light of day, exposed to gossip and calumny; a man clothed in glory, to whom, my dear father, I was but a dramatic, literary personage—a

girl of Shakespeare's—until the moment when I felt I must
know whether the man was as attractive as his soul is beautiful."

"Bless me, my poor child, you are dreaming of poetry in
connection with marriage. But if in all ages girls have been
cloistered in the family; if God and social law have placed
them under the stern yoke of parental sanction, it is precisely
and on purpose to spare them the misfortunes to which the
poetry that fascinates you must lead while it dazzles you, and
which you therefore cannot estimate at its true worth. Poetry
is one of the graces of life; it is not the whole of life."

"Papa, it is an action for ever undecided before the tribunal of facts, for there is a constant struggle between our
hearts and the family authority."

"Woe to the girl who should find happiness by means of
such resistance!" said the colonel gravely. "In 1813 one
of my fellow-officers, the Marquis d'Aiglemont, married his
cousin against her father's warnings, and the household paid
dearly for the obstinacy that a girl could mistake for love.
In these matters the family is supreme."

"My fiancé has told me all that," said she. "He assumed
the part of Orgon for some time, and had the courage to run
down the personal character of poets."

"I have read the correspondence," said her father, with a
meaning smile that made Modeste uneasy. "And I may, on
that point, remark that your last letter would hardly be allowable in a girl who had been seduced—in a Julie d'Étanges.
Good God! what mischief comes of romances!"

"If they were never written, my dear father, we should
still enact them. It is better to read them. There are fewer
romantic adventures now than in the time of Louis XIV. and
Louis XV., when fewer novels were published. Beside, if you
have read our letters, you must have perceived that I have found
you for a son-in-law the most respectful son, the most angelic
nature, the strictest honesty, and that we love each other at

least as much as you and mamma did. Well, I will admit
that the affair has not been conducted exactly as etiquette
requires. I made a mistake, if you like——"

"I have read your letters," repeated her father, interrupting her, "so I know how he justified you in your own eyes
for a step which might perhaps be excusable in a woman who
knows life, who is carried away by passion, but which in a
girl of twenty is a monstrous fault——"

"A fault in common people's eyes, in those of narrow-
minded Gobenheims, who measure out life with a T-square!
But do not let us go beyond the artistic and poetic world,
papa. We young girls live between two alternatives: we
may show a man that we love him by mincing graces, or we
may go to meet him frankly. And is not this last method
really great and noble? We French girls are disposed of by
our family like merchandise, at three months' date, sometimes
much sooner, like Mademoiselle Vilquin; but in England,
Switzerland, and Germany they are married more nearly on
the system I have adopted. What can you say to that? Am
I not half-German?"

"Child," exclaimed the colonel, looking at his daughter,
"the superiority of France lies precisely in the commonsense,
the strict logic to which our splendid language compels the
mind. France is the reason of the world! England and
Germany are romantic in this point; but even there the great
families follow our custom. You girls would rather not believe, then, that your parents, who know life, have the charge
of your souls and your happiness, and that it is their duty to
steer you clear of the rocks! Good God!" he went on, "is
this their fault or ours? Ought we to bend our children under
a yoke of iron? Must we always be punished for the tenderness which prompts us to make them happy, which, unfortunately, makes them heart of our heart!"

As she heard this ejaculation, spoken almost with tears,
Modeste cast a side glance at her father.

" Is it wrong in a girl whose heart is free," said she, " to choose for her husband a man who is not only charming in himself, but who is also a man of genius, of good birth, and in a fine position—a gentleman as gentle as myself?"

"Then you love him?" said the colonel.

"I tell you, father," said she, laying her head on his breast, "if you do not want to see me die——"

"That is enough," said the colonel, " your passion is, I see, unchangeable."

" Unchangeable."

" Nothing could move you?"

" Nothing in the world."

"You can conceive of no alteration, no betrayal," her father went on.   " You love him for better, for worse, for the sake of his personal charms ; and if he should be a d'Estourny, you still would love him?"

" Oh, papa, you do not know your child !   Could I love a coward, a man devoid of truth and honor—a gallows-bird?"

" Then supposing you have been deceived?"

" By that charming young fellow, so candid—almost melancholy?   You are laughing at me, or you have not seen him."

" I see ; happily your love is not so imperative as you say. I have suggested conditions which might modify your poem. Well, then, you will admit that fathers are of some use?"

" You wanted to give me a lesson, papa—a sort of object-lesson, it would seem."

" Poor misled girl ! " said her father severely ; "the lesson is not of my giving ; I have nothing to do with it beyond trying to soften the blow."

" Say no more, papa ; do not trifle with my very life," said Modeste, turning pale.

" Nay, my child, summon up your courage. It is you who have trifled with life, and life now laughs you to scorn."

Modeste looked at her father in bewilderment.

"Listen; if the young man you love, whom you saw in church at le Havre four days ago, were a contemptible wretch——"

"It is not true!" said she. "That pale, dark face, so noble and full of poetry——"

"Is a lie!" said the colonel, interrupting her. "He is no more Monsieur de Canalis than I am that fisherman hauling up his sail to go out——"

"Do you know what you are killing in me?" returned Modeste.

"Be comforted, my child; though fate has made your fault its own punishment, the mischief is not irreparable. The youth you saw, with whom you have exchanged hearts by correspondence, is an honest fellow; he came to me to confess his dilemma. He loves you, and I should not object to him as a son-in-law."

"And if he is not Canalis, who is he?" asked Modeste, in a broken voice.

"His secretary. His name is Ernest de la Brière. He is not of superior birth, but he is one of those average men, with solid virtues and sound morals, whom parents like. And what does it matter to us, after all? You have seen him; nothing can change your feelings; you have chosen him, you know his soul—it is as noble as he is good-looking."

The Comte de la Bastie was checked by a sigh from Modeste. The poor child, perfectly white, her eyes fixed on the sea, and as rigid as the dead, had been struck as by a pistol-shot by the words, "*One of those average men, with solid virtues and sound morals, whom parents like.*"

"Deceived!" she said at last.

"As your poor sister was, but less seriously."

"Let us go home, papa," she said, rising from the knoll on which they had been sitting. "Listen, father; I swear before God to obey your wishes, whatever they may be, in the business of marriage."

"Then you have already ceased to love?" asked her father sarcastically.

"I loved a true man without a falsehood on his face, as honest as you yourself, incapable of disguising himself like an actor, of dressing himself up in another man's glory."

"You said that nothing could move you!" said the colonel ironically.

"Oh, do not make game of me!" cried she, clasping her hands, and looking at her father in an agony of entreaty. "You do not know how you are torturing my heart and my dearest beliefs by your satire——"

"God forbid! I have said the exact truth."

"You are very good, father," she replied, after a pause, with a certain solemnity.

"And he has your letters! Heh?" said Charles Mignon. "If those crazy effusions of your soul had fallen into the hands of one of those poets who, according to Dumay, use them for pipe-lights——"

"Oh, that is going too far."

"So Canalis told him."

"He saw Canalis?"

"Yes," replied the colonel.

They walked on a little way in silence.

"That, then," said Modeste, when they had gone a few steps, "was why that gentleman spoke so ill of poets and poetry! Why did that little secretary talk of?—— But, however," she added, interrupting herself, "were not his virtues, his qualities, his fine sentiments, a mere epistolary make-up? The man who can steal another one's fame and name may very well——"

"Pick locks, rob the treasury, murder on the highway," said Charles Mignon, smiling. "That is just like you—you girls, with your uncompromising feelings and your ignorance of life. A man who can deceive a woman has either escaped the scaffold or must end there."

This raillery checked Modeste's effervescence, and again they were both silent.

"My child," the colonel added, "men in the world—as in nature, for that matter—are bound to try to win your hearts, and you to defend them. You have reversed the position. Is that well? In a false position everything is false. Yours, then, was the first wrong step. No, a man is not a monster because he tries to attract a woman; our rights allow us to be the aggressors, with all the consequences, short of crime and baseness. A man may still have virtues even after throwing over a woman, for this simply means that he has failed to find the treasure he sought in her; while no woman but a queen, an actress, or a woman so far above the man in rank that to him she is like a queen, can take the initiative without incurring much blame. But a girl! She is false to everything that God has given her, every flower of saintliness, dignity, and sweetness, whatever grace, poetry, or precaution she may infuse into the act."

"To seek the master and find the servant! To play the old farce of Love and Chance on one side only!" she exclaimed, with bitter feeling. "Oh, I shall never hold up my head again!"

"Foolish child! Monsieur Ernest de la Brière is, in my eyes, at least the equal of Monsieur de Canalis; he has been private secretary to a prime minister, he is referendary to the court of exchequer, he is a man of heart, he adores you—but he does not write verses. No, I confess it, he is not a poet; but he may have a heart full of poetry. However, my poor child," he added, in reply to Modeste's face of disgust, "you will see them both—the false and the real Canalis——"

"Oh, papa!"

"Did you not swear to obey me in everything that concerns the *business* of your marriage? Well, you may choose between them the man you prefer for your husband. You began with a poem, you may end with a page of bucolics by

11

trying to detect the true nature of these gentlemen in some
rustic excursions, a shooting or a fishing party.''

Modeste bent her head and returned to the chalet with her
father, listening to what he said, and answering in monosylla-
bles.   She had fallen humiliated into the depths of a bog,
from the Alp where she fancied she had flown up to an eagle's
nest.   To adopt the poetical phraseology of an author of that
period, ''After feeling the soles of her feet too tender to
tread on the glass sherds of reality, fancy, which had united
every characteristic of woman in that fragile form, from the
day-dreams of a modest girl, all strewn with violets, to the
unbridled desires of a courtesan, had now led her into the
midst of her enchanted gardens, where, hideous surprise !
instead of an exquisite blossom, she found growing from the
soil the hairy and twisted limbs of the Mandragora.''

From the mystic heights of her love Modeste had dropped
on to the dull, flat road, lying between ditches and ploughed
lands—the road, in short, that is paved with vulgarity.   What
girl with an ardent spirit but would be broken by such a fall?
At whose feet had she cast her promises ?

The Modeste who returned to the chalet bore no more resemblance to the girl who had gone out two hours before,
than the actress in the street resembles the heroine on the
stage.   She sank into a state of apathy that was painful to be-
hold.   The sun was darkened, nature was under a shroud, the
flowers had no message for her.   Like every girl of a vehement disposition, she drank a little too deeply of the cup of
disenchantment.   She rebelled against reality, without choosing as yet to bend her neck to the yoke of the family and of
society ; she thought it too heavy, too hard, too oppressive.
She would not even listen to the comfort offered by her father
and mother, and felt an indescribable savage delight in
abandoning herself wholly and unrestrainedly to her mental
sufferings.

" Then poor Butscha was right! " she exclaimed one evening.

This speech shows how far she had traveled in so short a time on the barren plains of reality, guided by her deep dejection. Grief, when it comes of the upheaval of all our hopes, is an illness; it often ends in death. It would be no mean occupation for modern physiology to investigate the process and means by which a thought can produce the same deadly effects as a poison; how despair can destroy the appetite, injure the pylorus, and change all the functions of the strongest vitality. This was the case with Modeste. In three days she presented an image of morbid melancholy; she sang no more, it was impossible to make her smile; her parents and friends were alarmed. Charles Mignon, uneasy at seeing nothing of the two young men, was thinking of going to Paris, remind la Brière of his promise, and fetch them; but on the fourth day Monsieur Latournelle had news of them, and this was how:

Canalis, immensely tempted by such a rich marriage, would neglect no means of outdoing la Brière, while Ernest could not complain of his having violated the laws of friendship. The poet thought that nothing put a lover at a greater disadvantage in a young lady's eyes than figuring in an inferior position; so he proposed, in the most innocent manner possible, that he and la Brière should keep house together, taking a little country place at Ingouville, where they might live for a month under pretext of recruiting their health.

As soon as la Brière had consented to this proposal, at first regarding it as very natural, Canalis insisted on his being his guest, and made all the arrangements himself. He sent his manservant to le Havre, desiring him to apply to Monsieur Latournelle for the choice of a country cottage at Ingouville, thinking that the notary would certainly talk over the matter with the Mignon family. Ernest and Canalis, it may be supposed, had discussed every detail of their adven-

ture; and la Brière, always prolix, had given his rival a
thousand valuable hints.

The servant, understanding his master's intentions, carried
them out to admiration; he trumpeted the advent of the
great poet, to whom his doctors had ordered some sea-baths
to recruit him after the double fatigues of politics and literature. This grand personage required a house of at least so
many rooms; for he was bringing his secretary, his cook, two
menservants, and a coachman, not to mention Monsieur Germain Bonnet, his body-servant. The traveling carriage the
poet selected and hired for a month was very neat, and could
serve for making some excursions; and Germain was in search
of two saddle-horses for hire in the neighborhood, as Monsieur
le Baron and his secretary were fond of horse exercise. In
the presence of little Latournelle, Germain, as he went over
various houses, spoke much of the secretary, and rejected two
villas on the ground that Monsieur de la Brière would not be
well accommodated.

"Monsieur le Baron," said he, "regards his secretary as
his best friend. Oh, I should catch it handsomely if Monsieur
de la Brière was not as well served as Monsieur le Baron
himself. And, after all, Monsieur de la Brière is referendary
to the court of exchequer."

Germain was never seen dressed otherwise than in a suit of
black, with good gloves and boots, turned out like a gentleman. Imagine the effect he produced, and the notion that
was formed of the great poet from this specimen. A clever
man's servant becomes clever too; the master's cleverness
presently "runs" and colors the man. Germain did not
overact his part; he was straightforward and genial, as Canalis
had, instructed him to be. Poor la Brière had no suspicion
of the injury Germain was doing him, or of the depreciation
to which he had exposed himself; for some echoes of public
report arose from the lower depths to Modeste's ears. Thus
Canalis was bringing his friend in his retinue, in his carriage;

and Ernest's simple nature did not allow him to perceive his
false position soon enough to remedy it.

The delay which so provoked Charles Mignon was caused
by the poet's desire to have his arms painted on the doors of
the chaise, and by his orders to the tailor; for Canalis took
in the wide world of such trivialities, of which the least may
influence a girl.

"Make yourself easy," said Latournelle to the colonel on
the fifth day. "Monsieur de Canalis' man came to a determination this morning. He has taken Madame Amaury's
cottage at Sanvic, furnished, for seven hundred francs, and
has written to his master that he can start, and will find everything ready on his arrival. So the gentlemen will be here by
Sunday. I have also had this note from Butscha. Here—it
is not long: 'My dear master, I cannot get back before
Sunday. Between this and then I must get some important
information which nearly concerns some one in whom you are
interested.'"

The announcement of this arrival did not make Modeste at
all less sad; the sense of a fall, of humiliation, still held sway
over her, and she was not such a born coquette as her father
thought her. There is a charming and permissible kind of
flirtation, the coquetry of the soul, which might be called the
good breeding of love; and Charles Mignon, when reproving
his daughter, had failed to distinguish between the desire to
please and the factitious love of the mind, between the craving
of love and self-interest. Just like a soldier of the Empire, he
saw in the letters he had so hastily read a girl throwing herself
at a poet's head; but in many letters—omitted here for the
sake of brevity—a connoisseur would have admired the maidenly and graceful reserve which Modeste had immediately
substituted for the aggressive and frivolous pertness of her first
effusions—a transition very natural in a woman.

On one point her father had been cruelly right. It was her
last letter—in which Modeste, carried away by threefold love,

had spoken as though their marriage was a decided thing, which really brought her to shame. Still, she thought her father very hard, very cruel, to compel her to receive a man so unworthy of her, toward whom her soul had flown almost unveiled. She had questioned Dumay as to his interview with the poet; she had ingeniously extracted from him every detail, and she could not think Canalis such a barbarian as the lieutenant thought him. She could smile at the fine papal chest containing the letters of the *mille et trois* ladies of this literary Don Giovanni. Again and again she was on the point of saying to her father, "I am not the only girl who writes to him; the cream of womankind sends leaves for the poet's crown of bay."

In the course of this week Modeste's character underwent a transformation. This catastrophe—and it was a great one to so poetical a nature—aroused her latent acumen and spirit of mischief, and her suitors were to find her a formidable adversary. For, in fact, in any girl, if her heart is chilled, her head grows clear; she then observes everything with a certain swiftness of judgment and a spirit of mockery, such as Shakespeare has admirably painted in the person of Beatrice in "Much Ado about Nothing." Modeste was seized by intense disgust of mankind, since the most distinguished of them had deceived her hopes. In love, what a woman mistakes for disgust is simply seeing clearly; but in matters of feeling no woman, especially no young girl, ever sees truly. When she ceases to admire, she contemns. So Modeste, after going through fearful tortures of mind, inevitably put on the armor on which, as she declared, she had stamped the word Contempt; thenceforward she could look on as a disinterested spectator at what she called the Farce of Suitors; although she filled the part of leading lady. More especially was she bent on pertinaciously humiliating and scornfully treating Monsieur de la Brière.

"Modeste is saved," said Madame Mignon to her husband

with a smile. "She means to be revenged on the false Canalis by trying to fall in love with the true one."

This was, indeed, Modeste's plan. It was so obvious that her mother, to whom she confided her vexation, advised her to treat Monsieur de la Brière with oppressive civility.

"These two young fellows," said Madame Latournelle on the Saturday, "have no suspicion of the troop of spies at their heels, for here are eight of us to keep an eye on them."

"What, my dear—two?" cried little Latournelle; "there are three of them! Gobenheim is not here yet, so I may speak."

Modeste had looked up, and all the others, following her example, gazed at the notary.

"A third lover, and he is a lover, has put himself on the list——"

"Bless me!" said Charles Mignon.

"But he is no less a person," the notary went on pompously, "than his lordship Monsieur le Duc d'Hérouville, Marquis de Saint-Séver, Duc de Nivron, Comte de Bayeux, Vicomte d'Essigny, High Equerry of France, and Peer of the Realm, Knight of the Orders of the Spur and of the Golden Fleece, Grandee of Spain, and son of the last Governor of Normandy. He saw Mademoiselle Modeste when he was staying with the Vilquins, and he then only regretted—as his notary told me, who arrived yesterday from Bayeux—that she was not rich enough for him, since his father, on his return from exile, had found nothing left but his château of Hérouville, graced by his sister's presence. The young Duke is three-and-thirty. I am definitely charged to make overtures, Monsieur le Comte," added Latournelle, turning respectfully to the colonel.

"Ask Modeste," said her father, "whether she wishes to have another bird in her aviary; for, so far as I am concerned, I am quite willing that this fine gentleman equerry should pay his addresses to her."

Notwithstanding the care with which Charles Mignon avoided seeing anybody, for he stayed in the chalet and never went out but with Modeste; Gobenheim, whom they could hardly cease to receive at the chalet, had gossiped about Dumay's wealth; for Dumay, a second father to Modeste, had said to Gobenheim when he left his service, "I shall be my colonel's steward, and all my money, excepting what my wife may keep, will go to my little Modeste's children."

So every one at le Havre had echoed the plain question that Latournelle had asked himself—

"Must not Monsieur Charles Mignon have made an enormous fortune if Dumay's share amounts to six hundred thousand francs and if Dumay is to be his steward?"

"Monsieur Mignon came home in a ship of his own," said the gossips on 'Change, "loaded with indigo. The freight alone, not to mention the vessel, is worth more than he gives out to be his fortune."

The colonel would not discharge the servants he had so carefully chosen during his travels, so he was obliged to hire a house for six months in the lower part of Ingouville; he had a body-servant, a cook, and a coachman—both negroes—and a mulatto woman and two mulatto men on whose faithfulness he could rely. The coachman was inquiring for riding horses for mademoiselle and his master, and for carriage horses for the chaise in which the colonel and the lieutenant had come home. This traveling carriage, purchased in Paris, was in the latest fashion, and bore the arms of la Bastie with a Count's coronet. All these things, mere trifles in the eyes of a man who had been living for four years in the midst of the unbounded luxury of the Indies, of the Hong merchants, and the English at Canton, were the subject of comment to the traders of le Havre and the good folks of Graville and Ingouville. Within five days there was a hubbub of talk which flashed across Normandy like a fired train of gunpowder.

"Monsieur Mignon has come home from China with millions," was said at Rouen, "and it would seem that he has become a Count in the course of his travels."

"But he was Comte de la Bastie before the revolution," somebody remarked.

"So a Liberal, who for five-and twenty years was known as Charles Mignon, is now called Monsieur le Comte ! What are we coming to ? "

Thus, in spite of the reserve of her parents and intimates, Modeste was regarded as the richest heiress in Normandy, and all eyes could now see her merits. The Duc d'Hérouville's aunt and sister, in full drawing-room assembly at Bayeux, confirmed Monsieur Charles Mignon's right to the arms and title of Count conferred on Cardinal Mignon, whose cardinal's hat and cords were, out of gratitude, assumed in place of a crest and supporters. These ladies had caught sight of Mademoiselle de la Bastie from the Vilquins', and their solicitude for the impoverished head of the house at once scented an opportunity.

"If Mademoiselle de la Bastie is as rich as she is handsome," said the young Duke's aunt, "she will be the best match in the province. And she, at any rate, is of noble birth ! "

The last words were a shot at the Vilquins, with whom they could not come to terms after enduring the humiliation of paying them a visit.

Such were the little events which led to the introduction of another actor in this domestic drama, contrary to all the laws of Aristotle and Horace. But the portrait and biography of this personage, so tardy in his appearance, will not detain us long, since he is of the smallest importance. Monsieur le Duc will not fill more space here than he will in history.

Monsieur le Duc d'Hérouville, the fruit of the matrimonial autumn of the last Governor of Normandy, was born at Vienna in 1796, during the emigration. The old marshal,

who returned with the King in 1814, died in 1819 without
seeing his son married, though he was Duc de Nivron ; he
had nothing to leave him but the immense château of Hérouville, with the park, some outlying ground and a farm, all
painfully repurchased, and worth about fifteen thousand francs
a year. Louis XVIII. gave the young Duke the post of
master of the horse ; and under Charles X. he received the
allowance of twelve thousand francs a year granted to impe-
cunious peers.

But what were twenty-seven thousand francs a year for such
a family ?   In Paris, indeed, the young Duke had the use of
the royal carriages, and his official residence at the King's
stables in the Rue Saint-Thomas du Louvre ; his salary paid
the expenses of the winter, and the twenty-seven thousand
francs paid those of the summer in Normandy.

Though this great man was still a bachelor, the fault was
less his own than that of his aunt, who was not familiar
with La Fontaine's fables.   Mademoiselle d'Hérouville's pretensions were stupendous, quite out of harmony with the spirit
of the age ; for great names without money can hardly meet
with any wealthy heiresses among the high French nobility,
which finds it difficult enough to enrich its sons, ruined by
the equal division of property.   To find an advantageous
match for the young Duc d'Hérouville she should have cultivated the great financial houses, but this haughty daughter of
the noble house offended them all by her cutting speeches.
During the early years of the restoration, between 1817 and
1825, while looking out for millions, Mademoiselle d'Hérouville refused Mademoiselle Mongenod, the banker's daughter,
with whom Monsieur de Fontaine was content.   And now,
after various good matches had been marred by her pride, she
had just decided that the fortune of the Nucingens had been
amassed by too vile means to allow of her lending herself to
Madame de Nucingen's ambitious desire to see her daughter
a duchess.   The King, anxious to restore the splendor of the

Hérouvilles, had almost made the match himself, and he publicly taxed Mademoiselle d'Hérouville with folly. Thus the aunt made her nephew ridiculous, and the Duke laid himself open to ridicule.

It is a fact that when the great things of humanity vanish they leave some fragments (*frusteaux*, Rabelais would call them); and the French nobility in our day shows too many fag-ends. In this long study of manners neither the clergy nor the nobility have anything to complain of. Those two great and magnificent social necessaries are well represented ; but would it not be false to the proud title of historian to be other than impartial, to fail to show here the degeneracy of the race—just as you will elsewhere find the study of an émigré, the Comte de Mortsauf (*le Lys dans la vallée*), and every noblest feature of the noble, in the Marquis d'Espard (*l'Interdiction*).

How was it that a race of brave and strong men, that the house of d'Hérouville, which gave the famous marshal to the royal cause, cardinals to the church, captains to the Valois, and brave men to Louis XIV., ended in a frail creature smaller than Butscha? It is a question we may ask ourselves in many a Paris drawing-room, as we hear one of the great names of France announced, and see a little slender slip of a man come in who seems only to breathe, or a prematurely old fellow, or some eccentric being, in whom the observer seeks, but scarcely finds, a feature in which imagination can see a trace of original greatness. The dissipations of the reign of Louis XV., the orgies of that selfish time, have produced the etiolated generation in which fine manners are the sole survivors of extinct great qualities. Style is the only inheritance preserved by the nobility. Thus, apart from certain exceptions, the defection which left Louis XVI. to perish may be to some extent explained by the miserable heritage of the reign of Madame de Pompadour.

The master of the horse, a young man with blue eyes,

fair, pale, and slight, had a certain dignity of mind ; but his small size, and his aunt's mistake in having led him to be uselessly civil to the Vilquins, made him excessively shy. The d'Hérouvilles had had a narrow escape of dying out in the person of a cripple (*l'Enfant maudit*). But the Grand Marshal—as the family always called the d'Hérouville whom Louis XIII. had created Duke—had married at the age of eighty-two, and, of course, the family had been continued. The young Duke liked women ; but he placed them too high, he respected them too much, he adored them, and was not at his ease but with those whom no one respects. This character had led to his living a twofold life. He avenged himself on women of easy life for the worship he paid in the drawing-rooms, or, if you like, the boudoirs, of Saint-Germain. His ways and his tiny figure, his weary face, his blue eyes, with their somewhat ecstatic expression, had added to the ridicule poured on him, most unjustly, for he was full of apprehensiveness and wit ; but his wit had no sparkle, and was never seen excepting when he was quite at his ease. Fanny Beaupré, the actress, who was supposed to be his highly paid and most intimate friend, used to say of him, " It is good wine, but so tightly corked up that you break your corkscrews."

The handsome Duchesse de Maufrigneuse, whom the master of the horse could only adore, crushed him by a speech which, unluckily, was repeated, as all clever but ill-natured speeches are.

" He reminds me," said she, "of a trinket, beautifully wrought, but which we show more than we use and always keep in cotton wool."

Even his title of master of the horse would, by force of contrast, make good King Charles X. laugh, though the Duc d'Hérouville was a capital horseman. Men, like books, are sometimes valued too late. Modeste had had a glimpse of the Duke during his fruitless visit to the Vilquins, and, as he went by, all these remarks involuntarily recurred to her mind ;

but in the position in which she now stood, she perceived how valuable the Duc d'Hérouville's suit would be to save her from being at the mercy of a Canalis.

"I do not see," said she to Latournelle, "why the Duc d'Hérouville should not be allowed to call. In spite of our indigence," she added, with a mischievous glance at her father, "I am supposed to be an heiress. I shall have at last to publish a card of the field. Have you not noticed how Gobenheim's looks have changed in the course of this week ? He is in despair because he cannot set down his faithful attendance for whist to the score of mute admiration of me ! "

"Hush, my darling ! here he is," said Madame Latournelle.

"Old Althor is in despair," said Gobenheim to Monsieur Mignon as he came in.

"What about ? " asked the Comte de la Bastie.

"Vilquin is going to fail, they say, and on 'Change here you are said to have several millions——" ,

"No one knows," said Charles Mignon very drily, "what my obligations in India may amount to, and I do not care to admit the public to my confidence in business matters. Dumay," he said in his friend's ear, " if Vilquin is in difficulties we may be able to get the place back for what he gave for it in ready money."

Such was the state of affairs brought about by chance when, on Sunday morning, Canalis and la Brière, preceded by a courier, arrived at Madame Amaury's villa. They were told that the Duc d'Hérouville and his sister had arrived on the previous Tuesday at a hired house in Graville, for the benefit of their health. This competition led to a jest in the town that rents would rise at Ingouville.

"She will make the place a perfect hospital if this goes on ! " remarked Mademoiselle Vilquin, disgusted at not becoming a duchess.

The perennial comedy of "The Heiress," now to be per-

formed at the chalet, might certainly, from the frame of mind
in which it found Modeste, have been, as she had said in jest,
a competition, for she was firmly resolved, after the overthrow of her illusions, to give her hand only to the man
whose character should prove perfectly satisfactory.

On the morrow of their arrival, the rivals—still bosom
friends—prepared to make their first visit to the chalet that
evening. They devoted the whole of Sunday and all Monday morning to unpacking, to taking possession of Madame
Amaury's house, and to settling themselves in it for a month.
Beside, the poet, justified by his position as minister's apprentice in allowing himself some craft, had thought of everything ; he wished to get the benefit of the excitement that
might be caused by his arrival, of which some echoes might
reach the chalet. Canalis, supposed to be much fatigued,
did not go out ; la Brière went twice to walk past the chalet,
for he loved with a sort of desperation, he had the greatest
dread of having repelled Modeste, his future seemed wrapped
in thick clouds.

The two friends came down to dinner on that Monday in
array for their first visit, the most important of all. La Brière
was dressed as he had been in church on that famous Sunday ;
but he regarded himself as the satellite to a planet, and trusted
wholly to the chance of circumstances. Canalis, on his part,
had not forgotten his black coat, nor his orders, nor the
drawing-room grace perfected by his intimacy with the Duchesse de Chaulieu, his patroness, and with the finest company
of the Faubourg Saint-Germain. Canalis had attended to
every detail of dandyism, while poor Ernest was prepared to
appear in the comparative carelessness of a hopeless man.

As he waited on the two gentlemen at table, Germain could
not help smiling at the contrast. At the second course he
came in with a diplomatic, or, to be exact, a disturbed air.

"Monsieur le Baron," said he to Canalis in a low voice,
"did you know that monsieur the master of the horse is

coming to Graville to be cured of the same complaint as you and Monsieur de la Brière?"

"The little Duc d'Hérouville?" cried Canalis.

"Yes, sir."

"Can he have come for Mademoiselle de la Bastie?" asked la Brière, coloring.

"For Mademoiselle Mignon," replied Germain.

"We are done!" said Canalis, looking at la Brière.

"Ah!" Ernest eagerly replied, "that is the first time you have said *we* since we left Paris. Till this moment you have said *I.*"

"You know me!" cried Melchior with a burst of laughter. "Well, we are not in a position to hold our own against an officer of the household, against the title of duke and peer, nor against the marsh-lands which the privy council has just conferred, on the strength of my report, on the House of Hérouville."

"His highness," said la Brière with mischievous gravity, "offers you a plum of consolation in the person of his sister."

Just at this moment the Comte de la Bastie was announced. The two young men arose to receive him, and la Brière hastened to meet him and introduce Canalis.

"I had to return the visit you paid me in Paris," said Charles Mignon to the young referendary, "and I knew that by coming here I should have the added pleasure of seeing one of our living great poets."

"Great?—monsieur," the poet replied with a smile; "there can be nothing great henceforth in an age to which the reign of Napoleon was the preface. To begin with, we are a perfect tribe of so-called great poets. And beside, second-rate talent apes genius so well that it has made any great distinction impossible."

"And is that what has driven you into politics?" asked the Comte de la Bastie.

"It is the same in that field too," said Canalis. "There

will be no more great statesmen; there will be only men who are more or less in touch with events. Under the system produced by the charter, monsieur, which regards the schedule of the rates you pay as a patent of nobility, there is nothing substantial but what you went to find in China—a fortune."

Melchior, well pleased with himself, and satisfied with the impression he was making on his future father-in-law, now turned to Germain.

"Give us coffee in the drawing-room," said he, bowing to the merchant to leave the dining-room.

"I must thank you, Monsieur le Comte," said la Brière, "for having spared me the embarrassment of not knowing how I might introduce my friend at your house. To your kind heart you add a happy wit——"

"Oh, such wit as is common to the natives of Provence," returned Mignon.

"Ah, you come from Provence?" cried Canalis.

"Forgive my friend," said la Brière, "he has not studied the history of the la Basties, as I have."

At the word friend, Canalis shot a deep look at Ernest.

"If your health permits," said the Provençal to the great poet, "I claim the honor of receiving you this evening under my roof. It will be a day to mark, as the ancients have it, *albo notanda lapillo*. Though we are somewhat shy of receiving so great a glory in so small a house, you will gratify my daughter's impatience, for her admiration has led her even to set your verses to music."

"You possess what is better than glory," said Canalis. "You have beauty in your home, if I may believe Ernest."

"Oh, she is a good girl, whom you will find quite provincial," said the father.

"Provincial as she is, she has a suitor in the Duc d'Hérouville," cried Canalis in a hard tone.

"Oh," said Monsieur Mignon, with the deceptive frankness of a southerner, "I leave my daughter free to choose. Dukes,

princes, private gentlemen, they are all the same to me, even
men of genius. I will pledge myself to nothing; the man my
Modeste may prefer will be my son-in-law, or rather my son,"
and he looked at la Brière. "Madame de la Bastie is a German; she cannot tolerate French etiquette, and I allow myself
to be guided by my two women. I would always rather ride
inside a carriage than on the box. We can discuss such
serious matters in jest, for we have not yet seen the Duc
d'Hérouville, and I do not believe in marriages arranged
by proxy any more than in suitors forced on girls by their
parents."

"That is a declaration equally disheartening and encouraging to two young men who seek in marriage the philosopher's
stone of happiness," said Canalis.

"Do you not think it desirable, necessary, and indeed good
policy to stipulate for perfect liberty for the parents, the
daughter, and the suitors?" asked Charles Mignon.

Canalis, at a glance from la Brière, made no reply, and the
conversation continued on indifferent subjects. After walking
two or three times round the garden, the father withdrew,
begging the two friends to pay their visit.

"That is our dismissal," cried Canalis. "You understood
it as I did. After all, in his place I should not hesitate between
the master of the horse and either of us, charming fellows as
we may be."

"I do not think so," said la Brière, "I believe that the
worthy officer came simply to gratify his own impatience to
see you, and to declare his neutrality while opening his house
to us. Modeste, bewitched by your fame and misled as to my
identity, finds herself between poetry and hard fact. It is my
misfortune to be the hard fact."

"Germain," said Canalis to the servant who came in to
clear away the coffee, "order the carriage round. We will
go out in half an hour and take a drive before going to the
chalet."

12

The two young men were equally impatient to see Modeste, but la Brière dreaded the meeting, while Canalis looked forward to it with a confidence inspired by conceit. Ernest's impulsive advances to her father, and the flattery by which he had soothed the merchant's aristocratic pride while showing up the poet's awkwardness, made Canalis determine that he would play a part. He resolved that he would display all his powers of attraction, but at the same time affect indifference, seem to disdain Modeste, and so goad the girl's vanity. A disciple of the beautiful Duchesse de Chaulieu, he here showed himself worthy of his reputation as a man who knew women well; though he did not really know them, since no man does who is the happy victim of an exclusive passion. While the luckless Ernest, sunk in a corner of the carriage, was crushed by the terrors of true love and the anticipated wrath, scorn, contempt—all the lightnings of an offended and disappointed girl—and kept gloomy silence, Canalis, not less silent, was preparing himself like an actor studying an important part in a new play.

Neither of them certainly looked like a happy man.

For Canalis, indeed, the matter was serious. To him the mere fancy for marrying involved the breach of the serious friendship which had bound him for nearly ten years to the Duchesse de Chaulieu. Though he had screened his journey under the common excuse of overwork—in which no woman ever believes, even if it is true—his conscience troubled him somewhat; but to la Brière the word conscience seemed so jesuitical that he only shrugged his shoulders when the poet spoke of his scruples.

"Your conscience, my boy, seems to me to mean simply your fear of losing the gratifications of vanity, some solid advantages, and a pleasant habit in sacrificing Madame de Chaulieu's affection; for, if you are successful with Modeste, you will certainly have nothing to regret in the aftermath of a passion so constantly reaped during these eight years past.

If you tell me that you are afraid of offending your protectress, should she learn the real reason of your visit here, I can easily believe you. To throw over the Duchess and fail at the chalet is staking too much! And you mistake the distress of this alternative for remorse!"

"You know nothing about sentiment!" cried Canalis, nettled, as a man always is when he asks for a compliment and hears the truth.

"That is just what a bigamist would say to a dozen jurymen," said la Brière, laughing.

This epigram made a yet more disagreeable impression on Canalis; he thought la Brière much too clever and too free for a secretary.

The arrival of a handsome carriage, with a coachman in Canalis' livery, made all the greater sensation at the chalet because the two gentlemen were expected, and all the persons of this tale, excepting only the Duke and Butscha, were assembled there.

"Which is the poet?" asked Madame Latournelle of Dumay, as they stood in the window-bay, where she had posted herself, on hearing the carriage wheels, to inspect the visitors.

"The one who marches like a drum-major," replied the cashier.

"Ah, hah!" said the lady, studying Melchior, who strutted like a man on whom the world has its eye.

Though rather severe, Dumay's judgment—a simple soul, if ever man was—had hit the mark. Canalis was, morally speaking, a sort of Narcissus; this was the fault of the great lady who flattered him immensely, and spoilt him as women older than their adorers always will flatter and spoil men. A woman past her first youth, who means to attach a man permanently, begins by glorifying his faults, so as to make all rivalry impossible; for her rival cannot at once be in the secret of that subtle flattery to which a man so easily becomes

accustomed.   Coxcombs are the product of this feminine industry when they are not coxcombs by nature.

Hence Canalis, caught young by the beautiful Duchess,
justified himself for his airs and graces by telling himself that
they pleased a woman whose taste was law.   Subtle as these
shades of feeling are, it is not impossible to render them.
Thus Melchior had a real talent for reading aloud, which had
been much admired, and too flattering praise had led him into
an exaggerated manner, which neither poet nor actor can set
bounds to, and which made de Marsay say—always de Marsay
—that he did not declaim, but brayed out his verses, so fully
would he mouth the vowels as he listened to himself.   To use
the slang of the stage, he pumped himself out, and made too
long pauses.   He would examine his audience with a knowing
look, and give himself self-satisfied airs, with the aids to
emphasis of " sawing the air " and " windmill action "—
picturesque phrases, as the catchwords of art always are.
Canalis indeed had imitators, and was the head of a school
in this style.   This melodramatic emphasis had slightly in-
fected his conversation and given it a declamatory tone, as
will have been seen in his interview with Dumay.   When
once the mind has become foppish, manners show the influence.   Canalis had come at last to a sort of rhythmic gait, he
invented attitudes, stole looks at himself in the glass, and
made his language harmonize with the position he assumed.
He thought so much of the effect to be produced, that more
than once Blondet, a mocking spirit, had bet he would pull
him up short—and had done it—merely by fixing a set gaze
on the poet's hair, or boots, or the tail of his coat.

At the end of ten years these antics, which at first had
passed under favor of youthful exuberance, had grown stale,
and all the more so as Melchior himself seemed somewhat worn.
Fashionable life is as fatiguing for men as for women, and perhaps the Duchess' twenty years' seniority weighed on Canalis
more than on her ; for the world saw her still handsome, with-

out a wrinkle, without rouge, and without heart. Alas! neither
men nor women have a friend to warn them at the moment
when the fragrance of modesty turns rancid, when a caressing
look is like a theatrical trick, when the expressiveness of a
face becomes a grimace, when the mechanism of their liveliness shows its rusty skeleton. Genius alone can renew its
youth like the serpent, and in grace, as in all else, only the
heart never grows stale. Persons of genuine feeling are single-
hearted. Now in Canalis, as we know, the heart was dry.
He wasted the beauty of his gaze by assuming at inappropriate
moments the intensity that deep thought gives to the eyes.

And, then, praise to him was an article of exchange, in
which he wanted to have all the advantage. His way of paying compliments, which charmed superficial persons, to those
of more refined taste might seem insultingly commonplace,
and the readiness of his flattery betrayed a set purpose. In
fact, Melchior lied like a courtier. To the Duc de Chaulieu,
who had proved an ineffective speaker when, as minister for
foreign affairs, he had been obliged to mount the tribune,
Canalis had unblushingly said, "Your excellency was sublime!"

Many men like Canalis might have had their affectations
eradicated by failure administered in small doses. Trifling,
indeed, as such faults are in the gilded drawing-rooms of the
Faubourg Saint-Germain—where every one contributes a quota
of absurdities, and this kind of audacity, artificiality, infla-
tion if you will, has a background of excessive luxury and
magnificent dress which is perhaps an excuse for it—they are
monstrously conspicuous in the depths of the country, where
what is thought ridiculous is the very opposite of all this.
Canalis, indeed, at once pompous and mannered, could not
now metamorphose himself; he had had time to set in the
mould into which the Duchess had cast him, and he was,
moreover, very Parisian, or, if you prefer it, very French.
The Parisian is amazed that everything, everywhere, is not

what it is in Paris, and the Frenchman that it is not what it
is in France. Good taste consists in accommodating one's self
to the manners of other places without losing too much of one's
native character, as Alcibiades did—the model of a gentleman.
True grace is elastic. It yields to every circumstance, it is in
harmony with every social atmosphere, it knows how to walk
in the street in a cheap dress, remarkable only for its fitness,
instead of parading the feathers and gaudy hues which some
vulgar people flaunt.

Now, Canalis, influenced by a woman who loved him for
her own sake rather than for his, wanted to be himself a law,
and to remain what he was wherever he might go. He believed that he carried his private public with him—a mistake
shared by some other great men in Paris.

While the poet made a studied entrance into the little
drawing-room, la Brière sneaked in like a dog that is afraid
of being beaten.

"Ah, here is my soldier!" said Canalis, on seeing Dumay,
after paying Madame Mignon his respects, and bowing to the
other women. "Your anxieties are relieved, I hope?" he
went on, offering him his hand with a flourish. "But the
sight of mademoiselle sufficiently explains their gravity. I
spoke only of earthly beings, not of angels."

The hearers by their expression asked for a clue to this
riddle.

"Yes, I shall regard it as a triumph," the poet went on,
understanding that everybody wanted an explanation, "that
I succeeded in alarming one of those men of iron whom Napoleon succeeded in finding to form the piles on which he
tried to found an empire too vast to be permanent. Only
time can serve to cement such a structure! But have I any
right to boast of my triumph? I had nothing to do with it;
it was the triumph of fancy over fact. Your battles, dear
Monsieur Dumay; your heroic cavalry charges, Monsieur le
Comte; in short, war was the form assumed by Napoleon's

thoughts. And of all these things what remains? The grass
that grows over them knows nothing of them, nor will har-
vests mark the spot; but for history, but for writing, the
future might know nothing of this heroic age! Thus your
fifteen years of struggle are no more than ideas, and that is
what will save the Empire; poets will make a poem of it.
A land that can win such battles ought to be able to sing
them!"

Canalis paused to collect, by a sweeping glance at their
faces, the tribute of admiration due to him from these country
folk.

"You cannot doubt, monsieur," said Madame Mignon,
"how much I regret being unable to see you, from the way
you indemnify me by the pleasure I feel in listening to you."

Modeste, dressed as she had been on the day when this
story opens, having made up her mind to think Canalis sublime, sat speechless, and dropped her embroidery, which hung
from her fingers at the end of the needleful of cotton.

"Modeste, this is Monsieur de la Brière. Monsieur Ernest
—my daughter," said Charles Mignon, thinking that the secretary was thrown rather too much into the background.

The young lady bowed coldly to Ernest, giving him a look
intended to convey to the whole party that she had never
seen him before.

"I beg your pardon," said she, without a blush, "the fer-
vent admiration I profess for our greatest poet is, in my
friends' eyes, a sufficient excuse for my having seen no one
else."

The clear, young voice, with a ring in it like the famous
tones of Mademoiselle Mars, enchanted the poor referendary,
already dazzled by Modeste's beauty, and in his amazement
he spoke a few words which, had they been true, would have
been sublime——

"But he is my friend," said he.

"Then you will have forgiven me," she replied.

"He is more than a friend," cried Canalis, taking Ernest by the shoulder, and leaning on him as Alexander leaned on Hephaestion. "We love each other like two brothers——"

Madame Latournelle cut the poet short in the middle of his speech by saying to her husband—

"Surely monsieur is the gentleman we saw in church?"

"Why not?" said Charles Mignon, seeing Ernest color.

Modeste gave no sign, but took up her work again.

"You may be right; I have been twice to le Havre," said la Brière, sitting down by the side of Dumay after again saluting him.

Canalis, bewildered by Modeste's beauty, misunderstood the admiration she expressed, and flattered himself that his efforts had been perfectly successful.

"I should think a man of genius devoid of heart if he had not about him some attached friend," said Modeste, to revive the subject interrupted by Madame Latournelle's awkwardness.

"Mademoiselle, Ernest's devotion is enough to make me believe that I am good for something," said Canalis. "For my dear Pylades is full of talent; he was quite half of the greatest minister we have had since the peace. Though he fills a distinguished position, he consents to be my tutor in politics. He teaches me business, he feeds me with his experience, while he might aspire to the highest office. Oh! he is much superior to me——"

At a gesture from Modeste, Melchior added gracefully—

"The poetry I write he bears in his heart; and if I dare speak so to his face, it is because he is as diffident as a nun."

"Come, come, that will do," said la Brière, who did not know how to look. "My dear fellow, you might be a mother wanting to get her daughter married."

"How can you think, monsieur, of becoming a politician?" said Charles Mignon to Canalis.

"For a poet it is abdication!" said Modeste. "Politics are the stand-by of men without imagination," she added as an after-thought.

"Nay, mademoiselle, in these days the tribune is the grandest stage in the world; it has taken the place of the lists of chivalry; it will be the meeting-place of every kind of intellect, as of old the army was of every form of courage."

Canalis had mounted his war-horse; for ten minutes he declaimed on the subject of political life: Poetry was the preface to a statesman. In these days the orator's province was lofty generalization; he was the pastor of ideas. If a poet could show his countrymen the road of the future, did he cease to be himself? He quoted Chateaubriand, asserting that he would some day be more important on his political than on his literary side. The French Chambers would be the guiding light of humanity. Contests by words henceforth had taken the place of fighting on the battlefield. Such or such a sitting had been a second Austerlitz and the speakers had risen to the dignity of generals; they spent as much of their life, courage, and strength, they wore themselves out as much as generals in war. Was not speech almost the most exhausting expenditure of vital power that man could indulge in, etc., etc.

This long harangue, made up of modern commonplace, but clothed in high-sounding phrases, newly coined words, and intended to prove that the Baron de Canalis must some day be one of the glories of the tribune, made a deep impression on the notary, on Gobenheim, on Madame Latournelle, and Madame Mignon. Modeste felt as if she were at the play and fired with enthusiasm for the actor, exactly as Ernest was in her presence; for though the secretary knew all these fine phrases by heart, he was listening to them by the light of the girl's eyes, and falling in love to the verge of madness. To this genuine lover Modeste had eclipsed all the different Modestes he had pictured to himself when reading or answering her letters.

This visit, of which Canalis had fixed the limits beforehand, for he would not give his admirers time to get tired of him, ended by an invitation to dinner on the following Monday.

"We shall no longer be at the chalet," said the Comte de la Bastie. "It is Dumay's home once more. I am going back to my old house by an agreement for six months, with the right of redemption, which I have just signed with Monsieur Vilquin in my friend Latournelle's office."

"I only hope," said Dumay, "that Vilquin may not be in a position to repay the sum you have loaned him on it."

"You will be in a home suitable to your fortune," said Canalis.

"To the fortune I am supposed to have," Charles Mignon put in.

"It would be a pity," said the poet, with a charming bow to Modeste, "that this Madonna should lack a frame worthy of her divine affections."

This was all that Canalis said about Modeste, for he had affected not to look at her, and to behave like a man who is not at liberty to think of marriage.

"Oh, my dear Madame Mignon, he is immensely clever!" exclaimed the notary's wife, when the gravel was heard crunching under the Parisians' feet.

"Is he rich? that is the question," said Gobenheim.

Modeste stood at the window, not missing a single gesture of the great poet's, and never casting a glance on Ernest de la Brière. When Monsieur Mignon came into the room again, and Modeste, after receiving a parting bow from the two young men as the carriage turned, had resumed her seat, a deep discussion ensued, such as country people indulge in on Paris visitors after a first meeting. Gobenheim reiterated his remark, is he rich?" in reply to the trio of praise sung by Madame Latournelle, Modeste, and her mother.

"Rich?" retorted Modeste. "What can it matter? Can you not see that Monsieur de Canalis is a man destined to fill the highest posts in the government? He has more than wealth; he has the means of acquiring wealth!"

"He will be an ambassador or a minister," said Monsieur Mignon.

"The taxpayers may have to pay for his funeral nevertheless," said little Lautournelle.

"Why?" asked Charles Mignon.

"He strikes me as being a man to squander all the fortunes which Mademoiselle Modeste so liberally credits him with the power of earning."

"How can Modeste help being liberal to a man who regards her as a Madonna?" said Dumay, faithful to the aversion Canalis had roused in him.

Gobenheim was preparing the whist-table, with all the more eagerness because since Monsieur Mignon's return Latournelle and Dumay had allowed themselves to play for ten sous a point.

"Now, my little darling," said the father to his daughter in the window recess, "you must own that papa thinks of everything. In a week, if you send orders this evening to the dressmaker you used to employ in Paris and to your other tradesmen, you may display yourself in all the magnificence of an heiress, while I take time to settle into our old house. You shall have a nice pony, so take care to have a habit made—the master of the horse deserves that little attention."

"All the more so as we must show our friends the country," said Modeste, whose cheeks were recovering the hues of health.

"The secretary," observed Madame Mignon, "is not much to speak of."

"He is a little simpleton," said Madame Latournelle. "The poet was very attentive to everybody. He remembered to thank Latournelle for finding him a house, by saying to me that he seemed to have consulted a lady's taste. And the other stood there as gloomy as a Spaniard, staring hard, looking as if he could swallow Modeste. If he had looked at me so, I should have been frightened."

"He has a very pleasant voice," Madame Mignon observed.

"He must have come to le Havre to make inquiries about the house of Mignon for the poet's benefit," said Modeste, with a sly look at her father. "He is certainly the man we saw in church."

Madame Dumay and the Latournelles accepted this explanation of Ernest's former journey.

"I tell you what, Ernest," said Canalis when they had gone twenty yards, "I see no one in the Paris world, not a single girl to marry, that can compare with this adorable creature !"

"Oh ! it is all settled," replied la Brière, with concentrated bitterness; "she loves you—or, if you choose, she will love you. Your fame half-won the battle. In short, you have only to command. You can go there alone next time; Modeste has the deepest contempt for me, and she is right; but I do not see why I should condemn myself to the torture of going to admire, desire, and adore what I can never possess."

After a few condoling speeches, in which Canalis betrayed his satisfaction at having produced a new edition of Cæsar's famous motto, he hinted at his wish to be "off" with the Duchesse de Chaulieu. La Brière, who could not endure the conversation, made an excuse of the loveliness of a rather doubtful night to get out and walk; he flew like a madman to the cliffs, where he stayed till half-past ten, given up to a sort of frenzy, sometimes walking at a great pace and spouting soliloquies, sometimes standing still or sitting down, with-

out observing the uneasiness he was giving to two coastguards
on the lookout. After falling in love with Modeste's mental
culture and aggressive candor, he now added his adoration of
her beauty, that is to say, an unreasoning and inexplicable
passion, to all the other causes that had brought him ten days
ago to church at le Havre.

Then he wandered back to the chalet, where the Pyrenean
dogs barked at him so furiously that he could not allow himself the happiness of gazing at Modeste's windows. In love,
all these things are of no more account than the under-paint-
ing covered by the final touches is to the painter; but they
are nevertheless the whole of love, as concealed painstaking is
the whole of art: the outcome is a great painter and a perfect
lover, which the public and the woman worship at last—often
too late.

"Well!" cried he aloud, "I will stay, I will endure. I
shall see her and love her selfishly, for my own joy! Modeste
will be my sun, my life, I shall breathe by her breath, I shall
rejoice in her joys, I shall pine over her sorrows, even if she
should be the wife of that egoist Canalis——"

"That is something like love, monsieur!" said a voice
proceeding from a bush by the wayside. "Bless me! is
everybody in love with Mademoiselle de la Bastie?"

Butscha started forth and gazed at la Brière. Ernest
sheathed his wrath as he looked at the dwarf in the moonlight, and walked on a few steps without replying.

"Two soldiers serving in the same company should be on
better terms than that," said Butscha. "If you are not in
love with Canalis, I am not very sweet on him myself."

"He is my friend," said Ernest, earnestly scrutinizing the
speaker.

"Oh! then you are the little secretary?" replied the
hunchback.

"I would have you to know, monsieur," said la Brière,
"that I am no man's secretary. I have the honor to call my-

self councilor to one of the high courts of justice of this realm."

"I have the honor, then, of making my bow to Monsieur de la Brière," said Butscha. "I have the honor to call my-self head clerk to Maître Latournelle, the first notary in le Havre, and I certainly am better off than you are. Yes—for I have had the happiness of seeing Mademoiselle Modeste de la Bastie almost every afternoon for the last four years, and I propose to live within her ken as one of the King's house-hold lives at the Tuileries. If I were offered the throne of Russia, I should reply, 'I like the sun too well!' Is not that as much as to say, monsieur, that I care more for her than for myself—with all respect and honor? And do you suppose that the high and mighty Duchesse de Chaulieu will look with a friendly eye on the happiness of Madame de Canalis, when her maid, who is in love with Monsieur Ger-main, and is already uneasy at that fascinating valet's long absence at le Havre, as she dresses her mistress' hair com-plains?"

"How do you know all this?" said la Brière, interrupting him.

"In the first place, I am a notary's clerk," replied Butscha. "And have you not observed that I have a hump? It is full of ingenuity, monsieur. I made myself cousin to Made-moiselle Philoxène Jacmin, of Honfleur, where my mother was born, also a Jacmin—there are eleven branches of Jac-mins at Honfleur. And so my fair cousin, tempted by the hope of a highly improbable legacy, told me a good many things."

"And the Duchess is vindictive?" said la Brière.

"As vengeful as a queen, says Philoxène. She has not yet forgiven the Duke for being only her husband," replied Butscha. "She hates as she loves. I am thoroughly in-formed as to her temper, her dress, her tastes, her religion, and her meanness, for Philoxène stripped her soul and

body. I went to the opera to see Madame de Chaulieu, and
I do not regret my ten francs—I am not thinking of the piece.
If my hypothetical cousin had not told me that her mistress
had seen fifty springs, I should have thought it lavish to give
her thirty ; she has known no winter, my lady the Duchess."

"True," said la Brière, "she is a cameo preserved by the
onyx. Canalis would be in great difficulties if the Duchess
knew of his plans ; and I hope, monsieur, that you will go no
further in an espionage so unworthy of an honest man."

"Monsieur," said Butscha proudly, "to me Modeste is the
State. I do not spy, I forestall ! The Duchesse de Chaulieu
will come here if necessary, or will remain quietly where she
is if I think it advisable."

"You ?"

"I."

"And by what means?" asked la Brière.

"Ah, that is the question," said the little hunchback. He
plucked a blade of grass. "This little plant imagines that
man builds palaces for its accommodation, and one day it dis-
lodges the most firmly cemented marble, just as the populace,
having found a foothold in the structure of the feudal system,
overthrew it. The power of the weakest that can creep in
everywhere is greater than that of the strong man who relies
on his cannon. There are three of us, a Swiss league, who
have sworn that Modeste shall be happy, and who would sell
our honor for her sake. Good-night, monsieur. If you love
Mademoiselle de la Bastie, forget this conversation, and give
me your hand to shake, for you seem to me to have a heart !
I was pining to see the chalet ; I got here just as she put out
her candle. I saw you when the dogs gave tongue, I heard
you raving; and so I took the liberty of telling you that we
serve under the same colors, in the regiment of loyal devotion ! "

"Good," replied la Brière, pressing the hunchback's hand.
"Then be kind enough to tell me whether Mademoiselle

Modeste ever fell in love with a man before her secret correspondence with Canalis?"

"Oh!" cried Butscha, "the mere question is an insult!
And even now who knows whether she is in love? Does she
herself know? She has rushed into enthusiasm for the mind,
the genius, the spirit of this verse-monger, this vendor of
literary pinchbeck; but she will study him—we shall all study
him; I will find some means of making his true character peep
out from beneath the carapace of the well-mannered man, and
we shall see the insignificant head of his ambition and his
vanity," said Butscha, rubbing his hands. "Now, unless
mademoiselle is mad enough to die of it——"

"Oh, she sat entranced before him, as if he were a miracle!" cried la Brière, revealing the secret of his jealousy.

"If he is really a good fellow, and loyal, and loves her, if
he is worthy of her," Butscha went on, "if he gives up his
Duchess, it is the Duchess I will spread a net for! There, my
dear sir, follow that path, and you will be at home in ten
minutes."

But Butscha presently turned back and called to the hapless
Ernest, who, as an ardent lover, would have stayed all night
to talk of Modeste.

"Monsieur," said Butscha, "I have not yet had the honor
of seeing our great poet; I am anxious to study that splendid
phenomenon in the exercise of his functions; do me the kindness to come and spend the evening at the chalet the day after
to-morrow; and stay some time, for a man does not completely betray himself in an hour. I shall know, before any
one, if he loves, or ever will love, or ever could love Mademoiselle Modeste."

"You are very young to——"

"To be a professor!" interrupted Butscha. "Ah, monsieur, the deformed come into the world a hundred years old.
Besides, a sick man, you see, when he has been ill a long
time, becomes more knowing than his doctor; he understands

the ways of the disease, which is more than a conscientious
doctor always does. Well, in the same way, a man who loves
a woman, while the woman cannot help scorning him for his
ugliness or his misshapen person, is at last so qualified in love
that he could pass as a seducer, as the sick man at last recovers
his health. Folly alone is incurable. Since the age of six,
and I am now five-and-twenty, I have had neither father nor
mother; public charity has been my mother and the King's
commissioner my father. Nay, do not be distressed," he
said, in reply to Ernest's expression, "I am less miserable
than my position—— Well, since I was six years old, when
the insolent eyes of a servant of Madame Latournelle's told
me that I had no right to wish to love, I have loved and have
studied women. I began with ugly ones—it is well to take
the bull by the horns. So I took for the first subject of my
studies Madame Latournelle herself, who has been really
angelic to me. I was perhaps wrong; however, so it was.
I distilled her in my alembic, and I at last discovered hidden
in a corner of her soul this idea, 'I am not as ugly as people
think!' And in spite of her deep piety, by working on that
idea, I could have led her to the brink of the abyss—to leave
her there."

"And have you studied Modeste?"

"I thought I had told you," replied the hunchback, "that
my life is hers, as France is the King's! Now do you understand my playing the spy in Paris? I alone know all the
nobleness and pride, the unselfishness, and unexpected sweetness that lie in the heart and soul of that adorable creature—
the indefatigable kindness, the true piety, the light-hearted-
ness, information, refinement, affability——"

Butscha drew out his handkerchief to stop two tears from
falling, and la Brière held his hand for some time.

"I shall live in her radiance! It comes from her, and it
ends in me, that is how we are united, somewhat as nature is
to God by light and the word. Good-night, monsieur, I

13

never chattered so much in my life; but seeing you below her windows, I guessed that you loved her in my way."

Butscha, without waiting for an answer, left the unhappy lover, on whose heart this conversation had shed a mysterious balm. Ernest determined to make Butscha his friend, never suspecting that the clerk's loquacity was chiefly intended to open communication with Canalis' house. In what a flow and ebb of thoughts, resolutions, and schemes was Ernest lapped before falling asleep; and his friend Canalis was sleeping the sleep of the triumphant, the sweetest slumber there is next to that of the just.

At breakfast the friends agreed to go together to spend the evening of the following day at the chalet, and be initiated into the mild joys of provincial whist. To get rid of this day they ordered out the horses, both guaranteed to ride and drive, and ventured forth into a country certainly as unknown to them as China; for the least known thing in France to a Frenchman, is France.

As he reflected on his position as a lover rejected and scorned, the secretary made such a study of himself as he had been led to make by the question Modeste had put to him at the beginning of their correspondence. Though misfortune is supposed to develop virtues, it only does so in virtuous people; for this sort of cleaning up of the conscience takes place only in naturally cleanly persons. La Brière determined to swallow his griefs with Spartan philosophy, to preserve his dignity, and never allow himself to be betrayed into a mean action; while Canalis, fascinated by such an enormous fortune, vowed to himself that he would neglect nothing that might captivate Modeste. Egoism and unselfishness, the watchwords of these two natures, brought them by a moral law, which sometimes has whimsical results, to behave in opposition to their characters. The selfish man meant to act self-sacrifice, the man who was all kindliness would take refuge on the Aventine Hill of pride. This phenomenon may also be seen in poli-

tics. Men often turn their natures inside out, and not unfre-
quently the public does not know the right side from the
wrong.

After dinner they heard from Germain that the master of
the horse had arrived ; he was introduced at the chalet that
evening by Monsieur Latournelle. Mademoiselle d'Hérouville managed to offend the worthy lawyer at once, by sending a message through a footman, desiring him to call at her
house, instead of simply sending her nephew to take up the
lawyer, who would certainly have talked till his dying day of
the visit paid by the master of the horse. So when his lordship offered to take him to Ingouville in his carriage the little
notary merely said that he must return home to accompany
his wife. Seeing by his sullen manner that there was something wrong, the Duke graciously replied, " If you will allow
me, I shall have the honor of going round to fetch Madame
Latournelle."

In spite of an emphatic shrug of his despotic aunt's shoulders, the Duke set out with the little notary. Intoxicated
with the delight of seeing a magnificent carriage at her door,
and men in the royal livery to let down the steps, the lawyer's
wife did not know which way to turn for her gloves, her para-
sol, her bag, and her dignity, when it was announced to her
that the master of the horse had come to fetch her. As
soon as she was in the carriage, while pouring out civilities to
the little Duke, she suddenly exclaimed with kindly impulse—

" Oh, and Butscha ? "

" Bring Butscha, too," said the Duke, smiling.

As the harbor-men, who had collected around the dazzling
vehicle, saw these three little men with that tall meagre
woman, they looked at each other and laughed.

" If you stuck them together end-to-end, perhaps you might
make a man tall enough for that long May-pole," said a sailor
from Bordeaux.

" Have you anything else to take with you, madame?" the

Duke asked jestingly, as the footman stood waiting for his orders.

" No, monseigneur," replied she, turning scarlet, and looking at her husband as much as to say, " What have I done wrong ? "

" His lordship," said Butscha, " does me too much honor in speaking of me as a thing ; a poor clerk like me is a nameless object."

Though he spoke lightly, the Duke colored and made no reply. Grand folk are always in the wrong to bandy jests with those below them. Banter is a game, and a game implies equality. And, indeed, it is to obviate the unpleasant results of such a transient familiarity that, when the game is over, the players have a right to not recognize each other.

The Duke's visit to le Havre was ostensibly for the settlement of an immense undertaking, namely, the reclaiming of a vast tract of land, left dry by the sea between two streams, of which the ownership had just been confirmed to the Hérouville family by the high court of appeals. The proposed scheme was no less a matter than the adjustment of sluice gates to two bridges, to drain a tract of mud-flats extending for about a kilometre, with a breadth of three or four hundred acres, to embank roads and dig ditches. When the Duc d'Hérouville had explained the nature and position of the land, Charles Mignon observed that he would have to wait until nature had enabled the soil to settle by the consolidation of its still shifting natural constituents.

" Time, which has providentially enriched your estate, Monsieur le Duc, must be left to complete its work," said he, in conclusion. " You will do well to wait another fifty years before setting to work."

" Do not let that be your final opinion, Monsieur le Comte," said the Duke. " Come to Hérouville, see, and judge for yourself."

Charles Mignon replied that some capitalist would need to

look into the matter with a cool head; and this remark had given Monsieur d'Hérouville an excuse for calling at the chalet.

Modeste made a deep impression on him; he begged the favor of a visit from her, saying that his aunt and sister had heard of her, and would be happy to make her acquaintance. On this, Charles Mignon proposed to introduce his daughter to the two ladies, and invited them to dine with him on the day when he should be re-established in his former home; this the Duke accepted. The nobleman's blue ribbon, his title, and, above all, his rapturous glances, had their effect on Modeste; still, she was admirably calm in speech, manner, and dignity. The Duke when he left seemed loath to depart, but he had received an invitation to go to the chalet every evening, on the pretext that, of course, no courtier of Charles X. could possibly endure an evening without a game of whist.

So, on the following evening, Modeste was to see her three admirers all on the stage at once.

Say what she will, it is certainly flattering to a girl to see several rivals fluttering around her, men of talent, fame, or high birth, all trying to shine and please her, though the logic of the heart will lead her to sacrifice everything to personal predilection. Even if Modeste should lose credit by the admission, she owned, at a later day, that the feelings expressed in her letters had paled before the pleasure of seeing three men, so different, vying with each other—three men, each of whom would have done honor to the most exacting family pride. At the same time, this luxury of vanity gave way before the misanthropical spirit of mischief engendered by the bitter affront which she already thought of merely as a disappointment. So when her father said to her with a smile—

"Well, Modeste, would you like to be a duchess?"

"Ill fortune has made me philosophical," she replied, with a mocking curtsey.

"You are content to be baroness?" asked Butscha quietly.

"Or viscountess?" replied her father.

"How could that be?" said Modeste quickly.

"Why, if you were to accept Monsieur de la Brière, he would certainly have influence enough with the King to get leave to take my title and bear my arms."

"Oh, if it is a matter of borrowing a disguise, he will make no difficulties!" replied Modeste bitterly.

Butscha did not understand this sarcasm, of which only Monsieur and Madame Mignon and Dumay knew the meaning.

"As soon as marriage is in question, every man assumes a disguise," said Madame Latournelle, "and women set them the example. Ever since I can remember I have heard it said, 'Monsieur this or mademoiselle that is making a very good match'—so the other party must be making a bad one, I suppose?"

"Marriage," quoth Butscha, "is like an action at law; one side is always left dissatisfied; and if one party deceives the other, half the married couples one sees certainly play the farce at the cost of the other."

"Whence you conclude, Sire Butscha?" asked Modeste.

"That we must always keep our eyes sternly open to the enemy's movements," replied the clerk.

"What did I tell you, my pet?" said Charles Mignon, alluding to his conversation with his daughter on the seashore.

"Men, to get married," interjected Latournelle, "play as many parts as mothers make their daughters play in order to get them off their hands."

"Then you think stratagem allowable?" rejoined Modeste.

"On both sides," cried Gobenheim. "Then the game is even."

This conversation was carried on in a fragmentary manner between the deals, and mixed up with the opinions each one allowed himself to express about Monsieur d'Hérouville, who was thought quite good-looking by the little notary, by little Dumay, and by little Butscha.

"I see," said Madame Mignon, with a smile, "that Madame Latournelle and my husband are quite monsters here!"

"Happily for him the colonel is not excessively tall," replied Butscha, while the lawyer was dealing, "for a tall man who is also intelligent is always a rare exception."

But for this little discussion on the legitimate use of matrimonial wiles, the account of the evening so anxiously expected by Butscha might seem lengthy; but wealth, for which so much secret meanness was committed, may perhaps lend to the minutiæ of private life the interest which is always aroused by the social feeling so frankly set forth by Ernest in his reply to Modeste.

In the course of the next morning Desplein arrived. He stayed only so long as was needful for sending to le Havre for a relay of post-horses, which were at once put in—about an hour. After examining Madame Mignon, he said she would certainly recover her sight, and fixed the date for the operation a month later. This important consultation was held, of course, in the presence of the family party at the chalet, all anxiously eager to hear the decision of the prince of science. The illustrious member of the Academy of Science asked the blind woman ten short questions, while examining her eyes in the bright light by the window. Modeste, amazed at the value of time to this famous man, noticed that his traveling chaise was full of books, which he intended to read on his way back to Paris, for he had come away on the previous evening, spending the night in sleeping and traveling.

The swiftness and clearness of Desplein's decisions on every answer of Madame Mignon's, his curt speech, his manner, all gave Modeste, for the first time, any clear idea of a

man of genius.   She felt the enormous gulf between Canalis,
a man of second-rate talents, and Desplein, a more than superior mind.

A man of genius has in the consciousness of his talent and
the assurance of his fame a domain, as it were, where his
legitimate pride can move and breathe freely without incom-
moding other people.   Then the incessant conflict with men
and things gives him no time to indulge the coquettish conceits in which the heroes of fashion indulge, as they hastily
reap the harvest of a passing season, while their vanity and
self-love are exacting and irritable, like a sort of custom-
house ever alert to seize a toll on everything that passes within
its ken.

Modeste was all the more delighted with the great surgeon
because he seemed struck by her extreme beauty—he, under
whose hands so many women had passed, and who for years
had been scrutinizing them with the lancet and microscope.

"It would really be too bad," said he, with the gallantry
which he could so well assume, in contrast to his habitual
abruptness, "that a mother should be deprived of seeing such
a lovely daughter."

Modeste herself waited on the great surgeon at the simple
luncheon he would accept.   She, with her father and Dumay,
escorted the learned man, for whom so many sick were longing, as far as the chaise which waited for him at the side gate,
and there, her eyes beaming with hope, she said once more to
Desplein—

"Then dear mamma will really see me?"

"Yes, my pretty will-o'-the-wisp, I promise you she shall,"
he replied, with a smile; "and I am incapable of deceiving
you, for I, too, have a daughter."

The horses whirled him off as he spoke the words, which
had an unexpected touch of feeling.   Nothing is more bewitching than the unforeseen peculiar to very clever men.

This visit was the event of the day, and it left a track of

light in Modeste's soul. The enthusiastic child admired without guile this man whose life was at everybody's command, and in whom the habit of contemplating physical suffering had overcome every appearance of egoism.

In the evening, when Gobenheim, the Latournelles, Canalis, Ernest, and the Duc d'Hérouville had assembled, they congratulated the Mignon family on the good news given them by Desplein. Then, of course, the conversation, led by Modeste, as we know her from her letters, turned on this man whose genius, unfortunately for his glory, could only be appreciated by the most learned men and the medical faculty. And Gobenheim uttered this speech, which is in our days the sanctifying anointing of genius in the ears of economists and bankers—

" He makes enormous sums."

" He is said to be very greedy ? " replied Canalis.

The praise lavished on Desplein by Modeste annoyed the poet. Vanity behaves like woman. They both believe that they lose something by praise or affection bestowed on another. Voltaire was jealous of the wit of a man whom Paris admired for two days, just as a duchess takes offense at a glance bestowed on her waiting-maid. So great is the avarice of these two feelings that they feel robbed of a pittance bestowed on the poor.

" And do you think, monsieur," asked Modeste, with a smile, " that a genius should be measured by the ordinary standard ? "

" It would first be necessary, perhaps," said Canalis, " to define a man of genius. One of his prime characteristics is inventiveness—the invention of a type, of a system, of a power. Napoleon was an inventor, apart from his other characteristics of genius. He invented his method of warfare. Walter Scott is an inventor, Linnæus was an inventor, so are Geoffroy Saint-Hilaire and Cuvier. Such men are geniuses above all else. They renew, or expand, or modify

science or art. But Desplein is a man whose immense talent
consists in applying laws that were previously discovered ; in
detecting, by natural intuition, the final tendency of every
temperament, and the hour marked out by nature for the
performance of an operation. He did not, like Hippocrates,
lay the foundations of the science itself. He has not discovered
a system, like Galen, Broussais, or Rasori. His is the genius
of the executant, like Moscheles on the piano, Paganini on
the violin, or Farinelli on his own larynx—men who display
immense powers, but who do not create music. Between
Beethoven and Madame Catalani you will allow that to him
should be awarded the crown of genius and suffering ; to her
a vast heap of five-franc pieces. We can pay our debt to
one, while the world must for ever remain in debt to the
other ! We owe more and more to Molière every day, and
we have already everpaid Baron."

"It seems to me that you are giving too large a share to
ideas, my dear fellow," said la Brière, in a sweet and gentle
voice that was in startling contrast to the poet's peremptory
style, for his flexible voice had lost its insinuating tone and
assumed the dominant ring of rhetoric. "Genius ought to
be estimated chiefly for its utility. Parmentier, Jacquard,
and Papin, to whom statues will one day be erected, were
also men of genius. They have in a certain direction altered,
or will alter, the face of nations. From this point of view
Desplein will always appear in the eyes of thinking men
accompanied by a whole generation whose tears and sufferings
have been alleviated by his mighty hand."

That Ernest should have expressed this opinion was enough
to prompt Modeste to contest it.

"In that case, monsieur," said she, "the man who should
find means to reap corn without spoiling the straw, by a machine that should do the work of ten laborers, would be a
man of genius?"

"Oh yes, my child," said Madame Mignon, " he would be

blessed by the poor, whose bread would then be cheaper; and he whom the poor bless is blessed by God."

"That is to give utility the preference over art," said Modeste, with a toss of her head.

"But for utility," said her father, "on what would art be founded? On what basis would it rest, on what would the poet live, and who would give him shelter, who would pay him?"

"Oh, my dear father, that is quite the view of a merchant captain, a Philistine, a counter-jumper. That Gobenheim or Monsieur de la Brière should hold it I can understand; they are interested in the solution of such social problems; but you, whose life has been so romantically useless to your age, since your blood spilt on the soil of Europe, and the terrible sufferings required of you by a Colossus, have not hindered France from losing ten departments which the Republic had conquered, how can you subscribe to a view so excessively 'out of date,' as the romantics have it? It is easy to see that you have dropped from China."

The disrespect of Modeste's speech was aggravated by the scornful and contemptuous-flippancy of the tone in which she intentionally spoke, and which astonished Madame Latournelle, Madame Mignon, and Dumay. Madame Latournelle, though she opened her eyes wide enough, could not see nor in the least comprehend what Modeste was driving at; Butscha, who was as alert as a spy, looked significantly at Monsieur Mignon on seeing his face flush with deep and sudden indignation.

"A little more, mademoiselle, and you would have failed in respect to your father," said the colonel with a smile, enlightened by Butscha's glance. "That is what comes of spoiling a child."

"I am an only daughter!" she retorted insolently.

"Unique!" said the notary, with emphasis.

"Monsieur," said Modeste to Latournelle, "my father is

very willing that I should educate him. He gave me life, I give him wisdom—he will still be my debtor.''

"But there is a way of doing it—and, above all, a time for it," interposed Madame Mignon.

"But mademoiselle is very right," said Canalis, rising, and placing himself by the ornate mantel in one of the finest postures of his collection of attitudes. "God in His foresight has given man food and clothing, and has not directly endowed him with art! He has said to man, ' To eat, you must stoop to the earth ; to think, you must uplift yourself to Me !' We need the life of the soul as much as the life of the body. Hence there are two forms of utility—obviously we do not wear books on our feet. From the utilitarian point of view, a canto of an epic is not to compare with a bowl of cheap soup from a charity kitchen. The finest idea in the world cannot take the place of the sail of a ship. An automatic boiler, no doubt, by lifting itself two inches, supplies us with calico thirty sous a yard cheaper ; but this machine and the inventions of industry do not breathe the life of the people, and will never tell the future that it has existed ; whereas Egyptian art, Mexican art, Greek or Roman art, with their masterpieces, stigmatized as useless, have borne witness to the existence of these nations through a vast space of time in places where great intermediate nations have vanished without leaving even a name-card, for lack of men of genius! Works of genius form the *summum* of a civilization and presuppose a great use. You, no doubt, would not think a pair of boots better in itself than a drama, nor prefer a windmill to the church of Saint-Ouen? Well, a nation is moved by the same spirit as an individual, and man's favorite dream is to survive himself morally, as he reproduces himself physically. What survives of a nation is the work of its men of genius.

"At this moment France is a vigorous proof of the truth of this proposition. She is assuredly outdone by England in industry, commerce, and navigation ; nevertheless, she leads the world, I believe, by her artists, her gifted men, and the taste of her products. There is not an artist, not a man of mark anywhere, who does not come to Paris to win his patent of mastery. There is at this day no school of painting but in France ; and we shall rule by the book more surely perhaps, and for longer, than by the sword.

"Under Ernest's system the flowers of luxury would be suppressed—the beauty of woman, music, painting, and poetry. Society would not, indeed, be overthrown; but who would accept life on such terms? All that is useful is horrible and ugly. The kitchen is indispensable in a house, but you take good care never to stay in it; you live in a drawing-room ornamented, as this is, with perfectly superfluous things. Of what use are those beautiful pictures and all this carved woodwork? Nothing is beautiful but what we feel to be useless. We have called the sixteenth century the age of the Renaissance with admirable accuracy of expression. That century was the dawn of a new world ; men will still talk of it when some preceding ages are forgotten, whose sole merit will be that they have existed—like the millions of beings that are of no account in a generation."

"'*Guenille, soit! ma guenille m'est chère*'* ('A poor thing, but mine own ')," said the Duc d'Hérouville playfully, during the silence that followed this pompous declamation of prose.

"But," said Butscha, taking up the cudgels against Canalis, "does the art exist which, according to you, is the sphere in which genius should disport itself? Is it not rather a magnificent fiction which social man is madly bent on believing? What need have I for a landscape in Normandy hanging in my room when I can go and see it so well done by God? We have in our dreams finer poems than the ' Iliad.' For a very moderate sum I can find at Valognes, at Carentan, as in Provence, at Arles, Venuses quite as lovely as Titian's. The ' Police News ' publishes romances, different, indeed, from

---

* Lit.: Be it rags! my rags are my entertainment.

Walter Scott's, but with terrible endings in real blood, and not in ink. Happiness and virtue are far above art and genius !"

"Bravo, Butscha!" cried Madame Latournelle.

"What did he say!" asked Canalis of la Brière,-ceasing to watch Modeste, in whose eyes and attitude he read the delightful evidence of her artless admiration.

The scorn with which he had been treated, and, above all, the girl's disrespectful speech to her father, had so depressed the unhappy la Brière that he made no reply; his gaze, sadly fixed on Modeste, betrayed absorbed meditation. The little clerk's argument was, however, repeated with some wit by the Duc d'Hérouville, who ended by saying that the raptures of Saint Theresa were far superior to the inventions of Lord Byron.

"Oh, Monsieur le Duc," remarked Modeste, "that is wholly personal poetry, while Lord Byron's or Molière's is for the benefit of the world——"

"Then you must make your peace with the Baron," interrupted her father quickly. "Now you are insisting that genius is to be useful, as much so as cotton; but you will, perhaps, think logic as stale and out of date as your poor old father."

Butscha, la Brière, and Madame Latournelle exchanged half-laughing glances, which spurred Modeste on in her career of provocation, all the more because for a moment she was checked.

"Nay, mademoiselle," said Canalis with a smile, "we have not fought nor even contradicted each other. Every work of art, whether in literature, music, painting, sculpture, or architecture, carries with it a positive social utility, like that of any other form of commercial produce. Art is the truest form of commerce; it takes it for granted. A book in these days helps its writer to pocket about ten thousand francs, and its production involves printing, paper-making,

type-founding, and the bookseller's trade ; that is to say, the
occupation of thousands of hands. The performance of a
symphony by Beethoven or of an opera by Rossini demands
quite as many hands, machines, and forms of industry.

"The cost of a building is a still more tangible answer to
the objection. It may, indeed, be said that works of genius
rest on a very costly basis, and are necessarily profitable to
the workingman."

Fairly started on this text, Canalis talked on for some minutes with a lavish use of imagery, and reveling in his own
words ; but it befell him, as often happens with great talkers,
to find himself at the end of his harangue just where he
started, and agreeing with la Brière, though he failed to perceive it.

"I discern with pleasure, my dear Baron," said the little
Duke slily, "that you will make a great constitutional
minister."

"Oh," returned Canalis, with an ostentatious flourish,
"what do we prove by all our discussions? The eternal truth
of this axiom, 'Everything is true and everything is false.'
Moral truths, like living beings, may be placed in an atmosphere where they change their appearance to the point of
being unrecognizable?"

"Society lives by condemned things," interposed the Duc
d'Hérouville.

"What flippancy!" said Madame Latournelle in a low
voice to her husband.

"He is a poet," said Gobenheim, who overheard her.

Canalis, who had soared ten leagues above his audience,
and who was, perhaps, right in his final philosophical dictum,
took the sort of chill he read on every face for a symptom of
ignorance ; but he saw that Modeste understood him, and was
content ; never discerning how offensive such a monologue is
to country folk, whose one idea is to prove to Parisians the
vitality, intelligence, and good judgment of the provinces.

" Is it long since you last saw the Duchesse de Chaulieu ? "
asked the Duke of Canalis, to change the subject.

" I saw her six days ago," replied Canalis.

" And is she well ? "

" Perfectly well."

" Remember me to her, pray, when you write."

" I hear she is charming," Modeste remarked to the Duke.

" Monsieur le Baron," said he, " knows more about that
than I do."

" She is more than charming," said Canalis, accepting the
Duke's perfidious challenge. " But I am partial, mademoiselle ; she has been my friend these ten years. I owe to her
all that may be good in me ; she has sheltered me from the
perils of the world. Beside, the Duc de Chaulieu started me
in the way I am going. But for their influence the King and
Princesses would often have forgotten a poor poet as I am ;
my affection, therefore, is always full of gratitude."

And he spoke with tears in his voice.

" How much we all ought to love the woman who has inspired you with such sublime song and such a noble sentiment," said Modeste with feeling. " Can one conceive of a
poet without a Muse ? "

" He would have no heart," said Canalis ; " he would
write verse as dry as Voltaire's—who never loved any one but
Voltaire."

" When I was in Paris," said Dumay, " did you not do me
the honor of assuring me that you felt none of the feelings
you expressed ? "

" A straight hit, my worthy soldier," replied the poet with
a smile ; " but you must understand that at the same time it
is allowable to have a great deal of heart in the intellectual
life as well as in real life. A man may express very fine sentiments without feeling them, or feel them without being able
to express them. La Brière, my friend there, loves to distraction," said he generously, as he looked at Modeste. "I, who

love at least as much as he does, believe—unless I am under
an illusion—that I can give my passion a literary form worthy
of its depth. Still, I will not answer for it, mademoiselle,"
he adroitly added, turning to Modeste with a rather over-elab-
orate grace, "that I shall not be bereft of my wits by to-
morrow——"

And thus the poet triumphed over every obstacle, burning
in honor of his love the sticks they tried to trip him up with,
while Modeste was dazzled by this Parisian brilliancy, which
was unfamiliar to her, and which lent a glitter to the orator's
rhetoric.

"What a mountebank!" said Butscha in a whisper to
Latournelle, after listening to a magniloquent tirade on the
Catholic religion, and the happiness of having a pious wife,
poured out in response to an observation from Madame
Mignon.

Modeste had a bandage over her eyes; the effect of his
delivery and the attention she intentionally devoted to Canalis
prevented her perceiving what Butscha saw and noted—the
declamatory tone, the lack of simplicity, rant taking the place
of feeling, and all the incoherence which prompted the clerk's
rather too severe epithet.

While Monsieur Mignon, Dumay, Butscha, and Latournelle
wondered at the poet's want of sequence, overlooking, indeed,
the inevitable digressions of conversation, which in France is
always very devious, Modeste was admiring the poet's versatility, saying to herself as she led him to follow the tortuous
windings of her fancy, "He loves me!"

Butscha, like all the other spectators of this performance,
as we must call it, was struck by the chief fault of all egoists,
which Canalis shows a little too much, like all men who are
accustomed to speechify in drawing-rooms. Whether he
knew beforehand what the other speaker meant to say, or
merely did not listen, or had the power of listening while
thinking of something else, Melchior wore the look of inat-

14

tention which is as disconcerting to another man's flow of
words as it is wounding to his vanity.

Not to attend to what is said is not merely a lack of politeness; it is an expression of contempt. And Canalis carries
this habit rather too far, for he often neglects to reply to a
remark that requires an answer, and goes off to the subject
he is absorbed in without any polite transition. Though this
form of impertinence may be accepted without protest from a
man of position, it nevertheless creates a leaven of hatred
and vengeful feeling at the bottom of men's hearts; in an
equal, it may even break up a friendship.

When by any chance Melchior compels himself to listen,
he falls into another failing—he only lends himself, he does
not give himself up. Nothing in social intercourse pays better
than the bestowal of attention. "Blessed are they that hear!"
is not only a precept of the Gospel, it is also an excellent
speculation; act on it, and you will be forgiven everything,
even vices. Canalis took much upon himself in the intention
of charming Modeste; but while he was sacrificing himself to
her, he was himself all the while with the others.

Modeste, pitiless for the ten persons she was martyrizing,
begged Canalis to read them some piece of his verse; she
wanted to hear a specimen of that much-praised elocution.

Canalis took the volume offered him by Modeste and cooed
—for that is the correct word—the poem that is supposed to
be his finest, an imitation of Moore's "Loves of the Angels,"
entitled "Vitalis," which was received with some yawns by
Mesdames Latournelle and Dumay, by Gobenheim and the
cashier.

"If you play whist well, monsieur," said Gobenheim,
offering him five cards spread out in a fan, "I have never met
with so accomplished a gentleman."

The remark made every one laugh, for it was the expression of the common wish.

"I play it well enough to be able to end my days in a

country town," replied Canalis. "There has, I dare say, been more of literature and conversation than whist players care to have," he added in an impertinent tone, flinging the book on to the side-table.

This incident shows what dangers are incurred by the hero of a salon when, like Canalis, he moves outside his orbit; he is then in the case of an actor who is a favorite with one particular public, but whose talent is wasted when he quits his own stage and ventures on to that of a superior theatre.

The Baron and the Duke were partners; Gobenheim played with Latournelle. Modeste sat down at the great poet's elbow, to the despair of Ernest, who marked on the capricious girl's countenance the progress of Canalis' fascination. La Brière had not known the power of seduction possessed by Melchior, and often denied by nature to genuine souls, who are generally shy. This gift demands a boldness and readiness of spirit which might be called the acrobatic agility of the mind; it even allows of a little part-playing; but is there not, morally speaking, always something of the actor in a poet? There is, indeed, a wide difference between expressing feelings we do not experience though we can imagine them in all their variety, and pretending to have them when they seem necessary to success on the stage of private life; and yet, if the hypocrisy needful to a man of the world has cankered the poet, he easily transfuses the powers of his talent into the expression of the required sentiment, just as a great man who has buried himself in solitude at last finds his heart overflowing into his brain.

"He is playing for millions," thought la Brière in anguish; "and he will act passion so well that Modeste will believe in it!"

And instead of showing himself more delightful and wittier than his rival, la Brière, like the Duc d'Hérouville, sat gloomy, uneasy, and on the watch; but while the courtier was studying the heiress' vagaries, Ernest was a prey to the misery of black and concentrated jealousy, and had not yet won a single glance from his idol. He presently went into the garden for a few minutes with Butscha.

"It is all over, she is crazy about him," said he. "I am worse than disagreeable—and, after all, she is right ! Canalis is delightful, he is witty even in his silence, he has passion in his eyes, poetry in his harangues——"

"Is he an honest man ?" asked Butscha.

"Oh, yes," replied la Brière. "He is loyal, chivalrous, and under Modeste's influence he is quite capable of getting over the little faults he has acquired under Madame de Chaulieu——"

"You are a good fellow !" exclaimed the little hunchback. "But is he capable of loving—will he love her ?"

"I do not know," replied Ernest. "Has she mentioned me ?" he asked after a short silence.

"Yes," said Butscha, and he repeated what Modeste had said about borrowing a disguise.

The young fellow threw himself on a seat and hid his face in his hands. He could not restrain his tears, and would not let Butscha see them; but the dwarf was the man to guess them.

"What is wrong, monsieur ?" asked he.

"She is right !" cried la Brière, suddenly sitting up. "I am a wretch."

He told the story of the trick he had been led into by Canalis, explaining to Butscha that he had wished to undeceive Modeste before she had unmasked ; and he overflowed in rather childish lamentations over the perversity of his fate. Butscha's sympathy recognized this as love in its most vigorous and youthful artlessness, in its genuine and deep anxiety.

"But why," said he, "do you not make the best of yourself to Mademoiselle Modeste, instead of leaving your rival to prance alone ?"

"Ah ! you evidently never felt your throat tighten as soon

as you tried to speak to her," said la Brière. "Do you not feel a sensation at the roots of your hair and all over your skin when she looks at you, even without seeing you?"

"Still you had your wits about you sufficiently to be deeply grieved when she as good as told her father that he was an old woman."

"Monsieur, I love her too truly not to have felt it like a dagger-thrust when I heard her thus belie the perfection I ascribed to her!"

"But Canalis, you see, justified her," replied Butscha.

"If she has more vanity than good feeling, she would not be worth regretting!" said Ernest.

At this moment Modeste came out to breathe the freshness of the starlit night with Canalis (who had been losing at cards), her father, and Madame Dumay. While his daughter walked on with Melchior, Charles Mignon left her and came up to la Brière.

"Your friend ought to have been an advocate, monsieur," said he with a smile, and looking narrowly at the young man.

"Do not be in a hurry to judge a poet with the severity you might exercise on an ordinary man, like me, for instance, Monsieur le Comte," said la Brière. "The poet has his mission. He is destined by nature to see the poetical side of every question, just as he expresses the poetry of everything; thus when you fancy that he is arguing against himself, he is faithful to his calling. He is a painter ready to represent either a Madonna or a courtesan. Molière is alike right in his pictures of old men and young men, and Molière certainly had a sound judgment. These sports of fancy which corrupt second-rate minds have no influence over the character of really great men."

Charles Mignon pressed the young fellow's hand, saying, "At the same time, this versatility might be used by a man to justify himself for actions diametrically antagonistic, especially in politics."

At this moment Canalis was saying in an insinuating voice, in reply to some saucy remark of Modeste's : " Ah, mademoiselle, never believe that the multiplicity of emotions can in any degree diminish strength of feeling.   Poets, more than other men, must love with constancy and truth.   In the first place, do not be jealous of what is called ' The Muse.' Happy is the wife of a busy man !   If you could but hear the lamentations of the wives who are crushed under the idleness of husbands without employment, or to whom wealth gives much leisure, you would know that the chief happiness of a Parisian woman is liberty, sovereignty in her home.   And we poets allow the wife to hold the sceptre, for we cannot possibly condescend to the tyranny exerted by small minds.   We have something better to do.   If ever I should marry, which I vow is a very remote disaster in my life, I should wish my wife to enjoy the perfect moral liberty which a mistress always preserves, and which is perhaps the source of all her seductiveness."

Canalis put forth all his spirit and grace in talking of love, marriage, the worship of woman, and arguing with Modeste, but presently Monsieur Mignon, who came to join them, seized a moment's silence to take his daughter by the arm and lead her back to Ernest, whom the worthy colonel had advised to attempt some explanation.

"Mademoiselle," said Ernest in a broken voice, " I cannot possibly endure to remain here the object of your scorn.   I do not defend myself, I make no attempt at justification ; I only beg to point out to you that before receiving your flattering letter addressed to the man and not to the poet—your last letter—I desired, and by a letter written at le Havre I intended, to dispel the mistake under which you wrote.   All the feelings I have had the honor of expressing to you are sincere.   A hope beamed on me when, in Paris, your father told me that he was poor ; but now, if all is lost, if nothing is left to me but eternal regrets, why should I stay where there is nothing for me but torture? Let me only take away with me one smile from you. It will remain graven on my heart."

"Monsieur," said Modeste, who appeared cold and absent-minded, "I am not the mistress here ; but I certainly should deeply regret keeping any one here who should find neither pleasure nor happiness in staying."

She turned away, and took Madame Dumay's arm to go back into the house. A few minutes later all the personages of this domestic drama, once more united in the drawing-room, were surprised to see Modeste sitting by the Duc d'Hérouville, and flirting with him in the best style of the most wily Parisienne. She watched his play, gave him advice when he asked it, and took opportunities of saying flattering things to him, placing the chance advantage of noble birth on the same level as that of talent or of beauty.

Canalis knew, or fancied he knew, the reason for this caprice; he had tried to pique Modeste by speaking of marriage as a disaster and seeming to be averse to it ; but, like all who play with fire, it was he who was burnt. Modeste's pride and disdain alarmed the poet ; he came up to her, making a display of jealousy all the more marked because it was assumed. Modeste, as implacable as the angels, relished the pleasure she felt in the exercise of her power, and naturally carried it too far. The Duc d'Hérouville had never been so well treated : a woman smiled on him !

At eleven o'clock, an unheard-of hour at the chalet, the three rivals left, the Duke thinking Modeste charming, Canalis regarding her as a coquette, and la Brière heart-broken by her relentlessness.

For a week the heiress still remained to her three admirers just what she had been on that evening, so that the poet seemed to have triumphed in spite of the whims and freaks which from time to time inspired some hopes in the Duc d'Hérouville. Modeste's irreverence to her father and the liberties she took with him ; her irritability toward her blind mother, as she half-grudgingly did her the little services which formerly had been the delight of her filial affection, seemed to be the outcome of a wayward temper and liveliness tolerated in her childhood. When Modeste went too far she would assert a code of her own, and ascribe her levity and fractiousness to her spirit of independence. She owned to Canalis and the Duke that she hated obedience, and regarded this as an obstacle in the way of marriage, thus sounding her suitors' character after the manner of those who pierce the soil to bring up gold, coal, stone, or water.

"I shall never find a husband," she said, the day before that on which the family were to reinstate themselves in the villa, "who will endure my caprices with such kindness as my father's, which has never failed for an instant, or the indulgence of my adorable mother."

"They know that you love them, mademoiselle," said la Brière.

"Be assured, mademoiselle, that your husband will know the full value of his treasure," added the Duke.

"You have more wit and spirit than are needed to break in a husband," said Canalis, laughing.

Modeste smiled, as Henri IV. may have smiled when, by extracting three answers to an insidious question, he had revealed to some foreign ambassador the character of his three leading ministers.

On the day of the dinner, Modeste, led away by her preference for Canalis, walked alone with him for some time up and down the graveled walk leading from the house to the lawn with its flower-beds. It was easy to perceive, from the poet's gestures and the young heiress' demeanor, that she was lending a favorable ear to Canalis, and the two Demoiselles d'Hérouville came out to interrupt a *tête-à-tête* that scandalized them. With the tact natural to women in such cases, they turned the conversation to the subject of the court, of the high position conferred by an office under the crown, explaining the difference subsisting between an appointment to the household and one held under the crown ; they tried, in fact, to intoxicate Modeste by appealing to her pride, and displaying to her one of the highest positions which a woman at that time could hope to attain.

"To have a duke in your son," cried the old lady, "is a positive distinction. The mere title is a fortune, out of reach of reverses, to bequeath to your children."

"To what ill-fortune," said Canalis, very ill pleased at this interruption to his conversation, "must we attribute the small success that the master of the horse has hitherto achieved in the matter in which that title is supposed to be of most service as supporting a man's pretensions?"

The two unmarried ladies shot a look at Canalis as full of venom as a viper's fangs, but were so put out of countenance by Modeste's sarcastic smile that they had not a word in reply.

"The master of the horse," said Modeste to Canalis, "has never blamed you for the diffidence you have learned from your fame ; why then grudge him his modesty?"

"Also," said the Duke's aunt, "we have not yet met with a wife worthy of my nephew's rank. Some we have seen who had merely the fortune that might suit the position ; others who, without the fortune, had indeed the right spirit ; and I must confess that we have done well to wait till God should give us the opportunity of making acquaintance with a young lady in whom should be united both the noble soul and the handsome fortune of a Duchesse d'Hérouville ! "

"My dear Modeste," said Hélène d'Hérouville, walking away a few steps with her new friend, "there are a thousand Barons de Canalis in the kingdom, and a hundred poets in Paris who are as good as he ; and he is so far from being a great man, that I, a poor girl, fated to take the veil for lack of a dower, would have nothing to say to him ! And you do not know, I dare say, that he is a man who has, for the last

ten years, been at the beck and call of the Duchesse de Chaulieu.   Really, none but an old woman of sixty could put up
with the endless little ailments with which, it is said, the poet
is afflicted, the least of which was unendurable in Louis XVI.
Still, the Duchess, of course, does not suffer from them as his
wife would; he is not so constantly with her as a husband
would be——"

And so by one of the manœuvres peculiar to woman against
woman, Hélène d'Hérouville whispered in every ear the
calumnies which women, jealous of Madame de Chaulieu,
propagated concerning the poet.   This trivial detail, not rare
in the gossip of young girls, shows that the Comte de la
Bastie's fortune was already made the object of ardent rivalry.

Within ten days, opinions at the chalet had varied consid-
erably about the three men who aspired to Modeste's hand.
This change, wholly to the disadvantage of Canalis, was
founded on considerations calculated to make the hero of any
form of fame reflect deeply.   When we see the passion with
which an autograph is craved, it is impossible to doubt that
public curiosity is strongly excited by celebrity.   Most pro-
vincials, it is evident, have no very exact idea of the manner
in which illustrious persons fasten their cravat, walk on the
boulevard, gape at the crows, or eat a cutlet; for, as soon as
they see a man wearing the halo of fashion, or resplendent
with popularity—more or less transient, no doubt, but always
the object of envy—they are ready to exclaim, "Ah! so
that is the thing!" or, "Well, that is odd!" or something
equally absurd.   In a word, the strange charm that is produced by every form of renown, even when justly acquired,
has no permanence.   To superficial minds, especially to the
sarcastic and the envious, it is an impression as swift as a
lightning-flash, and never repeated.   Glory, it would seem,
like the sun, is hot and luminous from afar, but, when we get
near, it is as cold as the peak of an Alp.   Perhaps a man is really
great only to his peers; perhaps the defects inherent in the

conditions of humanity are more readily lost to their eyes than to those of vulgar admirers. Thus, to be constantly pleasing, a poet would be compelled to display the deceptive graces of those persons who can win forgiveness for their obscurity by amiable manners and agreeable speeches, since, beside genius, the vapid drawing-room virtues and harmless domestic twaddle are exacted from him.

The great poet of the Faubourg Saint-Germain, who refused to yield to this law of society, found that insulting indifference soon took the place of the fascination at first caused by his conversation at evening parties. Cleverness too prodigally displayed produces the same effect on the mind as a shop full of cut-glass has on the eyes; this sufficiently explains that Canalis' glitter soon wearied those people who, to use their own words, like something solid. Then, under the necessity of appearing an ordinary man, the poet found many rocks ahead where la Brière could win the good opinion of those who, at first, had thought him sullen. They felt the desire to be revenged on Canalis for his reputation by making more of his friend. The most kindly people are so made. The amiable and unpretentious referendary shocked nobody's vanity; falling back on him, every one discerned his good heart, his great modesty, the discretion of a strong box, and delightful manners. On political questions the Duc d'Hérouville held Ernest far above Canalis. The poet, as erratic, ambitious, and mutable as Tasso, loved luxury and splendor, and ran into debt; while the young lawyer, even-minded, living prudently, and useful without officiousness, hoped for promotion without asking it, and was saving money meanwhile.

Canalis had indeed justified the good people who were watching him. For the last two or three days he had given way to fits of irritability, of depression, of melancholy, without any apparent cause—the caprices of temper that come of the nervous poetical temperament. These eccentricities—as they are called in a country town—had their cause in the wrong, which each day made worse, that he was doing to the Duchesse de Chaulieu, to whom he knew he ought to write, without being able to make up his mind to do it; they were anxiously noted by the gentle American and worthy Madame Latournelle, and more than once came under discussion between them and Madame Mignon. Canalis, knowing nothing of these discussions, felt their effect. He was no longer listened to with the same attention, the faces round him did not express the rapture of the first days, while Ernest was beginning to be listened to. For the last few days the poet had, therefore, been bent on captivating Modeste, and seized every moment when he could be alone with her to cast over her the tangles of the most impassioned language. Modeste's heightened color plainly showed the two Demoiselles d'Hérouville with what pleasure the heiress heard insinuating conceits charmingly spoken; and, uneasy at the poet's rapid advances, they had recourse to the *ultima ratio* of women in such predicaments—to calumny, which rarely misses its aim when it appeals to vehement physical repulsion.

As he sat down to dinner the poet saw a cloud on his idol's brow, and read in it Mademoiselle d'Hérouville's perfidy; so he decided that he must offer himself as a husband to Modeste at the first opportunity he should have of speaking to her. As he and the two noble damsels exchanged some subacid, though polite remarks, Gobenheim nudged Butscha, who sat next to him, to look at the poet and the master of the horse.

"They will demolish each other," said he in a whisper.

"Canalis has genius enough to demolish himself unaided," said the dwarf.

In the course of the dinner, which was extremely splendid and served to perfection, the Duke achieved a great triumph over Canalis. Modeste, whose riding-habit had arrived the evening before, talked of the various rides to be taken in the neighborhood. In the course of the conversation that ensued she was led to express a strong wish to see a hunt—a pleasure she had never known. The Duke at once proposed to arrange a hunt for Mademoiselle Mignon's benefit in one of the crown forest-lands a few leagues from le Havre. Thanks to his connection with the master of the King's hounds, the Prince de Cadignan, he had it in his power to show Modeste a scene of royal magnificence, to charm her by showing her the dazzling world of a court, and making her wish to enter it by marriage. The glances exchanged by the Duke and the two Demoiselles d'Hérouville, which Canalis happened to catch, distinctly said, "The heiress is ours!" enough to urge the poet, who was reduced to mere personal glitter, to secure some pledge of her affection without loss of time.

Modeste, somewhat scared at having gone further than she intended with the d'Hérouvilles, after dinner, when they were walking in the grounds, went forward a little distance in a rather marked manner, accompanied by Melchior. With a young girl's not illegitimate curiosity, she allowed him to guess the calumnies repeated by Hélène, and, on a remonstrance from Canalis, she pledged him to secrecy, which he promised.

"These lashes of the tongue," said he, "are fair war in the world of fashion; your simplicity is scared by them; for my part, I can laugh at them—nay, I enjoy them. Those ladies must think his lordship's interests seriously imperiled, or they would not have recourse to them."

Then, profiting by the opportunity given by such a piece of information, Canalis justified himself with so much mocking wit and passion so ingeniously expressed, while thanking Modeste for her confidence, in which he insisted in seeing a slight strain of love, that she found herself quite as deeply compromised toward the poet as she was toward the Duke. Canalis felt that daring was necessary; he declared himself in plain terms. He paid his vows to Modeste in a style

through which his poetic fancy shone like a moon ingeniously
staged, with a brilliant picture of herself—beautifully fair,
and arrayed to admiration for this family festival. The inspiration so cleverly called up, and encouraged by the complicity of the evening, the grove, the sky, and the earth, led
the grasping lover beyond all reason ; for he even talked of
his disinterestedness, and succeeded by the flowers of his eloquence in giving a new aspect to Diderot's stale theme of
" Five hundred francs and my Sophie," or the " Give me a
cottage and your heart ! " of every lover who knows that his
father-in-law has a fortune.

"Monsieur," said Modeste, after enjoying the music of
this concerto so admirably composed on "a familiar theme,"
"my parents leave me such freedom as has allowed me to
hear you ; but you must address yourself to them."

"Well, then," cried Canalis, "only tell me that if I get
their consent you will be quite satisfied to obey them."

"I know beforehand," said she, " that my father has some
wishes which might offend the legitimate pride of a family as
old as yours, for he is bent on transmitting his title and his
name to his grandsons."

"Oh, my dear Modeste, what sacrifice would I not make
to place my life in the hands of such a guardian angel as you
are ! "

"You must allow me not to decide my fate for life in
one moment," said she, going to join the Demoiselles
d'Hérouville.

These two ladies were at that minute flattering little Latournelle's vanity in the hope of securing him to their interests.
Mademoiselle d'Hérouville, to whom we must give the family
name to distinguish her from her niece Hélène, was convey-
ing to the notary that the place of president of the court at le
Havre, which Charles X. would give to a man recommended
by them, was an appointment due to his honesty and talents
as a lawyer. Butscha, who was walking with la Brière, in

great alarm at Melchior's audacity and rapid progress, found means to speak to Modeste for a few minutes at the bottom of the garden steps as the party went indoors to give themselves up to the vexations of the inevitable rubber.

"Mademoiselle, I hope you do not yet address him as Melchior," said he in an undertone.

"Not far short of it, my mysterious dwarf," she replied, with a smile that might have seduced an angel.

"Good God!" cried the clerk, dropping his hands, which almost touched the steps.

"Well, and is he not as good as that odious gloomy referendary in whom you take so much interest?" cried she, putting on for Ernest a haughty look of scorn, such as young girls alone have the secret of, as though their maidenhood lent them wings to soar so high. "Would your little Monsieur de la Brière take me without a settlement?" she added after a pause.

"Ask your father," replied Butscha, going a few steps on, so as to lead Modeste to a little distance from the windows. "Listen to me, mademoiselle. You know that I who speak to you am ready to lay down not my life only, but my honor for you, at any time, at any moment. So you can believe in me, you can trust me with things you would not perhaps tell your father. Well, has that sublime Canalis ever spoken to you in the disinterested way that allows you to cast such a taunt at poor Ernest?"

"Yes."

"And you believe him?"

"That, malignant clerk," said she, giving him one of the ten or twelve nicknames she had devised for him, "is, as it seems to me, casting a doubt on the strength of my self-respect."

"You can laugh, dear mademoiselle, so it cannot be serious. I can only hope that you are making a fool of him."

"What would you think of me, Monsieur Butscha, if I

thought I had any right to mock at either of the gentlemen who do me the honor to wish for me as a wife? I can tell you, Master John, that even when she appears to scorn the most contemptible admiration, a girl is always flattered at having it offered to her."

"Then I flatter you——?" said the clerk, his face lighting up as a town is illuminated on some great occasion.

" You——?" said she. " You give me the most precious kind of friendship, a feeling as disinterested as that of a mother for her child! Do not compare yourself to any one else, for even my father is obliged to yield to me." She paused. " I cannot tell you that I love you, in the sense men give to the word; but what I feel for you is eternal and can never know any change."

" Well, then," said Butscha, stooping to pick up a pebble that he might leave a kiss and a tear on the tip of Modeste's shoe, "let me watch over you as a dragon watches over a treasure. The poet spreads before you just now all the filigree of his elaborate phrases, the tinsel of his promises. He sang of love to the sweetest chord of his lyre, no doubt? If, when this noble lover is fully assured of your having but a small fortune, you should see his demeanor change; if you then find him cold and embarrassed, will you still make him your husband, still honor him with your esteem?"

" Can he be a Francisque Althor?" she asked, with an expression of the deepest disgust.

" Let me have the pleasure of working this transformation scene," said Butscha. " Not only do I intend that it shall be sudden, but I do not despair of restoring your poet to you afterward, in love once more, of making him blow hot and cold on your heart with as good a grace as when he argues for and against the same thing in the course of a single evening, sometimes without being aware of it——"

"And if you are right," said she, "whom can I trust?"

" The man who truly loves you."

"The little Duke?"

Butscha looked at Modeste. They both walked on a few steps in silence. The girl was impenetrable; she did not wince.

"Mademoiselle, will you allow me to put into words the thoughts that lurk at the bottom of your heart like water-mosses in a pool, and that you refuse to explain to yourself even?"

"Why, indeed!" cried Modeste, "is my privy councilor-in-waiting a mirror, too?"

"No, but an echo," he replied, with a little bow stamped with the utmost modesty. "The Duke loves you, but he loves you too well. I, a dwarf, have fully understood the exquisite delicacy of your soul. You would hate to be adored like the holy wafer in a monstrance. But, being so eminently a woman, you could no more bear to see a man of whom you were always secure perpetually at your feet, than you could endure an egoist like Canalis, who would always care more for himself than for you. Why? I know not. I would I could be a woman, and an old woman, to learn the reason of the pro-gramme I can read in your eyes, which is perhaps that of every girl.

"At the same time, your lofty soul craves for adoration. When a man is at your feet you cannot throw yourself at his. 'But you cannot go far in that way,' Voltaire used to say. So the little Duke has, morally speaking, too many genu-flexions, and Canalis not enough—not to say none at all. And I can read the mischief hidden in your smile when you are speaking to the master of the horse, when he speaks to you and you reply. You would never be unhappy with the Duke; everybody would be pleased if you chose him for your hus-band; but you would not love him. The coldness of egoism and the excessive fervor of perennial raptures no doubt have a negative effect on the heart of every woman.

"Obviously this is not the perpetual triumph that you would

15

enjoy in the infinite delights of such a marriage as that you dream of, in which you would find a submission to be proud of, great little sacrifices that are gladly unconfessed, successes looked forward to with rapture, and unforeseen magnanimity to which it is a joy to yield; in which a woman finds herself understood even to her deepest secrets, while her love is sometimes a protection to her protector——"

"You are a wizard!" cried Modeste.

"Nor will you meet with that enchanting equality of feeling, that constant sharing of life, and that certainty of giving happiness which makes marriage acceptable, if you marry a Canalis, a man who thinks only of himself, to whom *I* is the only note in the scale, and whose attention has not yet condescended so low as to listen to your father or the Duke. An ambitious man, not of the first class, to whom your dignity and supremacy matter little, who will treat you as a necessary chattel in his house, who insults you already by his indifference on points of honor. Yes, if you allowed yourself to go so far as to slap your mother, Monsieur Canalis would shut his eyes that he might not see your guilt, so hungry is he for your fortune!

"So, mademoiselle, I was not thinking of the great poet, who is but a little actor, nor of my lord Duke, who would be for you a splendid match, but not a husband——"

"Butscha, my heart is a blank page on which you yourself write what you read," replied Modeste. "You are carried away by your provincial hatred of everything that compels you to look above your head. You cannot forgive the poet for being a political man, for having an eloquent tongue, and a splendid future; you calumniate his purpose——"

"His, mademoiselle! He would turn his back on you within twenty-four hours with the meanness of a Vilquin."

"Well, make him play such a farcical scene, and——"

"Ay, and in every key; in three days—on Wednesday— do not forget. Until then, mademoiselle, amuse yourself by making the musical box play all its airs, that the vile discords of the antiphony may come out all the more clearly."

Modeste gayly returned to the drawing-room, where of all the men present, la Brière alone, seated in the recess of a window—whence, no doubt, he had been looking at his idol —rose at her entrance, as if an usher had shouted, "The Queen!" It was a respectful impulse, full of the eloquence peculiar to action, which surpasses that of the finest speech. Spoken love is not to be compared with love in action—every girl of twenty is fifty as concerns this axiom; this is the seducer's strongest argument.

Instead of looking Modeste in the face, as Canalis did, bowing to her as an act of public homage, the disdained lover watched her with a slow side-glance, as humble as Butscha's, almost timid. The young heiress observed this demeanor as she went to place herself by Canalis, in whose game she affected an interest. In the course of the conversation la Brière learned, from a remark she made to her father, that Modeste intended to begin riding again on the following Wednesday, and she mentioned that she had no riding-whip suitable to match with her handsome new habit. Ernest flashed a glance at the dwarf like a spark of fire, and a few minutes later they were walking together on the terrace.

"It is now nine o'clock," said la Brière. "I am off to Paris as fast as my horse will carry me. I can be there by ten to-morrow morning. My dear Butscha, from you she will accept a gift with pleasure, for she has a great regard for you; let me give her a riding-whip in your name; and, be-lieve me, in return for such an immense favor you have in me not indeed a friend, but a slave!"

"Go; you are happy," said the clerk. "You have money."

"Tell Canalis from me that I shall not be in to-night, and that he must invent some excuse for my absence for two days."

An hour later Ernest had set out on horseback for Paris, where he arrived after twelve hours' riding, his first care being to secure a place in the mail-coach for le Havre on the following day. He then went to the three first jewelers in Paris, comparing handles of riding-whips, and seeking what art could produce of the most royal perfection. He found one made by Stidmann for a Russian lady, who, after ordering it, had been unable to pay for it—a fox-hunt wrought in gold, with a ruby at the top, and exorbitantly expensive as compared with a referendary's stipend ; all his savings were swallowed up, amounting to seven thousand francs. Ernest gave a sketch of the arms of la Bastie, allowing twenty hours for them to be engraved instead of those that were on it. This handle, a masterpiece of workmanship, was fitted to an india-rubber whip, and placed in a red morocco case, lined with velvet, with a monogram of two M's on the top.

By Wednesday morning la Brière had returned by the mail, in time to breakfast with Canalis. The poet had explained his secretary's absence by saying that he was busy with some work forwarded from Paris. Butscha, who had gone to the coach office to hold out a welcoming hand to Ernest on the arrival of the mail, flew to give this work of art to Françoise Cochet, desiring her to place it on Modeste's dressing-table.

"You are going out riding, no doubt, with Mademoiselle Modeste," said Butscha, on returning to Canalis' villa to inform Ernest, by a side-glance, that the whip had safely reached its destination.

"I !" said la Brière. "I am going to bed."

"Well !" exclaimed Canalis, looking at his friend, "I do not understand you at all."

Breakfast was ready, and the poet naturally invited the clerk to sit down with them. Butscha had stayed, intending to get himself invited if necessary by la Brière, seeing on Germain's countenance the success of a hunchback's trick, of which his promise to Modeste may have given a hint.

"Monsieur was very wise to keep Monsieur Latournelle's clerk," said Germain in his master's ear. Canalis and Germain, on a hint from the latter, passed into the drawing-room. "'This morning I went out to see some fishing, an expedition to which I was invited the day before yesterday by the owner of a boat I have made acquaintance with.''

Germain did not confess that he had had such bad taste as to play billiards in a café in le Havre, where Butscha had surrounded him with a number of his friends in order to be able to work upon him.

"What then?" said Canalis. "Come to the point, and at once."

"Monsieur le Baron, I heard a discussion about Monsieur Mignon, which I did my best to keep going—no one knew who I lived with. I tell you, Monsieur le Baron, everybody in le Havre says that you are running your head against a wall. Mademoiselle de la Bastie's fortune is, like her name, very modest. The ship on which the father came home is not his own ; it belongs to some China merchants, with whom he has to settle, and things are said about it that are far from flattering to the colonel. Having heard that you and Monsieur le Duc were rivals for Mademoiselle de la Bastie, I take the liberty of mentioning it ; for, between you and him, it is better that his lordship should swallow the bait. On my way back I took a turn on the quay, past the theatre, where the merchants walk up and down, and I pushed my way boldly among them. These worthy folk, seeing a well-dressed man, began to talk about the affairs of the town ; from one thing to another I led them to speak of Colonel Mignon ; and they were so much of the same mind as the fishermen that I felt it my duty to speak. That is why I left you, sir, to get up and dress alone——"

"What is to be done?" cried Canalis, feeling that he was too deeply pledged to withdraw from his promises to Modeste.

"You know my attachment to you, sir," said Germain,

seeing that the poet was thunderstruck, " and you will not be
surprised if I offer a piece of advice. If you can make this
clerk drunk, he will let the cat out of the bag, and if he
won't open his mouth for two bottles of champagne, he certainly will for the third. It would be a strange thing, too,
if monsieur, who will certainly be an ambassador one day, for
Philoxène heard Madame la Duchesse say so—if you, sir,
cannot get round a country lawyer's clerk.''

At this moment Butscha, the unknown author of this fishing expedition, was begging the referendary to say nothing
about his journey to Paris, and not to interfere with his manœuvres at breakfast. Butscha meant to take advantage of a
reaction of feeling unfavorable to Charles Mignon, which had
set in at le Havre.

This was the cause of that reaction : Monsieur le Comte de
la Bastie had entirely ignored those of his former friends who,
during his absence, had neglected his wife and children. On
hearing that a dinner was to be given at the Villa Mignon,
each one flattered himself that he would be among the guests,
and expected an invitation ; but when it was known that only
Gobenheim, the Latournelles, the Duke, and the two Parisians were to be asked, there was a loud outcry at the merchant's arrogance ; his marked avoidance of seeing anybody
and of ever going down to le Havre was commented on and
attributed to scorn, on which the whole town avenged itself
by casting doubts on Mignon's sudden wealth. By dint of
gossip everybody soon ascertained that the money advanced
to Vilquin on the villa had been found by Dumay. This fact
gave the most malignant persons grounds for the libelous
supposition that Charles had confided to Dumay's known devotion the funds concerning which he anticipated litigation
on the part of his so-called partners in Canton. Charles' reti-
cence, for his constant aim was to conceal his wealth, and
the gossip of his servants, who had been put on their guard,
lent an appearance of truth to these monstrous fables, believed

by all who were governed by the spirit of detraction that animates rival traders. In proportion as parochial pride had formerly cried up his immense fortune as one of the makers of le Havre, so now provincial jealousy cast doubts on it.

Butscha, to whom the fishermen of the port owed more than one good turn, desired them to be secret, and to cram their new friend. He was well served. The owner of the boat told Germain that a cousin of his, a sailor, was coming from Marseilles, having just been paid off in consequence of the sale of the brig in which the colonel had come home. The vessel was being sold by order of one Castagnould, and the cargo—according to the cousin—was worth only three or four hundred thousand francs at most.

"Germain," said Canalis, as the servant was leaving the room, "bring us up some champagne and some bordeaux. A member of the legal factor of Normandy must carry away some memories of a poet's hospitality. And he has the wit of 'le Figaro,'" added Canalis, laying his hand on the dwarf's shoulder; "that *petit-journal* brilliancy must be made to sparkle and foam with the wine of champagne; we will not spare ourselves either, Ernest! Why, it is two years at least since I last got tipsy," he added, turning to la Brière.

"With wine? That I can quite understand," replied the clerk. "You get tipsy with yourself every day! In the matter of praise, you drink your fill. You are handsome; you are famous during your lifetime; your conversation is on a level with your genius; and you fascinate all the women, even my master's wife. Loved as you are by the most beautiful Sultana Valideh I ever saw—it is true, I have never seen another—you can, if you choose, marry Mademoiselle de la Bastie. Why, merely with making this inventory of your present advantages, to say nothing of the future—a fine title, a peerage, an embassy! I am quite fuddled, like the men who bottle wine for other people to drink."

"All this social magnificence is nothing," replied Canalis,

"without that which gives them value—a fortune! Here
we are men among men; fine sentiments are delightful in
stanzas."

"And in certain circum*stanzas*," said Butscha, with a significant shrug.

"You, a master of the mystery of settlements," said the
poet, smiling at the pun, "must know as well as I do that
cottage rhymes to nothing better than pottage."

At table Butscha played with signal success the part of le
Rigaudin in "la Maison en Loterie," alarming Ernest, to
whom the jests of a lawyer's office were unfamiliar; they are
a match for those of the studio. The clerk repeated all the
scandal of le Havre, the history of every fortune, of every
boudoir, and of all the crimes committed just outside the
pale of the law, what is called sailing as close hauled as possible (in Normandy, *se tirer d'affaire comme on peut*). He
spared no one, and his spirits rose with the stream of wine he
poured down his throat like storm-water through a gutter.

"Do you know, la Brière," said Canalis, filling up Butscha's
glass, "that this brave boy would be a first-rate secretary to
an ambassador?"

"And cut out his master!" retorted the dwarf with a look
at Canalis, of insolence redeemed by the sparkle of carbonic
acid gas. "I have enough spirit of intrigue and little enough
gratitude to climb on to your shoulders. A poet supporting
an abortion! Well, it has been seen, and pretty frequently—
in libraries. Why, you are staring at me as if I were swallowing swords. Heh! my dear, great genius, you are a very
superior man; you know full well that gratitude is a word for
idiots; it is to be found in the dictionary, but not in the
human heart. I O U is a formula unhonored on the green
banks of Parnassus or Pindus. Do you suppose I feel the
debt to my master's wife for having brought me up? Why,
the whole town has paid it off in esteem, praise, and admiration, the most precious of all coin. I do not see the virtue

"YOU WILL MAKE ME DRUNK," SAID THE CLERK.

that is merely an investment for the benefit of one's vanity.
Men make a trade of reciprocal services; the word gratitude
represents the debit side, that is all.

"As to intrigue, I adore it! What!" he went on, in reply
to a gesture from Canalis, "do you not delight in the faculty
which enables a crafty man to get the upper hand of a man
of genius, which requires constant observation of the vices
and weaknesses of our betters, and a sense of the nick of
time for everything? Ask diplomacy whether the triumph
of cunning over strength is not the most delightful success
there is. If I were your secretary, Monsieur le Baron, you
would soon be prime minister, because it would be to my
interest! Now, would you like a sample of my little talents
of that kind? Hearken! You love Mademoiselle Modeste
to distraction, and you are very right. In my opinion, the
girl is a genuine Parisienne, for here and there a Parisienne
sprouts in the country. Our Modeste would be a wife to
push a man. She has that sort of thing," said he, giving his
hand a twirl in the air. "You have a formidable rival in the
Duke. Now, what will you give me to pack him off within
three days?"

"Let us finish this bottle," said the poet, refilling Butscha's
glass.

"You will make me drunk!" said the clerk, swallowing
down his ninth glass of champagne. "Is there a bed where
I may sleep for an hour? My master is as sober as a camel,
the old fox, and Madame Latournelle too. They would both
be hard upon me, and they would have good reason, while I
should have lost mine, and I have some work to do."

Then going back to a former subject without any transition,
after the manner of a man when he is screwed, he exclaimed—

"And then, what a memory I have! It is a match for my
gratitude."

"Butscha!" exclaimed the poet, "just now you said that
you had no gratitude; you are contradicting yourself."

"Not at all," said the clerk. "Forgetting almost always means remembering! Now, then, on we go! I am made to be a secretary."

"And how will you set to work to get rid of the Duke?" asked Canalis, charmed to find the conversation tending naturally to the subjects he aimed at.

"That—is no concern of yours," said Butscha, with a tremendous hiccough.

Butscha rolled his head on his shoulders, and his eyes from Germain to la Brière, and from la Brière to Canalis, in the manner of a man who feels intoxication creeping over him, and wants to know in what esteem he is held; for in the wreck of drunkenness it may be noted that self-esteem is the last sentiment to float.

"Look here, great poet, you are a jolly fellow, you are. Do you take me for one of your readers, you who sent your friend to Paris to procure information concerning the house of Mignon. I humbug, you humbug, we humbug. Well and good; but do me the honor to believe that I am clear-headed enough always to keep as much conscience as I need in my sphere of life. As head clerk to Maître Latournelle my heart is a padlocked despatch-box, my lips never breathe a word of any paper concerning the clients. I know everything, and I know nothing. And then, passion is no secret: I love Modeste, she is a pupil of mine, she must marry well; and I could get round the Duke if necessary. But you are going to marry——"

"Germain, coffee and liqueurs," said Canalis to his man-servant.

"Liqueurs?" repeated Butscha, holding up a forbidding hand like a too knowing maiden putting aside some little temptation. "Oh, my poor work! By the way, there is a marriage contract to be drawn up, and my second clerk is as stupid as a matrimonial bargain, and quite capable of p-p-poking a penknife through the bride's personal property. He thinks himself a fine fellow because he measures nearly six feet—the idiot!"

"Here, this is créme de thé, a West India liqueur," said Canalis. "You who are Mademoiselle Modeste's most trusty adviser——"

"Her adviser?——"

"Well, do you think she loves me?"

"Ye-e-es, more than she loves the Duke," drawled the dwarf, rousing himself from a sort of torpor, which he acted to admiration. "She loves you for your disinterestedness. She told me that for you she felt equal to the greatest sacrifices, to giving up dress, spending only a thousand francs a year, devoting her life to prove to you that in marrying her you would have done a good stroke of business. And she is devilish honest (hiccough), I can tell you, and well informed ; there is nothing that girl does not know."

"That and three hundred thousand francs," said Canalis.

"Oh! there may be as much as you say," replied the clerk with enthusiasm. "Mignon Papa—and you see he is really a Mignon, a dear papa, that's what I like him for—to marry his only daughter—well, he would strip himself of everything. The colonel has been accustomed under your restoration to live on half-pay (hiccough), and he will be quite happy living with Dumay, speculating in a small way at le Havre ; he will be sure to give the child his three hundred thousand francs. Then we must not forget Dumay, who means to leave his fortune to Modeste. Dumay, you know, is a Breton ; his birth gives security to the bargain ; he never changes his mind, and his fortune is quite equal to his master's. At the same time, since they listen to me at least as much as to you, though I do not talk so much nor so well, I said to them, 'You are putting too much money into your house; if Vilquin leaves it on your hands, there are two hundred thousand francs that will bring you no return. There will be only a hundred thousand francs left to turn over,

and that, in my opinion, is not enough.' At this moment
the colonel and Dumay are talking it over. Take my word
for it, Modeste is rich. The people of the town talk nonsense, they are envious. Why, who in the department has
such a portion?" said Butscha, holding up his fingers to
count. "Two to three hundred thousand francs in hard
cash!" said he, folding down his left thumb with the fore-
finger of his right hand. "That is for one. The freehold
of the Villa Mignon," and he doubled down his left fore-
finger, "for two; Dumay's fortune for three," he added,
ticking it off on the middle finger. "Why, little Mother
Modeste is a lady with six hundred thousand francs of her
own when the two old soldiers shall have gone aloft to take
further orders from God A'mighty."

This blunt and artless communication, broken by sips of
liqueur, sobered Canalis as much as it seemed to intoxicate
Butscha. To the lawyer's clerk, a mere provincial, this fortune was evidently colossal. He let his head drop on the
palm of his right hand, and with the elbow majestically resting on the table, he sat blinking and talking to himself: "In
twenty years, at the pace the code is taking us, melting down
fortunes by the process of subdivision, an heiress with six
hundred thousand francs will be as rare as disinterestedness
in a money-lender. You may say that Modeste will spend at
least twelve thousand francs a year, the interest of her fortune; but she is a very nice girl—very nice—very nice. She
is as you may say—a poet must have imagery—she is an
ermine as knowing as a monkey."

"And what did you tell me?" cried Canalis in an undertone to la Brière. "That she had six millions?"

"My dear fellow," said Ernest, "allow me to remark
that I could say nothing. I am bound by an oath, and
it is perhaps saying more than I ought to tell you——"

"An oath! and to whom?"

"To Monsieur Mignon."

"Why, Ernest, when you know how indispensable fortune is to me"—Butscha was snoring—"you who know my position and all that I should lose in the Rue de Grenelle by marrying—you would have coolly allowed me to plunge in?" said Canalis, turning pale. "But this is a matter between friends; and our friendship, my boy, is a compact of a far older date than this that the wily Provençal has required of you."

"My dear fellow," said Ernest, "I love Modeste too well to——"

"Idiot, take her!" cried the poet. "So break your oath——"

"Do you solemnly promise, on your honor as a man, to forget what I tell you, and to be just the same to me as though I had never confided it to you, come what may?"

"I swear it by the sacred memory of my mother!"

"Well, when I was in Paris, Monsieur Mignon told me that he was very far from having such a colossal fortune as the Mongenods had spoken of. The colonel intends to give his daughter two hundred thousand francs. But then, Melchior, was the father suspicious? or was he sincere? It is no concern of mine to solve that question. If she should condescend to choose me, Modeste, with nothing, should be my wife."

"A blue-stocking, appallingly learned, who has read everything and knows everything—in theory," cried Canalis, in reply to a protesting gesture of la Brière's; "a spoilt child, brought up in luxury during her early years, and weaned from it for the last five. Oh, my poor friend, think, pause, consider——"

"Ode and Code!" said Butscha, rousing himself. "You go in for the Ode, and I for the Code; there is only a C between. Code, from coda, a tail! You have treated me handsomely, and I like you—don't have anything to do with the Code. Listen; a piece of good advice is not a bad return

for your wine and your crème de thé. Old Mignon is
cream too, the cream of good fellows. Well, trot out your
horse, he is riding out with his daughter; you can speak
frankly to him; ask him about her marriage portion; he will
give you a plain answer, and you will see to the bottom of
things as sure as I am tipsy and you are a great man; but then
there must be no mistake, we leave le Havre together, I
suppose? I am to be your secretary, since this little chap,
who thinks I am drunk and is laughing at me, is going to
leave you. Go ahead. March!—and leave him to marry
the girl."

Canalis went to dress.

"Not a word; he is rushing on suicide," said Butscha (as
cool as Gobenheim) to la Brière, very quietly; and he tele-
graphed behind Canalis a signal of scorn familiar to the Paris
street boy. "Good-by, master," he went on at the top of his
voice, "may I go and get forty winks in Madame Amaury's
summer-house?"

"Make yourself at home," replied the poet as Butscha
staggered out.

The clerk, loudly laughed at by Canalis' three servants,
made his way to the summer-house, plunging into flower-beds
and baskets with the perverse grace of an insect describing its
endless zigzags as it tries to escape through a closed window.
He scrambled up into the gazebo, and when the servants had
gotten indoors he sat down on a wooden bench and gave himself up to the joys of triumph. He had fooled the superior
man; not only had he snatched off his mask, but he had seen
him untie the strings, and he laughed as an author laughs at
his piece, with a full appreciation of the value of this *vis
comica*.

"Men are tops!" cried he; "you have only to find the
end of the string that is wound around them. Why, any one
could make me faint away by simply saying, 'Mademoiselle
Modeste has fallen off her horse and broken her leg.'"

A few minutes later, Modeste, wearing a bewitching habit of dark-green kerseymere, a little hat with a green veil, doe-skin gloves, and velvet boots, over which the lace frills of her drawers fell gracefully, had mounted her handsomely saddled pony, and was showing to her father and the Duc d'Hérou-ville the pretty gift she had just received; she was delighted with it, seeing in it one of those attentions which most flatter a woman.

"Was it you, Monsieur le Duc?" she said, holding out the sparkling end of her whip. "There was a card on it with the words, 'Guess if you can,' and a row of dots. Françoise and Madame Dumay ascribe this charming surprise to Butscha; but my dear Butscha is not rich enough to pay for such fine rubies! And my father, on my saying on Sunday evening that I had no whip, sent for that one from Rouen."

Modeste pointed to a whip in her father's hand with a handle set closely with turquoises, a fashionable novelty then, but now rather common.

"I only wish, mademoiselle—I would give ten years of my life to have the right of offering such a magnificent jewel," replied the Duke politely.

"Ah! then here is the audacious man," cried Modeste, seeing Canalis come up on horseback. "None but a poet can find such exquisite things. Monsieur," she went on to Melchior, "my father will be angry with you; you are justi-fying those who blame you for your extravagance."

"Hah!" cried Canalis simply, "then that is what took la Brière from le Havre to Paris as fast as he could ride."

"Your secretary took such a liberty!" said Modeste, turn-ing pale, and flinging the whip to Françoise Cochet with a vehemence expressive of the deepest contempt. "Give me back that whip, father!"

"The poor boy is lying on his bed broken with fatigue!" Melchior went on, as they followed the girl, who had gone off-at a gallop. "You are hard, mademoiselle. 'I have this chance alone of reminding her of my existence,' was what he said."

"And could you esteem a woman who was capable of preserving keepsakes from every comer?" asked Modeste.

Modeste, who was surprised at receiving no reply from Canalis, ascribed his inattention to the sound of the horse's hoofs.

"How you delight in tormenting those who are in love with you!" said the Duke. "Your pride and dignity so entirely belie your vagaries that I am beginning to suspect that you do yourself injustice by deliberately planning your malicious tricks!"

"What! you have just discovered that, Monsieur le Duc?" returned she, with a laugh. "You have exactly as much insight as a husband!"

For about a kilometre they rode on in silence. Modeste was surprised at being no longer aware of the flaming glances of Canalis, whose admiration for the beauties of the landscape seemed rather more than was natural. On the preceding evening Modeste had pointed out to the poet a beautiful effect of color in the sunset over the sea, and, finding him as speechless as a mute, had said—

"Well, do you not see it all?"

"I see nothing but your hand," he had replied.

"Does Monsieur de la Brière know how to ride?" Modeste asked, to pique him.

"He is not a very good horseman, but he goes," replied the poet, as cold as Gobenheim had been before the colonel's return.

As they went along a cross-road, down which Monsieur Mignon turned to go through a pretty valley to a hill overlooking the course of the Seine, Canalis let Modeste and the Duke go forward, slackening his speed so as to bring his horse side by side with the colonel's.

"Monsieur le Comte," said he, "you are a frank soldier, so you will regard my openness as a claim to your esteem. When an offer of marriage, with all the too barbarous, or, if you will, too civilized discussions to which it gives rise, is made through a third person, every one suffers. You and I are both men of perfect discretion, and you, like me, are past the age for surprises, so let us speak as man to man. I will set the example. I am nine-and-twenty, I have no landed estate, I am an ambitious man. That I ardently admire Mademoiselle Modeste you must have seen. Now, in spite of the faults your charming daughter delights in affecting——"

"To say nothing of those she really has," said the colonel, smiling.

"I should be glad, indeed, to make her my wife, and I believe I could make her happy. The whole question of my future life turns on the point of fortune. Every girl who is open to marriage must be loved whatever comes of it; at the same time you are not the man to get rid of your dear Modeste without a portion, and my position would no more allow of my marrying 'for love,' as the phrase is, than of my proposing to a girl without a fortune at least equal to my own. My salary and some sinecures, with what I get from the Academy, and my writings, come to about thirty thousand francs a year, a fine income for a bachelor. If my wife and I between us have sixty thousand francs a year, I could continue to live on much the same footing as at present. Have you a million francs to give Mademoiselle Modeste?"

"Oh! monsieur, we are very far from any agreement," said the colonel jesuitically.

"Well, then, we have said nothing about the matter—only whistled," said Canalis anxiously. "You will be quite satisfied with my conduct, Monsieur le Comte; I shall be one more of the unfortunate men crushed by that charming young lady. Give me your word that you will say nothing of this to anybody, not even to Mademoiselle Modeste; for," he

16

added, by way of consolation, "some change might occur in my position which would allow of my asking her hand without a settlement."

"I swear it," said the colonel. "You know, monsieur, with what exaggerated language the public, in the provinces as in Paris, talk of fortunes made and lost. Success and failure are alike magnified, and we are never so lucky or so unlucky as report says. In business there is no real security but investment in land when cash transactions are settled. I am awaiting with anxious impatience the reports of my various agents; nothing is as yet concluded—neither the sale of my merchandise and my ship, nor my account with China. I shall not for the next ten months know the amount of my capital. However, in Paris, when talking to Monsieur de la Brière, I guaranteed a settlement on my daughter of two hundred thousand francs in money down. I intend to purchase a landed estate and settle it in tail on my grandchildren, obtaining for them a grant of my titles and coat-of-arms."

After the first words of this speech Canalis had ceased to listen.

The four riders now came out on a wide road and rode abreast up to the plateau, which commands a view of the rich valley of the Seine towards Rouen, while on the other horizon they could still see the line of the sea.

"Butscha was indeed right, God is a great landscape-maker," said Canalis, as he looked down on the panorama, unique among those for which the hills above the Seine are justly famous.

"But it is when out hunting, my dear Baron," said the Duke, "when nature is roused by a voice, by a stir in the silence, that the scenery, as we fly past, seems most really sublime with the rapid change of effect."

"The sun has an inexhaustible palette," said Modeste, gazing at the poet in a sort of bewilderment. On her making a remark as to the absence of mind she observed in Canalis, he replied that he was "reveling in his own thoughts," an excuse which writers can make in addition to those common to other men.

"Are we really blest when we transfer our life to the centre of the world, and add to it a thousand factitious needs and overwrought vanities?" asked Modeste, as she contemplated the calm and luxuriant champaign which seemed to counsel philosophical quietude.

"Such bucolics, mademoiselle, are always written on tables of gold," said the poet.

"And imagined, perhaps, in a garret," interposed the colonel.

Modeste gave Canalis a piercing look, and saw him flinch; there was a sound of bells in her ears; for a moment everything grew dark before her; then, in a hard, cold tone, she exclaimed—

"Ah! it is Wednesday!"

"It is not with the idea of flattering a merely transient fancy of yours, mademoiselle," said the Duc d'Hérouville solemnly—for this little scene, so tragical to Modeste, had given him time for thought—"but, I assure you, I am so utterly disgusted with the world, the court, and Paris life, that, for my part, with a Duchesse d'Hérouville so full of charm and wit as you are, I could pledge myself to live like a philosopher in my château, doing good to those about me, reclaiming my alluvial flats, bringing up my children——"

"This shall be set down to your credit, Duke," said Modeste, looking steadily at the noble gentleman. "You flatter me," she added, "for you do not think me frivolous, and you believe that I have enough resources in myself to live in solitude. And that perhaps will be my fate," she added, looking at Canalis with a compassionate expression.

"It is the lot of all small fortunes," replied the poet. "Paris requires Babylonian luxury. I sometimes wonder how I have managed to live till now."

"The King is Providence to you and me," said the Duke frankly, "for we both live on his majesty's bounty. If, since the death of Monsieur le Grand, as Cinq-Mars was called, we had not always held his office in our family, we should have had to sell Hérouville to be demolished by the Black Gang. Believe me, mademoiselle, it is to me a terrible humiliation to mix up financial considerations with the thought of marriage——"

The candor of this avowal, which came from the heart, and the sincerity of this regret, touched Modeste.

"In these days," said the poet, "nobody in France, Monsieur le Duc, is rich enough to commit the folly of marrying a woman for her personal merits, her charm, her character, or her beauty——"

The colonel looked at Canalis with a strange expression, after studying his daughter, whose face no longer expressed any astonishment.

"Then for a man of honor," he said, "it is a noble use of riches to devote them to repair the ravages that time has wrought on our old historical families."

"Yes, papa," said the girl gravely.

The colonel asked the Duke and Canalis to dine at the villa, without ceremony, in their riding dress, and set them the example by not changing his for dinner. When, on their return, Modeste went to change her dress, she looked curiously at the trinket that had come from Paris, and that she had so cruelly disdained.

"How exquisitely such work is done nowadays," said she to Françoise Cochet, who was now her maid.

"And that poor young gentleman, mademoiselle, ill of a fever——"

"Who told you so?"

"Monsieur Butscha. He came here just now to bid me say you had no doubt found out that he had kept his word on the day he named."

Modeste went down stairs, dressed with queenly simplicity.

"My dear father," said she, quite audibly, taking the colonel's arm, "will you go and ask after Monsieur de la Brière, and oblige me by taking back his present. You may put it to him that my small fortune, as well as my own taste, prohibits my using such toys as are fit only for a queen or a courtesan. Beside, I can only accept presents from the man I may hope to marry. Beg our excellent young friend to keep the whip till you find yourself rich enough to buy it of him."

"Then my little girl is full of good sense!" replied the colonel, kissing her on the forehead.

Canalis took advantage of a conversation between the Duc d'Hérouville and Madame Mignon to go out on the terrace, where Modeste presently joined him, urged by curiosity, while he believed it was by her desire to become Madame Canalis. Somewhat alarmed at his own audacity in thus executing what a soldier would call "right about face," though, according to the jurisprudence of ambitious souls, every man in his place would have done the same, and just as suddenly, he tried to find some plausible reasons as he saw the ill-starred Modeste come out to him.

"Dear Modeste," said he, in insinuating tones, "as we are on such terms of friendship, will you be offended if I point out to you how painful your replies with regard to Monsieur d'Hérouville must be to a man who loves you, and, above all, to a poet, whose soul is a woman, is all nerves, and suffering from the myriad jealousies of a genuine passion. I should be a poor diplomat indeed if I had not understood that your preliminary flirtations, your elaborate recklessness, were the outcome of a plan to study our characters——"

Modeste raised her head with a quick, intelligent, and pretty movement, of a type that may perhaps be traced to certain animals to which instinct gives wonderful grace.

"And so, thrown back on myself, I was no longer deceived by them. I marveled at your subtle wit, in harmony with your character and your countenance. Be satisfied that I never imagined your assumed duplicity to be anything but an outer wrapper, covering the most adorable candor. No, your intelligence, your learning, have left untainted the exquisite innocence we look for in a wife. You are the very wife for a poet, a diplomatist, a thinker, a man fated to live through hazardous moments, and I admire you as much as I feel attached to you. I entreat you, unless you were merely playing with me yesterday when you accepted the pledges of a man whose vanity will turn to pride if he is chosen by you, whose faults will turn to virtues at your divine touch—I beseech you, do not crush the feeling he has indulged till it is a vice !

"Jealousy in me is a solvent, and you have shown me what its violence is ; it is fearful ; it eats into everything ! Oh ! it is not the jealousy of Othello ! " said he, in reply to a movement on Modeste's part. "No, no ! I myself am in question ; I am spoiled in this regard. You know of the one affection to which I owe the only form of happiness I have yet known—and that very incomplete." He shook his head.

"Love is depicted as a child by every nation, because it cannot be conceived of but as having all life before it. Well, this love of mine had its term fixed by nature ; it was stillborn. The most intuitive motherliness discerned and soothed this aching spot in my heart, for a woman who feels—who sees—that she is dying to the joys of love, has angelic consideration ; the Duchess has never given me a pang of that kind. In ten years not a word, not a look, has failed of its mark. I attach more importance than ordinary people do to words, thoughts, and looks. To me a glance is an infinite possession, the slightest doubt is a mortal poison, and acts instantaneously: I cease to love. In my opinion—which is opposed to that of the vulgar, who revel in trembling, hoping, waiting —love ought to dwell in absolute assurance, childlike, infinite.

To me the enchanting purgatory which women delight in inflicting on us with their caprices is an intolerable form of happiness to which I will have nothing to say ; to me, love is heaven or hell. Hell I will not have; I feel that I am strong enough to endure the sempiternal blue of paradise. I give myself unreservedly, I will have no secrets, no doubts, no delusions in my future life, and I ask for reciprocity. Perhaps I offend you by doubting you! But, remember, I am speaking only of myself——''

"And a great deal," said Modeste, hurt by all the lancet points of this harangue, in which the Duchesse de Chaulieu was used as a sledge-hammer, " but it can never be too much ; I have a habit of admiring you, my dear poet."

" Well, then, can you promise me the dog-like fidelity I offer you ? Is it not fine ? Is it not what you wish for ?"

" But why, my dear poet, do you not look for a wife who is dumb and blind and something of a fool ? I am quite pre-pared to please my husband in all things; but you threaten to deprive a girl of the very happiness you promise her, to snatch it from her at the slightest movement, the slightest word, the slightest look ! You cut the bird's wings and want to see it fly ! I knew that poets were accused of inconsist-ency. Oh! quite unjustly," she added, as Canalis protested by a gesture, " for the supposed fault is merely the result of a vulgar misapprehension of the suddenness of their impulses. Still, I had not thought that a man of genius would devise the contradictory conditions of such a game, and then call it life ! You insist on impossibilities just to have the pleasure of put-ting me in the wrong, like those enchanters who in fairy tales set tasks to persecuted damsels whom good fairies rescue——''

" In this case true love will be the fairy," said Canalis, rather drily, seeing that his motive for a separation had been detected by the acute and delicate intelligence which Butscha had put on the scent.

" You, at this moment, my dear poet, are like those parents

who inquire as to a girl's fortune before mentioning what their son's will be. You make difficulties with me, not knowing whether you have any right to do so. Love cannot be based on agreements discussed in cold blood. The poor Duke allows himself to be managed with all the submissiveness of Uncle Toby in Sterne's novel, with this difference, that I am not the widow Wadman, though bereaved at this moment of many illusions concerning poetry. Yes! we hate to believe anything, we girls, that can overthrow our world of fancy! I had been told all this beforehand! Oh! you are trying to quarrel with me in a way unworthy of you! I cannot recognize the Melchior of yesterday."

"Because Melchior has detected in you an ambition you still cherish?——"

Modeste looked at Canalis from head to foot with an imperial glance.

"But I shall some day be an ambassador and a peer as he is——"

"You take me for a vulgar school-girl!" she said, as she went up the steps. But she turned hastily, and added in some confusion, for she felt suffocating—

"That is less insolent than taking me for a fool. The change in your demeanor is due to the nonsense current in le Havre, which Françoise, my maid, has just repeated to me."

"Oh, Modeste, can you believe that?" cried Canalis, with theatrical emphasis. "Then you think that I want to marry you only for your fortune!"

"If I do you this injustice after your edifying remarks on the hills by the Seine, it lies with you to undeceive me, and thenceforth I will be what you would wish me to be," said she, blighting him with her scorn.

"If you think you can catch me in that trap, my lady," said the poet to himself as he followed her, "you fancy me younger than I am. What an ado, to be sure, for a little hussy for whose esteem I care no more than for that of the King of

Borneo. However, by ascribing to me an ignoble motive she justifies my present attitude. Isn't she cunning? La Brière will be saddled, like the little fool that he is; and five years hence we shall laugh at him well, she and I."

The coolness produced by this dispute between Modeste and Canalis was obvious to all eyes that evening. Canalis withdrew early, on the pretext of la Brière's illness, leaving the field free to the master of the horse. At about eleven Butscha, who had come to escort Madame Latournelle home, said in an undertone to Modeste—

"Was I right?"

"Alas, yes!" said she.

"But have you done as we agreed, and left the door ajar so that he may return?"

"My anger was too much for me," replied Modeste. "Such meanness brought the blood to my head, and I told him my mind."

"Well, so much the better! When you have quarreled so that you cannot speak civilly to each other, even then I undertake to make him so devoted and pressing that you yourself will be taken in by him."

"Come, come, Butscha; he is a great poet, a gentleman, and a man of intellect."

"Your father's eight millions will be more than all that."

"Eight millions!" said Modeste.

"My master, who is selling his business, is setting out for Provence to look into Castagnould's investments as your father's agent. The sum-total of the contracts for repurchasing the lands of la Bastie amounts to four millions of francs, and your father has consented to every item. Your settlement is to be two millions, and the colonel allows one for establishing you in Paris with a house and furniture. Calculate."

"Ah, then, I may be Duchesse d'Hérouville," said Modeste, looking at Butscha.

" But for that ridiculous Canalis, you would have kept *his*
whip, as sent by me," said Butscha, putting in a word for la
Brière.

"Monsieur Butscha, do you really expect me to marry the
man you may choose?" retorted Modeste, laughing.

" That worthy young fellow loves as truly as I do ; you
loved him yourself for a week, and he is a man of genuine
heart," replied the clerk.

"And can he compete with a crown appointment, do you
think ?   There are but six—the high almoner, the chancellor,
the lord chamberlain, the master of the horse, the high constable, the high admiral.   But there are no more lords high
constable."

" But in six months, mademoiselle, the people, composed
of an infinite number of malignant Butschas, may blow upon
all this grandeur.   Beside, what does nobility matter in these
days ?   There are not a thousand real noblemen in France.
The d'Hérouvilles are descended from an usher of the rod
under Robert of Normandy.   You will have many a vexation
from those two knife-faced old maids.   If you are bent on
being a duchess—well, you belong to Franche Comté, the
pope will have at least as much consideration for you as for the
tradespeople, he will sell you a duchy ending in *nia* or *agno*.
Do not trifle with your happiness for the sake of a crown appointment."

The reflections indulged in by Canalis during the night were
all satisfactory.   He could imagine nothing in the world
worse than the situation of a married man without a fortune.
Still tremulous at the thought of the danger he had been led
into by his vanity, which he had pledged, as it were, to Modeste by his desire to triumph over the Duc d'Hérouville, and
by his belief in Monsieur Mignon's millions, he began to
wonder what the Duchesse de Chaulieu must be thinking of
his stay at le Havre, aggravated by five days' cessation from

letter-writing, whereas in Paris they wrote each other four or five notes a week.

"And the poor woman is struggling to get me promoted to be commander of the Legion of Honor and to the place of minister to the Grand Duchy of Baden!" cried he.

Forthwith, with the prompt decisiveness which in poets, as in speculators, is the result of a clear intuition of the future, he sat down and wrote the following letter:

To Madame la Duchesse de Chaulieu.

"MY DEAR ÉLÉONORE:—You are, no doubt, astonished at having had no news of me, but my stay here is not merely a matter of health; I also have had to do my duty in some degree to our little friend la Brière. The poor boy has fallen desperately in love with a certain Demoiselle Modeste de la Bastie, a little pale-faced, insignificant thread-paper of a girl, who, by the way, has as a vice a mania for literature, and calls herself poetical to justify the whims, the tantrums, and changes of a pretty bad temper. You know Ernest, he is so easily made a fool of that I would not trust him alone. Mademoiselle de la Bastie set up a strange flirtation with your Melchior; she was very well inclined to be your rival, though she has lean arms and scraggy shoulders, like most young girls, hair more colorless than Madame de Rochefide's, and a very doubtful expression in her little gray eyes. I pulled up this Immodeste's advances pretty short—perhaps rather too roughly; but that is the way of an absorbing passion. What do I care for all the women on earth, who, all put together, are not worth you?

"The people with whom we spend our time, who surround this heiress, are *bourgeois* enough to make one sick. Pity me; I spend my evenings with notaries' clerks, their wives, their cashiers, and a provincial money-lender; wide indeed is the gulf between this and the evenings in the Rue de Grenelle.

The father's trumped-up fortune—he has just come home from China—has secured us the company of that omnipresent suitor the master of the horse, hungrier for millions than ever, since it will cost six or seven, they say, to reclaim and work the much-talked-of alluvion of Hérouville. The King has no idea what a fatal gift he has made to the little Duke. His grace, who does not suspect how small a fortune his hoped-for father-in-law possesses, is jealous only of me. La Brière is making his way with his idol under cover of his friend, who serves as a screen.

"In spite of Ernest's raptures, I, the poet, think of the substantial; and the information I have gathered as to the gentleman's wealth casts a gloomy hue over our secretary's prospects, for his lady-love has sharp enough teeth to eat a hole in any fortune. Now, if my angel would redeem some of our sins, she would try to find out the truth about this matter, by sending for her banker, Mongenod, and cross-questioning him with the skill that distinguishes her. Monsieur Charles Mignon, formerly a colonel in the cavalry of the Imperial Guard, has for seven years been in constant communication with Mongenod's house. They talk here of two hundred thousand francs in settlement, at most; and before making an offer in form for the young lady on Ernest's behalf, I should be glad to have positive data. As soon as the good folks are agreed, I return to Paris. I know a way of bringing the business to a satisfactory conclusion for our lover. All that is needed is to secure permission for Monsieur Mignon's son-in-law to take his title of Count, and no man is more likely to obtain such a grant than Ernest, in view of his services, especially when seconded by us three—you, the Duke, and myself. With his tastes, Ernest, who will undoubtedly rise to be a master of the exchequer, will be perfectly happy living in Paris if he is certain of twenty-five thousand francs a year, a permanent office, and a wife—poor wretch!

"Oh, my dear! how I long to see the Rue de Grenelle again! A fortnight's absence, when it does not kill love, revives the ardor of its early days, and you know, better perhaps than I, all the reasons that make my love eternal. My bones in the tomb will love you still! Indeed, I cannot hold out! If I am compelled to remain ten days longer, I must go to Paris for a few hours.

"Has the Duke got me rope to hang myself? And you, dear life, shall you have to take the Baden waters this season? The cooing of our secret love, as compared with the accents of happy love—always the same, and true to itself for nearly ten years past—has given me a deep contempt of marriage; I had never seen all this so close to my eyes before. Ah! my dear, what is called wrongdoing is a far closer tie between two souls than the law—is it not?"

This idea served as the text for two pages of reminiscences and of aspirations of too private a nature for publication.

On the day before Canalis posted this letter, Butscha, who wrote under the name of Jean Jacmin to his imaginary cousin Philoxène, had sent off his answer twelve hours in advance of the poet's letter. The Duchess, for the last fortnight extremely alarmed and offended by Melchior's silence, had dictated Philoxène's letter to her cousin; and now, after reading the clerk's reply—somewhat too decisive for the vanity of a lady of fifty—had made minute inquiries as to Colonel Mignon's fortune. Finding herself betrayed, deserted for money, Éléonore gave herself up to a paroxysm of rage, hatred, and cold malignancy. Philoxène, knocking at the door of her mistress' luxurious room, on going in, found her with tears in her eyes, and stood amazed at this unprecedented phenomenon, which she had never before seen during fifteen years of service.

"We expiate the happiness of ten years in ten minutes!" exclaimed the Duchess.

"A letter from le Havre, madame."

Éléonore read Canalis' effusion of prose without observing
Philoxène's presence, and the maid's surprise was heightened
as she saw the Duchess' face recover its serenity as she read
the letter. If you hold out to a drowning man a pole as
thick as a walking stick, he will regard it as the king's highway to safety; and so the happy Éléonore believed in the
poet's good faith as she perused these sheets in which love
and business, lies and truth, elbowed each other.

Just now, when the banker had left her, she had sent for
her husband to hinder Melchior's promotion if there were
time yet; but a generous regret came over her that rose to a
sublime impulse.

"Poor boy!" thought she, "he has not the smallest
thought of ill. He loves me as he did the first day; he tells
me everything. Philoxène!" said she, noticing her head
maid loitering about and affecting to arrange the toilet-table.

"Madame la Duchesse?"

"My hand-glass, child."

Éléonore looked at herself, noted the razor-fine lines groov-
ing her forehead, but invisible at a distance; and she sighed,
for she believed that in that sigh she was taking leave of love.
Then she had a man's thought, above the pettiness of woman
—a thought which is sometimes intoxicating; an intoxication which may perhaps account for the clemency of the
Semiramis of the North when she made her young and lovely
rival Momonoff's wife.

"Since he has not failed me, I will get the millions and
the girl for him," thought she, "if this little Mademoiselle
Mignon is as plain as he says she is."

Three knocks, delicately rapped out, announced the Duke,
for whom his wife herself opened the door.

"Ah! you are better, my dear," cried he, with the assumed gladness that courtiers so well know how to put on,
and by which simpletons are taken in.

"My dear Henri," said she, "it is really inconceivable

that you should not by this time have secured Melchior's appointment, after sacrificing yourself for the King during your year's ministry, knowing that it would scarcely endure so long!"

The Duke glanced at Philoxène; and the maid, by an almost imperceptible jerk of the head, showed him the letter from le Havre on the dressing-table. "You would be bored to death in Germany and quarrel with Melchior before your return," said the Duke artlessly.

"Why?"

"Well, would you not always be together?" replied the erewhile ambassador with comical candor.

"Oh! no," said she; "I mean to get him married."

"If d'Hérouville is to be believed, our dear Canalis has not waited for your good offices," replied the Duke, smiling. "Grandlieu yesterday read me some passages of a letter to him from the master of the horse, which was no doubt edited by his aunt to come to your ears; for Mademoiselle d'Hérouville, always on the lookout for a fortune, knows that Grandlieu and I play whist together almost every evening. That good little d'Hérouville invites the Prince de Cadignan to a royal hunt in Normandy, begging him to persuade the King to go, so as to turn the damsel's head when she finds herself the object of such a chivalrous procession. In fact, two words from Charles X. would settle everything. D'Hérouville says the girl is incomparably lovely."

"Henri, let us go to le Havre!" cried the Duchess, interrupting her husband.

"But on what excuse?" said he gravely—a man who had been in the intimate confidence of Louis XVIII.

"I never saw a hunt."

"That would be all very well if the King should be there, but to go so far for a hunt would be ridiculous; and he will not go, I have just spoken to him about it."

"Madame perhaps would go——"

"That is a better plan," said the Duke; "and the Duchesse de Maufrigneuse may help you to get her away from Rosny. Then the King would make no objection to his hounds being taken out. But do not go to le Havre, my dear," said the Duke, in a paternal tone; "it would make you conspicuous. Look here; this, I think, will be a better plan. Gaspard has his Château of Rosembray, on the further side of the forest of Brotonne; why not give him a hint to receive all the party there?"

"Through whom?"

"Why, his wife the Duchess, who attends the holy table with Mademoiselle d'Hérouville, might ask Gaspard to do it if the old maid hinted it to her."

"You are the dearest man!" said Éléonore. "I will write two lines to the old lady, and to Diane; for we must have hunting-suits made. The little hat, now I think of it, makes one look very much younger. Did you win yesterday at the English embassy?"

"Yes," said the Duke; "I wiped out my score."

"And, above all, Henri, set everything aside till Melchior's two promotions are settled."

After writing a few lines to the fair Diane de Maufrigneuse and a note to Mademoiselle d'Hérouville, Éléonore flung this reply like the smack of a horsewhip across Canalis' lies:

To Monsieur le Baron de Canalis.

"MY DEAR POET:—Mademoiselle de la Bastie is beautiful; Mongenod assures me that her father has eight millions of francs; I had thought of making her your wife, so I am deeply annoyed by your want of confidence in me. If before you started for le Havre, you aimed at getting la Brière married to her, I cannot imagine your not telling me so plainly before you went. And why pass a fortnight without writing a line to a friend so easily alarmed as I am?

"Your letter came a little late; I had already seen the banker. You are a child, Melchior; you try to be cunning with us. That is not right. Even the Duke is amazed at your behavior; he thinks you not quite gentlemanly—which casts a doubt on the virtue of your lady mother.

"Now, I want to see things for myself. I shall, I believe, have the honor of attending MADAME to the hunt arranged by the Duc d'Hérouville for Mademoiselle de la Bastie. I will contrive that you shall be invited to stay at Rosembray, as the hunt will probably take place at the Duc de Verneuil's.

"Believe me, none the less, my dear poet, your friend for life, ÉLÉONORE."

"There, Ernest," said Canalis, tossing this letter, which arrived at breakfast-time, across the table in la Brière's face. "That is the two thousandth love-letter I have received from that woman, and there is not one single 'thou.' The noble Éleonore never compromised herself further than what you find there. Get married, and make haste about it! The worst marriage in the world is more tolerable than the lightest of these halters. Well, I am the veriest Nicodemus that ever dropped from the moon. Modeste has millions; she is lost to me for ever; for no one ever comes back from the poles, where we now are, to the tropics, where we dwelt three days ago! Beside, I have all the more reason to wish for your triumph over the little Duke, because I told the Duchesse de Chaulieu that I came here only for your sake; so now I shall work for you."

"Alas, Melchior, Modeste must need have so superior, so mature a character, and such a noble mind, to resist the spectacle of the court, and all the splendor so skillfully displayed in her honor and glory by the Duke, that I cannot believe in the existence of such perfection; and yet—if she is still the Modeste of her letters, there may be a hope——"

"You are a happy fellow, young Boniface, to see the world

17

and your lady-love through such green spectacles!" exclaimed Canalis, going out to walk in the garden.

The poet, caught between two falsehoods, could not make
up his mind what to do next.

"Play the game by the rules, and you lose!" cried he as
he sat in the summer-house. "Every man of sense would
undoubtedly have acted as I did four days ago, and have
crept out of the trap in which I found myself. For in such
a case you don't wait to untie the knots; you break through
everything! Come, I must be cold, calm, dignified, hurt.
Honor will not allow of any other demeanor. English rigidity is the only way to recover Modeste's respect. After all,
if I only get out of the scrape by falling back on my old
felicity, my ten years' fidelity will be rewarded. Éléonore
will find me a suitable match."

The hunt was destined to be the rallying-point of all the
passions brought into play by the colonel's fortune and his
daughter's beauty. There was a sort of truce among the con-
tending parties during the few days needed to prepare this
solemn act of forestry; the drawing-room in the Villa Mignon
had the peaceful appearance of a very united family party.
Canalis, intrenched in his part of a much-injured man, made
a display of courtesy; he put aside his pretentiousness, gave
no more specimens of oratorical talent, and was charming, as
clever men are when they shed their affectations. He discussed the money-market with Gobenheim, war with the
colonel, Germany with Madame Mignon, and housekeeping
with Madame Latournelle, trying to win them over to la
Brière. The Duc d'Hérouville frequently left the field free
to the two friends, as he was obliged to go to Rosembray to
consult the Duc de Verneuil and superintend the execution of
the orders issued by the master of the hounds, the Prince de
Cadignan.

Meanwhile, the comic element was not lacking. Modeste

found herself between the disparagement Canalis tried to cast
on the Duke's gallant attentions and the exaggerated views
of the two Demoiselles d'Hérouville, who came every evening.
Canalis pointed out to Modeste that, far from being the heroine of the day, she would be scarcely noticed. MADAME
would be attended by the Duchesse de Maufrigneuse, the
daughter-in-law of the master of the hounds, by the Duchesse
de Chaulieu, and some other ladies of the court, and among
them a mere girl would produce no sensation. Some officers
would, no doubt, be invited from the garrison at Rouen, etc.
Hélène was never tired of repeating to the girl, whom she
looked upon as her sister-in-law, that she would, of course,
be presented to MADAME; that the Duc de Verneuil would
certainly invite her and her father to stay at Rosembray ; that
if the colonel had any favor to ask of the King—such as a peerage
—this would be a unique opportunity, for they did not despair
of getting the King there on the third day ; that she would
be surprised at the charming reception she would meet with
from the handsomest women of the court, the Duchesses de
Chaulieu, de Maufrigneuse, de Lenoncourt-Chaulieu, etc.;
Modeste's prejudices against the Faubourg Saint-Germain
would disappear—and so forth, and so forth. It was a most
amusing little warfare, with its marches and counter-marches
and strategy, which the Dumays, the Latournelles, Gobenheim, and Butscha looked upon and enjoyed, saying among
themselves all manner of hard things about the nobility, as
they watched their elaborate, cruel, and studied meanness.

The assurances of the d'Hérouville faction were justified by
an invitation, in the most flattering terms, from the Duc de
Verneuil and the master of the King's hounds to Monsieur
le Comte de la Bastie and his daughter to be present at a
royal hunt at Rosembray on the 7th, 8th, 9th, and 10th of
November.

La Brière, oppressed by gloomy presentiments, reveled in
Modeste's presence in that spirit of concentrated avidity

whose bitter joys are known only to lovers irrevocably and
for ever discarded. The flashes of happiness in his inmost
self, mingled with melancholy reflections on the same theme,
"She is lost to me!" made the poor youth a pathetic spectacle, all the more touching because his countenance and person were in harmony with this depth of feeling. There is
nothing more poetical than such a living elegy that has eyes,
that walks, and sighs without rhyming.

Finally, the Duc d'Hérouville came to arrange for Modeste's journey. After crossing the Seine, she was to proceed
in the Duke's traveling carriage with his aunt and sister.
The Duke was perfect in his courtesy; he invited Canalis and
la Brière, telling them, as he told Monsieur Mignon, that
they would find hunters at their service.

The colonel asked his daughter's three lovers to breakfast
on the day of the departure. Then Canalis tried to execute a
scheme that had ripened in his mind during the last few days
—namely, to reconquer Modeste, and to trick the Duchess,
the master of the horse, and la Brière. A graduate in diplomacy could not remain bogged in such a position as that in
which he found himself. La Brière, on his part, had made
up his mind to bid Modeste an eternal farewell. Thus each
suitor, as he foresaw the conclusion of a struggle that had
been going on for three weeks, proposed to put in a last word,
like a pleader to the judge before sentence is pronounced.

After dinner the day before, the colonel took his daughter
by the arm and impressed on her the necessity for coming to
a decision.

"Our position with the d'Hérouville family would be intolerable at Rosembray. Do you want to be a duchess?"
he asked Modeste.

"No, father," she replied.

"Then do you really love Canalis—— ?"

"Certainly not, papa; a thousand times, no!" said she,
with childish irritability.

The colonel looked at her with a sort of glee.

"Ah! I have not influenced you," cried the kind father. "But I may tell you now that even in Paris I had chosen my son-in-law when, on my impressing on him that I had no fortune, he threw his arms around me, saying that I had lifted a hundredweight from his heart."

"Of whom are you speaking?" asked Modeste, coloring.

"Of the man of solid virtues and sound morals," said he, mockingly repeating the phrase which, on the day after his return, had scattered Modeste's dreams.

"Oh, I am not thinking of him, papa! Leave me free to refuse the Duke myself; I know him, I know how to soothe him——"

"Then your choice is not made?"

"Not yet. I still have to guess a few syllables in the riddle of my future; but after having had a glimpse of the court, I will tell you my secret at Rosembray."

"You will join the hunt, will you not?" said the colonel to Ernest, whom he saw coming down the path where he was walking with Modeste.

"No, colonel," replied Ernest. "I have come to take leave of you and of mademoiselle. I am going back to Paris."

"You have no curiosity?" said Modeste, interrupting him, and looking at the bashful youth.

"Nothing is needed to keep me," said he, "but the expression of a wish I hardly hope for."

"If that is all, it will give me pleasure, at any rate," said the colonel, as he went forward to meet Canalis, leaving his daughter alone for a moment with the hapless Ernest.

"Mademoiselle," said the young man, looking up at her with the courage of despair; "I have a petition to make."

"To me?"

"Let me depart forgiven! My life can never be happy; I must endure the remorse of having lost my happiness, by my own fault no doubt; but at least——"

"Before we part for ever," replied Modeste, interrupting him à *la* Canalis, "I want to know one thing only; and though you once assumed a disguise, I do not think that you will now be such a coward as to deceive me——"

At the word "coward" Ernest turned pale.

"You are merciless!" he exclaimed.

"Will you be frank with me?"

"You have the right to ask me such a humiliating question," said he, in a voice made husky by the violent beating of his heart.

"Well, then, did you read my letters out to Monsieur de Canalis?"

"No, mademoiselle; and though I gave them to the colonel to read, it was only to justify my love, by showing him how my affection had had birth, and how genuine my efforts had been to cure you of your fancy."

"But what put this ignoble masquerading into your head?" she asked with a kind of impatience.

La Brière related, in all its details, the scene to which Modeste's first letter had given rise, and the challenge which had resulted from Ernest's high opinion in favor of a young lady yearning for glory, as a plant strives for its share of the sunshine.

"Enough," said Modeste, concealing her agitation. "If you have not my heart, monsieur, you have my highest esteem."

This simple speech made la Brière quite dizzy. He felt himself totter, and leaned against a tree, like a man whose senses are failing him. Modeste, who had walked away turned her head and hastily came back.

"What is the matter?" she exclaimed, taking him by the hand to save him from falling.

Modeste felt his hand like ice, and saw a face as white as a lily; all the blood had rushed to his heart.

"Forgive me, mademoiselle, I had fancied myself so despised——"

"Well," said she, with haughty scorn, "I did not say that I loved you."

And she again left la Brière, who, notwithstanding this hard speech, thought he was walking on the upper air. The earth felt soft beneath his feet, the trees seemed decked with flowers, the sky was rosy and the air blue, as in the temples of Hymen at the close of a fairy drama that ends happily. In such circumstances women are Janus-like, they see what is going on behind them without turning round; and Modeste saw in her lover's expression the unmistakable symptoms of a love such as Butscha's, which is beyond a doubt the *ne plus ultra* of a woman's desire. And the high value attached by la Brière to her esteem was to Modeste an infinitely sweet experience.

"Mademoiselle," said Canalis, leaving the colonel and coming to meet Modeste, "in spite of the small interest you take in my sentiments, it is a point of honor with me to wipe out a stain from which I have too long suffered. Here is what Madame the Duchess wrote me five days after my arrival here."

He made Modeste read the first few lines of the letter, in which the Duchess said that she had seen Mongenod, and wished that Melchior should marry Modeste; then, having torn off the rest, he placed them in her hand.

"I cannot show you the remainder," said he, putting the paper in his pocket; "but I intrust these few lines to your delicacy, that you may be able to verify the handwriting. The girl who could ascribe to me such ignoble sentiments is quite capable of believing in some collusion, some stratagem. This may prove to you how much I care to convince you that the difference between us was not based on the vilest interest on my part. Ah! Modeste," he went on, with tears in his voice, "your poet—Madame de Chaulieu's poet—has not less poetry in his heart than in his mind. You will see the Duchess. Suspend your judgment of me until then." And he left Modeste quite disconcerted.

"On my word! They are all angels," she muttered to herself. "All too fine for marriage! Only the Duke is a human being."

"Mademoiselle Modeste, this hunt makes me very uneasy," said Butscha, appearing on the scene with a parcel under his arm. "I dreamed that your horse ran away with you, so I have been to Rouen to get you a Spanish snaffle; I have been told that a horse can never get it between his teeth. I implore you to use it; I have shown it to the colonel, who has thanked me more than the thing is worth."

"Poor, dear Butscha!" cried Modeste, touched to tears by this motherly care.

Butscha went skipping off like a man who has suddenly heard of the death of an old uncle leaving a fortune.

"My dear father," said Modeste, on returning to the drawing-room, "I should like very much to have that handsome whip; supposing you were to offer to exchange with Monsieur de la Brière—that whip for your picture by Ostade?"

Modeste cast a side-glance at Ernest while the colonel made this proposal, standing in front of the picture—the only thing he possessed as a memorial of the campaigns he had fought in; he had bought it of a citizen of Ratisbon. And seeing the eagerness with which Ernest rushed from the room, "He will attend the hunt," said she to herself.

Thus, strange to say, Modeste's three lovers all went to Rosembray with hearts full of hope and enraptured by her adorable charms.

Rosembray, an estate recently purchased by the Duc de Verneuil with the money that fell to his share of the thousand million francs voted to legitimize the sale of national property, is remarkable for a château comparable for magnificence with those of Mesnière and Balleroy. This noble and imposing mansion is reached by an immense avenue of ancestral elms

four rows deep, and across a vast courtyard on a slope, like
that of Versailles, with a splendid iron screen and two gate
lodges, and surrounded by large orange trees in tubs. The
façade to this great court displays two stories of' nineteen
windows in each, between two wings at right angles—tall
windows with small panes, set in carved stone arches, and
separated by reeded pilasters. A cornice and balustrade screen
an Italian roof, whence rise stone chimneys marked by
trophies of arms, Rosembray having been built in the reign
of Lous XIV. by a farmer-general named Cottin. The front
toward the park differs from this, having a centre block of
five windows projecting from the main building, with columns
and a noble pediment. The Marigny family, to whom the
possessions of this Cottin came by marriage with his sole
heiress, had a group representing Dawn executed for this
pediment by Coysevox. Below it two genii support a scroll,
on which this motto is ascribed in honor of the King, instead
of the old family device : *Sol nobis benignus.* The great Louis
had made a duke of the Marquis de Marigny, one of his most
insignificant favorites.

From the top of the semicircular double-flight of steps there
is a view over a large lake, as long and wide as the grand
canal of Versailles, starting from the bottom of a slope of
turf worthy of the most English lawn, its banks dotted with
clumps displaying the brightest autumn flowers. Beyond, on
each side, a French formal parterre spreads its square beds
and paths—pages written in the most majestic style of our
time. These two gardens are set in a border of wood and
shrubbery, extending the whole length to the extent of thirty
acres, and cleared in places in the English fashion under
Louis XV. The view from the terrace is shut in beyond by
a forest belonging to Rosembray, adjoining two demesnes,
one belonging to the nation and one to the crown. It would
be hard to find a more beautiful landscape.

Modeste's arrival caused some sensation in the avenue

when the carriage was seen with the royal livery of France, escorted by the master of the horse, the colonel, Canalis, and la Brière, all riding, and preceded by an outrider in the royal livery; behind them came ten servants, among them the colonel's negro and mulatto, and his elegant britska, in which were the two ladies' maids and the luggage. The first carriage was drawn by four horses mounted by tigers, dressed with the spruce perfection insisted on by the master of the horse—often better served in such matters than the King himself.

Modeste, as she drove up and saw this minor Versailles, was dazzled by the magnificence of these great folk; she was suddenly conscious of having to meet these famous duchesses; she dreaded seeming affected, provincial, or parvenu, lost her head completely, and repented of ever having wished for this hunting party.

When the carriage stopped, Modeste happily saw before her an old man in a fair, frizzy wig, with small curls, whose calm, smooth, full face wore a paternal smile and an expression of monastic joviality, to which a half-downcast look lent something like dignity. The Duchess, a woman of deep devotion, the only daughter of a very wealthy president of the supreme court, who had died in 1800, was the mother of four children; very thin and erect, she bore some resemblance to Madame Latournelle, if imagination could be persuaded to embellish the lawyer's wife with the graces of a noble lady-prioress.

"Ah! how do you do, dear Hortense?" said Mademoiselle d'Hérouville, embracing the Duchess with all the sympathy that was a tie between these two proud spirits; "allow me to introduce to you and to our dear Duke, Mademoiselle de la Bastie, who is a little angel."

"We have heard so much about you, mademoiselle," said the Duchess, "that we have been most eager to have you here."

"We can but regret our lost time," added the Duc de Verneuil, bowing with gallant admiration.

"Monsieur le Comte de la Bastie," added the master of the horse, taking the colonel by the arm, and leading him up to the Duke and Duchess with a tinge of respect in his tone and manner.

The colonel bowed to the Duchess, the Duke gave him his hand.

"You are very welcome, Monsieur le Comte," said Monsieur de Verneuil. "You are the owner of many treasures," he added, glancing at Modeste.

The Duchess drew Modeste's hand through her arm and led her into a vast drawing-room, where half a score of women were sitting in groups around the fire. The men, led by the Duke, went to walk on the terrace, excepting only Canalis, who went in to pay his respects to the superb Éléonore. She, seated before a tapestry frame, was giving Mademoiselle de Verneuil some hints as to shading.

If Modeste had thrust her finger through with a needle when laying her hand on a cushion, she could not have felt a keener shock than she received from the icy glance, haughty and contemptuous, that the Duchesse de Chaulieu bestowed on her. From the first instant she saw no one but this woman, and guessed whom she was. To know to what a pitch the cruelty can go of those sweet creatures who are exalted by our passion, women must be seen together. Modeste might have disarmed any one but Éléonore by her amazed and involuntary admiration; for if she had not known her rival's age, she would have taken her to be a woman of six-and-thirty; but there were greater surprises in store for her !

The poet found himself flung against the wrath of a great lady. Such anger is the most ruthless Sphinx; the face is beaming, all else is savage. Even kings do not know how to reduce the stronghold of exquisitely cold politeness which a mistress can then hide under steel armor. The lovely woman's countenance smiles, and at the same time the steel strikes home : the hand is of steel, the arm, the body, all is steel. Canalis tried to clutch this steel, but his fingers slipped over it as his words slipped from her heart. And the gracious face, the gracious phrases, the gracious manner of the Duchess, concealed from every eye the steel of her cold fury —down to twenty-five degrees below zero. The sight of Modeste's supreme beauty, heightened by her journey, the appearance of the girl, as well dressed as Diane de Maufrigneuse, had fired the powder that reflection had stored up in Éléonore's brain.

All the women had gone to the window to see the wonder of the day step out of the carriage, followed by her three lovers.

"Do not let us show that we are so curious," said Madame de Chaulieu, struck to the heart by Diane's exclamation, "She is divine! Where can such a creature have dropped from?"

And they had fled back to the drawing-room, where each one had composed her countenance, while the Duchesse de Chaulieu felt in her heart a thousand vipers all crying at once to be satisfied.

Mademoiselle d'Hérouville remarked in an undertone and with marked meaning to the Duchesse de Verneuil—

"Éléonore is not cordial in her reception of her great Melchior."

"The Duchesse de Maufrigneuse thinks that there is a coolness between them," replied Laure de Verneuil simply. This phrase, so often spoken in the world of fashion, is full of meaning. We feel in it the icy polar blast.

"Why?" asked Modeste of the charming girl who had left the convent of the sacred heart not more than two months since.

"The great man," replied the Duchess, signing to her daughter to be silent, "left her for a fortnight without writing a word to her, after setting out for le Havre, and saying that he had gone for his health."

Modeste gave a little start which struck Laure, Hélène, and Mademoiselle d'Hérouville.

"And meanwhile," the devout Duchess went on, "she was getting him appointed commander of the Legion of Honor and minister to Baden."

"Oh, it is very wrong of Canalis, for he owes everything to her," said Mademoiselle d'Hérouville.

"Why did Madame de Chaulieu not come to le Havre?" asked Modeste guilelessly of Hélène.

"My child," said the Duchesse de Verneuil, "she would let herself be killed without speaking a word. Look at her. What a queen! With her head on the block she would still smile, like Mary Stuart—indeed, our handsome Éléonore has the same blood in her veins."

"And she did not write to him?" said Modeste.

"Diane told me," replied the Duchess, prompted to further confidences by an elbow nudge from Mademoiselle d'Hérouville, "that she had sent a very cutting answer to the first letter Canalis wrote to her about ten days ago."

This statement made Modeste color with shame for Canalis; she longed not to crush him under her feet, but to revenge herself by a piece of mischief more cruel than a poniard thrust. She looked proudly at Madame de Chaulieu. That glance was gilded with eight millions of francs.

"Monsieur Melchior!" said she.

All the women looked up, first at the Duchess, who was talking to Canalis over the work-frame, then at this young girl, so ill-bred as to disturb two lovers who were settling their quarrel—a thing which is never done in any rank of life.

Diane de Maufrigneuse gave her head a little toss, as much as to say, "The child is in her rights."

Finally, the twelve women smiled at each other, for they were all jealous of a woman of fifty-six who was still handsome enough to dip her hand in the common treasury and steal a young woman's share. Melchior glanced at Modeste with feverish irritability, the hasty look of a master to a servant, while the Duchess bent her head with the air of a lioness interrupted at her meal; her eyes, fixed on the canvas, shot flames of fire, almost red-hot, at the poet while she sifted his very soul with her epigrams, for each sentence was a vengeance for a triple injury.

"Monsieur Melchior!" repeated Modeste, in a voice that asserted its right to be heard.

"What is it, mademoiselle?" asked the poet.

He was obliged to rise, but he stood still half-way between the work-frame, which was near the window, and the fireplace, by which Modeste was sitting on the Duchess de Verneuil's sofa. What cruel reflections were forced on the ambitious man when he met Éléonore's steady eye. If he should obey Modeste, all was over for ever between the poet and his protectress. If he paid no heed to the girl, it would be an avowal of his serfdom, he would lose the advantages gained by five-and-twenty days of meanness, and fail in the simplest rules of gentlemanly politeness. The greater the folly, the more imperatively the Duchess insisted on it. Modeste's beauty and fortune, set in the opposite scale to Éléonore's influence and established rights, made this hesitancy between the man and his honor as terrible to watch as the peril of a matadore in the ring. A man never knows such frightful palpitations, as those that seemed to threaten Canalis with an aneurism, anywhere but in front of the gaming-table where his fortune or his ruin is settled within five minutes.

"Mademoiselle d'Hérouville made me get out of the carriage in such a hurry," said Modeste to Canalis, "that I dropped my handkerchief——"

Canalis gave a highly significant shrug.

"And," she went on, in spite of this impatient gesture, "I had, tied to it, the key of a blotting-case, containing an important fragment of a letter; will you be good enough, Melchior, to ask for it?——"

Between an angel and a tigress, equally irate, Canalis, who had turned pale, hesitated no longer; the tigress seemed the less dangerous. He was on the point of committing himself when la Brière appeared in the doorway, seeming to Canalis something like the archangel Michael descended from heaven.

"Here, Ernest, Mademoiselle de la Bastie wants you," said the poet, hastily retreating to his chair by the workframe.

Ernest, on his part, went at once to Modeste without bowing to any one else; he saw her alone, received her instructions with visible joy, and ran off with the unconfessed approbation of every woman present.

"What a position for a poet!" said Modeste to Hélène, pointing to the worsted work at which the Duchess was stitching furiously.

"If you speak to her, if you once look at her, all is ended," said Éléonore to Melchior in a low tone, for his middle course had not satisfied her. "And, mind, when I am absent I shall leave other eyes to watch you."

As she spoke, Madame de Chaulieu, a woman of medium height, but rather too fat—as all women are who are still handsome when past fifty—rose, walked toward the group with which Diane de Maufrigneuse was sitting, stepping out with small feet as firm and light as a fawn's. Under her full form the exquisite refinement was conspicuous with which women of that type are gifted, and which gives them that vigorous nervous system that controls and animates the development of the flesh. It was impossible otherwise to account for her light step, which was amazingly dignified. Only those women whose quarterings of nobility date back to Noah, like Éléonore's, know how to be majestic in spite of being as large as a farmer's wife. A philosopher might, perhaps, have pitied Philoxène, while admiring the happy

arrangement of the bodice and the careful details of a morning dress worn with the elegance of a queen and the ease of a
girl. Boldly wearing her own abundant and undyed hair,
plaited on the top of her head in a coronet like a tower,
Éléonore proudly displayed her white neck, her finely shaped
bust and shoulders, her dazzling bare arms, ending in hands
famous for their beauty. Modeste, like all the Duchess'
rivals, saw in her one of those women of whom the others
say, " She is past mistress of us all ! "

In fact, every one recognized her as one of those few great
ladies who are now become so rare in France. Any attempt to
describe how majestic was the carriage of her head, how refined and delicate this or that curve of her neck, what harmony there was in her movements, what dignity in her mien,
what nobleness in the perfect agreement of every detail with
the whole result in the little arts that are a second nature, and
make a woman holy and supreme—this would be to try to
analyze the sublime. We delight in such poetry, as in that
of Paganini, without seeking the means, for the cause is a soul
making itself visible.

The Duchess bowed, saluting Hélène and her aunt ; then
she said to Diane in a clear, bright voice without a trace of
emotion—

" Is it not time to dress, Duchess ? "

And she swept out of the room, accompanied by her
daughter-in-law and Mademoiselle d'Hérouville, each giving
her an arm. She was speaking in a low voice as she went
away with the old maid, who pressed her to her heart, saying,
" You are quite charming ! " which was as much as to say, " I
am wholly yours in return for the service you have just
done us."

Mademoiselle d'Hérouville returned to the drawing-room to
play her part as spy, and her first glance told Canalis that the
Duchess' last words were no vain threat. The apprentice to
diplomacy felt he knew too little of this minor science for so

severe a struggle, and his wit served him at any rate so far as
to enable him to assume a straightforward, if not a dignified,
attitude. When Ernest returned with Modeste's handkerchief, he took him by the arm and led him out on the lawn.

"My dear fellow," said he, "I am, of all men, not the
most unhappy, but the most ridiculous. So I have recourse to
you to help me out of the wasps' nest I have gotten into. Modeste is a demon; she saw my embarrassment, she mocks at it;
she has just spoken to me of two lines of a letter of Madame
de Chaulieu's that I was fool enough to trust her with. If
she were to show them, I could never make it up again with
Éléonore. So, pray, at once ask Modeste for that paper, and
tell her from me that I have no views—no pretensions to her
hand; I rely on her delicacy, on her honesty as a lady, to
behave to me as though we had never met; I entreat her not
to speak to me; I beseech her to vouchsafe to be implacable,
though I dare not hope that her spite will move her to a sort
of jealous wrath that would serve my ends to a miracle——
Go, I will wait here."

On re-entering the room, Ernest de la Brière saw there a
young officer of Havré's company of the Guards, the Vicomte
de Sérizy, who had just arrived from Rosny to announce that
MADAME was obliged to be present at the opening of the
session. This constitutional solemnity was, as is well known,
a very important function. Charles X. pronounced a speech
in the presence of his whole family, the Dauphiness and MA-
DAME being present in their seats. The choice of the envoy
charged with expressing the Princess' regrets was a compliment to Diane. She was supposed to be the immediate object
of this fascinating youth's adoration; he was the son of a
minister of state, gentleman-in-waiting, and hopeful of high
destinies, as being an only son and heir to an immense fortune. The Duchesse de Maufrigneuse, however, only accepted
the Viscount's attentions in order to throw light on the age of
Madame de Sérizy, who, according to the chronicle repeated

18

behind fans, had won from her the heart of handsome Lucien de Rubempré.

"You, I hope, will do us the pleasure of remaining at Rosembray," said the severe Duchess to the young man.

While keeping her ears open to evil-speaking, the pious lady shut her eyes to the peccadilloes of her guests, who were carefully paired by the Duke; for no one knows what such excellent women will tolerate on the plea of bringing a lost sheep back to the fold by treating it with indulgence.

"We reckoned without the constitutional government," said the Duc d'Hérouville, "and Rosembray loses a great honor, Madame la Duchesse——"

"We shall feel all the more at our ease," observed a tall, lean old man of about seventy-five, dressed in blue cloth, and keeping on his hunting cap by leave of the ladies.

This personage, who was very like the Duc de Bourbon, was no less a man than the Prince de Cadignan, the master of the hounds, and also one of the last of the French Great Lords.

Just as la Brière was about to slip behind the sofa to beg a minute's speech with Modeste, a man of about eight and thirty came in, short, fat, and common looking.

"My son, the Prince de Loudon," said the Duchesse de Verneuil to Modeste, who could not control an expression of amazement on her youthful features as she saw the man who now bore the name which the general of the Vendée Cavalry had made so famous by his daring and by his execution.

The present Duc de Verneuil was the third son taken by his father into exile, and the only survivor of four children.

"Gaspard," said the Duchess, calling her son to her. The Prince obeyed his mother, who went on as she introduced Modeste—

"Mademoiselle de la Bastie, my dear."

The heir presumptive, whose marriage to Desplein's only daughter was a settled thing, bowed to the girl without seeming struck by her beauty, as his father had been. Modeste thus had an opportunity of comparing the young men of to-day with the old men of the past; for the old Prince de Cadignan had already made her two or three very pretty speeches, proving that he was not less devoted to women than to royalty. The Duc de Rhétoré, Madame de Chaulieu's eldest son, noted for the style which combines impertinence with easy freedom, had, like the Prince de Loudon, treated Modeste almost cavalierly.

The reason of this contrast between the sons and the fathers may, perhaps, lie in the fact that the heirs no longer feel themselves to be objects of importance, as their ancestors were, and excuse themselves from the duties of power, since they no longer have anything but its shadow. The fathers still have the fine manners inherent in their vanished grandeur, like mountains gilded by the sunshine, when all around them is in darkness.

At last Ernest succeeded in saying two words to Modeste, who arose.

"My little beauty!" said the Duchess, as she pulled a bell, thinking that Modeste was going to change her dress, "you shall be taken to your rooms."

Ernest went with Modeste to the foot of the great staircase to make the unhappy Melchior's request, and he tried to touch her by describing the poet's miseries.

"He loves her, you see! He is a captive who thought he could break his chains."

"Love! In a man who calculates everything so closely?" retorted Modeste.

"Mademoiselle, you are at the beginning of your life; you do not know its narrow places. Every sort of inconsistency must be forgiven to a man who places himself under the dominion of a woman older than himself, for he is not responsible. Consider how many sacrifices Canalis has offered to that divinity! how he has sown too much seed to scorn the harvest; the Duchess represents to him ten years of devotion and of happiness. You had made the poet forget everything, for, unhappily, he has more vanity than pride; he knew not what he was losing till he saw Madame de Chaulieu again. If you knew Canalis, you would help him. He is a mere child, and is spoiling his life for ever. You say he calculates everything, but he calculates very badly, like all poets indeed —creatures of impulse, full of childishness, dazzled, like children, by all that shines, and running after it! He has been fond of horses, of pictures; he has yearned for glory; he sells his pictures to get armor and furniture of the style of the Renaissance and of Louis XV.; he now has a grudge against the government. Admit that his whims are on a grand scale!"

"That will do," said Modeste. "Come," she added, as she saw her father, and beckoned to him to ask him to accompany her, "I will give you that scrap of paper; you can take it to the great man, and assure him of my entire consent to all he wishes, but on one condition, I beg you to give him my best thanks for the pleasure I have enjoyed in seeing him perform for my sole benefit one of the finest pieces of the German theatre. I know now that Goethe's *chef-d'œuvre* is neither 'Faust' nor 'Egmont'"—and, as Ernest looked at the sprightly girl with a puzzled expression—"it is 'Torquato Tasso,'" she added. "Desire Monsieur Canalis to read it once more," she went on, smiling. "I particularly desire that you will repeat this to your friend word for word, for it is not an epigram; it is the justification of his conduct—with this difference, that I hope he will become quite sane, thanks to his Éléonore's folly."

The Duchess' head waiting-maid led Modeste and her father to their rooms, where Françoise Cochet had already arranged everything. Their choice elegance surprised the colonel, and Françoise told him that there were thirty guest-chambers in the same style in the château.

"This is my idea of a country-house," said Modeste.

"The Comte de la Bastie will have such another built for you," replied the colonel.

"Here, monsieur," said Modeste, handing the scrap of paper to Ernest, "go and reassure our friend."

The words "our friend" struck the young man. He looked at Modeste to see if there were seriously some community of sentiment such as she seemed to acknowledge; and the girl, understanding the implied question, added—

"Well, go; your friend is waiting."

La Brière colored violently, and went, in a state of doubt, anxiety, and disturbance more terrible than despair. The approach to happiness is to true lovers very like what the poetry of catholicism has called the straits of paradise, to express a dark, difficult, and narrow way, echoing with the last cries of supreme anguish.

An hour later the distinguished party had all met again in the drawing-room, some playing at whist, others chatting, the women busy with fancy-work, while awaiting the dinner-hour. The master of the hounds led Monsieur Mignon to talk of China, of his campaigns, of the great Provençal families of Portenduère, l'Estorade, and Maucombe; and he remonstrated with him on not asking for employment, assuring him that nothing would be easier than to obtain a post in the Guards with his full rank as colonel.

"A man of your birth and fortune can never class himself with the present opposition," said the Prince with a smile.

This aristocratic society pleased Modeste; and not only that, during her visit she gained a perfection of manner which, but for this revelation, she would never in her life have acquired. If you show a clock to a natural mechanic, it is always enough to reveal to him what mechanism means; the germs within him are at once developed. In the same way, Modeste intuitively assimilated everything that gave distinction to the Duchesses de Maufrigneuse and de Chaulieu. To

her each detail was a lesson, where a commonplace woman
would have fallen into absurdity by imitating mere manners.
A girl of good birth, well informed, with the instincts of
Modeste, fell naturally into the right key, and discerned the
differences which divide the aristocratic from the middle-class,
and provincial life from that of the Faubourg Saint-Germain;
she caught the almost imperceptible shades; in short, she
recognized the grace of a really fine lady, and did not despair
of acquiring it.

In the midst of this Olympus she saw that her father and la
Brière were infinitely superior to Canalis. The great poet,
abdicating his real and indisputable power, that of the intellect,
was nothing but a master of appeals, eager to become a minister, anxious for the collar of the Legion of Honor, and obliged
to subserve every constellation. Ernest de la Brière, devoid
of ambition, was simply himself; while Melchior, eating
humble pie, to use a vulgar phrase, paid court to the Prince
de Loudon, the Duc de Rhétoré, the Vicomte de Sérizy, the
Duc de Maufrigneuse, as though he had no liberty of speech
like Colonel Mignon the Comte de la Bastie, proud of his services and of the Emperor Napoleon's esteem. Modeste saw the
continued preoccupation of a wit seeking a point to raise a
laugh, a brilliant remark to surprise, or a compliment to flatter
the high and mighty personages, on whose level he aimed at
keeping himself. In short, here the peacock shed his glittering plumes.

In the course of the evening Modeste went to sit with the
master of the horse in a recess of the drawing-room; she took
him there to put an end to a struggle she could no longer
encourage without lowering herself in her own eyes.

"Monsieur le Duc," she began, "if you knew me well,
you would know how deeply I am touched by your attentions.
It is precisely the high esteem I have for your character, the
friendship inspired by such a nature as yours, which makes
me anxious not to inflict the smallest wound on your self-

respect. Before you came to le Havre I loved sincerely, deeply, and for ever a man who is worthy to be loved, and from whom my affection is still a secret; but I may tell you— and in this I am more sincere than most girls—that, if I had not been bound by this voluntary engagement, you would have been my choice, so many and so great are the good qualities I have found in you. A few words dropped by your sister and aunt compel me to say this. If you think it neces- sary, by to-morrow, before the hunt, my mother shall recall me home under the excuse of serious indisposition. I will not be present without your consent at an entertainment ar- ranged by your kind care, where, if my secret should escape me, I might aggrieve you by an insult to your legitimate pre- tensions.

"'Why did I come?' you may ask. I might have de- clined. Be so generous as not to make a crime of an inevi- table curiosity. This is not the most delicate part of what I have to communicate. You have firmer friends than you know of in my father and me; and as my fortune was the prime motive in your mind when you came to seek me, with- out wishing to treat it as a solace to the grief your gallantry requires of you, I may tell you that my father is giving his mind to the matter of the Hérouville lands. His friend Du- may thinks the scheme feasible, and has been feeling his way to the formation of a company. Gobenheim, Dumay, and my father are each ready with fifteen hundred thousand francs, and undertake to collect the remainder by the confidence they will inspire in the minds of capitalists by taking substantial interest in the business.

"Though I may not have the honor of being the Duchesse d'Hérouville, I am almost certain of putting you in the posi- tion to choose her one day with perfect freedom in the exalted sphere to which she belongs. Oh, let me finish," said she, at a gesture of the Duke's.

"It is easy to see from my brother's agitation," said Mademoiselle d'Hérouville to her niece, "that you have gained a sister."

"Monsieur le Duc, I decided on this on the day of our first ride together, when I heard you lamenting your position. This is what I wanted to tell you ; on that day my fate was sealed. If you have not won a wife, you have, at any rate, found friends at Ingouville, if, indeed, you will accept us as friends."

This little speech which Modeste had prepared was uttered with such soul-felt charm that tears rose to the Duke's eyes. He seized Modeste's hand and kissed it.

"Remain here for the hunt," said he. "My small merit has accustomed me to such refusals. But while I accept your friendship and the colonel's, allow me to assure myself, by inquiring of the most competent experts, that the reclaiming of the marsh-lands of Hérouville will involve the company of which you speak in no risks, but may bring in some profits, before I accept the liberality of your friends.

"You are a noble girl, and though it breaks my heart to be no more than your friend, I shall glory in the title and prove it to you whenever and wherever I find occasion."

"At any rate, Monsieur le Duc, let us keep the secret to ourselves. My choice will not be announced, unless I am greatly mistaken, till my mother is completely cured ; for it is my desire that my plighted husband and I should be blessed with her first glances."

"Ladies," said the Prince de Cadignan at the moment when all were going to bed, "I remember that several of you proposed to follow the hunt with us to-morrow ; now I think it my duty to inform you that, if you are bent on being Dianas, you must rise with the dawn. The meet is fixed for half-past eight. I have often in the course of my life seen women display greater courage than men, but only for a few minutes, and you will all need a certain modicum of determination to remain on horseback for a whole day excepting during the halt called for luncheon—a mere snack, as beseems sportsmen and sportswomen.   Are you all still resolved to prove yourselves gallant horsewomen?"

"I, Prince, cannot help myself," said Modeste slily.

"I can answer for myself," said the Duchesse de Chaulieu.

"I know my daughter Diane ; she is worthy of her name," replied the Prince.   "Well, then, you are all primed for the sport.   However, for the sake of Madame and Mademoiselle de Verneuil, who remain at home, I shall do my best to turn the stag to the further end of the pool."

"Do not be uneasy, ladies, the hunters' snack will be served under a splendid marquee," said the Prince de Loudon when the master of the hounds had left the room.

Next morning at daybreak everything promised fine weather. The sky, lightly veiled with gray mist, showed through it here and there in patches of pure blue, and it would be entirely cleared before noon by a northwest breeze, which was already sweeping up some little, fleecy clouds.   As they left the château, the master of the hounds, the Prince de Loudon, and the Duc de Rhétoré, who, having no ladies under their care, started first for the meet, saw the chimneys of the house piercing through the veil-mist in white masses against the russet foliage, which the trees in Normandy never lose till quite the end of a fine autumn.

"The ladies are in luck," said the Prince to the Duc de Rhétoré.

"Oh, in spite of their bravado last night, I fancy they will leave us to hunt without them," replied the Duc de Verneuil.

"Yes, if they have not each a gentleman-in-waiting," retorted the Duke.

At this moment these determined sportsmen—for the Prince de Loudon and the Duc de Rhétoré are of the race of Nimrod, and supposed to be the finest shots of the Faubourg Saint-Germain—heard the noise of an altercation, and rode forward at a gallop to the clearing appointed for the meet,

at one of the openings into the forest of Rosembray, and
remarkable for a mossy knoll. This was the subject of the
quarrel : The Prince de Loudon, bitten by Anglomania, had
placed at the Duc de Verneuil's orders the whole of his stable
and kennel, in the English style throughout. On one side of
the clearing stood a young Englishman, short, fair, insolent-
looking and cool, speaking French after a fashion, and
dressed with the neatness that characterizes Englishmen even
of the lowest class. John Barry had a tunic-coat of scarlet
cloth belted round the waist, silver buttons with the arms of
Verneuil, white doeskin breeches, top-boots, a striped waistcoat, and a black velvet collar and cap. In his right hand he
held a hunting-crop, and in his left, hanging by a silk cord,
was a brass horn. This chief huntsman had with him two
large thoroughbred hounds, pure fox-hounds with white coats
spotted with tan, high on their legs, with keen noses, small
heads, and short ears, high up. This man, one of the most
famous huntsmen of the country whence the Prince had sent
for him at great expense, ruled over fifteen hunters and sixty
English-bred dogs, which annually cost the Duc de Verneuil
enormous sums ; though he cared little for sport, he indulged
his son in this truly royal taste. The subordinates, men and
horses, stood some little way off and kept perfect silence.

Now on arriving on the ground, John found there three
huntsmen with three packs of the King's hounds that had
arrived before him in carts ; the Prince de Cadignan's three
best men, whose figures, both in character and costumes, were
a perfect contrast with the representative of insolent Albion.
These, the Prince's favorites, all wearing three-cornered
cocked hats, very low and flat, beneath which grinned tanned,
wrinkled, weather-beaten faces, lighted up as it were by their
twinkling eyes, were curiously dry, lean, and sinewy men,
burnt up with the passion for sport. Each was provided with
a large bugle hung about with green worsted cord that left
nothing visible but the bell of the trumpet ; they kept their

dogs in order by the eye and voice. The noble brutes, all splashed with liver-color and black, each with his individual expression, as distinct as Napoleon's soldiers, formed a posse of subjects more faithful than those whom the King was at that moment addressing—their eyes lighting up at the slightest sound with a spark that glittered like a diamond—this one from Poitou, short in the loins, broad-shouldered, low on the ground, long-eared; that one an English dog, white, slim in the belly, with short ears, and made for coursing; all the young hounds eager to give tongue, while their elders, seamed with scars, lay quiet, at full length, their heads resting on their fore-paws, and listening on the ground like wild men of the woods.

On seeing the English contingent the dogs and the King's men looked at each other, asking without saying a word—

"Are we not to hunt by ourselves? Is not this a slur on his majesty's royal hunt?"

After beginning with some banter, the squabble had grown warm between Monsieur Jacquin la Roulie, the old chief huntsman of the French force, and John Barry, the young Briton.

While still at some distance the princes guessed what had given rise to the quarrel, and the master of the hounds, putting spurs to his horse, ended the matter by asking in a commanding tone—

"Who beat the wood?"

"I, monseigneur," said the Englishman.

"Very good," said the Prince de Cadignan, listening to John Barry's report.

Men and dogs, all alike, were respectful in the presence of the master of the hounds, as though all alike recognized his supreme authority. The Prince planned the order of the day; for a hunt is like a battle, and Charles X.'s master of the hounds was a Napoleon of the forest. Thanks to the admirable discipline carried out by his orders in stable and

kennel, he could give his whole mind to strategy and the
science of the chase. He assigned a place in the proceedings
of the day to the Prince de Loudon's hounds and men, re-
serving them, like a cavalry corps, to turn the stag back on
the pool, in the event of the King's packs succeeding, as he
hoped, in forcing the game into the royal demesne lying in
the distance in front of the château. He gratified the self-
respect of his own old retainers by giving them the hardest
work, and that of the Englishman, whom he employed in his
own special line, by giving him an opportunity of displaying
the strength of limb of his dogs and horses. Thus the two
methods would work against each other, and do wonders to
excite reciprocal emulation.

"Are we to wait any longer, monsiegneur?" asked la
Roulie respectfully.

"I understand you, old friend," replied the Prince. "It
is late, but——"

"Here come the ladies, for Jupiter scents the fetish
odors," said the second huntsman, observing the nose of his
favorite hound.

"Fetish?" repeated the Prince de Loudon with a smile.

"He probably means fetid," said the Duc de Rhétoré.

"That is it, no doubt, for everything that does not smell
of the kennel is poisonous, according to Monsieur Laravine,"
replied the Prince.

In point of fact, the three gentlemen could see in the distance a party of sixteen riders, and fluttering at their head the
green veils of four ladies. Modeste, with her father, the Duc
d'Hérouville, and little la Brière, was in front, with the
Duchesse de Maufrigneuse attended by the Vicomte de Sérizy.
Then came the Duchesse de Chaulieu with Canalis at her side,
she smiling at him with no sign of rancor. On reaching the
clearing, where the huntsmen, dressed in red, holding their
hunting horns and surrounded by dogs and beaters, formed a
group worthy of the brush of Van der Meulen, the Duchesse

de Chaulieu, an admirable figure on horseback, though somewhat too stout, drew up close to Modeste, feeling it beneath her dignity to sulk with the young person to whom, the day before, she had not spoken a word.

Just at the moment when the master of the hounds had ended his compliments on such fabulous punctuality, Éléonore condescended to remark the splendid whip-handle that sparkled in Modeste's little hand, and she very graciously begged to examine it.

"It is the finest thing in its way that I have ever seen," said she, showing the gem to Diane de Maufrigneuse; "but, indeed, it is in harmony with the owner's whole person," she added, as she returned it to Modeste.

"You will confess, madame," replied Mademoiselle de la Bastie, with a mischievous but tender glance at la Brière, in which he could read an avowal, "that it is a very strange gift as coming from a future husband——"

"Indeed," exclaimed Madame de Maufrigneuse, "I should regard it as a recognition of my rights, remembering always Louis XIV."

There were tears in la Brière's eyes; he dropped his bridle, and was ready to fall; but another look from Modeste recalled him to himself by warning him not to betray his supreme happiness.

The cavalcade set out.

The Duc d'Hérouville said in a low voice to la Brière: "I hope, monsieur, that you will make your wife happy, and if I can in any way serve you, command me; for I should be delighted to contribute to the happiness of two such charming people."

This great day, when such important interests of hearts and fortunes were definitely settled, to the master of the hounds offered no other problem but that as to whether the stag would cross the pool, and be killed on the grass-slope within sight of the château; for huntsmen of such experience are like chess

players, who can foresee a checkmate many moves ahead.
The fortunate old gentleman succeeded to the height of his
wishes; the run was splendid, and the ladies relieved him of
their presence on the next day but one, which proved to be
rainy.

The Duc de Verneuil's guests remained three days at
Rosembray. On the last morning the "Gazette de France"
contained the announcement that M. le Baron de Canalis was
appointed to the rank of commander of the Legion of Honor
and the post of minister at Carlsruhe.

When early in the month of December the Comtesse de la
Bastie was operated on by Desplein, and could at last see
Ernest de la Brière, she pressed Modeste's hand and said in
her ear—

"I should have chosen him."

Toward the end of February all the documents relating to
the acquisition of the estates were signed by the worthy and
excellent Latournelle, Monsieur Mignon's attorney in Provence. At this time the family of la Bastie obtained from his
majesty the distinguished honor of his signature to the marriage contract and the transmission of the title and the arms
of la Bastie to Ernest de la Brière, who was authorized to call
himself the Vicomte de la Bastie-La Brière. The estate of la
Bastie, reconstituted to yield more than a hundred thousand
francs a year, was entailed by letters patent registered by the
court in the month of April.

La Brière's witnesses were Canalis and the minister, whose
private secretary he had been for five years. Those who
signed for the bride were the Duc d'Hérouville and Desplein,
for whom the Mignons cherished enduring gratitude, after
giving him magnificent proofs of it.

By-and-by, perhaps, in this long record of our manners, we
may meet again with Monsieur and Madame de la Brière-La
Bastie, and connoisseurs will then perceive how easy and

sweet a tie is marriage when the wife is well informed and clever; for Modeste, who kept her promise of avoiding all the absurdities of pedantry, is still the pride and delight of her husband, of her family, and of her circle of friends.

PARIS, *March-July*, 1844.

HONORINE.

To Monsieur Achille Devéria.

An affectionate remembrance from the Author.

If the French have as great an aversion for traveling as the
English have a propensity for it, both English and French
have perhaps sufficient reasons.   Something better than
England is everywhere to be found; whereas, it is excessively difficult to find the charms of France outside France.
Other countries can show admirable scenery, and they frequently offer greater comfort than that of France, which
makes but slow progress in that particular.   They sometimes
display a bewildering magnificence, grandeur, and luxury;
they lack neither grace nor noble manners; but the life of
the brain, the talent for conversation, the "Attic salt" so
familiar at Paris, the prompt apprehension of what one is
thinking, but does not say, the spirit of the unspoken, which
is half the French language, is nowhere else to be met with.
Hence a Frenchman, whose raillery, as it is, finds so little
comprehension, would wither in a foreign land like an up-
rooted tree.   Emigration is counter to the instincts of the
French nation.   Many Frenchmen, of the kind here in question, have owned to pleasure at seeing the custom-house
officers of their native land, which may seem the most daring
hyperbole of patriotism.
    This little preamble is intended to recall to such French-
men as have traveled the extreme pleasure they have felt on
occasionally finding their native land, like an oasis, in the
drawing-room of some diplomatist: a pleasure hard to be
understood by those who have never left the asphalt of the

(288)

Boulevard des Italiens, and to whom the quais of the left
bank of the Seine are not really Paris. To find Paris again !
Do you know what that means, O Parisians? It is to find—
not indeed the cookery of the *Rocher de Cancale* as Borel
elaborates it for those who can appreciate it, for that exists
only in the Rue Montorgueil—but a meal which reminds you
of it ! It is to find the wines of France, which out of France
are to be regarded as myths, and as rare as the woman of
whom I write ! It is to find—not the most fashionable pleas-
antry, for it loses its aroma between Paris and the frontier—
but the witty understanding, the critical atmosphere in which
the French live, from the poet down to the artisan, from the
duchess to the boy in the street.

In 1836, when the Sardinian court was residing at Genoa,
two Parisians, more or less famous, could fancy themselves
still in Paris when they found themselves in a palazzo, taken
by the French consul-general, on the hill forming the last
fold of the Apennines between the gate of San Tomaso and
the well-known lighthouse, which is to be seen in all the
keepsake views of Genoa. This palazzo is one of the magnificent villas on which Genoese nobles were wont to spend
millions at the time when the aristocratic republic was a
power.

If the early night is beautiful anywhere, it surely is at
Genoa, after it has rained as it can rain there, in torrents, all
the morning ; when the clearness of the sea vies with that of
the sky ; when silence reigns on the quay and in the groves
of the villa, and over the marble heads with yawning jaws,
from which water mysteriously flows ; when the stars are
beaming ; when the waves of the Mediterranean lap one after
another like the avowal of a woman, from whom you drag it
word by word. It must be confessed that the moment when
the perfumed air brings fragrance to the lungs and to our day-
dreams ; when voluptuousness, made visible and ambient as
the air, holds you in your easy-chair ; when, a spoon in your

19

hand, you sip an ice or a sherbet, the town at your feet and
fair women opposite—such Boccaccio hours can be known
only in Italy and on the shores of the Mediterranean.

Imagine to yourself, round the table, the Marquis di Negro,
a knight hospitaler to all men of talent on their travels, and
the Marquis Damaso Pareto, two Frenchmen disguised as
Genoese, a consul-general with a wife as beautiful as a Madonna, and two silent children—silent because sleep has fallen
on them—the French ambassador and his wife, a secretary to
the embassy who believes himself to be crushed and mischievous; finally, two Parisians, who have come to take leave of the
consul's wife at a splendid dinner, and you will have the picture presented by the terrace of the villa about the middle of
May—a picture in which the predominant figure was that of a
celebrated woman, on whom all eyes centred now and again,
the heroine of this improvised festival.

One of the two Frenchmen was the famous landscape painter,
Léon de Lora; the other a well-known critic, Claude Vignon.
They had both come with this lady, one of the glories of the
fair sex, Mademoiselle des Touches, known in the literary
world by the name of Camille Maupin.

Mademoiselle des Touches had been to Florence on business. With the charming kindness of which she is prodigal,
she had brought with her Léon de Lora to show him Italy, and
had gone on as far as Rome that he might see the Campagna.
She had come by the Simplon, and was returning by the Cornice road to Marseilles. She had stopped at Genoa, again on
the landscape painter's account. The consul-general had, of
course, wished to do the honors of Genoa, before the arrival
of the court, to a woman whose wealth, name, and position
recommend her no less than her talents. Camille Maupin,
who knew her Genoa down to its smallest chapels, had left
her landscape painter to the care of the diplomatist and the
Genoese marquises, and was miserly of her minutes. Though
the ambassador was a distinguished man of letters, the cele-

brated lady had refused to yield to his advances, dreading
what the English call an exhibition; but she had drawn in
the claws of her refusals when it was proposed that they should
spend a farewell day at the consul's villa. Léon de Lora had
told Camille that her presence at the villa was the only return
he could make to the ambassador and his wife, the two Genoese noblemen, the consul and his wife. So Mademoiselle des
Touches had sacrificed one of those days of perfect freedom,
which are not always to be had in Paris by those on whom the
world has its eye.

Now, the meeting being accounted for, it is easy to understand that etiquette had been banished, as well as a great
many women even of the highest rank, who were curious to
know whether Camille Maupin's manly talent impaired her
grace as a pretty woman, and to see, in a word, whether the
trousers showed below her petticoats. After dinner till nine
o'clock, when a collation was served, though the conversation
had been gay and grave by turns, and constantly enlivened
by Léon de Lora's sallies—for he is considered the most
roguish wit of Paris to-day—and by the good taste which will
surprise no one after the list of guests, literature had scarcely
been mentioned. However, the butterfly flittings of this
French tilting match were certain to come to it, were it only
to flutter over this essentially French subject. But before
coming to the turn in the conversation which led the consul-
general to speak, it will not be out of place to give some account of him and his family.

This diplomatist, a man of four-and-thirty, who had been
married about seven years, was a living portrait of Lord Byron.
The familiarity of that face makes a description of the consul's unnecessary. It may, however, be noted that there was
no affectation in his dreamy expression. Lord Byron was
a poet, and the consul was poetical; women know and recognize the difference, which explains without justifying some
of their attachments. His handsome face, thrown into relief

by a delightful nature, had captivated a Genoese heiress. A Genoese heiress! the expression might raise a smile at Genoa, where, in consequence of the inability of daughters to inherit, a woman is rarely rich; but Onorina Pedrotti, the only child of a banker without heirs male, was an exception. Notwithstanding all the flattering advances prompted by a spontaneous passion, the consul-general had not seemed to wish to marry. Nevertheless, after living in the town for two years, and after certain steps taken by the ambassador during his visits to the Genoese court, the marriage was decided on. The young man withdrew his former refusal, less on account of the touching affection of Onorina Pedrotti than by reason of an unknown incident, one of those crises of private life which are so instantly buried under the daily tide of interests that, at a subsequent date, the most natural actions seem inexplicable.

This involution of causes sometimes affects the most serious events of history. This, at any rate, was the opinion of the town of Genoa, where, to some women, the extreme reserve, the melancholy of the French consul could be explained only by the word passion. It may be remarked, in passing, that women never complain of being the victims of a preference; they are very ready to immolate themselves for the common weal. Onorina Pedrotti, who might have hated the consul if she had been altogether scorned, loved her *sposo* no less, and perhaps more, when she knew that he had loved. Women allow precedence in love affairs. All is well if other women are in question.

A man is not a diplomatist with impunity: the *sposo* was as secret as the grave—so secret that the merchants of Genoa chose to regard the young consul's attitude as premeditated, and the heiress might perhaps have slipped through his fingers if he had not played his part of a love-sick *malade imaginaire.* If it was real, the women thought it too degrading to be believed.

Pedrotti's daughter gave him her love as a consolation;

she lulled these unknown griefs in a cradle of tenderness and
Italian caresses.

The Signor Pedrotti had indeed no reason to complain of the
choice to which he was driven by his beloved child. Powerful protectors in Paris watched over the young diplomatist's
fortunes. In accordance with a promise made by the ambassador to the consul-general's father-in-law, the young man
was created Baron and commander of the Legion of Honor.
Signor Pedrotti himself was made a Count by the King of
Sardinia. Onorina's dower was a million of francs. As to
the fortune of the Casa Pedrotti, estimated at two millions,
made in the corn trade, the young couple came into it within
six months of their marriage, for the first and last Count
Pedrotti died in January, 1831.

Onorina Pedrotti is one of those beautiful Genoese women
who, when they are beautiful, are the most magnificent creatures in Italy. Michael Angelo took his models in Genoa for
the tomb of Giuliano. Hence the fullness and singular placing of the breast in the figures of Day and Night, which so
many critics have thought exaggerated, but which is peculiar
to the women of Liguria. A Genoese beauty is no longer to
be found excepting under the *mezzaro*, as at Venice it is met
with only under the *fazzioli*. This phenomenon is observed
among all fallen nations. The noble type survives only among
the populace, as after the burning of a town coins are found
hidden in the ashes. And Onorina, an exception as regards
her fortune, is no less an exceptional patrician beauty. Recall to mind the figure of Night which Michael Angelo has
placed at the feet of the " Pensieroso," dress her in modern
garb, twist that long hair around the magnificent head, a little
dark in complexion, set a spark of fire in those dreamy eyes,
throw a scarf about the massive bosom, see the long dress,
white, embroidered with flowers, imagine the statue sitting
upright, with her arms folded like those of Mademoiselle
Georges, and you will see before you the consul's wife, with

a boy of six, as handsome as a mother's desire, and a little
girl of four on her knees, as beautiful as the type of childhood
so laboriously sought out by the sculptor David to grace a
tomb.

This beautiful family was the object of Camille's secret
study. It struck Mademoiselle des Touches that the consul
looked rather too absent-minded for a perfectly happy man.

Although, throughout the day, the husband and wife had
offered her the pleasing spectacle of complete happiness,
Camille wondered why one of the most superior men she had
ever met, and whom she had seen, too, in Paris drawing-rooms,
remained as consul-general at Genoa when he possessed a fortune of a hundred-odd thousand francs a year. But, at the
same time, she had discerned, by many of the little nothings
which women perceive with the intelligence of the Arab sage
in "Zadig," that the husband was faithfully devoted. These
two handsome creatures would no doubt love each other without a misunderstanding till the end of their days. So Camille
said to herself alternately, "What is wrong? Nothing is
wrong," following the misleading symptoms of the consul's
demeanor; and he, it may be said, had the absolute calmness
of Englishmen, of savages, of Orientals, and of consummate
diplomatists.

In discussing literature, they spoke of the perennial stock-
in-trade of the republic of letters—woman's sin. And they
presently found themselves confronted by two opinions :
When a woman sins, is the man or the woman to blame?
The three women present—the ambassadress, the consul's
wife, and Mademoiselle des Touches, women, of course, of
blameless reputations—were without pity for the woman. The
men tried to convince these three fair flowers of their sex
that some virtues might remain in a woman after she had
fallen.

"How long are we going to play at hide-and-seek in this
way?" asked Léon de Lora.

"Dear life, go and put your children to bed, and send me by Gina the little black pocket-book that lies on my boule cabinet," said the consul to his wife.

She arose without a reply, which showed that she loved her husband very truly, for she already knew French enough to understand that her husband was getting rid of her.

"I will tell you a story in which I played a part, and after that we can discuss it, for it seems to me childish to practice with the scalpel on an imaginary body. Begin by dissecting a corpse."

Every one prepared to listen, with all the greater readiness because they had all talked enough, and this is the moment to be chosen for telling a story. This, then, is the consul-general's tale :

"When I was twenty-two, and had taken my degree in law, my old uncle, the Abbé Loraux, then seventy-two years old, felt it necessary to provide me with a protector and to start me in some career. This excellent man, if not indeed a saint, regarded each year of his life as a fresh gift from God. I need not tell you that the father confessor of a royal highness had no difficulty in finding a place for a young man brought up by himself, his sister's only child. So one day, toward the end of the year 1824, this venerable old man, who for five years had been curé of the white friars at Paris, came up to the room I had in his house, and said in his mild, gentle way—

"'Get yourself dressed, my dear boy; I am going to in-troduce you to some one who is willing to engage you as secretary. If I am not mistaken, he may fill my place in the event of God's taking me to Himself. I shall have finished mass by nine o'clock ; you have three-quarters of an hour be-fore you. Be ready.'

"'What, uncle ! must I say good-by to this room, where for four years I have been so happy?'

"'I have no fortune to leave you,' said he.

" ' Have you not the reputation of your name to leave me, the memory of your good works—— ? '

" ' We need say nothing of that inheritance,' he replied, smiling. 'You do not yet know enough of the world to be aware that a legacy of that kind is hardly likely to be paid, whereas by taking you this morning to M. le Comte '—Allow me," said the consul, interrupting himself, "to speak of my protector by his Christian name only, and to call him Comte Octave.—' By taking you this morning to M. le Comte Octave, I hope to secure you his patronage, which, if you are so fortunate as to please that virtuous statesman—as I make no doubt you can—will be worth, at least, as much as the fortune I might have accumulated for you, if my brother-in-law's ruin and my sister's death had not fallen on me like a thunderbolt from a clear sky.'

" ' Are you the Count's director ? '

" ' If I were, could I place you with him ? What priest could be capable of taking advantage of the secrets which he learns at the tribunal of repentance ? No ; you owe this position to his highness the keeper of the seals. My dear Maurice, you will be as much at home there as in your father's house. The Count will give you a salary of two thousand four hundred francs, rooms in his house, and an allowance of twelve hundred francs in lieu of feeding you. He will not admit you to his table, nor give you a separate table, for fear of leaving you to the care of servants. I did not accept the offer when it was made to me till I was perfectly certain that Comte Octave's secretary was never to be a mere upper servant. You will have an immense amount of work, for the Count is a great worker ; but when you leave him you will be qualified to fill the highest posts. I need not warn you to be discreet ; that is the first virtue of any man who hopes to hold public appointments.'

"You may conceive of my curiosity. Comte Octave, at that time, held one of the highest legal appointments ; he was in the confidence of Madame the Dauphiness, who had just got him made a state minister; he led such a life as the Comte de Sérizy, whom you all know, I think; but even more quietly, for his house was in the Marais, Rue Payenne, and he hardly ever entertained. His private life escaped public comment by its hermit-like simplicity and by constant hard work.

"Let me describe my position to you in a few words. Having found in the solemn headmaster of the Collége Saint-Louis a tutor to whom my uncle delegated his authority, at the age of eighteen I had gone through all the classes; I left school as innocent as a seminarist, full of faith, on quitting Saint-Sulpice. My mother, on her death-bed, had made my uncle promise that I should not become a priest, but I was as pious as though I had to take orders. On leaving college, the Abbé Loraux took me into his house and made me study law. During the four years of study requisite for passing all the examinations, I worked hard, but chiefly at things outside the arid fields of jurisprudence. Weaned from literature as I had been at college, where I lived in the headmaster's house, I had a thirst to quench. As soon as I had read a few modern masterpieces, the works of all the preceding ages were greedily swallowed. I became crazy about the theatre, and for a long time I went every night to the play, though my uncle gave me only a hundred francs a month. This parsimony, to which the good old man was compelled by his regard for the poor, had the effect of keeping a young man's desires within reasonable limits.

"When I went to live with Comte Octave I was not indeed an innocent, but I thought of my rare escapades as crimes. My uncle was so truly angelic, and I was so much afraid of grieving him, that in all those four years I had never spent a night out. The good man would wait till I came in to go to bed. This almost-maternal care had more power to keep me within bounds than the sermons and reproaches with which the life of a young man is diversified in a puritanical home. I was a

stranger to the various circles which make up the world of
Paris society; I only knew some women of the better sort,
and none of the inferior class but those I saw as I walked
about, or in the boxes at the play, and then only from the
depths of the pit where I sat. If, at that period, any one
had said to me, 'You will see Canalis or Camille Maupin,' I
should have felt hot coals on my head and in my bowels.
Famous people were to me as gods, who neither spoke, nor
walked, nor ate like other mortals.

"How many tales of the 'Thousand-and-one Nights' are
comprehended in the ripening of a youth! How many wonderful lamps must we have rubbed before we understand that
the true wonderful lamp is either luck, or work, or genius!
In some men this dream of the aroused spirit is but brief;
mine has lasted until now! In those days I always went to
sleep as Grand Duke of Tuscany—as a millionaire—as beloved
by a princess—or famous! So to enter the service of Comte
Octave, and have a hundred louis a year, was entering on
independent life. I had glimpses of some chance of getting
into society, and seeking for what my heart desired most, a
protectress, who would rescue me from the paths of danger,
which a young man of twenty-two can hardly help treading,
however prudent and well brought up he may be. I began
to be afraid of myself.

"The persistent study of other people's rights into which I
had plunged was not always enough to repress painful imaginings. Yes, sometimes in fancy I threw myself into theatrical
life; I thought I could be a great actor; I dreamed of endless
triumphs and loves, knowing nothing of the disillusion hidden
behind the curtain, as everywhere else—for every stage has its
reverse behind the scenes. I have gone out sometimes, my
heart boiling, carried away by an impulse to rush hunting
through Paris, to attach myself to some handsome woman I
might meet, to follow her to her door, watch her, write to
her, throw myself on her mercy, and conquer her by sheer

force of passion. My poor uncle, a heart consumed by charity, a child of seventy years, as clear-sighted as God, as guileless as a man of genius, no doubt read the tumult of my soul ; for when he felt the tether by which he held me strained too tightly and ready to break, he would never fail to say, ' Here, Maurice, you too are poor ! Here are twenty francs ; go and amuse yourself, you are not a priest ! ' And if you could then have seen the dancing light that gilded his gray eyes, the smile that relaxed his fine lips, puckering the corners of his mouth, the adorable expression of that august face, whose native ugliness was redeemed by the spirit of an apostle, you would understand the feeling which made me answer the curé of white friars only with a kiss, as if he had been my mother.

" ' In Comte Octave you will find not a master, but a friend,' said my uncle on the way to the Rue Payenne. ' But he is distrustful, or, to be more exact, he is cautious. The statesman's friendship can be won only with time ; for in spite of his deep insight and his habit of gauging men, he was deceived by the man you are succeeding, and nearly became a victim to his abuse of confidence. This is enough to guide you in your behavior to him.'

" When we knocked at the enormous outer door of a house as large as the Hôtel Carnavalet, with a courtyard in front and a garden behind, the sound rang as in a desert. While my uncle inquired of an old porter in livery if the Count were at home, I cast my eyes, seeing everything at once, over the courtyard where the cobblestones were hidden in grass, the blackened walls where little gardens were flourishing above the decorations of the elegant architecture, and on the roof, as high as that of the Tuileries. The balustrade of the upper balconies was eaten away. Through a magnificent colonnade I could see a second court on one side, where were the offices ; the door was rotting. An old coachman was there cleaning an old carriage. The indifferent air of this servant allowed

me to assume that the handsome stables, where of old so many
horses had whinnied, now sheltered two at most.   The handsome façade of the house seemed to me gloomy, like that of a
mansion belonging to the state or the crown, and given up to
some public office.   A bell rang as we walked across, my
uncle and I, from the porter's lodge—'Enquire of the Porter'
was still written over the door—toward the outside steps,
where a footman came out in a livery like that of Labranche
at the Théâtre Français in the old stock plays.   A visitor was
so rare that the servant was putting his coat on when he
opened a door glazed with small panes, on each side of which
the smoke of a lamp had traced patterns on the wall.

"A hall so magnificent as to be worthy of Versailles ended
in a staircase such as will never again be built in France,
taking up as much space as the whole of a modern house.
As we went up the marble steps, as cold as tombstones and
wide enough for eight persons to walk abreast, our tread
echoed under sonorous vaulting.   The banister charmed the
eye by its miraculous workmanship—goldsmith's work in iron
—wrought by the fancy of an artist of the time of Henri III.
Chilled as by an icy mantle that fell on our shoulders, we
went through anterooms, drawing-rooms, opening one out of
the other, with carpetless parquet floors, and furnished with
such splendid antiquities as from thence would find their way
to the curiosity dealers.   At last we reached a large study in
a cross wing, with all the windows looking into an immense
garden.

"'Monsieur le Curé of the White Friars and his nephew,
Monsieur de L'Hostal,' said Labranche, to whose care the
other theatrical servant had consigned us in the first ante-
chamber.

"Comte Octave, dressed in long trousers and a gray flannel
morning-coat, rose from his seat by a huge writing-table,
came to the fireplace and signed to me to sit down, while he
went forward to take my uncle's hands, which he pressed.

"'Though I am in the parish of Saint-Paul,' said he, 'I could scarcely have failed to hear of the curé of the white friars, and I am happy to make his acquaintance.'

"'Your excellency is most kind,' replied my uncle. 'I have brought to you my only remaining relation. While I believe that I am offering a good gift to your excellency, I hope at the same time to give my nephew a second father.'

"'As to that, I can only reply, Monsieur l'Abbé, when we shall have tried each other,' said Comte Octave. 'Your name?' he added to me.

"'Maurice.'

"'He has taken his doctor's degree in law,' my uncle observed.

"'Very good, very good!' said the Count, looking at me from head to foot. 'Monsieur l'Abbé, I hope that for your nephew's sake in the first instance, and then for mine, you will do me the honor of dining here every Monday. That will be our family dinner, our family party.'

"My uncle and the Count then began to talk of religion from the political point of view, of charitable institutes, the repression of crime, so I could at my leisure study the man on whom my fate would henceforth depend. The Count was of middle height; it was impossible to judge of his build on account of his dress, but he seemed to me to be lean and spare. His face was harsh and hollow; the features were refined. His mouth, which was rather large, expressed both irony and kindliness. His forehead, perhaps too spacious, was as intimidating as that of a madman, all the more so from the contrast of the lower part of the face, which ended squarely in a short chin very near the lower lip. Small eyes, of turquoise blue, were as keen and bright as those of the Prince de Talleyrand—which I admired at a later time— and endowed, like the Prince's, with a faculty of becoming expressionless to the verge of gloom; and they added to the singularity of a face that was not pale but yellow. This complexion seemed to bespeak an irritable temper and violent passions. His hair, already silvered and carefully dressed, seemed to furrow his head with streaks of black and white alternately. The trimness of this head spoiled the resemblance I had remarked in the Count to the wonderful monk described by Lewis after Schedoni in the 'Confessional of the Black Penitents,' a superior creation, as it seems to me, to 'The Monk.'

"The Count was already shaved, having to attend early at the law courts. Two candelabra with four lights, screened by lamp-shades, were still burning at the opposite ends of the writing-table, and showed plainly that the magistrate rose long before daylight. His hands, which I saw when he took hold of the bell-pull to summon his servant, were extremely fine and as white as a woman's.

"As I tell you this story," said the consul-general, interrupting himself, "I am altering the titles and the social position of this gentleman, while placing him in circumstances analogous to what his really were. His profession, rank, luxury, fortune, and style of living were the same; all these details are true, but I will not be false to my benefactor, nor to my usual habits of discretion.

"Instead of feeling—as I really was, socially speaking—an insect in the presence of an eagle," the narrator went on after a pause, "I felt I know not what indefinable impression from the Count's appearance, which, however, I can now account for. Artists of genius" (and he bowed gracefully to the ambassador, the distinguished lady, and the two Frenchmen), "real statesmen, poets, a general who has commanded armies—in short, all really great minds are simple, and their simplicity places you on a level with themselves. You who are all of superior minds," he said, addressing his guests, "have perhaps observed how feeling can bridge over the distances created by society. If we are inferior to you in intellect, we can be your equals in devoted friendship. By the temperature—allow me the word—of our hearts I felt myself as near my patron as I was far below him in rank. In short, the soul has its clairvoyance; it has presentiments of suffering, grief, joy, antagonism, or hatred in others.

"I vaguely discerned the symptoms of a mystery, from recognizing in the Count the same effects of physiognomy that I had observed in my uncle. The exercise of virtue, serenity of conscience, and purity of mind had transfigured my uncle, who from being ugly had become quite beautiful. I detected a metamorphosis of a reverse kind in the Count's face; at the first glance I thought he was about fifty-five, but after an attentive examination I found youth entombed under the ice of a great sorrow, under the fatigue of persistent study, under the glowing hues of some suppressed passion. At a word from my uncle the Count's eyes recovered for a moment the softness of the periwinkle flower and he had an admiring smile, which revealed what I believed to be his real age, about forty. These observations I made, not then but afterward, as I recalled the many different circumstances of my visit.

"The manservant came in carrying a tray with his master's breakfast on it.

"'I did not ask for breakfast,' remarked the Count; 'but leave it, and show monsieur to his rooms.'

"I followed the servant, who led the way to a complete set of pretty rooms, under a terrace, between the great courtyard and the servants' quarters, over a corridor of communication between the kitchens and the grand staircase. When I returned to the Count's study, I overheard, before opening the door, my uncle pronouncing this judgment on me—

"'He may do wrong, for he has strong feelings, and we are all liable to honorable mistakes; but he has no vices.'

"'Well,' said the Count to me, with a kindly look, 'do you like yourself there? Tell me. There are so many rooms in this barrack that, if you were not comfortable, I could put you elsewhere.'

"'At my uncle's I had but one room,' I replied.

"'Well, you can settle yourself this evening,' said the Count, 'for your possessions, no doubt, are such as all students own and a hackney coach will be enough to convey them. To-day we will all three dine together,' and he looked at my uncle.

"A splendid library opened from the Count's study, and he took us in there, showing me a pretty little recess decorated with paintings, which had formerly served, no doubt, as an oratory.

"'This is your cell,' said he. 'You will sit there when you have to work with me, for you will not be tethered by a chain;' and he explained in detail the kind and duration of my employment with him. As I listened I felt that he was a great political teacher.

"It took me about a month to familiarize myself with people and things, to learn the duties of my new office, and accustom myself to the Count's methods. A secretary necessarily watches the man who makes use of him. That man's tastes, passions, temper, and manias become the subject of involuntary study. The union of their two minds is at once more and less than a marriage.

"During these months the Count and I reciprocally studied each other. I learned with astonishment that Comte Octave was but thirty-seven years old. The merely superficial peacefulness of his life and the propriety of his conduct were the outcome not solely of a deep sense of duty and of stoical reflection; in my constant intercourse with this man—an extraordinary man to those who knew him well—I felt vast depths beneath his toil, beneath his acts of politeness, his mask of benignity, his assumption of resignation, which so closely resembled calmness that it was easy to mistake it. Just as when walking through forest lands certain soils give

forth under our feet a sound which enables us to guess whether
they are dense masses of stone or a void; so intense egoism,
though hidden under the flowers of politeness, and subterranean caverns eaten out by sorrow sound hollow under the
constant touch of familiar life. It was sorrow and not de- .
spondency that dwelt in that really great soul. The Count
had understood that actions, deeds, are the supreme law of
social man. And he went on his way in spite of secret
wounds, looking to the future with a tranquil eye, like a
martyr full of faith.

"His concealed sadness, the bitter disenchantment from
which he suffered, had not led him into philosophical deserts
of incredulity; this brave statesman was religious, but without
ostentation; he always attended the earliest mass at Saint-
Paul's for pious workmen and servants. Not one of his friends,
no one at court, knew that he so punctually fulfilled the practice of religion. He was addicted to God as some men are
addicted to a vice, with the greatest mystery. Thus one day
I came to find the Count at the summit of an Alp of woe
much higher than that on which many are who think themselves the most tried; who laugh at the passions and the
beliefs of others because they have conquered their own; who
play variations in every key of irony and disdain. He did
not mock at those who still follow hope into the swamps
whither she leads, nor those who climb a peak to be alone,
nor those who persist in the fight, reddening the arena with
their blood and strewing it with their illusions. He looked
on the world as a whole; he mastered its beliefs; he listened
to its complaining; he was doubtful of affection, and yet
more of self-sacrifice; but this great and stern judge pitied
them, or admired them, not with transient enthusiasm, but
with silence, concentration, and the communion of a deeply
touched soul. He was a sort of catholic Manfred, and un-
stained by crime, carrying his choiceness into his faith,
melting the snows by all the deeply hidden and smoldering

20

fires of a sealed volcano, holding converse with a star seen by himself alone!

"I detected many dark riddles in his ordinary life. He evaded my gaze, not like a traveler who, following a path, disappears from time to time in dells or ravines according to the formation of the soil, but like a sharpshooter who is being watched, who wants to hide himself, and seeks a cover. I could not account for his frequent absences at times when he was working the hardest, and of which he made no secret from me, for he would say, 'Go on with this for me,' and trust me with the work in hand.

"This man, wrapped in the threefold duties of the statesman, the judge, and the orator, charmed me by a taste for flowers, which shows an elegant mind, and which is shared by almost all persons of refinement. His garden and his study were full of the rarest plants, but he always bought them half-withered. Perhaps it pleased him to see such an image of his own fate! He was faded like these dying flowers, whose almost decaying fragrance mounted strangely to his brain. The Count loved his country; he devoted himself to public interests with the frenzy of a heart that seeks to cheat some other passion; but the studies and work into which he threw himself were not enough for him; there were frightful struggles in his mind, of which some echoes reached me. Finally, he would give utterance to harrowing aspirations for happiness, and it seemed to me he ought yet to be happy; but what was the obstacle? Was there a woman he loved? This was a question I asked myself. You may imagine the extent of the circles of torment that my mind had searched before coming to so simple and so terrible a question. Notwithstanding his efforts, my patron did not succeed in stifling the movements of his heart. Under his austere manner, under the reserve of the magistrate, a passion rebelled, though coerced with such force that no one but I who lived with him ever guessed the secret. His motto seemed to be, 'I suffer and am silent.'

The escort of respect and admiration which attended him; the friendship of workers as valiant as himself—Grandville and Sérizy, both presiding judges—had no hold over the Count: either he told them nothing or they knew all. Impassible and lofty in public, the Count betrayed the man only on rare intervals when, alone in his garden or his study, he supposed himself unobserved; but then he was a child again, he gave course to the tears hidden beneath the toga, to the excitement which, if wrongly interpreted, might have damaged his credit for perspicacity as a statesman.

"When all this had become to me a matter of certainty, Comte Octave had all the attractions of a problem, and won on my affection as much as though he had been my own father. Can you enter into the feeling of curiosity, tempered by respect? What catastrophe had blasted this learned man, who, like Pitt, had devoted himself from the age of eighteen to the studies indispensable to power, while he had no ambition; this judge, who thoroughly knew the law of nations, political law, civil and criminal law, and who could find in these a weapon against every anxiety, against every mistake; this profound legislator, this serious writer, this pious celibate whose life sufficiently proved that he was open to no reproach? A criminal could not have been more hardly punished by God than was my master; sorrow had robbed him of half his slumbers; he never slept more than four hours. What struggle was it that went on in the depths of these hours apparently so calm, so studious, passing without a sound or a murmur, during which I often detected him, when the pen had dropped from his fingers, with his head resting on one hand, his eyes like two fixed stars, and sometimes wet with tears? How could the waters of that living spring flow over the burning strand without being dried up by the subterranean fire? Was there below it, as there is under the sea, between it and the central fires of the globe, a bed of granite? And would the volcano burst at last?

"Sometimes the Count would give me a look of that sagacious and keen-eyed curiosity by which one man searches another when he desires an accomplice; then he shunned my eye as he saw it open a mouth, so to speak, insisting on a reply, and seeming to say, 'Speak first!' Now and then Comte Octave's melancholy was surly and gruff. If these spurts of temper offended me, he could get over it without thinking of asking my pardon; but then his manners were gracious to the point of Christian humility.

"When I became attached like a son to this man—to me such a mystery, but so intelligible to the outer world, to whom the epithet eccentric is enough to account for all the enigmas of the heart—I changed the state of the house. Neglect of his own interests was carried by the Count to the length of folly in the management of his affairs. Possessing an income of about a hundred and sixty thousand francs, without including the emoluments of his appointments—three of which did not come under the law against plurality—he spent sixty thousand, of which at least thirty thousand went to his servants. By the end of the first year I had rid him of all these rascals, and begged his excellency to use his influence in helping me to get honest servants. By the end of the second year the Count, better fed and better served, enjoyed the comforts of modern life; he had fine horses, supplied by a coachman to whom I paid so much a month for each horse; his dinners on his reception days, furnished by Chevet at a price agreed upon, did him credit; his daily meals were prepared by an excellent cook found by my uncle, and helped by two kitchen-maids. The expenditure for housekeeping, not including purchases, was no more than thirty thousand francs a year; we had two additional menservants, whose care restored the poetical aspect of the house; for this old palace, splendid even in its rust, had an air of dignity which neglect had dishonored.

"'I am no longer astonished,' said he, on hearing of these

results, 'at the fortunes made by my servants. In seven years I have had two cooks, who have become rich restaurant-keepers.'

"'And in seven years you have lost a hundred thousand francs,' replied I. 'You, a judge, who in your court sign summonses against crime, encouraged robbery in your own house.'

"Early in the year 1826 the Count had, no doubt, ceased to watch me, and we were as closely attached as two men can be when one is subordinate to the other. He had never spoken to me of my future prospects, but he had taken an interest, both as a master and as a father, in training me. He often required me to collect materials for his most arduous labors; I drew up some of his reports and he corrected them, showing the difference between his interpretation of the law, his views and mine. When at last I had produced a document which he could give in as his own he was delighted; this satisfaction was my reward, and he could see that I took it so. This little incident produced an extraordinary effect on a soul which seemed so stern. The Count pronounced sentence on me, to use a legal phrase, as supreme and royal judge; he took my head in his hands, and kissed me on the forehead.

"'Maurice,' he exclaimed, 'you are no longer my apprentice; I know not yet what you will be to me—but if no change occurs in my life, perhaps you will take the place of a son.'

"Comte Octave had introduced me to the best houses in Paris, whither I went in his stead with his servants and carriage, on the too frequent occasions when, on the point of starting, he changed his mind and sent for a hackney cab to take him—Where?—that was the mystery. By the welcome I met with I could judge of the Count's feelings toward me and the earnestness of his recommendations. He supplied all my wants with the thoughtfulness of a father, and with all the greater liberality because my modesty left it to him always to think of me. Toward the end of January, 1827, at the house of the Comtesse de Sérizy, I had such persistent ill-luck at play that I lost two thousand francs, and I would not draw them out of my savings. Next morning I asked myself, ' Had I better ask my uncle for the money, or put my confidence in the Count ? '

"I decided on the second alternative.

" ' Yesterday,' I said, when he was at breakfast, 'I lost persistently at play; I was provoked, and went on; I owe two thousand francs. Will you allow me to draw the sum on account of my year's salary ? '

" ' No,' said he, with the sweetest smile; ' when a man plays in society, he must have a gambling purse. Draw six thousand francs; pay your debts. Henceforth we must go halves ; for since you are my representative on most occasions, your self-respect must not be made to suffer for it.'

"I made no speech of thanks. Thanks would have been superfluous between us. This shade shows the character of our relations. And as yet we had not unlimited confidence in each other ; he did not open to me the vast subterranean chambers which I had detected in his secret life ; and I, for my part, never said to him, ' What ails you? From what are you suffering ? '

"What could he be doing during those long evenings ? He would often come in on foot or in a hackney cab when I returned in a carriage—I, his secretary ! Was so pious a man a prey to vices hidden under hypocrisy ? Did he expend all the powers of his mind to satisfy a jealousy more dexterous than Othello's ? Did he live with some woman unworthy of him ? One morning, on returning from I have forgotten what store, where I had just paid a bill, between the church of Saint-Paul and the Hôtel de Ville, I came across Comte Octave in such eager conversation with an old woman that he did not see me. The appearance of this hag filled me with strange suspicions, suspicions that were all the better founded because I never found that the Count invested his savings. Is it not shocking to think of? I was constituting myself my patron's censor. At that time I knew that he had more than six hundred thousand francs to invest; and if he had bought securities of any kind his confidence in me was so complete, in all that concerned his pecuniary interests, that I certainly should have known it.

"Sometimes, in the morning, the Count took exercise in his garden, to and fro, like a man to whom a walk is the hippogryph ridden by dreamy melancholy. He walked and walked! And he rubbed his hands enough to rub the skin off. And then, if I met him unexpectedly as he came to the angle of a path, I saw his face beaming. His eyes, instead of the hardness of a turquoise, had that velvety softness of the blue periwinkle, which had so much struck me on the occasion of my first visit, by reason of the astonishing contrast in the two different looks: the look of a happy man and the look of an unhappy man. Two or three times at such a moment he had taken me by the arm and led me on; then he had said, 'What have you come to ask?' instead of pouring out his joy into my heart that opened to him. But more often, especially since I could do his work for him and write his reports, the unhappy man would sit for hours staring at the gold fish that swarmed in a handsome marble basin in the middle of the garden, round which grew an amphitheatre of the finest flowers. He, an accomplished statesman, seemed to have succeeded in making a passion, a reigning hobby, of the mechanical amusement of crumbling bread to fishes.

"This is how the drama was disclosed of this second inner life, so deeply ravaged and storm-tossed, where, in a circle overlooked by Dante in his 'Inferno,' horrible joys had their birth."

The consul-general paused.

"On a certain Monday," he resumed, "as chance would have it, M. le Président de Grandville and M. de Sérizy (at that time vice-president of the council of state) had come to hold a meeting at the Comte Octave's house. They formed a committee of three, of which I was the secretary. The Count had already gotten me the appointment of auditor to the council of state. All the documents requisite for their inquiry into the political matter privately submitted to these three gentlemen were laid out on one of the long tables in the library. Messrs. de Grandville and de Sérizy had trusted to the Count to make the preliminary examination of the papers relating to the matter. To avoid the necessity for carrying all the papers to M. de Sérizy, as president of the commission, it was decided that they should meet first in the Rue Payenne. The cabinet at the Tuileries attached great importance to this piece of work, of which the chief burden fell on me—and to which, and my patron's efforts, I owed my appointment, in the course of that year, to be master of appeals.

"Though the Comtes de Grandville and de Sérizy, whose habits were much the same as my patron's, never dined away from home, we were still discussing the matter at a late hour, when we were startled by the manservant calling me aside to say, 'Messrs. the Curés of Saint-Paul and of the White Friars have been waiting in the drawing-room for two hours.'

"It was nine o'clock.

"'Well, gentlemen, you find yourselves compelled to dine with priests,' said Comte Octave to his colleagues. 'I do not know whether Grandville can overcome his horror of a priest's gown——'

"'It depends on the priest.'

"'One of them is my uncle and the other is the Abbé Gaudron,' said I. 'Do not be alarmed; the Abbé Fontanon is no longer second priest at Saint-Paul——'

"'Well. let us dine,' replied the Président de Grandville.

'A bigot frightens me, but there is no one so cheerful as a truly pious man.'

"We went into the drawing-room. The dinner was delightful. Men of real information, politicians to whom business gives both consummate experience and the practice of speech, are admirable story-tellers, when they tell stories. With them there is no medium; they are either heavy or they are sublime. In this delightful sport Prince Metternich is as good as Charles Nodier. The fun of a statesman, cut in facets like a diamond, is sharp, sparkling, and full of sense. Being sure that the proprieties would be observed by these three superior men, my uncle allowed his wit full play, a refined wit, gentle, penetrating, and elegant, like that of all men who are accustomed to conceal their thoughts under the black robe. And you may rely upon it, there was nothing vulgar nor idle in this light talk, which I would compare, for its effect on the soul, to Rossini's music.

"The Abbé Gaudron was, as M. de Grandville said, a Saint Peter rather than a Saint Paul, a peasant full of faith, as square on his feet as he was tall, a sacerdotal of whose ignorance in matters of the world and of literature enlivened the conversation by guileless amazement and unexpected questions. They came to talking of one of the plague spots of social life, of which we were just now speaking—adultery. My uncle remarked on the contradiction which the legislators of the code, still feeling the blows of the revolutionary storm, had established between civil and religious law, and which he maintained and insisted was at the root of all the mischief.

"'In the eyes of the church,' said he, 'adultery is a crime; in those of your tribunals it is a misdemeanor. Adultery drives to the police court in a carriage instead of standing at the bar to be tried. Napoleon's council of state, touched with tenderness toward erring women, was quite inefficient. Ought they not in this case to have harmonized the civil and the religious law, and have sent the guilty wife to a convent, as of old?'

"'To a convent!' said M. de Sérizy. 'They must first have created convents, and in those days monasteries were being turned into barracks. Beside, think of what you say, Monsieur l'Abbé — give to God what society would have none of?'   .

"'Oh!' said the Comte de Grandville, 'you do not know France. They were obliged to leave the husband free to take proceedings; well, there are not ten cases of adultery brought up in a year.'

"'M. l'Abbé preaches for his own saint, for it was Jesus Christ who invented adultery,' said Comte Octave. 'In the East, the cradle of the human race, woman was merely a luxury, and was there regarded as a chattel; no virtues were demanded of her but obedience and beauty. By exalting the soul above the body, the modern family in Europe—a daughter of Christ—invented indissoluble marriage and made it a sacrament.'

"'Ah! the church saw all the difficulties,' exclaimed M. de Grandville.

"'This institution has given rise to a new world,' the Count went on with a smile. 'But the practice of that world will never be that of a climate where women are marriageable at seven years of age and more than old at five-and-twenty. The Catholic Church overlooked the needs of half the globe. So let us discuss Europe only.

"'Is woman our superior or our inferior? That is the real question so far as we are concerned. If woman is our inferior, by placing her on so high a level as the church does, fearful punishment for adultery were needful. And formerly that was what was done. The cloister or death sums up early legislation. But since then practice has modified the law, as is always the case. The throne served as a hot-bed for adultery, and the increase of this inviting crime marks the decline of the dogmas of the Catholic Church. In these days, in cases where the church now exacts no more than sincere repentance from the erring wife, society is satisfied with a brand-mark instead of an execution. The law still condemns the guilty, but it no longer terrifies them. In short, there are two standards of morals: that of the world and that of the code. Where the code is weak, as I admit with our dear abbé, the world is audacious and satirical. There are so few judges who would not gladly have committed the fault against which they hurl the rather stolid thunders of their "Inasmuch." The world, which gives the lie to the law alike in its rejoicings, in its habits, and in its pleasures, is severer than the code and the church; the world punishes a blunder after encouraging hypocrisy. The whole economy of the law on marriage seems to me to require reconstruction from the bottom to the top. The French law would be perfect perhaps if it excluded daughters from inheriting.'

" 'We three among us know the question very thoroughly,' said the Comte de Grandville with a laugh. 'I have a wife I cannot live with. Sérizy has a wife who will not live with him. As for you, Octave, yours ran away from you. So we three represent every case of the conjugal conscience, and, no doubt, if ever divorce is brought in again, we shall form the committee.'

"Octave's fork dropped on his glass, broke it, and broke his plate. He had turned pale as death, and flashed a thunderous glare at M. de Grandville, by which he hinted at my presence, and which I caught.

" 'Forgive me, my dear fellow. I did not see Maurice,' the president went on. 'Sérizy and I, after being the witnesses to your marriage, became your accomplices; I did not think I was committing an indiscretion in the presence of these two venerable priests.'

" M. de Sérizy changed the subject by relating all he had done to please his wife without ever succeeding. The old man concluded that it was impossible to regulate human sympathies and antipathies; he maintained that social law was never more perfect than when it was nearest to natural law. Now, nature takes no account of the affinities of souls; her aim is fulfilled by the propagation of the species. Hence, the code, in its present form, was wise in leaving a wide latitude to chance. The incapacity of daughters to inherit so long as there were male heirs was an excellent provision, whether to hinder the degeneration of the race, or to make households happier by abolishing scandalous unions and giving the sole preference to moral qualities and beauty.

" ' But then,' he exclaimed, lifting his hand with a gesture of disgust, ' how are we to perfect legislation in a country which insists on bringing together seven or eight hundred legislators? After all, if I am sacrificed,' he added, ' I have a child to succeed me.'

" ' Setting aside all the religious question,' my uncle said, ' I would remark to your excellency that nature only owes us life, and that it is society that owes us happiness. Are you a father?' asked my uncle.

" ' And I—have I any children?' said Comte Octave in a hollow voice, and his tone made such an impression that there was no more talk of wives or marriage.

"When coffee had been served, the two Counts and the two priests stole away, seeing that poor Octave had fallen into a fit of melancholy, which prevented his noticing their disappearance. My patron was sitting in an armchair by the fire, in the attitude of a man crushed.

" ' You now know the secret of my life,' said he to me on noticing that we were alone. ' After three years of married life, one evening when I came in I found a letter in which the Countess announced her flight. The letter did not lack dignity, for it is in the nature of women to preserve some virtues even when committing that horrible sin. The story now is that my wife went abroad in a ship that was wrecked;

she is supposed to be dead. I have lived alone for seven years! Enough for this evening, Maurice. We will talk of my situation when I have grown used to the idea of speaking of it to you. When we suffer from a chronic disease, it needs time to become accustomed to improvement. That improvement often seems to be merely another aspect of the complaint.'

"I went to bed greatly agitated; for the mystery, far from being explained, seemed to me more obscure than ever. I foresaw some strange drama indeed, for I understood that there could be no vulgar difference between the woman the Count could choose and such a character as his. The events which had driven the Countess to leave a man so noble, so amiable, so perfect, so loving, so worthy to be loved, must have been singular, to say the least. M. de Grandville's remark had been like a torch flung into the caverns over which I had so long been walking; and though the flame lighted them but dimly, my eyes could perceive their wide extent! I could imagine the Count's sufferings without knowing their depth or their bitterness. That sallow face, those parched temples, those overwhelming studies, those moments of absent-mindedness, the smallest details of the life of this married bachelor, all stood out in luminous relief during the hour of mental questioning, which is, as it were, the twilight before sleep, and to which any man would have given himself up, as I did.

"Oh! how I loved my poor master! He seemed to me sublime. I read a poem of melancholy, I saw perpetual activity in the heart I had accused of being torpid. Must not supreme grief always come at last to stagnation? Had this judge, who had so much in his power, ever revenged himself? Was he feeding himself on her long agony? Is it not a remarkable thing in Paris to keep anger always seething for ten years? What had Octave done since this great misfortune—for the separation of husband and wife is a great

misfortune in our day, when domestic life has become a social
question, which it never was of old?

"We allowed a few days to pass on the watch, for great
sorrows have a diffidence of their own; but at last, one evening, the Count said in a grave voice—

"'Stay.'

"This, as nearly as may be, is his story:

"'My father had a ward, rich and lovely, who was sixteen
at the time when I came back from college to live in this old
house. Honorine, who had been brought up by my mother,
was just awaking to life. Full of grace and of childlike ways,
she dreamed of happiness as she would have dreamed of
jewels; perhaps happiness seemed to her the jewels of the
soul. Her piety was not free from puerile pleasures; for
everything, even religion, was poetry to her ingenuous heart.
She looked to the future as a perpetual fête. Innocent and
pure, no delirium had disturbed her dream. Shame and grief
had never tinged her cheek nor moistened her eye. She did
not even inquire into the secret of her involuntary emotions
on a fine spring day. And, then, she felt that she was weak
and destined to obedience, and she awaited marriage without
wishing for it. Her smiling imagination knew nothing of the
corruption—necessary perhaps—which literature imparts by
depicting the passions; she knew nothing of the world, and
was ignorant of all the dangers of society. The dear child had
suffered so little that she had not even developed her courage.
In short, her guilelessness would have led her to walk fear-
lessly among serpents, like the ideal figure of Innocence a
painter once created. We lived together like two brothers.
An ideal life.

"'At the end of a year I said to her one day, in the garden
of this house, by the basin, as we stood throwing crumbs to
the fish—

"'"Would you like that we should be married? With me

you could do whatever you please, while another man would make you unhappy."

" ' " Mamma," said she to my mother, who came out to join us, " Octave and I have agreed to be married——"

" ' " What ! at seventeen?" said my mother. "No; you must wait eighteen months ; and if eighteen months hence you like each other, well, your birth and fortunes are equal, you can make a marriage which is suitable, as well as being a love match."

" ' When I was six-and-twenty and Honorine nineteen, we were married. Our respect for my father and mother, old folk of the Bourbon court, hindered us from making this house fashionable or renewing the furniture; we lived on, as we had done in the past, as children. However, I went into society ; I initiated my wife into the world of fashion ; and I regarded it as one of my duties to instruct her.

" ' I recognized afterward that marriages contracted under such circumstances as ours bear in themselves a rock against which many affections are wrecked, many prudent calculations, many lives. The husband becomes a pedagogue, or, if you like, a professor, and love perishes under the rod which, soon or later, gives pain ; for a young and handsome wife, at once discreet and laughter-loving, will not accept any superiority above that with which she is endowed by nature. Perhaps I was in the wrong. During the difficult beginnings of a household I, perhaps, assumed a magisterial tone. On the other hand, I may have made the mistake of trusting too entirely to that artless nature ; I kept no watch over the Countess, in whom revolt seemed to me impossible. Alas! neither in politics nor domestic life has it yet been ascertained whether empires and happiness are wrecked by too much confidence or too much severity ! Perhaps, again, the husband failed to realize Honorine's girlish dreams? Who can tell, while happy days last, what precepts he has neglected.'

" I remember only the broad outlines of the reproaches the

Count addressed to himself, with all the good faith of an
anatomist seeking the cause of a disease which might be overlooked by his brethren; but his merciful indulgence struck
me then as equally worthy as that of Jesus Christ when He
rescued the woman taken in adultery.

"'It was eighteen months after my father's death—my
mother followed him to the tomb in a few months—when the
fearful night came which surprised me by Honorine's farewell
letter. What poetic delusion had seduced my wife? Was it
through her senses? Was it the magnetism of misfortune or
of genius? Which of these powers had taken her by storm
or misled her? I would not know. The blow was so terrible that for a month I remained stunned. Afterward, reflection counseled me to continue in ignorance, and Honorine's misfortunes have since taught me too much about all
these things. So far, Maurice, the story is commonplace
enough; but one word will change it all: I love Honorine,
I have never ceased to worship her. From the day when she
left me I have lived on memory; one by one I recall the
pleasures for which Honorine, no doubt, had no taste.

"'Oh!' said he, seeing the amazement in my eyes, 'do
not make a hero of me, do not think me such a fool, as a
colonel of the Empire would say, as to have sought no diversion. Alas, my boy! I was either too young or too much in
love; I have not in the whole world met with another woman.
After frightful struggles with myself, I tried to forget; money
in hand, I stood on the very threshold of infidelity, but there
the memory of Honorine rose before me like a white statue.
As I recalled the infinite delicacy of that exquisite skin,
through which the blood might be seen coursing and the
nerves quivering; as I saw in fancy that ingenuous face, as
guileless on the eve of my sorrows as on the day when I said
to her, "Shall we marry?" as I remembered a heavenly
fragrance, the very odor of virtue, and the light in her eyes,
the prettiness of her movements, I fled like a man preparing

to violate a tomb, who sees emerging from it the transfigured soul of the dead. At consultations, in court, by night, I dream so incessantly of Honorine that only by excessive strength of mind do I succeed in attending to what I am doing and saying. This is the secret of my labors.

"'Well, I felt no more anger with her than a father can feel on seeing his beloved child in some danger it has imprudently rushed into. I understood that I had made a poem of my wife—a poem I delighted in with such intoxication that I fancied she shared the intoxication. Ah! Maurice, an indiscriminating passion in a husband is a mistake that may lead to any crime in a wife. I had no doubt left all the faculties of this child, loved as a child, entirely unemployed; I had perhaps wearied her with my love before the hour of loving had struck for her! Too young to understand that in the constancy of the wife lies the germ of the mother's devotion, she mistook this first test of marriage for life itself, and the refractory child cursed life, unknown to me, not daring to complain to me, out of sheer modesty perhaps! In so cruel a position she would be defenseless against any man who stirred her deeply. And I, so wise a judge as they say—I, who have a kind heart, but whose mind was absorbed—I understood too late these unwritten laws of the woman's code; I read them by the light of the fire that wrecked my roof. Then I constituted my heart a tribunal by virtue of the law, for the law makes the husband a judge: I acquitted my wife, and I condemned myself. But love took possession of me as a passion, the mean, despotic passion which comes over some old men. At this day I love the absent Honorine as a man of sixty loves a woman whom he must possess at any cost, and yet I feel the strength of a young man. I have the insolence of the old man and the reserve of a boy. My dear fellow, society only laughs at such a desperate conjugal predicament. Where it pities a lover, it regards a husband as ridiculously inept; it makes sport of those who cannot keep

21

the woman they have secured under the canopy of the church
and before the mayor's scarf of office. And I had to keep
silence.

"'Sérizy is happy. His indulgence allows him to see his
wife; he can protect and defend her; and, as he adores her,
he knows all the perfect joys of a benefactor whom nothing
can disturb, not even ridicule, for he pours it himself on his
fatherly pleasures. "I remain married only for my wife's
sake," he said to me one day on coming out of court.

"'But I—I have nothing; I have not even to face ridicule,
I who live solely on a love which is starving! I who can
never find a word to say to a woman of the world! I who
loathe prostitution! I who am faithful under a spell! But
for my religious faith, I should have killed myself. I have
defied the gulf of hard work; I have thrown myself into it,
and come out again alive, fevered, burning, ever bereft of
sleep!——'

"I cannot remember all the words of this eloquent man, to
whom passion gave an eloquence indeed so far above that of
the pleader that, as I listened to him, I, like him, felt my
cheeks wet with tears. You may conceive of my feelings
when, after a pause, during which we dried them away, he
finished his story with this revelation:

"'This is the drama of my soul, but it is not the actual
living drama which is at this moment being acted in Paris!
The interior drama interests nobody. I know it; and you
will one day admit that it is so, you, who at this moment
shed tears with me; no one can burden his heart or his skin
with another's pain. The measure of our sufferings is in ourselves. You even understand my sorrows only by very vague
analogy. Could you see me calming the most violent frenzy
of despair by the contemplation of a miniature in which I
can see and kiss her brow, the smile on her lips, the shape of
her face, can breathe the whiteness of her skin; which enables
me almost to feel, to play with the black masses of her curling

hair? Could you see me when I leap with hope—when I writhe under the myriad darts of despair—when I tramp through the mire of Paris to quell my irritation by fatigue? I have fits of collapse comparable to those of a comsumptive patient, moods of wild hilarity, terrors as of a murderer who meets a sergeant of police. In short, my life is a continual paroxysm of fears, joy, and dejection.

" 'As to the drama—it is this: You imagine that I am occupied with the council of state, the chamber, the courts, politics. Why, dear me, seven hours at night are enough for all that, so much are my faculties overwrought by the life I lead! Honorine is my real concern. To recover my wife is my only study; to guard her in her cage, without her suspecting that she is in my power; to satisfy her needs, to supply the little pleasure she allows herself, to be always about her like a sylph without allowing her to see or to suspect me, for, if she did, the future would be lost—that is my life, my true life. For seven years I have never gone to bed without going first to see the light of her night-lamp or her shadow on the window curtains.

" 'She left my house, choosing to take nothing but the dress she wore that day. The child carried her magnanimity to the point of folly! Consequently, eighteen months after her flight she was deserted by her lover, who was appalled by the cold, cruel, sinister, and revolting aspect of poverty—the coward! The man had, no doubt, counted on the easy and luxurious life in Switzerland or Italy which fine ladies indulge in when they leave their husbands. Honorine has sixty thousand francs a year of her own. The wretch left the dear creature expecting an infant, and without a penny. In the month of November, 1820, I found means to persuade the best accoucheur in Paris to play the part of a humble suburban apothecary. I induced the priest of the parish in which the Countess was living to supply her needs as though he were performing an act of charity. Then to hide my wife, to

secure her against discovery, to find her a housekeeper who
would be devoted to me and be my intelligent confidante—it
was a task worthy of Figaro! You may suppose that to discover where my wife had taken refuge I had only to make up
my mind to it.

"'After three months of desperation rather than despair,
the idea of devoting myself to Honorine, with God only in
my secret, was one of those poems which occur only to the
heart of a lover through life and death! Love must have its
daily food. And ought I not to protect this child, whose
guilt was the outcome of my imprudence, against fresh disaster—to fulfill my part, in short, as a guardian angel? At
the age of seven months her infant died, happily for her and
for me. For nine months more my wife lay between life and
death, deserted at the time when she most needed a manly
arm; but this arm,' said he, holding out his own with a
gesture of angelic dignity, 'was extended over her head.
Honorine was nursed as she would have been in her own
home. When, on her recovery, she asked how and by whom
she had been assisted, she was told—"By the sisters of charity
in the neighborhood—by the maternity society—by the parish
priest, who took an interest in her."

"'This woman, whose pride amounts to a vice, has shown
a power of resistance in misfortune, which on some evenings
I call the obstinacy of a mule. Honorine was bent on earning her living. My wife works! For five years past I have
lodged her in the Rue Saint-Maur, in a charming little house,
where she makes artificial flowers and articles of fashion.
She believes that she sells the product of her elegant fancy-
work to a shop, where she is so well paid that she makes
twenty francs a day, and in these six years she has never had
a moment's suspicion. She pays for everything she needs at
about the third of its value, so that on six thousand francs a
year she lives as if she had fifteen thousand. She is devoted
to flowers, and pays a hundred crowns to a gardener, who

costs me twelve hundred in wages and sends me in a bill for
two thousand francs every three months. I have promised the
man a market-garden with a house on it close to the porter's
lodge in the Rue Saint-Maur. I hold this ground in the name
of a clerk of the law courts. The smallest indiscretion would
ruin the gardener's prospects. Honorine has her little house,
a garden, and a splendid hot-house, for a rent of five hundred
francs a year. There she lives under the name of her housekeeper, Madame Gobain, the old woman of impeccable discretion whom I was so lucky as to find, and whose affection
Honorine has won. But her zeal, like that of the gardener,
is kept hot by the promise of reward at the moment of success.
The porter and his wife cost me dreadfully dear for the same
reasons. However, for three years Honorine has been happy,
believing that she owes to her own toil all the luxury of
flowers, dress, and comfort.

" 'Oh! I know what you are about to say,' cried the
Count, seeing a question in my eyes and on my lips. 'Yes,
yes; I have made the attempt. My wife was formerly living
in the Faubourg Saint-Antoine. One day when, from what
Gobain told me, I believed in some chance of a reconcilia-
tion, I wrote by post a letter, in which I tried to propitiate
my wife—a letter written and re-written twenty times! I
will not describe my agonies. I went from the Rue Payenne
to the Rue de Reuilly like a condemned wretch going from
the Palais de Justice to his execution; but he goes on a cart,
and I was on foot. It was dark—there was a fog; I went to
meet Madame Gobain, who was to come and tell me what
my wife had done. Honorine, on recognizing my writing,
had thrown the letter into the fire without reading it.
"Madame Gobain," she had exclaimed, "I leave this to-
morrow."

" ' What a dagger-stroke was this to a man who found inexhaustible pleasure in the trickery by which he gets the finest
Lyons velvet at twelve francs a yard, a pheasant, a fish, a dish

of fruit, for a tenth of their value, for a woman so ignorant as
to believe that she is paying ample wages with two hundred
and fifty francs to Madame Gobain, a cook fit for a bishop.

" ' You have sometimes found me rubbing my hands in the
enjoyment of a sort of happiness. Well, I had just succeeded
in some ruse worthy of the stage. I had just deceived my
wife—I had sent her by a purchaser of wardrobes an India
shawl, to be offered to her as the property of an actress who
had hardly worn it, but in which I—the solemn lawyer whom
you know—had wrapped myself for a night! In short, my
life at this day may be summed up in the two words which
express the extremes of torment—I love and I wait! I have
in Madame Gobain a faithful spy on the heart I worship. I
go every evening to chat with the old woman, to hear from
her all that Honorine has done during the day, the lightest
word she has spoken, for a single exclamation might betray
to me the secrets of that soul which is willfully deaf and
dumb. Honorine is pious; she attends the church services
and prays, but she has never been to confession or taken the
communion; she foresees what a priest would tell her. She
will not listen to the advice, to the injunction, that she should
return to me. This horror of me overwhelms me, dismays
me, for I have never done her the smallest harm. I have
always been kind to her. Granting even that I may have
been a little hasty when teaching her, that my man's irony
may have hurt her legitimate girlish pride, is that a reason for
persisting in a determination which only the most implacable
hatred could have inspired? Honorine has never told Madame Gobain whom she is; she keeps absolute silence as to her
marriage, so that the worthy and respectable woman can
never speak a word in my favor, for she is the only person in
the house who knows my secret. The others know nothing;
they live under the awe caused by the name of the prefect of
police, and their respect for the power of a minister. Hence
it is impossible for me to penetrate that heart; the citadel is

mine, but I cannot get into it. I have not a single means of action. An act of violence would ruin me for ever.

"'How can I argue against reasons of which I know nothing? Should I write a letter and have it copied by a public writer, and laid before Honorine? But that would be to run the risk of a third removal. The last cost me fifty thousand francs. The purchase was made in the first instance in the name of the secretary whom you succeeded. The unhappy man, who did not know how lightly I sleep, was detected by me in the act of opening the box in which I had put the private agreement; I coughed, and he was seized with a panic; next day I compelled him to sell the house to the man in whose name it now stands, and I turned him out.

"'If it were not that I feel all my noblest faculties as a man satisfied, happy, expansive; if the part I am playing were not that of divine fatherhood; if I did not drink in delight by every pore, there are moments when I should believe that I was a monomaniac. Sometimes at night I hear the jingling bells of madness. I dread the violent transitions from a feeble hope, which sometimes shines and flashes up, to complete despair, falling as low as man can fall. A few days since I was seriously considering the horrible end of the story of Lovelace and Clarissa Harlowe, and saying to myself, " If Honorine were the mother of a child of mine, must she not necessarily return under her husband's roof?"

"'And I have such complete faith in a happy future that, ten months ago, I bought and paid for one of the handsomest houses in the Faubourg Saint-Honoré. If I win back Honorine, I will not allow her to see this house again, nor the room from which she fled. I mean to place my idol in a new temple, where she may feel that life is altogether new. That house is being made a marvel of elegance and taste. I have been told of a poet who, being almost mad with love for an actress, bought the handsomest bed in Paris without knowing how the actress would reward his passion. Well, one of the

coldest of lawyers, a man who is supposed to be the gravest
adviser of the crown, was stirred to the depths of his heart by
that anecdote.   The orator of the legislative chamber can
understand the poet who fed his ideal on material possibilities.
Three days before the arrival of Maria Louisa, Napoleon flung
himself on his wedding-bed at Compiègne.   All stupendous
passions have the same impulses.   I love as a poet—as an
emperor ! '

"As I heard the last words, I believed that Comte Octave's
fears were realized ; he had risen, and was walking up and
down, and gesticulating, but he stopped as if shocked by the
vehemence of his own words.

" 'I am very ridiculous,' he added, after a long pause,
looking at me, as if craving a glance of pity.

" ' No, monsieur, you are very unhappy.'

" ' Ah, yes ! ' said he, taking up the thread of his confidences.   'From the violence of my speech you may, you
must believe in the intensity of a physical passion which for
nine years has absorbed all my faculties ; but that is nothing
in comparison with the worship I feel for the soul, the mind,
the heart, all in that woman that is not mere woman ; the
enchanting divinities in the train of love, with whom we pass
our life, and who form the daily poem of a fugitive delight.
By a phenomenon of retrospection I see now the graces of
Honorine's mind and heart, to which I paid little heed in the
time of my happiness—like all who are happy.   From day to
day I have appreciated the extent of my loss, discovering the
exquisite gifts of that capricious and refractory young creature
who has grown so strong and so proud under the heavy hand
of poverty and the shock of the most cowardly desertion.   And
that heavenly blossom is fading in solitude and hiding !   Ah !
The law of which we were speaking,' he went on with bitter
irony, ' the law is a squad of gendarmes—my wife seized and
dragged away by force !   Would not that be to triumph over
a corpse ? Religion has no hold on her ; she craves its poetry,

she prays, but she does not listen to the commandments of the church. I, for my part, have exhausted everything in the way of mercy, of kindness, of love ; I am at my wits' end. Only one chance of victory is left to me : the cunning and patience with which bird-catchers at last entrap the wariest birds, the swiftest, the most capricious, and the rarest. Hence, Maurice, when Monsieur de Grandville's indiscretion betrayed to you the secret of my life, I ended by regarding this incident as one of the decrees of fate, one of the utterances for which gamblers listen and pray in the midst of their most impassioned play. Have you enough affection for me to show me romantic devotion ?'

" 'I see what you are coming to, Monsieur le Comte,' said I, interrupting him ; 'I guess your purpose. Your first secretary tried to open your deed box. I know the heart of your second—he might fall in love with your wife. And can you devote him to destruction by sending him into the fire ? Can any one put his hand into a brasier without burning it ?'

" 'You are a foolish boy,' replied the Count. 'I will send you well gloved. It is no secretary of mine that will be lodged in the Rue Saint-Maur in the little garden-house which I have at his disposal. It is my distant cousin, Baron de L'Hostal, a lawyer high in office.'

"After a moment of silent surprise, I heard the gate bell ring, and a carriage came into the courtyard. Presently the footman announced Madame de Courteville and her daughter. The Count had a large family connection on his mother's side. Madame de Courteville, his cousin, was the widow of a judge on the bench of the Seine division, who had left her a daughter and no fortune whatever. What could a woman of nine-and-twenty be in comparison with a young girl of twenty, as lovely as imagination could wish for an ideal mistress ?

" 'Baron and master of appeals, till you get something better, and this old house settled on her—would you not

have enough good reasons for not falling in love with the
Countess?' he said to me in a whisper, as he took me by
the hand and introduced me to Madame de Courteville and
her daughter.

"I was dazzled, not so much by these advantages of
which I had never dreamed, but by Amélie de Courteville,
whose beauty was thrown into relief by one of those well-
chosen toilets which a mother can achieve for a daughter
when she wants to see her married.

"But I will not talk of myself," said the consul after
a pause.

"Three weeks later I went to live in the gardener's
cottage, which had been cleaned, repaired, and furnished
with the celerity which is explained by three words: Paris;
French workmen; money! I was as much in love as the
Count could possibly desire as a security. Would the prudence of a young man of twenty-five be equal to the part
I was undertaking, involving a friend's happiness? To settle
that matter, I may confess that I counted very much on
my uncle's advice; for I had been authorized by the Count
to take him into confidence in any case where I deemed
his interference necessary. I engaged a garden; I devoted
myself to horticulture; I worked frantically, like a man
whom nothing can divert, turning up the soil of the market-
garden, and appropriating the ground to the culture of flowers. Like the maniacs of England, or of Holland, I gave it
out that I was devoted to one kind of flower, and especially
grew dahlias, collecting every variety. You will understand
that my conduct, even in the smallest detail, was laid down
for me by the Count, whose whole intellectual powers were
directed to the most trifling incidents of the tragi-comedy
enacted in the Rue Saint-Maur. As soon as the Countess
had gone to bed, at about eleven at night, Octave, Madame
Gobain, and I sat in council. I heard the old woman's report
to the Count of his wife's least proceedings during the day.

He inquired into everything: her meals, her occupations, her
frame of mind, her plans for the morrow, the flowers she proposed to imitate. I understood what love in despair may be
when it is the threefold passion of the heart, the mind, and
the senses. Octave lived only for that hour.

"During two months, while my work in the garden lasted,
I never set eyes on the little house where my fair neighbor
dwelt. I had not even inquired whether I had a neighbor,
though the Countess' garden was divided from mine by a
paling, along which she had planted cypress trees already four
feet high. One fine morning Madame Gobain announced to
her mistress, as a disastrous piece of news, the intention, expressed by an eccentric creature who had become her neighbor,
of building a wall between the two gardens, at the end of the
year. I will say nothing of the curiosity which consumed me
to see the Countess! The wish almost extinguished my budding love for Amélie de Courteville. My scheme for building
a wall was indeed a serious threat. There would be no more
fresh air for Honorine, whose garden would then be a sort of
narrow alley shut in between my wall and her own little
house. This dwelling, formerly a summer villa, was like a
house of cards; it was not more than thirty feet deep and
about a hundred feet long. The garden front, painted in the
German fashion, imitated a trellis with flowers up to the
second floor, and was a really charming example of the pompadour style, so well called rococo. A long avenue of limes
led up to it. The gardens of the pavilion and my plot of
ground were in the shape of a hatchet, of which this avenue
was the handle. My wall would cut away three-quarters of
the hatchet.

"The Countess was in despair.

"'My good Gobain,' said she, 'what sort of a man is this
florist?'

"'On my word,' said the housekeeper, 'I do not know
whether it will be possible to tame him. He seems to have

a horror of women.   He is the nephew of a Paris curé.   I
have seen the uncle but once ; a fine old man of sixty, very
ugly, but very amiable.   It is quite possible that this priest
encourages his nephew, as they say in the neighborhood, in
his love of flowers, that nothing worse may happen——'

"'Why—what ?'

"'Well, your neighbor is a little cracked!' said Gobain,
tapping her head !

"Now a harmless lunatic is the only man whom no woman
ever distrusts in the matter of sentiment.   You will see how
wise the Count had been in choosing this disguise for me.

"'What ails him then?' asked the Countess.

"'He has studied too hard,' replied Gobain; 'he has
turned misanthropic.   And he has his reasons for disliking
women—well, if you want to know all that is being said about
him——'

"'Well,' said Honorine, 'madmen frighten me less than
sane folk ; I will speak to him myself!   Tell him that I beg
him to come here.   If I do not succeed, I will send for the
curé.'

"The day after this conversation, as I was walking along
my graveled path, I caught sight of the half-opened curtains
on the second floor of the little house, and of a woman's face
curiously peeping out.   Madame Gobain called me.   I hastily
glanced at the Countess' house, and by a rude shrug expressed,
'What do I care for your mistress?'

"'Madame,' said Gobain, called upon to give an account
of her errand, 'the madman bid me leave him in peace, saying that even a charcoal-seller is master in his own premises,
especially when he has no wife.'

"'He is perfectly right,' said the Countess.

"'Yes, but he ended by saying, "I will go," when I told
him that he would greatly distress a lady living in retirement,
who found her greatest solace in growing flowers.'

"Next day a signal from Gobain informed me that I was

expected. After the Countess' breakfast, when she was walking to and fro in front of her house, I broke out some palings and went toward her. I had dressed myself like a countryman, in an old pair of gray flannel trousers, heavy wooden shoes, and shabby shooting coat, a peaked cap on my head, a ragged bandana round my neck, hands soiled with mold, and a dibble in my hand.

"'Madame,' said the housekeeper, 'this good man is your neighbor.'

"The Countess was not alarmed. I saw at last the woman whom her own conduct and her husband's confidences had made me so curious to meet. It was in the early days of May. The air was pure, the weather serene ; the verdure of the first foliage, the fragrance of spring formed a setting for this creature of sorrow. As I then saw Honorine I understood Octave's passion and the truthfulness of his description, 'A heavenly flower ! '

"Her pallor was what first struck me by its peculiar tone of white—for there are as many tones of white as of red or blue. On looking at the Countess, the eye seemed to feel that tender skin, where the blood flowed in the blue veins. At the slightest emotion the blood mounted under the surface in rosy flushes like a cloud. When we met, the sunshine, filtering through the light foliage of the acacias, shed on Honorine the pale gold, ambient glory in which Raphael and Titian, alone of all painters, have been able to enwrap the Virgin. Her brown eyes expressed both tenderness and vivacity ; their brightness seemed reflected in her face through the long downcast lashes. Merely by lifting her delicate eyelids, Honorine could cast a spell ; there was so much feeling, dignity, terror, or contempt in her way of raising or dropping those veils of the soul. She could freeze or give life by a look. Her light-brown hair, carelessly knotted on her head, outlined a poet's brow, high, powerful, and dreamy. The mouth was wholly voluptuous. And to crown all by a grace,

rare in France, though common in Italy, all the lines and
forms of the head had a stamp of nobleness which would
defy the outrages of time.

"Though slight, Honorine was not thin, and her figure
struck me as being one that might revive love when it believed itself exhausted. She perfectly represented the idea
conveyed by the word *mignonne* (darling), for she was one of
those pliant little women who allow themselves to be taken
up, petted, set down, and taken up again like a kitten. Her
small feet, as I heard them on the gravel, made a light sound
essentially their own, that harmonized with the rustle of her
dress, producing a feminine music which stamped itself on
the heart, and remained distinct from the footfall of a thousand other women. Her gait bore all the quarterings of her
race with so much pride, that, in the street, the least respectful
workingman would have made way for her. Gay and tender,
haughty and imposing, it was impossible to understand her,
excepting as gifted with these apparently incompatible qualities, which, nevertheless, had left her still a child. But it
was a child who might be as strong as an angel; and, like the
angel, once hurt in her nature, she would be implacable.

"Coldness on that face must no doubt be death to those
on whom her eyes had smiled, for whom her set lips had
parted, for those whose soul had drunk in the melody of that
voice, lending to her words the poetry of song by its peculiar
intonation. Inhaling the perfume of violets that accompanied
her, I understood how the memory of this wife had arrested
the Count on the threshold of debauchery, and how impossible it would be ever to forget a creature who really was a
flower to the touch, a flower to the eye, a flower of fragrance,
a heavenly flower to the soul—— Honorine inspired devotion, chivalrous devotion, regardless of reward. A man on
seeing her must say to himself—

"'Think, and I will divine your thought; speak, and I
will obey. If my life, sacrificed in torments, can procure

you one day's happiness, take my life; I will smile like a
martyr at the stake, for I shall offer that day to God, as a
token to which a father responds on recognizing a gift to his
child.' Many women study their expression, and succeed in
producing effects similar to those which would have struck
you at first sight of the Countess; only, in her, it all was the
outcome of a delightful nature, an inimitable nature that went
at once to the heart. If I tell you all this, it is because her
soul, her thoughts, the exquisiteness of her heart, are all we
are concerned with, and you would have blamed me if I had
not sketched them for you.

"I was very near forgetting my part as a half-crazy lout,
clumsy, and by no means chivalrous.

"'I have been told, madame, that you are very fond of
flowers?'

"'I am an artificial flower-maker,' said she. 'After growing flowers, I imitate them, like a mother who is artist enough
to have the pleasure of painting portraits of her children.
That is enough to tell you that I am poor and unable to pay
for the concession that I am anxious to obtain from you?'

"'But how,' said I, as grave as a judge, 'can a lady of such
rank as yours would seem to be, ply so humble a calling?
Have you, like me, good reasons for employing your fingers
so as to keep your brain from working?'

"'Let us stick to the question of the wall,' said she with a
smile.

"'Why we have begun at the foundations,' I rejoined.
'Must I not know which of us ought to yield to the other in
behalf of our suffering, or, if you choose, of our mania? Oh!
what a charming clump of narcissus! They are as fresh as this
spring morning!'

"I assure you, she had made for herself a perfect museum
of flowers and shrubs, which none might see but the sun, and
of which the arrangement had been prompted by the genius
of an artist; the most heartless of landlords must have treated

it with respect. The masses of plants, arranged according to their height, or in single clumps, were really a joy to the soul. This retired and solitary garden breathed comforting scents, and suggested none but sweet thoughts and graceful, nay, voluptuous pictures. On it was set that inscrutable sign-manual, which our true character stamps on everything, as soon as nothing compels us to obey the various hypocrisies, necessary as they are, which society insists upon. I looked alternately at the mass of narcissus and at the Countess, affecting to be far more in love with the flowers than with her, to carry out my part.

"'So you are very fond of flowers?' said she.

"'They are,' I replied, 'the only beings that never disappoint our cares and affection.' And I went on to deliver such a diatribe while comparing botany and the world, that we ended miles away from the dividing wall, and the Countess must have supposed me to be a wretched and wounded sufferer worthy of her pity. However, at the end of half an hour my neighbor naturally brought me back to the point; for women, when they are not in love, have all the cold blood of an experienced attorney.

"'If you insist on my leaving the paling,' said I, 'you will learn all the secrets of gardening that I want to hide; I am seeking to grow a blue dahlia, a blue rose; I am crazy for blue flowers. Is not blue the favorite color of superior souls? We are neither of us really at home; we might as well make a little door of open railings to unite our gardens. You, too, are fond of flowers; you will see mine, I shall see yours. If you receive no visitors at all, I, for my part, have none but my uncle, the curé of the white friars.'

"'No,' said she, 'I will give you the right to come into my garden, my premises, at any hour. Come and welcome; you will always be admitted as a neighbor with whom I hope to keep on good terms. But I like my solitude too well to burden it with any loss of independence.'

" 'As you please,' said I, and with one leap I was over the paling.

" 'Now, of what use would a door be?' said I, from my own domain, turning round to the Countess, and mocking her with a madman's gesture and grimace.

"For a fortnight I seemed to take no heed of my neighbor. Toward the end of May, one lovely evening, we happened both to be out on opposite sides of the paling, both walking slowly. Having reached the end, we could not help exchanging a few civil words; she found me in such deep dejection, lost in such painful meditations, that she spoke to me of hopefulness, in brief sentences that sounded like the songs with which nurses lull their babes. I then leaped the fence and found myself for the second time at her side. The Countess led me into the house, wishing to subdue my sadness. So at last I had penetrated the sanctuary where everything was in harmony with the woman I have tried to describe to you.

"Exquisite simplicity reigned there. The interior of the little house was just such a dainty box as the art of the eighteenth century devised for the pretty profligacy of a fine gentleman. The dining-room, on the first floor, was painted in fresco, with garlands of flowers, admirably and marvelously executed. The staircase was charmingly decorated in monochrome. The little drawing-room, opposite the dining-room, was very much faded; but the Countess had hung it with panels of tapestry of fanciful designs, taken off old screens. A bath-room came next. Upstairs there was but one bedroom, with a dressing-room, and a library which she used as her workroom. The kitchen was beneath in the basement on which the house was raised, for there was a flight of several steps outside. The balustrade of a balcony in garlands *à la* pompadour concealed the roof; only the lead cornices were visible. In this retreat one was a hundred leagues from Paris.

"But for the bitter smile which occasionally played on the beautiful red lips of this pale woman, it would have been

22

possible to believe that this violet buried in her thicket of flowers was happy. In a few days we had reached a certain degree of intimacy, the result of our close neighborhood and of the Countess' conviction that I was indifferent to women. A look would have spoilt all, and I never allowed a thought of her to be seen in my eyes. Honorine chose to regard me as an old friend. Her manner to me was the outcome of a kind of pity. Her looks, her voice, her words, all showed that she was a hundred miles away from the coquettish airs which the strictest virtue might have allowed under such circumstances. She soon gave me the right to go into the pretty workshop where she made her flowers, a retreat full of books and curiosities, as smart as a boudoir, where elegance emphasized the vulgarity of the tools of her trade. The Countess had in the course of time poetized, as I may say, a thing which is at the antipodes to poetry—a manufacture.

"Perhaps of all the work a woman can do, the making of artificial flowers is that of which the details allow her to display most grace. For coloring prints she must sit bent over a table and devote herself, with some attention, to this half-painting. Embroidering tapestry, as diligently as a woman must who is to earn her living by it, entails consumption or curvature of the spine. Engraving music is one of the most laborious, by the care, the minute exactitude, and the intelligence it demands. Sewing and white embroidery do not earn thirty sous a day. But the making of flowers and light articles of wear necessitates a variety of movements, gestures, ideas even, which do not take a pretty woman out of her sphere; she is still herself; she may chat, laugh, sing, or think.

"There was certainly a feeling for art in the way in which the Countess arranged on a long pine table the myriad-colored petals which were used in composing the flowers she was to produce. The saucers of color were of white china, and always clean, arranged in such order that the eye could at once see the required shade in the scale of tints. Thus the aristocratic artist saved time. A pretty little cabinet with a hundred tiny drawers, of ebony inlaid with ivory, contained the little steel moulds in which she shaped the leaves and some forms of petals. A fine Japanese bowl held the paste, which was never allowed to turn sour, and it had a fitted cover with a hinge so easy that she could lift it with a finger-tip. The wire, of iron and brass, lurked in a little drawer of the table before her.

"Under her eyes, in a Venetian glass, shaped like a flower-cup on its stem, was the living model she strove to imitate. She had a passion for achievement; she attempted the most difficult things, close racemes, the tiniest corollas, heaths, nectaries, of the most variegated hues. Her hands, as swift as her thoughts, went from the table to the flower she was making, as those of an accomplished pianist fly over the keys. Her fingers seemed to be fairies, to use Perrault's expression, so infinite were the different actions of twisting, fitting, and pressure needed for the work, all hidden under grace of movement, while she adapted each motion to the result with the lucidity of instinct.

"I could not tire of admiring her as she shaped a flower from the materials sorted before her, padding the wire-stem and adjusting the leaves. She displayed the genius of a painter in her bold attempts; she copied faded flowers and yellowing leaves; she struggled even with wild-flowers, the most artless of all, and the most elaborate in their simplicity.

"'This art,' she would say, 'is in its infancy. If the women of Paris had a little of the genius which the slavery of the harem brings out in Oriental women, they would lend a complete language of flowers to the wreaths they wear on their heads. To please my own taste as an artist, I have made drooping flowers with leaves of the hue of Florentine bronze, such as are found before or after the winter. Would not such a crown on the head of a young woman whose life is a failure have a certain poetical fitness? How many things a woman

might express by her head-dress! Are there not flowers for
drunken Bacchantes, flowers for gloomy and stern bigots, pen-
sive flowers for women who are bored? Botany, I believe,
may be made to express every sensation and thought of the
soul, even the most subtle?'

"She would employ me to stamp out the leaves, cut up
material, and prepare wires for the stems. My affected desire
for occupation soon made me skillful. We talked as we
worked. When I had nothing to do, I read new books to
her, for I had my part to keep up as a man weary of life, worn
out with griefs, gloomy, skeptical, and soured. My person
led to adorable banter as to my purely physical resemblance—
with the exception of his club-foot—to Lord Byron. It was
tacitly acknowledged that her own troubles, as to which she
kept the most profound silence, far outweighed mine, though
the causes I assigned for my misanthropy might have satisfied
Young or Job.

"I will say nothing of the feelings of shame which tormented
me as I inflicted on my heart, like the beggars in the street,
false wounds to excite the compassion of that enchanting
woman. I soon appreciated the extent of my devotedness by
learning to estimate the baseness of a spy. The expressions
of sympathy bestowed on me would have comforted the
greatest grief. This charming creature, weaned from the
world, and for so many years alone, having, beside love, treasures of kindliness to bestow, offered these to me with childlike
effusiveness and such compassion as would inevitably have
filled with bitterness any profligate who should have fallen in
love with her; for, alas! it was all charity, all sheer pity.
Her renunciation of love, her dread of what is called happiness
for women, she proclaimed with equal vehemence and candor.
These happy days proved to me that a woman's friendship is
far superior to her love.

"I suffered the revelations of my sorrows to be dragged
from me with as many grimaces as a young lady allows herself

before sitting down to the piano, so conscious are they of the annoyance that will follow. As you may imagine, the necessity for overcoming my dislike to speak had induced the Countess to strengthen the bonds of our intimacy; but she found in me so exact a counterpart of her own antipathy to love that I fancied she was well content with the chance which had brought to her desert island a sort of Man Friday. Solitude was, perhaps, beginning to weigh on her. At the same time there was nothing of the coquette in her; nothing survived of the woman; she did not feel that she had a heart, she told me, excepting in the ideal world where she found refuge. I involuntarily compared these two lives—hers and the Count's: his, all activity, agitation, and emotion; hers, all inaction, quiescence, and stagnation. The woman and the man were admirably obedient to their nature. My misanthropy allowed me to utter cynical sallies against men and women both, and I indulged in them, hoping to bring Honorine to the confidential point; but she was not to be caught in any trap, and I began to understand that mulish obstinacy which is commoner among women than is generally supposed.

" 'The Orientals are right,' I said to her one evening, ' when they shut you up and regard you merely as the playthings of their pleasure. Europe has been well punished for having admitted you to form an element of society and for accepting you on an equal footing. In my opinion, woman is the most dishonorable and cowardly being to be found. Nay, and that is where her charm lies. Where would be the pleasure of hunting a tame thing? When once a woman has inspired a man's passion, she is to him for ever sacred; in his eyes she is hedged round by an imprescriptible prerogative. In men gratitude for past delights is eternal. Though he should find his mistress grown old or unworthy, the woman still has rights over his heart; but to you women the man you have loved is as nothing to you; nay, more, he is unpardonable in one thing—he lives on! You dare not own it, but you all have in your hearts the feeling which that popular calumny called tradition ascribes to the Lady of the Tour de Nesle: "What a pity it is that we cannot live on love as we live on fruit, and that, when we have had our fill, nothing should survive but the remembrance of pleasure!"'

"'God has, no doubt, reserved such perfect bliss for paradise,' said she. 'But,' she added, 'if your argument seems to you very witty, to me it has the disadvantage of being false. What can those women be who give themselves up to a succession of loves?' she asked, looking at me as the Virgin in Ingres' picture looks at Louis XIII. offering her his kingdom.

"'You are an actress in good faith,' said I, 'for you gave me a look just now which would make the fame of an actress. Still, lovely as you are, you have loved; *ergo,* you forget.'

"'I!' she exclaimed, evading my question, 'I am not a woman. I am a nun, and seventy-two years old!'

"'Then, how can you so positively assert that you feel more keenly than I? Sorrow has but one form for women. The only misfortunes they regard are disappointments of the heart.'

"She looked at me sweetly, and, like all women when stuck between the issues of a dilemma or held in the clutches of truth, she persisted, nevertheless, in her willfulness.

"'I am a nun,' she said, 'and you talk to me of a world where I shall never again set foot.'

"'Not even in thought?' said I.

"'Is the world so much to be desired?' she replied. 'Oh! when my mind wanders, it goes higher. The angel of perfection, the beautiful angel Gabriel, often sings in my heart. If I were rich, I should work all the same, to keep me from soaring too often on the many-tinted wings of the angel, and wandering in the world of fancy. There are meditations which are the ruin of us women! I owe much

peace of mind to my flowers, though sometimes they fail to
occupy me. On some days I find my soul invaded by a pur-
poseless expectancy ; I cannot banish some idea which takes
possession of me, which seems to make my fingers clumsy. I
feel that some great event is impending, that my life is about
to change ; I listen vaguely, I stare into the darkness, I have
no liking for my work, and after a thousand fatigues I find
life once more—every-day life. Is this a warning from heaven?
I ask myself——'

"After three months of this struggle between two diplomatists, concealed under the semblance of youthful melancholy, and a woman whose disgust of life made her invulner-
able, I told the Count that it was impossible to drag this
tortoise out of her shell ; it must be broken. The evening
before, in our last quite friendly discussion, the Countess
had exclaimed—

"'Lucretia's dagger wrote in letters of blood the watchword of woman's charter : *"Liberty !"*'

"From that moment the Count left me free to act.

"'I have been paid a hundred francs for the flowers and
caps I made this week !' Honorine exclaimed gleefully one
Saturday evening when I went to visit her in the little sitting-
room on the ground floor, which the unavowed proprietor
had had regilt.

"It was ten o'clock. The twilight of July and a glorious
moon lent us their misty light. Gusts of mingled perfumes
soothed the soul ; the Countess was clinking in her hand the
five gold-pieces given to her by a supposititious dealer in
fashionable frippery, another of Octave's accomplices found
for him by a judge, M. Popinot.

"'I earn my living by amusing myself,' she said ; 'I am
free, when men, armed with their laws, have tried to make us
slaves. Oh, I have transports of pride every Saturday ! In
short, I like Monsieur Gaudissart's gold-pieces as much as
Lord Byron, your double, liked Mr. Murray's.'

" 'This is not in the least becoming in a woman,' said I.

" 'Pooh! Am I a woman? I am a boy gifted with a soft soul, that is all; a boy whom no woman can ever torture——'

" 'Your life is the negation of your whole being,' I replied. 'What? You, on whom the good God has lavished His choicest treasures of love and beauty, do you never wish——'

" 'For what?' said she, somewhat disturbed by a speech which, for the first time, gave the lie to the part I had assumed.

" 'For a pretty little child with curling hair, running, playing among the flowers, like a flower itself of life and love, and calling you mother!'

" I waited for an answer. A too-prolonged silence led me to perceive the terrible effect of my words, though the darkness at first concealed it. Leaning on her sofa, the Countess had not indeed fainted, but frozen under a nervous attack of which the first chill, as gentle as everything that was part of her, felt, as she afterward said, like the influence of a most insidious poison. I called Madame Gobain, who came and led away her mistress, laid her on her bed, unlaced her, undressed her, and restored her, not to life, it is true, but to the consciousness of some dreadful suffering. I meanwhile walked up and down the path behind the house, weeping, and doubting my success. I only wished to give up this part of the bird-catcher which I had so rashly assumed. Madame Gobain, who came down and found me with my face wet with tears, hastily went upstairs and into the bedroom again to say to the Countess——

" 'What has happened, madame? Monsieur Maurice is crying like a child.'

" Roused to action by the evil interpretation that might be put on our mutual behavior, she summoned superhuman strength to put on a wrapper and come down to me.

"'You are not the cause of this attack,' said she. 'I am subject to these spasms, a sort of cramp of the heart——'

"'And you will not tell me of your troubles?' I asked, in a voice which cannot be affected, as I wiped away my tears. 'Have you not just now told me that you have been a mother, and have been so unhappy as to lose your child?'

"'Marie!' she called as she rang the bell. Gobain came in.

"'Bring lights and some tea,' said she, with the calm decision of a 'mylady' clothèd in the armor of pride by the dreadful English training which you know too well.

"When the housekeeper had lighted the tapers and closed the shutters, the Countess showed me a mute countenance; her indomitable pride and gravity, worthy of a savage, had already asserted their mastery. She said—

"'Do you know why I like Lord Byron so much? It is because he suffered as animals do. Of what use are complaints when they are not an elegy like Manfred's, nor bitter mockery like Don Juan's, nor a reverie like Childe Harold's? Nothing shall be known of me. My heart is a poem that I lay before God.'

"'If I chose——' said I.

"'If?' she repeated.

"'I have no interest in anything,' I replied, 'so I cannot be inquisitive; but, if I chose, I could know all your secrets by to-morrow.'

"'I defy you!' she exclaimed, with ill-disguised uneasiness.

"'Seriously?'

"'Certainly,' said she, tossing her head. 'If such a crime is possible, I ought to know it.'

"'In the first place, madame,' I went on, pointing to her hands, 'those pretty fingers, which are enough to show that you are not a mere girl—were they made for toil? Then you call yourself Madame Gobain, you, who, in my presence the other day on receiving a letter, said to Marie: "Here, this is for you?" Marie is the real Madame Gobain; so you conceal your name behind that of your housekeeper. Fear nothing, madame, from me. You have in me the most devoted friend you will ever have : Friend, do you understand me? I give this word its sacred and pathetic meaning, so profaned in France, where we apply it to our enemies. And your friend, who will defend you against everything, only wishes that you should be as happy as such a woman ought to be. Who can tell whether the pain I have involuntarily caused you was not a voluntary act?'

"'Yes,' replied she with threatening audacity, 'I insist on it. Be curious, and tell me all that you can find out about me ; but,' and she held up her finger, 'you must also tell me by what means you obtain your information. The preservation of the small happiness I enjoy here depends on the steps you take.'

"'That means that you will fly——'

"'On wings!' she cried, 'to the New World——'

"'Where you will be at the mercy of the brutal passions you will inspire,' said I, interrupting her. 'Is it not the very essence of genius and beauty to shine, to attract men's gaze, to excite desires and evil thoughts? Paris is a desert with Bedouins; Paris is the only place in the world where those who must work for their livelihood can hide their life. What have you to complain of? Who am I? An additional servant—M. Gobain, that is all. If you have to fight a duel, you may need a second.'

"'Never mind ; find out whom I am. I have already said that I insist. Nay, I beg that you will,' she went on, with the grace which you ladies have at command," said the consul, looking at the ladies.

"'Well, then, to-morrow, at the same hour, I will tell you what I may have discovered,' replied I. 'But do not therefore hate me! Will you behave like other women?'

"'What do other women do?'

" ' They lay upon us immense sacrifices, and when we have made them, they reproach us for it some time later as if it were an injury.'

" ' They are right if the thing required appears to be a sacrifice ! ' replied she pointedly.

" ' Instead of sacrifices, say efforts and——'

" ' It would be an impertinence,' she said.

" ' Forgive me,' I replied. ' I forgot that woman and the pope are infallible.'

" ' Good heavens ! ' she went on, after a long pause, ' only two words would be enough to destroy the peace so dearly bought, and which I enjoy like a fraud——'

" She arose and paid no further heed to me.

" ' Where can I go ? ' she asked. ' What is to become of me ? Must I leave this quiet retreat that I had arranged with such care to end my days in ? '

" ' To end your days ! ' exclaimed I with visible alarm. ' Has it never struck you that a time would come when you could no longer work, when competition will lower the price of flowers and articles of fashion——? '

" ' I have already saved a thousand crowns,' she returned.

" ' Heavens ! what privations must such a sum represent ! ' I exclaimed.

" ' Leave me,' she said, ' till to-morrow. This evening I am not myself; I must be alone. Must I not save my strength in case of disaster? For, if you should learn anything, others beside you would be informed. and then—Good-night,' she added shortly, dismissing me with an imperious gesture.

" ' The battle is to-morrow, then,' I replied with a smile, to keep up the appearance of indifference I had given to the scene. But as I went down the avenue I repeated the words—

" ' The battle is to-morrow.'

" Octave's anxiety was equal to Honorine's. The Count and I remained together until two in the morning, walking back and forth by the trenches of the bastile, like two generals

who, on the eve of a battle, calculate all the chances, examine
the ground, and perceive that the victory must depend on an
opportunity to be seized half-way through the fight. These
two divided beings would each lie awake, one in the hope, the
other in the agonizing dread of reunion. The real dramas of
life are not in circumstances, but in feelings; they are played
in the heart, or, if you please, in that vast realm which we
ought to call the spiritual world. Octave and Honorine
moved and lived altogether in the world of lofty spirits.

"I was punctual. At ten next evening I was, for the first
time, shown into a charming bedroom furnished with white
and blue—the nest of this wounded dove. The Countess
looked at me and was about to speak, but was stricken dumb
by my respectful demeanor.

"'Madame la Comtesse,' said I with a grave smile.

"The poor woman, who had risen, dropped back into her
chair and remained there, sunk in an attitude of grief, which
I should have liked to see perpetuated by a great painter.

"'You are,' I went on, 'the wife of the noblest and most
highly respected of men; of a man who is acknowledged to
be great, but who is far greater in his conduct to you than he
is in the eyes of the world. You and he are two lofty natures.
Where do you suppose yourself to be living?' I asked her.

"'In my own house, she replied,' opening her eyes with a
wide stare of astonishment.

"'In Count Octave's,' I replied. .'You have been tricked.
M. Lenormand, the usher of the court, is not the real owner;
he is only a screen for your husband. The delightful seclusion
you enjoy is the Count's work, the money you earn is paid by
him, and his protection extends to the most trivial details of
your existence. Your husband has saved you in the eyes of
the world; he has assigned plausible reasons for your disappearance; he professes to hope that you were not lost in the
wreck of the "Cécile," the ship in which you sailed for Ha-
vana to secure the fortune to be left to you by an old aunt, who

might have forgotten you; you embarked, escorted by two
ladies of her family and an old manservant. The Count says
that he has sent agents to various spots, and received letters
which give him great hopes. He takes as many precautions to
hide you from all eyes as you take yourself. In short, he obeys
you——'

" ' That is enough,' she said. ' I want to know but one
thing more. From whom have you obtained all these details?'

" ' Well, madame, my uncle got a place for a penniless
youth as secretary to the commissary of police in this part of
Paris. That young man told me everything. If you leave
this house this evening, however stealthily, your husband will
know where you are gone and his care will follow you everywhere. How could a woman so clever as you are believe that
shopkeepers buy flowers and caps as dear as they sell them?
Ask a thousand crowns for a bouquet, and you will get it.
No mother's tenderness was ever more ingenious than your
husband's ! I have learned from the porter of this house that
the Count often comes behind the fence when all are asleep,
to see the glimmer of your night-light. Your large cashmere
shawl cost six thousand francs—your old-clothes-seller brings
you, as second hand, things fresh from the best makers. In
short, you are living here like Venus in the toils of Vulcan ;
but you are alone in your prison by the devices of a sublime
magnanimity, sublime for seven years past, and at every hour.'

" The Countess was trembling as a trapped swallow trem-
bles while, as you hold it in your hand, it strains its neck to
look about it with wild eyes. She shook with a nervous
spasm, studying me with a defiant look. Her dry eyes glittered with a light that was almost hot : still, she was a woman !
The moment came when her tears forced their way, and she
wept—not because she was touched, but because she was helpless ; they were tears of desperation. She had believed herself independent and free ; marriage weighed on her as the
prison cell does on the captive.

" ' I will go ! ' she cried through her tears. ' He forces me to it ; I will go where no one certainly will come after me.'

" ' What,' I said, ' you would kill yourself ? Madame, you must have some very powerful reasons for not wishing to return to Comte Octave.'

" ' Certainly I have ! '

" ' Well, then, tell them to me ; tell them to my uncle. In us you will find two devoted advisers. Though in the confessional my uncle is a priest, he is never one in a drawing-room. We will hear you ; we will try to find a solution of the problems you may lay before us ; and if you are the dupe or the victim of some misapprehension, perhaps we can clear the matter up. Your soul, I believe, is pure ; but if you have done wrong, your fault is fully expiated—— At any rate, remember that in me you have a most sincere friend. If you should wish to evade the Count's tyranny, I will find you the means ; he shall never find you.'

" ' Oh ! there is always a convent ! ' said she.

" ' Yes. But the Count, as minister of state, can procure your rejection by every convent in the world. Even though he is powerful, I will save you from him ; but—only when you have demonstrated to me that you cannot and ought not to return to him. Oh ! do not fear that you would escape his power only to fall into mine,' I added, noticing a glance of horrible suspicion, full of exaggerated dignity. ' You shall have peace, solitude, and independence ; in short, you shall be as free and as little annoyed as if you were an ugly, cross old maid. I myself would never be able to see you without your consent.'

" ' And how ? By what means ? '

" ' That is my secret. I am not deceiving you, of that you may be sure. Prove to me that this is the only life you can lead, that it is preferable to that of the Comtesse Octave, rich, admired, in one of the finest houses in Paris, beloved

by her husband, a happy mother—— and I will decide in your
favor.'

" ' But,' said she, ' will there never be a man who understands me ? '

" ' No. And that is why I appeal to religion to decide
between us. The curé of the white friars is a saint, seventy-
five years of age. My uncle is not a grand inquisitor, he is a
Saint John ; but for you he will be Fénelon—the Fénelon
who said to the Duc de Bourgogne : " Eat a calf on a Friday
by all means, monseigneur. But be a Christian." '

" ' Nay, nay, monsieur, the convent is my last hope and
my only refuge. There is none but God who can understand
me. No man, not Saint Augustine himself, the tenderest of
the fathers of the church, could enter into the scruples of my
conscience, which are to me as the circles of Dante's hell,
whence there is no escape. Another than my husband, a
different man, however unworthy of the offering, has had all
my love. No, he has not had it, for he did not take it ; I
gave it him as a mother gives her child a wonderful toy, which
it breaks. For me there never could be two loves. In some
natures love can never be on trial ; it is, or it is not. When
it comes, when it rises up, it is complete. Well, that life of
eighteen months was to me a life of eighteen years ; I threw
into it all the faculties of my being, which were not impoverished by their effusiveness ; they were exhausted by that
delusive intimacy in which I alone was genuine. For me the
cup of happiness is not drained, nor empty ; and nothing can
refill it, for it is broken. I am out of the fray ; I have no
weapons left. Having thus utterly abandoned myself, what
am I ?—the leavings of a feast. I had but one name bestowed
on me, Honorine, as I had but one heart. My husband had
the young girl, a worthless lover had the woman—there is
nothing left ! Then let myself be loved ! that is the great idea
that you mean to utter to me. Oh ! but I still am something,
and I rebel at the idea of being a prostitute ! Yes, by the

light of the conflagration I saw clearly; and I tell you—well, I could imagine surrendering to another man's love, but to Octave's? No, never.'

" ' Ah! you love him,' I said.

" ' I esteem him, respect him, venerate him ; he has never done me the smallest hurt ; he is kind, he is tender ; but I can never more love him. However,' she went on, ' let us talk no more of this. Discussion makes everything small. I will express my notions on this subject in writing to you, for at this moment they are suffocating me ; I am feverish, my feet are standing in the ashes of my paraclete. All that I see, these things which I believed I had earned by my labor, now remind me of everything I wish to forget. Ah! I must fly from hence as I fled from my home.'

" ' Where will you go ?' I asked. ' Can a woman exist unprotected? At thirty, in all the glory of your beauty, rich in powers of which you have no suspicion, full of tenderness to be bestowed, are you prepared to live in the wilderness where I could hide you? Be quite easy. The Count, who for nine years has never allowed himself to be seen here, will never go there without your permission. You have his sublime devotion of nine years as a guarantee for your tranquillity. You may therefore discuss the future in perfect confidence with my uncle and me. My uncle has as much influence as a minister of state. So compose yourself; do not exaggerate your misfortune. A priest whose hair has grown white in the exercise of his functions is not a boy ; you will be understood by him to whom every passion has been confided for nearly fifty years now, and who weighs in his hands the ponderous heart of kings and princes. If he is stern under his stole, in the presence of your flowers he will be as tender as they are, and as indulgent as his Divine Master.'

" I left the Countess at midnight ; she was apparently calm, but depressed, and had some secret purpose which no perspicacity could guess. I found the Count a few paces off,

HONORINE.

353

in the Rue Saint-Maur. Drawn by an irresistible attraction he had quitted the spot on the boulevards where we had agreed to meet.

"'What a night my poor child will go through!' he exclaimed, when I had finished my account of the scene that had just taken place. 'Supposing I were to go to her?' he added; 'supposing she were to see me suddenly?'

"'At this moment she is capable of throwing herself out of the window,' I replied. 'The Countess is one of those Lucretias who could not survive any violence, even if it were done by a man into whose arms she could throw herself.'

"'You are young,' he answered; 'you do not know that in a soul tossed by such dreadful alternatives the will is like the waters of a lake lashed by a tempest; the wind changes every instant, and the waves are driven now to one shore, now to the other. During this night the chances are quite as great that on seeing me Honorine might rush into my arms as that she should throw herself out of the window.'

"'And you would accept the equal chances?' said I interrogatively.

"'Well, come,' said he, 'I have at home, to enable me to wait until to-morrow, a dose of opium which Desplein prepared for me to send me to sleep without any risk!'

"Next day at noon Gobain brought me a letter, telling me that the Countess had gone to bed at six, worn out with fatigue, and that, having taken a soothing draught prepared by the chemist, she had now fallen asleep.

"This is her letter, of which I kept a copy—for you, mademoiselle," said the consul, addressing Camille, "know all the resources of art, the tricks of style, and the efforts made in their compositions by writers who do not lack skill; but you will acknowledge that literature could never find such language in its assumed pathos; there is nothing so terrible as truth. Here is the letter written by this woman, or rather by this anguish:

23

"'MONSIEUR MAURICE:—I know all your uncle could say
to me; he is not better informed than my own conscience.
Conscience is the interpreter of God to man. I know that
if I am not reconciled to Octave, I shall be damned; that is
the sentence of religious law. Civil law condemns me to
obey, cost what it may. If my husband does not reject me,
the world will regard me as pure, as virtuous, whatever I may
have done. Yes, that much is sublime in marriage : society
ratifies the husband's forgiveness; but it forgets that the forgiveness must be accepted. Legally, religiously, and from
the world's point of view I ought to go back to Octave.
Keeping only to the human aspect of the question, is it not
cruel to refuse him happiness, to deprive him of children, to
wipe his name out of the "Golden Book" and the list of
peers? My sufferings, my repugnance, my feelings, all my
egoism—for I know that I am an egoist—ought to be sacrificed to the family. I shall be a mother; the caresses of my
child will wipe away many tears ! I shall be very happy; I
certainly shall be much looked up to. I shall ride, haughty
and wealthy, in a handsome carriage ! I shall have servants
and a fine house, and be the queen of as many parties as there
are weeks in the year. The world will receive me handsomely. I shall not have to climb up again to the heaven of
aristocracy, I shall never have come down from it. So God,
the law, society are all in accord.

"'"What are you rebelling against?" I am asked from
the height of heaven, from the pulpit, from the judge's bench,
and from the throne, whose august intervention may at need
be invoked by the court. Your uncle, indeed, at need, would
speak to me of a certain celestial grace which will flood my
heart when I know the pleasure of doing my duty.

"'God, the law, the world, and Octave all wish me to live,
no doubt. Well, if there is no other difficulty, my reply cuts
the knot : I will not live. I will become quite white and
innocent again; for I will lie in my shroud, white with the

blameless pallor of death. This is not in the least " mulish obstinacy." That mulish obstinacy of which you jestingly accused me is in a woman the result of confidence, of a vision of the future. Though my husband, sublimely generous, may forget all, I shall not forget. Does forgetfulness depend on our will? When a widow remarries, love makes a girl of her; she marries a man she loves. But I cannot love the Count. It all lies in that, do you not see?

" ' Every time my eyes met his I should see my sin in them, even when his were full of love. The greatness of his generosity would be the measure of the greatness of my crime. My eyes, always uneasy, would be for ever reading an invisible condemnation. My heart would be full of confused and struggling memories; marriage can never move me to the cruel rapture, the mortal delirium of passion. I should kill my husband by my coldness, by comparisons with which he would guess, though hidden in the depths of my conscience. Oh! on the day when I should read a trace of involuntary, even of suppressed reproach in a furrow on his brow, in a saddened look, in some imperceptible gesture, nothing could hold me: I should be lying with a fractured skull on the pavement, and find that less hard than my husband. It might be my own over-susceptibility that would lead me to this horrible but welcome death; I might die the victim of an impatient mood in Octave caused by some matter of business, or be deceived by some unjust suspicion. Alas! I might even mistake some proof of love for a sign of contempt!

" ' What torture on both sides! Octave would be always doubting me, I doubting him. I, quite involuntarily, should give him a rival wholly unworthy of him, a man whom I despise, but with whom I have known raptures branded on me with fire, which are my shame, but which I cannot forget.

" ' Have I shown you enough of my heart? No one, monsieur, can convince me that love may be renewed, for I neither can nor will accept love from any one. A young bride

is like a plucked flower ; but a guilty wife is like a flower that
has been walked over. You, who are a florist, you know
whether it is ever possible to restore the broken stem, to
revive the faded colors, to make the sap flow again in the
tender vessels of which the whole vegetative function lies in
their perfect rigidity.   If some botanist should attempt the
operation, could his genius smooth out the folds of the
bruised corolla ?   If he could remake a flower, he would be
God.   God alone can remake me !   I am drinking the bitter
cup of expiation ; but as I drink it I painfully spell out this
sentence : Expiation is not annihilation.

"'In my little house, alone, I eat my bread soaked in
tears ; but no one sees me eat nor sees me weep.   If I go
back to Octave, I must give up my tears—they would offend
him.   Oh ! monsieur, how many virtues must a woman tread
under foot, not to give herself, but to restore herself to a
betrayed husband ?   Who could count them ?   God alone ;
for He alone can know and encourage the horrible refinements
at which the angels must turn pale.   Nay, I will go further.
A woman has courage in the presence of her husband if he
knows nothing ; she shows a sort of fierce strength in her
hypocrisy ; she deceives him to secure him double happiness.
But common knowledge is surely degrading.   Supposing I
could exchange humiliation for ecstasy?   Would not Octave
at last feel that my consent was sheer depravity?   Marriage
is based on esteem, on sacrifices on both sides ; but neither
Octave nor I could esteem each other the day after our reunion.   He would have disgraced me by a love like that of
an old man for a courtesan, and I should for ever feel the
shame of being a chattel instead of a lady.   I should represent pleasure, and not virtue, in his house.   These are the
bitter fruits of such a sin.   I have made myself a bed of anguish upon which I can only toss on burning coals, a sleepless
pillow.

"'Here, when I suffer, I bless my sufferings ; I say to God,

"I thank Thee!" But in my husband's house I should be full of terror, tasting joys to which I have no right.

"'All this, monsieur, is not argument; it is the feeling of a soul made vast and hollow by seven years of suffering. Finally, must I make a horrible confession? I shall always feel at my bosom the lips of a child conceived in rapture and joy, and in the belief in happiness, of a child I nursed for seven months, that I shall bear in my womb all the days of my life. If other children should draw their nourishment from me, they would drink in tears mingling with the milk and turning it sour. I seem a light thing, you regard me as a child—Ah yes! I have a child's memory, the memory which returns to us on the verge of the tomb. So, you see, there is not a situation in that beautiful life to which the world and my husband's love want to recall me, which is not a false position, which does not cover a snare or reveal a precipice down which I must fall, torn by pitiless rocks. For five years now I have been wandering in the sandy desert of the future without finding a place convenient to repent in, because my soul is possessed by true repentance.

"'Religion has its answers ready to all this, and I know them by heart. This suffering, these difficulties, are my punishment, she says, and God will give me strength to endure them. This, monsieur, is an argument to certain pious souls gifted with an energy which I have not. I have made my choice between this hell, where God does not forbid my blessing Him, and the hell that awaits me under Count Octave's roof.

"'One word more. If I were still a girl, with the experience I now have, my husband is the man I should choose; but that is the very reason of my refusal. I could not bear to blush before that man. What! I should be always on my knees, he always standing upright; and if we were to exchange positions, I should scorn him! I will not be better treated by him in consequence of my sin. The angel who

might venture under such circumstances on certain liberties,
which are permissible when both are equally blameless, is not
on earth; he dwells in heaven! Octave is full of delicate
feeling, I know; but even in his soul (which, however generous, is a man's soul after all) there is no guarantee for the
new life I should lead with him.

"'Come, then, and tell me where I may find the solitude,
the peace, the silence, so kindly to irreparable woes, which
you promised me.'

"After making this copy of the letter to preserve it complete, I went to the Rue Payenne. Anxiety had conquered
the power of opium. Octave was walking up and down his
garden like a madman.

"'Answer that!' said I, giving him his wife's letter.
'Try to reassure the modesty of experience. It is rather
more difficult than conquering the modesty of ignorance,
which curiosity helps to betray.' .

"'She is mine!' cried the Count, whose face expressed
joy as he went on reading the letter.

"He signed to me with his hand to leave him to himself.
I understood that extreme happiness and extreme pain obey
the same laws: I went in to receive Madame de Courteville
and Amélie, who were to dine with the Count that day.
However handsome Mademoiselle de Courteville might be, I
felt, on seeing her once more, that love has three aspects,
and that the women who can inspire us with perfect love are
very rare. As I involuntarily compared Amélie with Honorine, I found the erring wife more attractive than the pure
girl. To Honorine's heart fidelity had not been a duty, but
the inevitable; while Amélie would serenely pronounce the
most solemn promises without knowing their purport or to
what they bound her. The crushed, the dead woman, so to
speak, the sinner to be reinstated, seemed to me sublime;
she incited the special generosities of a man's nature; she

22222

demanded all the treasures of the heart, all the resources of strength; she filled his life and gave the zest of a conflict to happiness; whereas Amélie, chaste and confiding, would settle down into the sphere of peaceful motherhood, where the commonplace must be its poetry, and where my mind would find no struggle and no victory.

"Of the plains of Champagne and the snowy, storm-beaten but sublime Alps, what young man would choose the chalky, monotonous level? No; such comparisons are fatal and wrong on the threshold of the mairie. Alas! only the experience of life can teach us that marriage excludes passion, that a family cannot have its foundation on the tempests of love. After having dreamed of impossible love, with its infinite caprices, after having tasted the tormenting delights of the ideal, I saw before me modest reality. Pity me, for what could be expected! At twenty-five I did not trust myself; but I took a manly resolution.

"I went back to the Count to announce the arrival of his relations, and I saw him grown young again in the reflected light of hope.

"'What ails you, Maurice?' said he, struck by my changed expression.

"'Monsieur le Comte——'

"'No longer Octave? You, to whom I shall owe my life, my happiness——'

"'My dear Octave, if you should succeed in bringing the Countess back to her duty, I have studied her well'—(he looked at me as Othello must have looked at Iago when Iago first contrived to insinuate a suspicion into the Moor's mind) —'she must never see me again; she must never know that Maurice was your secretary. Never mention my name to her, or all will be undone—— You have gotten me an appointment as maître des requêtes *—well, get me instead some diplomatic post abroad, a consulship, and do not think of my

* Chief of Requests (a Court Judge).

marrying Amélie. Oh ! do not be uneasy,' I added, seeing him draw himself up, ' I will play my part to the end.'

"'Poor boy !' said he, taking my hand, which he pressed, while he kept back the tears that were starting to his eyes.

"'You gave me gloves,' I said, laughing, ' but I have not put them on ; that is all.'

"We then agreed as to what I was to do that evening at Honorine's house, whither I presently returned. It was now August ; the day had been hot and stormy, but the storm hung overhead, the sky was like copper ; the scent of the flowers was heavy, I felt as if I were in an oven, and caught myself wishing that the Countess might have set out for the Indies ; but she was sitting on a wooden bench shaped like a sofa, under an arbor, in a loose dress of white muslin fastened with blue bows, her hair unadorned in waving bands over her cheeks, her feet on a small wooden stool, and showing a little way beyond her skirt. She did not rise ; she showed me with her hand to the seat by her side, saying—

"'Now, is not life at a deadlock for me ?'

"'Life as you have made it,' I replied. ' But not the life I propose to make for you ; for, if you choose, you may be very happy——'

"'How ?' said she ; her whole person was a question.

"'Your letter is in the Count's hands.'

"Honorine started like a frightened doe, sprang to a few paces off, walked down the garden, turned about, remained standing for some minutes, and finally went in to sit alone in the drawing-room, where I joined her, after giving her time to get accustomed to the pain of this poniard thrust.

"'You—a friend ? Say rather a traitor ! A spy, perhaps, sent by my husband.'

"Instinct in women is as strong as the perspicacity of great men.

"'You wanted an answer to your letter, did you not? And there was but one man in the world who could write it. You

must read the reply, my dear Countess; and if after reading
it you still find that your life is a deadlock, the spy will prove
himself a friend; I will place you in a convent whence the
Count's power cannot drag you. But, before going there, let
us consider the other side of the question. There is a law,
alike divine and human, which even hatred affects to obey,
and which commands us not to condemn the accused without
hearing his defense. Till now you have passed condemnation, as children do, with your ears stopped. The devotion
of seven years has its claims. So you must read the answer
your husband will send you. I have forwarded to him,
through my uncle, a copy of your letter, and my uncle asked
him what his reply would be if his wife wrote him a letter in
such terms. Thus you are not compromised. He will himself bring the Count's answer. In the presence of that saintly
man, and in mine, out of respect for your own dignity, you
must read it, or you will be no better than a willful, passionate
child. You must make this sacrifice to the world, to the law,
and to God.'

"As she saw in this concession no attack on her womanly
resolve, she consented. All the labor of four or five months
had been building up to this moment. But do not the pyra-
mids end in a point on which a bird may perch? The Count
had set all his hopes on this supreme instant, and he had
reached it.

"In all my life I remember nothing more formidable than
my uncle's entrance into that little pompadour drawing-room,
at ten that evening. The fine head with its silver hair thrown
into relief by the entirely black dress, and the divinely calm
face, had a magical effect on the Comtesse Honorine; she
had the feeling of cool balm on her wounds, and beamed in
the reflection of that virtue which gave light without knowing it.

"'Monsieur the Curé of the White Friars,' said old Gobain.

"'Are you come, uncle, with a message of happiness and peace?' said I.

"''Happiness and peace are always to be found in obedience to the precepts of the church,' replied my uncle, and he handed the Countess the following letter:

"'My dear Honorine:—If you had but done me the favor of trusting me, if you had read the letter I wrote to you five years since, you would have spared yourself five years of useless labor and of privations which have grieved me deeply. In it I proposed an arrangement of which the stipulations will relieve all your fears, and make our domestic life possible. I have much to reproach myself with, and in seven years of sorrow I have discovered all my errors. I misunderstood marriage. I failed to scent danger when it threatened you. An angel was in my house. The Lord bade me guard it well! The Lord has punished me for my audacious confidence.

"'You cannot give yourself a single lash without striking me. Have mercy on me, my dear Honorine. I so fully appreciated your susceptibilities that I would not bring you back to the old house in the Rue Payenne, where I can live without you, but which I could not bear to see again with you. I am decorating, with great pleasure, another house, in the Faubourg Saint-Honoré, to which, in hope, I conduct not a wife whom I owe to her ignorance of life, and secured to me by law, but a sister who will allow me to press on her brow such a kiss as a father gives the daughter he blesses every day.

"'Will you bereave me of the right I have conquered from your despair—that of watching more closely over your needs, your pleasures, your life even? Women have one heart always on their side, always abounding in excuses—their mother's; you never knew any mother but my mother, who would have brought you back to me. But how is it that you never guessed that I had for you the heart of a mother, both of my mother

and of your own? Yes, dear, my affection is neither mean
nor grasping; it is one of those which will never let any
annoyance last long enough to pucker the brow of the child
it worships. What can you think of the companion of your
childhood, Honorine, if you believe him capable of accepting
kisses given in trembling, of living between delight and
anxiety? Do not fear that you will be exposed to the laments
of a suppliant passion; I would not want you back until I felt
certain of my own strength to leave you in perfect freedom.

"'Your solitary pride has exaggerated the difficulties. You
may, if you will, look on at the life of a brother, or of a father,
without either suffering or joy; but you will find neither
mockery nor indifference, nor have any doubt as to his intentions. The warmth of the atmosphere in which you live will
be always equable and genial, without tempests, without a
possible squall. If, later, when you feel secure that you are
as much at home as in your own little house, you desire to
try some other elements of happiness, pleasures, or amusements, you can expand their circle at your will. The tenderness of a mother knows neither contempt nor pity. What is
it? Love without desire. Well, in me admiration shall hide
every sentiment in which you might see an offense.

"'Thus, living side by side, we may both be magnanimous.
In you the kindness of a sister, the affectionate thoughtfulness
of a friend, will satisfy the ambition of him who wishes to be
your life's companion; and you may measure his tenderness
by the care he will take to conceal it. Neither you nor I will
be jealous of the past, for we may each acknowledge that the
other has sense enough to look only straightforward.

"'Thus you will be at home in your new house exactly as
you are in the Rue Saint-Maur; unapproachable, alone, occupied as you please, living by your own law; but having in
addition the legitimate protection, of which you are now
exacting the most chivalrous labors of love, with the consideration which lends so much lustre to a woman, and the

fortune which will allow of your doing many good works. Honorine, when you long for an unnecessary absolution, you have only to ask for it; it will not be forced upon you by the church or by the law; it will wait on your pride, on your own impulsion. My wife might indeed have to fear all the things you dread; but not my friend and sister, toward whom I am bound to show every form and refinement of politeness. To see you happy is enough happiness for me; I have proved this for these seven years past. The guarantee for this, Honorine, is to be seen in all the flowers made by you, carefully preserved, and watered by my tears. Like the *quipos*, the tally cords of the Peruvians, they are the record of our sorrows.

"'If this secret compact does not suit you, my child, I have begged the saintly man who takes charge of this letter not to say a word in my behalf. I will not owe your return to the terrors threatened by the church, nor to the bidding of the law. I will not accept the simple and quiet happiness that I ask from any one but yourself. If you persist in condemning me to the lonely life, bereft even of a fraternal smile, which I have led for nine years, if you remain in your solitude and show no sign, my will yields to yours. Understand me perfectly: you shall be no more troubled than you have been until this day. I will get rid of the crazy fellow who has meddled in your concerns and has, perhaps, caused you some annoyance——'

"'Monsieur,' said Honorine, folding up the letter, which she placed in her bosom, and looking at my uncle, 'thank you very much. I will avail myself of Monsieur le Comte's permission to remain here——'

"'Ah!' I exclaimed.

"This exclamation made my uncle look at me uneasily, and won from the Countess a mischievous glance which enlightened me as to her motives.

" Honorine had wanted to ascertain whether I was an actor, a bird-snarer; and I had the melancholy satisfaction of deceiving her by my exclamation, which was one of those cries from the heart which women understand so well.

" ' Ah, Maurice,' said she, ' you know how to love.'

" The light that flashed in my eyes was another reply which would have dissipated the Countess' uneasiness if she still had any. Thus the Count found me useful to the very last.

" Honorine then took out the Count's letter again to finish reading it. My uncle signed to me, and I arose.

" ' Let us leave the Countess,' said he.

" ' You are going already, Maurice?' she said, without looking at me.

" She arose, and still reading, followed us to the door. On the threshold she took my hand, pressed it very affectionately, and said, ' We shall meet again——'

" ' No,' I replied, wringing her hand, so that she cried out. ' You love your husband. I leave to-morrow.'

" And I rushed away, leaving my uncle, of whom she asked:

" ' Why, what is the matter with your nephew?'

" The good Abbé completed my work by pointing to his head and heart, as much as to say, ' He is mad, madame; you must forgive him!' and with all the more truth, because he really thought it.

" Six days after I set out with an appointment as vice-consul in Spain, in a large commercial town, where I could quickly qualify to rise in the career of a consul, to which I now restricted my ambition. After I had established myself there, I received this letter from the Count:

" ' MY DEAR. MAURICE:—If I were happy, I should not write to you, but I have entered on a new life of suffering. I have grown young again in my desires, with all the impatience of a man of forty and the prudence of a diplomatist, who has learned to moderate his passion. When you left I had

not yet been admitted to the pavilion in the Rue Saint-Maur,
but a letter had promised me that I should have permission—
the mild and melancholy letter of a woman who dreaded the
agitations of a meeting. After waiting for more than a month,
I made bold to call, and desired Gobain to inquire whether I
could be received. I sat down in a chair in the avenue near
the lodge, my head buried in my hands, and there I remained
for almost an hour.

" " " Madame had to dress," said Gobain, to hide Honorine's
hesitancy under a pride of appearance which was flattering
to me.

" ' During a long quarter of an hour we both of us were
possessed by an involuntary nervous trembling as great as that
which seizes a speaker on the platform, and we spoke to each
other in scared phrases like those of persons taken by surprise
who " make believe " a conversation.

" " " You see, Honorine," said I, my eyes full of tears, " the
ice is broken, and I am so tremulous with happiness that you
must forgive the incoherency of my language. It will be so
for a long time yet."

" ' " There is no crime in being in love with your wife,"
she returned with a forced smile.

" ' " Do me the favor," said I, " no longer to work as you
do. I have heard from Madame Gobain that for three weeks
you have been living on your savings ; you have sixty thousand
francs a year of your own, and if you cannot give me back
your heart at least do not abandon your fortune to me."

" ' " I have long known your kindness," said she.

" ' " Though you should prefer to remain here," I added
impressively, " and to preserve your independence; though the
most ardent love should find no favor in your eyes, still do
not toil."

" ' I gave her three certificates for twelve thousand francs a
year each ; she took them, opened them languidly, and after
reading them through she gave me only a look as my reward.

"I AM CONQUERED," SAID SHE.

She fully understood that I was not offering her money, but freedom.

" ' "I am conquered," said she, holding out her hand, which I kissed. "Come and see me as often as you like."

" 'So she had done herself a violence in receiving me. Next day I found her armed with affected high spirits, and it took two months of habit before I saw her in her true character. But then it was like a delicious May, a springtime of love that gave me ineffable bliss; she was no longer afraid; she was studying me. Alas! when I proposed that she should go to England to return ostensibly to me, to our home, that she should resume her rank and live in our new residence, she was seized with alarm.

" ' "Why not live always as we are!" she said.

" 'I submitted without saying a word.

" ' "Is she making an experiment?" I asked myself as I left her. On my way from my own house to the Rue Saint-Maur thoughts of love had swelled in my heart, and I had said to myself, like a young man, "This evening she will yield."

" 'All my real or affected force was blown to the winds by a smile, by a command from those proud, calm eyes, untouched by passion. I remembered the terrible words you once quoted to me, "Lucretia's dagger wrote in letters of blood the watchword of woman's charter—Liberty!" and they froze me. I felt imperatively how necessary to me was Honorine's consent, and how impossible it was to wring it from her. Could she guess the storms that distracted me when I left as when I came?

" 'At last I painted my situation in a letter to her, giving up the attempt to speak of it. Honorine made no answer, and she was so sad that I made as though I had not written. I was deeply grieved by the idea that I could have distressed her; she read my heart and forgave me. And this was how. Three days ago she received me, for the first time, in her own blue-and-white room. It was bright with flowers, dressed, and lighted up. Honorine was in a dress that made her bewitching. Her hair framed that face that you know in its light curls; and in it were some sprays of Cape heath; she wore a white muslin gown, a white sash with long floating ends. You know what she is in such simplicity, but that day she was a bride, the Honorine of long past days. My joy was chilled at once, for her face was terribly grave; there were fires beneath the ice.

" ' "Octave," she said, "I will return as your wife when you will. But understand clearly that this submission has its dangers. I can be resigned——"

" ' I made a movement.

" ' "Yes," she went on, "I understand : resignation offends you, and you want what I cannot give—Love. Religion and pity led me to renounce my vow of solitude ; you are here ! " She paused.

" ' "At first," she went on, " you asked no more. Now you demand your wife. Well, here I give you Honorine, such as she is, without deceiving you as to what she will be. What shall I be ? A mother ? I hope it. Believe me, I hope it eagerly. Try to change me ; you have my consent ; but if I should die, my dear, do not curse my memory, and do not set down to obstinacy what I should call the worship of the ideal, if it were not more natural to call the indefinable feeling which must kill me the worship of the Divine ! The future will be nothing to me ; it will be your concern ; consult your own mind."

" ' And she sat down in the calm attitude you used to admire, and watched me turning pale with the pain she had inflicted. My blood ran cold. On seeing the effect of her words she took both my hands, and, holding them in her own, she said—

" ' " Octave, I do love you, but not in the way you wish to be loved. I love your soul —— Still, understand that I love you enough to die in your service like an Eastern slave, and without a regret. It will be my expiation."

" 'She did more; she knelt before me on a cushion, and in a spirit of sublime charity she said—

" ' " And perhaps I shall not die ! "

" 'For two months now I have been struggling with myself. What shall I do? My heart is too full; I therefore seek a friend, and send out this cry, " What shall I do?"

" ' OCTAVE.'

"I did not answer this letter. Two months later the newspapers announced the return on board an English vessel of the Comtesse Octave, restored to her family after adventures by land and sea, invented with sufficient probability to arouse no contradiction.

"When I moved to Genoa I received a formal announcement of the happy event of the birth of a son to the Count and Countess. I held that letter in my hand for two hours, sitting on this terrace—on this bench. Two months after, urged by Octave, by Monsieur de Grandville, and Monsieur de Sérizy, my kind friends, and broken by the death of my uncle, I agreed to take a wife.

"Six months after the revolution of July I received this letter, which concludes the story of this couple :

" ' MONSIEUR MAURICE :—I am dying 'though I am a mother—perhaps because I am a mother. I have played my part as a wife well; I have deceived my husband. I have had happiness not less genuine than the tears shed by actresses on the stage. I am dying for society, for the family, for marriage, as the early Christians died for God ! I know not of what I am dying, and I am honestly trying to find out, for I am not perverse ; but I am bent on explaining my malady to you—you who brought that heavenly physician your uncle, at whose word I surrendered. He was my di-

24

rector ; I nursed him in his last illness, and he showed me the way to heaven, bidding me persevere in my duty.

" ' And I have done my duty.

" ' I do not blame those who forget. I admire them as strong and necessary natures ; but I have the malady of memory ! I have not been able twice to feel that love of the heart which identifies a woman with the man she loves. To the last moment, as you know, I cried to your heart, in the confessional, and to my husband, " Have mercy ! " But there was no mercy. Well, and I am dying, dying with stupendous courage. No courtesan was ever more gay than I. My poor Octave is happy ; I let his love feed on the illusions of my heart. I throw all my powers into this terrible masquerade ; the actress is applauded, feasted, smothered in flowers ; but the invisible rival comes every day to seek its prey—a fragment of my life. I am rent and I smile. I smile on two children, but it is the elder, the dead one, that will triumph ! I told you so before. The dead child calls me, and I am going to him.

" ' The intimacy of marriage without love is a position in which my soul feels degraded every hour. I can never weep or give myself up to dreams but when I am alone. The exigencies of society, the care of my child, and that of Octave's happiness never leave me a moment to refresh myself, to renew my strength, as I could in my solitude. The incessant need for watchfulness startles my heart with constant alarms. I have not succeeded in implanting in my soul the sharp-eared vigilance that lies with facility, and has the eyes of a lynx. It is not the lip of one I love that drinks my tears and kisses my eyelids ; it is a handkerchief that dries them ; my burning eyes are cooled with water, and not with tender lips. It is my soul that acts a part, and that perhaps is why I am dying ! I lock up my grief with so much care that nothing is to be seen of it ; it must eat into something, and it has attacked my life.

. " ' I said to the doctors, who discovered my secret, " Make me die of some plausible complaint, or I shall drag my husband with me."

" ' So it is quite understood by M. Desplein, Bianchon, and myself that I am dying of the softening of some bone which science has fully described. Octave believes that I adore him, do you understand? So I am afraid lest he should follow me. I now write to beg you in that case to be the little Count's guardian. You will find with this a codicil in which I have expressed my wish; but do not produce it excepting in case of need, for perhaps I am fatuously vain. My devotion may perhaps leave Octave inconsolable but willing to live. Poor Octave! I wish him a better wife than I am, for he deserves to be well loved.

" ' Since my spiritual spy is married, I bid him remember what the florist of the Rue Saint-Maur hereby bequeaths to him as a lesson: May your wife soon be a mother! Fling her into the vulgarest materialism of household life; hinder her from cherishing in her heart the mysterious flower of the ideal—of that heavenly perfection in which I believed, that enchanted blossom with glorious colors, and whose perfume disgusts us with reality. I am a Saint-Theresa who has not been suffered to live on ecstasy in the depths of a convent, with the Holy Infant, and a spotless winged angel to come and go as she wished.

" ' You saw me happy among my beloved flowers. I did not tell you all: I saw love budding under your affected madness and I concealed from you my thoughts, my poetry; I did not admit you to my kingdom of beauty. Well, well; you will love my child for love of me if he should one day lose his poor father. Keep my secrets as the grave will keep them. Do not mourn for me; I have been dead this many a day, if Saint-Bernard was right in saying that where there is no more love there is no more life.

" ' HONORINE.'

"And the Countess died," said the consul, putting away.
the letters and locking the pocket-book.

"Is the Count still living?" asked the ambassador, "for
since the revolution of July he has disappeared from the
political stage."

"Do you remember, Monsieur de Lora," asked the consul-
general, turning to him, "having seen me going to the steamboat with?——"

"A white-haired man! an old man?" said the painter.

"An old man of forty-five, going in search of health and
amusement in Southern Italy. That old man was my poor
friend, my patron, passing through Genoa to take leave of me
and place his will in my hands. He appoints me his son's
guardian. I had no occasion to tell him of Honorine's
wishes."

"Does he suspect himself of murder?" said Mademoiselle
des Touches to the Baron de L'Hostal.

"He suspects the truth," replied the consul, "and that is
what is killing him. I remained on board the steamship that
was to take him to Naples until it was out of the roadstead ;
a small boat brought me back. We sat for some little time
taking leave of each other—for ever, I fear. God only knows
how much we love the confidant of our love when she who
inspired it is no more.

"'That man,' said Octave, 'holds a charm and wears an
aureola.' The Count went to the prow and looked down on
the Mediterranean. It happened to be fine, and, moved no
doubt by the spectacle, he spoke these last words: 'Ought
we not, in the interests of human nature, to inquire what is
the irresistible power which leads us to sacrifice an exquisite
creature to the most fugitive of all pleasures, and in spite of
our reason? In my conscience I heard cries. Honorine was
not alone in her anguish. And yet I would have it!—— I
am consumed by remorse. In the Rue Payenne I was dying
of the joys I had not; now I shall die in Italy of the joys I

have had—— Wherein lay the discord between two natures, equally noble, I dare assert?' "

For some minutes profound silence reigned on the terrace. Then the consul, turning to the two women, asked, " Was she virtuous?"

Mademoiselle des Touches arose, took the consul's arm, went a few steps away, and said to him—

"Are not men wrong, too, when they come to us and make a young girl a wife while cherishing at the bottom of their heart some angelic image, and comparing us to those unknown rivals, to perfections often borrowed from a remembrance, and always finding us wanting?"

"Mademoiselle, you would be right if marriage were based on passion; and that was the mistake of those two, who will soon be no more. Marriage with heart-deep love on both sides would be paradise."

Mademoiselle des Touches turned from the consul, and was immediately joined by Claude Vignon, who said in her ear—

"A bit of a coxcomb is M. de L'Hostal."

"No," replied she, whispering to Claude these words: "for he has not yet guessed that Honorine would have loved him. Oh!" she exclaimed, seeing the consul's wife approaching, "his wife was listening! Unhappy man!"

Eleven was striking by all the clocks and the guests went home on foot along the seashore.

"Still, that is not life," said Mademoiselle des Touches. "That woman was one of the rarest, and perhaps the most extraordinary exceptions in intellect—a pearl! Life is made up of various incidents, of pain and pleasure alternately. The paradise of Dante, that sublime expression of the ideal, that perpetual blue, is to be found only in the soul; to ask it of the facts of life is a luxury against which nature protests every hour. To such souls as those the six feet of a cell and the kneeling chair are all they need."

"You are right," said Léon de Lora; " but good-for-nothing as I may be, I cannot help admiring a woman who is capable, as that one was, of living by the side of a studio, under a painter's roof, and never coming down, nor seeing the world, nor dipping her feet in the street mud."

"Such a thing has been known—for a few months," said Claude Vignon, with deep irony.

"Comtesse Honorine was not unique of her kind," replied the ambassador to Mademoiselle des Touches.   "A man, nay, and a politician, a bitter writer, was the object of such a passion ; and the pistol-shot which killed him hit not him alone ; the woman who loved lived like a nun ever after."

"Then there are yet some great souls in this age !" said Camille Maupin, and she stood for some minutes pensively leaning on the balustrade of the quay.

PARIS, *January*, 1843.

FACINO CANE.

I ONCE used to live in a little street which probably is not known to you—the Rue de Lesdiguières. It is a turning out of the Rue Saint-Antoine, beginning just opposite a fountain near the Place de la Bastille, and ending in the Rue de la Cerisaie. Love of knowledge stranded me in a garret; my nights I spent in work, my days in reading at the Orleans' Library, close by. I lived frugally, I had accepted the conditions of the monastic life, necessary conditions for every worker, scarcely permitting myself a walk along the Boulevard Bourdon when the weather was fine. One passion only had power to draw me from my studies; and yet, what was that passion but a study of another kind? I used to watch the manners and customs of the faubourg, its inhabitants, and their characteristics. As I dressed no better than a working-man and cared nothing for appearances, I did not put them on their guard; I could join a group and look on while they drove bargains or wrangled among themselves on their way home from work. Even then observation had come to be an instinct with me; a faculty of penetrating to the soul without neglecting the body; or, rather, a power of grasping external details so thoroughly that they never detained me for a moment and at once I passed beyond and through them. I could enter into the life of the human creatures whom I watched, just as the dervish in the "Arabian Nights" could pass into any soul or body after pronouncing a certain formula.

If I met a workingman and his wife in the streets between eleven o'clock and midnight on their way home from the Ambigu Comique, I used to amuse myself by following them from the Boulevard du Pont aux Choux to the Boulevard Beau-

marchais. The good folk would begin by talking about the
play; then from one thing to another they would come to
their own affairs, and the mother would walk on and on,
heedless of complaint or question from the little one that
dragged at her hand, while she and her husband reckoned up
the wages to be paid on the morrow, and spent the money in
a score of different ways. Then came domestic details,
lamentations over the excessive dearness of potatoes, or the
length of the winter and the high price of block fuel, together
with forcible representations of amounts owing to the baker,
ending in an acrimonious dispute, in the course of which such
couples reveal their characters in picturesque language. As I
listened, I could make their lives mine, I felt their rags on
my back, I walked with their gaping shoes on my feet; their
cravings, their needs, had all passed into my soul, or my soul
had passed into theirs. It was the dream of a waking man.
I waxed hot with them over the foreman's tyranny, or the
bad customers that made them call again and again for payment.

To come out of my own way of life, to be another than
myself through a kind of intoxication of the intellectual faculties, and to play this game at will, such was my recreation.
Whence comes the gift? Is it a kind of second-sight? Is it
one of those powers which, when abused, ends in madness?
I have never tried to discover its source; I possess it, I use it,
that is all. But this it behooves you to know, that in those
days I began to resolve the heterogeneous mass known as the
People into its elements, and to evaluate its good and bad
qualities. Even then I realized the possibilities of my suburb,
that hot-bed of revolution in which heroes, inventors, and
practical men of science, rogues and scoundrels, virtues and
vices, were all packed together by poverty, stifled by necessity,
drowned in drink, and consumed by ardent spirits.

You would not imagine how many adventures, how many
tragedies, lie buried away out of sight in that dolorous city;

how much horror and beauty lurks there. No imagination can reach the truth; no one can go down into that city to make discoveries; for one must needs descend too low into its depths to see the wonderful scenes of tragedy or comedy enacted there, the masterpieces brought forth by chance.

I do not know how it is that I have kept the following story so long untold. It is one of the curious things that stop in the bag from which memory draws out stories at haphazard, like numbers in a lottery. There are plenty of tales just as strange and just as well hidden still left; but some day, you may be sure, their turn will come:

One day my charwoman, a workingman's wife, came to beg me to honor her sister's wedding with my presence. If you are to realize what this wedding was like, you must know that I paid my charwoman, poor creature, four francs a month; for which sum she came every morning to make my bed, clean my shoes, brush my clothes, sweep the room, and make ready my breakfast, before going to her day's work of turning the handle of a machine, at which hard drudgery she earned ten sous. Her husband, a cabinet maker, made four francs a day at his trade; but as they had three children, it was all that they could do to gain an honest living. Yet I have never met with more sterling honesty than in this man and his wife. For five years after I left the quarter, Mère Vaillant used to come on my birthday with a bunch of flowers and some oranges for me—she that had never one franc to put by! Want had drawn us together. I never could give her more than a ten-franc piece, and often I had to borrow the money for the occasion. This will perhaps explain my promise to go to the wedding; I hoped to efface myself in these poor people's merry-making.

The banquet and the ball were given on the first floor above a wineshop in the Rue de Charenton. It was a large room, lighted by oil lamps with tin reflectors. A row of wooden

benches ran round the walls, which were black with grime to
the height of the tables. Here some eighty persons, all in
their Sunday best, tricked out with ribbons and bunches of
flowers, all of them on pleasure bent, were dancing away with
heated visages as if the world were about to come to an end.
Bride and bridegroom exchanged salutes to the general satisfaction, amid a chorus of facetious " Oh, ohs ! " and " Ah,
ahs ! " less really indecent than the furtive glances of young
girls that have been well brought up. There was something
indescribably infectious about the rough, homely enjoyment
in all countenances.

But neither the faces, nor the wedding, nor the wedding-
guests have anything to do with my story. Simply bear them
in mind as the odd setting to it. Try to realize the scene,
the shabby, red-painted wineshop, the smell of wine, the yells
of merriment ; try to feel that you are really in the faubourg,
among old people, workingmen and poor women giving
themselves up to a night's enjoyment.

The band consisted of a fiddle, a clarionet, and a flageolet
from the Blind Asylum. The three were paid seven francs in
a lump sum for the night. For the money, they gave us, not
Beethoven certainly, nor yet Rossini ; they played as they
had the will and the skill ; and every one in the room (with
charming delicacy of feeling) refrained from finding fault.
The music made such a brutal assault on the drum of my ear,
that after a first glance round the room my eyes fell at once
upon the blind trio, and the sight of their uniform inclined
me from the first to indulgence. As the artists stood in a
window recess, it was difficult to distinguish their faces except
at close quarters, and I kept away at first ; but when I came
nearer (I hardly know why) I thought of nothing else ; the
wedding-party and the music ceased to exist, my curiosity was
aroused to the highest pitch, for my soul passed into the body
of the clarionet player.

The fiddle and the flageolet were neither of them interest-

ing ; their faces were of the ordinary type among the blind—
earnest, attentive, and grave. Not so the clarionet player ;
any artist or philosopher must have come to a stop at the sight
of him.

Picture to yourself a plaster-mask of Dante in the red lamp-
light, with a forest of silver-white hair above the brows.
Blindness intensified the expression of bitterness and sorrow
in that grand face of his ; the dead eyes were lighted up, as it
were, by a thought within that broke forth like a burning
flame, lit by one sole insatiable desire, written large in vigorous characters upon an arching brow scored across with as many
lines as an old stone-wall.

The old man was playing at random, without the slightest
regard for time or tune. His fingers traveled mechanically
over the worn keys of his instrument ; he did not trouble
himself over a false note now and again (a *canard*, in the language of the orchestra), neither did the dancers, nor, for that
matter, did my old Italian's acolytes ; for I had made up my
mind that he must be an Italian, and an Italian he was.
There was something great, something too of the despot about
this old Homer bearing within him an "Odyssey" doomed
to oblivion. The greatness was so real that it triumphed
over his abject position ; the despotism so much a part of
him, that it rose above his poverty.

There are violent passions which drive a man to good or
evil, making of him a hero or a convict ; of these there was
not one that had failed to leave its traces on the grandly
hewn, lividly Italian face. You trembled lest a flash of
thought should suddenly light up the deep sightless hollows
under the grizzled brows, as you might fear to see brigands
with torches and poniards in the mouth of a cavern. You
felt that there was a lion in that cage of flesh, a lion spent
with useless raging against iron bars. The fires of despair
had burned themselves out into ashes, the lava had cooled ;
but the tracks of the flames, the wreckage, and a little smoke

remained to bear witness to the violence of the eruption, the ravages of the fire. These images crowded up at the sight of the clarionet player, till the thoughts now grown cold in his face burned hot within my soul.

The fiddle and the flageolet took a deep interest in bottles and glasses; at the end of a country dance they hung their instruments from a button on their reddish-colored coats, and stretched out their hands to a little table set in the window recess to hold their liquor supply. Each time they did so they held out a full glass to the Italian, who could not reach it for himself because he sat in front of the table, and each time the Italian thanked them with a friendly nod. All their movements were made with the precision which always amazes one so much at the Blind Asylum. You could almost think that they can see. I came nearer to listen; but when I stood beside them, they evidently guessed I was not a workingman and kept themselves to themselves.

"What part of the world do you come from, you that are playing the clarionet?"

"From Venice," he said, with a trace of Italian accent.

"Have you always been blind, or did it come on afterward——?"

"Afterward," he answered quickly. "A cursed gutta serena."

"Venice is a fine city; I have always had a fancy to go there."

The old man's face lighted up, the wrinkles began to work, he was violently excited.

"If I went with you, you would not lose your time," he said.

"Don't talk about Venice to our doge," put in the fiddle, "or you will start him off, and he has stowed away a couple of bottles as it is—has the prince!"

"Come, strike up, Daddy Canard!" added the flageolet, and the three began to play. But while they executed the four figures of a square dance, the Venetian was scenting my thoughts; he guessed the great interest I felt in him. The dreary dispirited look died out of his face, some mysterious hope brightened his features and slid like a blue flame over his wrinkles. He smiled and wiped his brow, that fearless, terrible brow of his, and at length grew gay like a man mounted on his hobby.

"How old are you?" I asked.

"Eighty-two."

"How long have you been blind?"

"For very nearly fifty years," he said, and there was that in his tone which told me that his regret was for something more than his lost sight, for great power of which he had been robbed.

"Then why do they call you 'the doge?'" I asked.

"Oh, it is a joke. I am a Venetian noble and I might have been a doge like any one else."

"What is your name?"

"Here, in Paris, I am Père Canet," he said. "It was the only way of spelling my name on the register. But in Italy I am Marco Facino Cane, Prince of Varese."

"What, are you descended from the great *condottiere* Facino Cane, whose lands won by the sword were taken by the Dukes of Milan?"

"Of a truth," returned he. "His son's life was not safe under the Visconti; he fled to Venice, and his name was inscribed on the Golden Book. And now neither Cane nor Golden Book is in existence." His gesture startled me; it told of patriotism extinguished and weariness of life.

"But if you were once a Venetian senator, you must have been a wealthy man. How did you lose your fortune?"

"In evil days."

He waved away the glass of wine handed to him by the flageolet, and bowed his head. He had no heart to drink. These details were not calculated to extinguish my curiosity.

As the three ground out the music of the square dance I
gazed at the old Venetian noble, thinking thoughts that set a
young man's mind afire at the age of twenty. I saw Venice
and the Adriatic; I saw her ruin in the ruin of the face before
me. I walked to and fro in that city, so beloved of her citi-
zens; I went from the Rialto Bridge, along the Grand Canal,
and from the Riva degli Schiavoni to the Lido, returning to
St. Mark's, that cathedral so unlike all others in its sublimity.
I looked up at the windows of the Casa Doro, each with its
different sculptured ornaments; I saw old palaces rich in
marbles, saw all the wonders which a student beholds with
the more sympathetic eyes because visible things take their
color of his fancy, and the sight of realities cannot rob him
of the glory of his dreams. Then I traced back a course of
life for this latest scion of a race of condottieri, tracking
down his misfortunes, looking for the reasons of the deep
moral and physical degradation out of which the lately revived sparks of greatness and nobility shone so much the
more brightly. My ideas, no doubt, were passing through
his mind, for all processes of thought-communications are far
more swift, I think, in blind people, because their blindness
compels them to concentrate their attention. I had not long
to wait for proof that we were in sympathy in this way.
Facino Cane left off playing and came up to me. "Let us
go out!" he said; his tones thrilled through me like an
electric shock. I gave him my arm, and we went.

Outside on the street he said, "Will you take me back to
Venice? will you be my guide? Will you put faith in me?
You shall be richer than ten of the richest houses in Amsterdam or London, richer than Rothschild; in short, you shall
have the fabulous wealth of the 'Arabian Nights.'"

The man was mad, I thought; but in his voice there was a
potent something which I obeyed. I allowed him to lead,
and he went in the direction of the Fossés de la Bastille, as
if he could see; walking till he reached a lonely spot down

by the river, just where the bridge has since been built at the junction of the Canal Saint-Martin and the Seine. Here he sat down on a stone, and I, sitting opposite to him, saw the old man's hair gleaming like threads of silver in the moonlight. The stillness was scarcely troubled by the sound of the far-off thunder of traffic along the boulevards; the clear night air and everything about us combined to make a strangely unreal scene.

"You talk of millions to a young man," I began, "and do you think that he will shrink from enduring any number of hardships to gain them? Are you not laughing at me?"

"May I die unshriven," he cried vehemently, "if all that I am about to tell you is not true. I was one-and-twenty years old, like you at this moment. I was rich, I was handsome, and a noble by birth. I began with the first madness of all—with love. I loved as no one can love nowadays. I have hidden myself in a chest, at the risk of a dagger thrust, for nothing more than the promise of a kiss. To die for her—it seemed to me to be a whole life in itself. In 1760 I fell in love with a lady of the Vendramin family; she was eighteen years old, and married to a Sagredo, one of the richest senators, a man of thirty, madly in love with his wife. My mistress and I were guiltless as cherubs when the *sposo* caught us together talking of love. He was armed, I was not, but he missed me; I sprang upon him and killed him with my two hands, wringing his neck as if he had been a chicken. I wanted Bianca to fly with me; but she would not. That is the way with women! So I went alone. I was condemned to death, and my property was confiscated and made over to my next-of-kin; but I had carried off my diamonds, five of Titian's pictures taken down from their frames and rolled up, and all my gold.

"I went to Milan, no one molested me, my affair in nowise interested the state. One small observation before I go further," he continued, after a pause, "whether it is true or

not that the mother's fancies at the time of conception or in
the months before birth can influence her child, this much is
certain, my mother during her pregnancy had a passion for
gold, and I am the victim of a monomania, of a craving for
gold which must be gratified.   Gold is so much a necessity
of life for me that I have never been without it ; I must have
gold to toy with and finger.   As a young man I always wore
jewelry, and carried two or three hundred ducats about with
me wherever I went."

He drew a couple of gold coins from his pocket and showed
them to me as he spoke.

" I can tell by instinct when gold is near.   Blind as I am,
I stop before the jewelers' store windows.   That passion was
the ruin of me ; I took to gambling to play with gold.   I
was not a cheat—I was cheated ; I ruined myself.   I lost all
my fortune.   Then the longing to see Bianca once more possessed me like a frenzy.   I stole back to Venice and found
her again.   For six months I was happy ; she hid me in her
house and fed me.   I thought thus deliciously to finish my
days.   But the Provveditore courted her, and guessed that he
had a rival ; we in Italy can feel that.   He played the spy
upon us, and surprised us together in bed, base wretch !   You
may judge what a fight for life it was ; I did not kill him out-
right, but I wounded him dangerously.

"That adventure broke my luck.   I have never found
another Bianca ; I have known great pleasures ; but among
the most celebrated women of the court of Louis XV. I never
found my beloved Venetian's charm, her love, her great
qualities.

" The Provveditore called his servants, the palace was surrounded and entered.   I fought for my life that I might die
beneath Bianca's eyes ; Bianca helped me to kill the Provveditore.   Once before she had refused flight with me ; but
after six months of happiness she wished only to die with me,
and received several thrusts.   I was entangled in a great

cloak that they flung over me, carried down to a gondola and
hurried to the Pozzi dungeons. I was twenty-two years old;
I gripped the hilt of my broken sword so hard that they
could only have taken it from me by cutting off my hand at
the wrist. A curious chance, or rather the instinct of self-
preservation, led me to hide the fragment of the blade in a
corner of my cell, as if it might still be of use. They tended
me; none of my wounds were serious. At two-and-twenty
one can recover from anything. I was to lose my head on
the scaffold. I shammed illness to gain time. It seemed to
me that the canal lay just outside my cell. I thought to
make my escape by boring a hole through the wall and swimming for my life. I based my hopes on the following reasons:

"Every time that the gaoler came with my food there was
light enough to read directions written on the walls—'Side
of the Palace,' 'Side of the Canal,' 'Side of the Vaults.'
At last I saw a design in this, but I did not trouble myself
much about the meaning of it; the actual incomplete condition of the Ducal Palace accounted for it. The longing to
regain my freedom gave me something like genius. Groping
about with my fingers, I spelled out an Arabic inscription on
the wall. The author of the work informed those to come
after him that he had loosened two stones in the lowest course
of masonry and hollowed out eleven feet beyond under-
ground. As he went on with his excavations, it became necessary to spread the fragments of stone and mortar over the
floor of his cell. But even if gaolers and inquisitors had not
felt sure that the structure of the buildings was such that no
watch was needed below, the level of the Pozzi dungeons
being several steps below the threshold, it was possible gradually to raise the earthen floor without exciting the warder's
suspicions.

"The tremendous labor had profited nothing—nothing at
least to him that began it. The very fact that it was left

25

unfinished told of the unknown worker's death. Unless his devoted toil was to be wasted for ever, his successor must have some knowledge of Arabic, but I had studied Oriental languages at the Armenian convent. A few words written on the back of the stone recorded the unhappy man's fate; he had fallen a victim to his great possessions; Venice had coveted his wealth and seized upon it. A whole month went by before I obtained any result; but whenever I felt my strength failing as I worked, I heard the chink of gold, I saw gold spread before me, I was dazzled by diamonds. Ah! wait.

"One night my blunted steel struck on wood. I whetted the fragment of my blade and cut a hole; I crept on my belly like a serpent; I worked naked and mole-fashion, my hands in front of me, using the stone itself to gain a purchase. I was to appear before my judges in two days' time; I made a final effort, and that night I bored through the wood and felt that there was space beyond.

" Judge of my surprise when I applied my eye to the hole. I was in the ceiling of a vault, heaps of gold were dimly visible in the faint light. The doge himself and one of the Ten stood below; I could hear their voices and sufficient of their talk to know that this was the secret treasury of the republic, full of the gifts of doges and reserves of booty called the Tithe of Venice from the spoils of military expeditions. I was saved!

" When the gaoler came I proposed that he should help me to escape and fly with me, and that we should take with us as much as we could carry. There was no reason for hesitation; he agreed. Vessels were about to sail for the Levant. All possible precautions were taken. Bianca furthered the schemes which I suggested to my accomplice. It was arranged that Bianca should only rejoin us in Smyrna for fear of exciting suspicion. In a single night the hole was enlarged and we dropped down into the secret treasury of Venice.

" What a night that was! Four great casks full of gold

stood there. In the outer room silver pieces were piled in heaps, leaving a gangway between by which to cross the chamber. Banks of silver coins surrounded the walls to the height of five feet.

"I thought the gaoler would go mad. He sang and laughed and danced and capered among the gold, till I threatened to strangle him if he made a sound or wasted time. In his joy he did not notice at first the table where the diamonds lay. I flung myself upon these, and deftly filled the pockets of my sailor's jacket and trousers with the stones. Ah! heaven, I did not take the third of them. Gold ingots lay underneath the table. I persuaded my companion to fill as many bags as we could carry with the gold, and made him understand that this was our only chance of escaping detection abroad.

"'Pearls, rubies, and diamonds might be recognized,' I told him.

"Covetous though we were, we could not possibly take more than two thousand livres weight of gold, which meant six journeys across the prison to the gondola. The sentinel at the water-gate was bribed with a bag containing ten livres weight of gold; and as for the two gondoliers, they believed they were serving the republic. At daybreak we set out.

"Once upon the open sea, when I thought of that night, when I recollected all that I had felt, when the vision of that great hoard arose before my eyes, and I computed that I had left behind thirty millions in silver, twenty in gold, and many more in diamonds, pearls, and rubies—then a sort of madness began to work in me. I had the gold fever.

"We landed at Smyrna and took ship at once for France. As we went on board the French vessel, heaven favored me by ridding me of my accomplice. I did not think at the time of all the possible consequences of this mishap and rejoiced not a little. We were so completely unnerved by all that had happened that we were stupid, we said not a word

to each other, we waited until it should be safe to enjoy ourselves at our ease.   It was not wonderful that the rogue's
head was dizzy.   You shall see how heavily God has punished
me.

"I never knew a quiet moment until I had sold two-thirds
of my diamonds in London or Amsterdam, and held the value
of my gold dust in a negotiable shape.   For five years I hid
myself in Madrid, then in 1770 I came to Paris with a Spanish name, and led as brilliant a life as may be.   Then, in the
midst of my pleasures, as I enjoyed a fortune of six millions,
I was smitten with blindness.   I do not doubt but that my
infirmity was brought on by my sojourn in the cell and my
work in the stone, if, indeed, my peculiar faculty for 'seeing'
gold was not an abuse of the power of sight which predes-
tined me to lose it.   Bianca was dead.

"At this time I had fallen in love with a woman to whom
I thought to link my fate.   I had told her the secret of my
name ; she belonged to a powerful family ; she was a friend
of Madame du Barry ; I hoped everything from the favor
shown me by Louis XV. ; I trusted in her.   Acting on her
advice I went to England to consult a famous oculist, and
after a stay of several months in London she deserted me in
Hyde Park.   She had stripped me of all that I had, and left
me without resource.   Nor could I make complaint, for to
disclose my name was to lay myself open to the vengeance of
my native city ; I could appeal to no one for aid, I feared
Venice.   The woman put spies about me to exploit my infirmity.   I spare you a tale of adventures worthy of Gil Blas.
Your revolution followed.   For two whole years that creature
kept me at the Bicêtre as a lunatic, then she gained admit-
tance for me at the Blind Asylum ; there was no help for it,
I went.   I could not kill her ; I could not see ; and I was so
poor that I could not pay another arm.

"If only I had taken counsel with my gaoler, Benedetto
Carpi, before I lost him, I might have known the exact posi-

tion of my cell, I might have found my way back to the treasury and returned to Venice when Napoleon crushed the republic——

"Still, blind as I am, let us go back to Venice! I shall find the door of my prison, I shall see the gold through the prison walls, I shall hear it where it lies under the water; for the events which brought about the fall of Venice befell in such a way that the secret of the hoard must have perished with Bianca's brother, Vendramin, a doge to whom I looked to make my peace with the Ten. I sent memorials to the First Consul; I proposed an agreement with the Emperor of Austria; every one sent me about my business for a lunatic. Come! we will go to Venice; let us set out as beggars, we shall come back millionaires. We will buy back my estates, and you shall be my heir! You shall be Prince of Varese!"

My head was swimming. For me his confidences reached the proportions of tragedy; at the sight of that white head of his and beyond it the black water in the trenches of the bastile lying still as a canal in Venice, I had no words to answer him. Facino Cane thought, no doubt, that I judged him, as the rest had done, with a disdainful pity; his gesture expressed the whole philosophy of despair.

Perhaps his story had taken him back to happy days and to Venice. He caught up his clarionet and made plaintive music, playing a Venetian boat-song with something of his lost skill, the skill of the young patrician lover. It was a sort of *Super flumina Babylonis*. Tears filled my eyes. Any belated persons walking along the Boulevard Bourdon must have stood still to listen to an exile's last prayer, a last cry of regret for a lost name, mingled with memories of Bianca. But gold soon gained the upper hand, the fatal passion quenched the light of youth.

"I see it always," he said, "dreaming or waking, I see it; and as I pace to and fro, I pace in the treasury, and the diamonds sparkle. I am not so blind as you think; gold and diamonds light up my night, the night of the last Facino Cane, for my title passes to the Memmi. My God! the murderer's punishment was not long delayed! *Ave Maria*," and he repeated several prayers that I did not heed.

"We will go to Venice!" I said, when he arose.

"Then I have found a man!" he cried, with his face on fire.

I gave him my arm and went home with him. We reached the gates of the Blind Asylum just as some of the wedding-guests were returning along the street, shouting at the top of their voices. He squeezed my hand.

"Shall we start to-morrow?" he asked.

"As soon as we can get some money."

"But we can go on foot. I will beg. I am strong, and you feel young when you see gold before you."

Facino Cane died before the winter was out, after a two months' illness. The poor man had taken a chill.

PARIS, *March*, 1836.

www.ingramcontent.com/pod-product-compliance
Lightning Source LLC
Chambersburg PA
CBHW032309280326
41932CB00009B/756